60 HIKES WITHIN 60 MILES

SACRAMENTO

INCLUDING DAVIS, ROSEVILLE, AND AUBURN

JORDAN SUMMERS

DISCLAIMER

This book is meant only as a guide to select trails in the Sacramento area and does not guarantee hiker safety in any way—you hike at your own risk. Neither Menasha Ridge Press nor Jordan Summers is liable for property loss or damage, personal injury, or death that result in any way from accessing or hiking the trails described in the following pages. Please be aware that hikers have been injured in the Sacramento area. Be especially cautious when walking on or near boulders, steep inclines, and drop-offs, and do not attempt to explore terrain that may be beyond your abilities. To help ensure an uneventful hike, please read carefully the introduction to this book, and perhaps get further safety information and guidance from other sources. Familiarize yourself thoroughly with the areas you intend to visit before venturing out. Ask questions, and prepare for the unforeseen. Familiarize yourself with current weather reports, maps of the area you intend to visit, and any relevant park regulations.

Copyright © 2008 Jordan Summers
All rights reserved
Printed in the United States of America
Published by Menasha Ridge Press
Distributed by Publishers Group West
First edition, fourth printing 2010

Library of Congress Cataloging-in-Publication Data

Summers, Jordan, 1951–
    60 hikes within 60 miles, Sacramento: including Davis, Roseville, and Auburn/
    Jordan Summers. —1st ed.
      p. cm.
    Includes bibliographical references and index.
    ISBN-13: 978-0-89732-556-1
    ISBN-10: 0-89732-556-7
        1. Hiking—California—Sacramento Region—Guidebooks. 2. Sacramento Region
    (Calif.)—Guidebooks. I. Title. II. Title: Sixty hikes within sixty miles, Sacramento.

    GV199.42.C22S239 2008
    796.5109794'5—dc22
                              2007048705

Text and cover design by Steveco International
Cover photograph by Jordan Summers
Author photograph by Karin Connolly
Cartography and elevation profiles by Scott McGrew and Jordan Summers
Indexing by Rich Carlson

Menasha Ridge Press
P.O. Box 43673
Birmingham, AL 35243
www.menasharidge.com

TO MY CHILDREN, ASHLEY AND JASON, WHO BEGAN HIKING WITH ME
WHEN THEY WERE TODDLERS—AND WHO HAVE BEEN WITH ME ON EVERY
HIKE SINCE, WHETHER THEY WERE THERE OR NOT. — JORDAN SUMMERS

HIKE LIST

URBAN HIKES
1 Capitol Park Loop
2 Old Sacramento State Historic Park
3 William Land Park Trail
4 Effie Yeaw Nature Center Trails
5 Riverwalk Park
6 UC Davis Arboretum Trail
7 Davis–Covell Greenbelt

WEST SACRAMENTO VALLEY HIKES
8 Johnson Ridge–Gunsight Rock Trail
9 Homestead–Blue Ridge Trail
10 Redbud Trail
11 Perkins Creek Ridge Trail
12 High Bridge Trail
13 Judge Davis Trail
14 Blue Ridge–Fiske Peak Trail
15 Blue Ridge–Fiske Creek Trail

DELTA AREA HIKES
16 Cosumnes River Preserve Trails
17 Lodi Lake Nature Trail
18 River Bend–Majestic Oaks Loop Trail
19 Grizzly Island Wildlife Area Trail

FOOTHILLS SOUTH HIKES
20 River of Skulls Trail
21 China Gulch Trail
22 Indian Grinding Rock Loop Trails
23 Big Trees North Grove Trails
24 Big Trees South Grove Trails

FOOTHILLS NORTH HIKES A
25 Jenkinson Lake Trail
26 Monroe Ridge Trail
27 Sweetwater Trail
28 Pioneer Express Trail

29 Avery's Pond Trail
30 Rattlesnake Bar–Horseshoe Bar Trail
31 Cronan Ranch Trails
32 Wendell T. Robie Trail
33 American Canyon–Dead Truck Trail
34 Olmstead Loop Trail
35 Hidden Falls Trails
36 Lake Clementine Trail
37 Confluence Trail
38 Quarry Road Trail to American Canyon Falls
39 Robie Point Firebreak Trail
40 Foresthill Divide Loop Trail
41 Codfish Falls Trail
42 North Fork Middle Fork American River Trail

FOOTHILLS NORTH HIKES B
43 Yankee Jim's–Indian Creek Trail
44 Ruck-A-Chucky Rapids Trail
45 Michigan Bluff–Deadwood Trail
46 Green Valley Trail
47 Mumford Bar Trail
48 American River–Beacroft Trail
49 Sugar Pine Mountain Trail
50 Windy Point Trail
51 Stevens Trail
52 Stevens Trail South
53 Euchre Bar Trail to Humbug Canyon
54 American Eagle Mine Trail
55 Hardrock Trail
56 Independence Trail: West Branch
57 Buttermilk Bend Trail
58 Point Defiance Trail
59 Diggins Loop Trail
60 Fairy Falls Trail

MENASHA RIDGE PRESS
Birmingham, Alabama

TABLE OF CONTENTS

ACKNOWLEDGMENTS

The opportunity to author this book may have come to one person, but it is not realized without the guidance, knowledge, and support of many people—many of whom may be unaware of their contributions.

First, let me thank Russell Helms and the staff at Menasha Ridge Press for providing me the opportunity to share the vast outdoor beauty of the Sacramento region. Their advice, guidance, and support made it possible for me to write this book.

A sincere recognition is due to the many volunteers and trail crews who have worked so hard to create or maintain the trails reported in this book. We would not be able to visit these beautiful wild places without their valuable contributions.

Let me acknowledge as well the many rangers and park volunteers who gladly answered my questions, helped me pinpoint features, or told me about interesting hikes and trails.

Thanks also to all of my fellow hikers whom I met on the trail and who shared their insights on trailheads, conditions, scenery, natural history, and a dozen other topics.

I appreciate the help provided by Andy Fisher of the Placer County Facilities Planning Department for excellent work on the Hidden Falls Trails and for his suggestion of the Sugar Pine Mountain Trail.

Thanks to Joel Berringer for tipping me off to the spectacular Fairy Falls and Ruck-A-Chucky Rapids along with his insights on natural history.

Huge thanks are due to Russell Towle, whose relentless efforts have helped preserve several historic trails, or access to them, in the North Fork region. I am grateful for his efforts and his thoughtful input on hiking the south side of Stevens Trail.

I am indebted to my hiking partners, Randy Peterson and Eric Nichols, trout- and wildlife-management experts who always want to go hiking again. Their continuous encouragement as the book developed was invaluable. They also tipped me off to several hikes and trailheads around Folsom Lake and Auburn.

I am understandably obliged to all of my friends for their patience, understanding, and immeasurable support throughout this project. Thanks to my friend Frank Freudberg, whose encouragement and advice came at just the right time.

I owe a long-held debt of gratitude to Georgia Saviers, Jack Frost, and the many other professionals at the National Outdoor Leadership School in Lander, Wyoming, for teaching me how to share the depth and breadth of the outdoors with others.

A special thanks is due to my son, Jason, for ferrying my car from the Mumford Bar Trailhead to the Beacroft Trailhead as well as for joining me on the trails in the South Yuba region.

I am deeply grateful to my wonderful partner, Karin—who wanted to be with me on every hike but waited patiently for me at home for most; who kept me supplied with trail bars and hydrating mix; who made breakfast for every predawn departure; who tolerated my feather, cone, leaf, rock, and flower collecting; who approved of each of my new gear requirements; and who cheerfully encouraged me with her excitement for each new hike.

—*Jordan Summers*
Elk Grove, California

ABOUT THE AUTHOR

JORDAN SUMMERS, a native of North Carolina, grew up near the Smoky Mountains of Tennessee and the Blue Ridge Mountains of Virginia. His teen years in La Jolla, California, introduced him to new terrain and to the Sierra Club.

Summers's undergraduate years at the U.S. Air Force Academy in Colorado exposed him to even more diverse hiking in the Four Corners region—desert, canyon, forest, and mountain.

A high-tech career in Southern California brought him near the mountains for hikes of all kinds—day hikes, ultralight weekends, or weeklong treks. As friends asked him to arrange and lead trips, it became apparent that some new skills were needed. An educational expedition in Wyoming's Wind River Range not only enhanced those skills but taught Summers how to safely share the outdoor experience using Leave No Trace techniques.

As his daughter and son grew to become more constant hiking partners, Summers had to tackle the problem of how to move their gear into the wilderness. Llamas worked well at this, as it turned out, and by 1991 Summers was leading treks with llamas into wilderness areas of Oregon and California. Summers also served during this time as a local chapter president of the Sierra Club.

Sacramento has been Summers's gateway to the Sierra Nevada and Coast Range for more than a decade.

PREFACE

MY FIRST HIKES as a 6-year-old were wonderful experiences among the frogs and snakes, the turtles and crayfish, the poison ivy and mosquitoes. I would literally drag my army-surplus pup tent to a clear spot in the big trees near the creek at my home in Virginia. A sandwich was dinner. The stars were my night-light. And I was always home by breakfast. Honestly, the first song I ever learned was "The Bear Went over the Mountain."

So it is no exaggeration to say that I truly have a passion for hiking. I have had the good fortune to have lived on both coasts, both north and south, and in between. I can sincerely say that hiking has never been better than it is here now in the Sacramento region.

Sacramento is considered the gateway to the central Sierra Nevada. Interstate 80 and US 50 lead from Sacramento to the crystal-clear waters of Lake Tahoe and the snowcapped ridges of the Pacific Crest. Millions of avid outdoor enthusiasts annually pass through the Sacramento Valley and the foothills on their way to these natural treasures.

In the days prior to European settlement, this area served as an important gateway for Native Americans. The Maidu, Nisenan, Miwok, and others capitalized on this lush riparian land for trading opportunities, valuable food crops, and plentiful game migrations.

Then the gold rush opened up Sacramento as the gateway for the miners, ranchers, farmers, anglers, loggers, and engineers who followed them. And the Sacramento region continues today as a gateway for outdoor recreation.

From strolls down a riverside promenade in the city to near-vertical monster slopes in a remote river canyon, there is something here for all types of hikers. Broad tidal marshlands, verdant riverine woodlands, crystal-clear creeks, cascading streams, plummeting waterfalls, ice-cold swimming holes, wild rushing rivers, old-growth forests, historic mining towns, colorful profusions of wildflowers, and a dozen other wonderful things can be found within a 60-mile radius of Sacramento.

The expected things are going to be there: wildflowers, rivers, trees, and photo opportunities on every hike. However, this book touches on the special things, the hidden gems that make each hike memorable in its way. Stand on the porch of a forty-niner's cabin and behold his view of the river. Walk through a grove of valley oaks more than half a millennium old whose acorns the Miwok women turned into flour on the ancient grinding rock. Walk across the windswept grasses atop a levee where you might see, on one day, endangered, threatened, and migrating bird species that nest or feed here.

Whether you are new to the area or are a resident trail vet, you are going to discover something new in this book. The Web sites included here should lead you to further investigation about hikes and history in this region. *Did you know that Yankee Jim was hanged for attempting to steal a schooner in San Diego?*

If you are an experienced hiker but you want to learn more natural history, several of the hikes I've profiled have excellent interpretive displays. You may rediscover a trail that you haven't thought about for years, or you could learn about a new one just around the corner.

Preparing for the hikes is just part of the fun. Check the details and, with the information in this book, some maps, and pleasant weather, you're off—as that song from my childhood says—to see what you can see.

ABOUT THE HIKES

With the help of Google Earth, we can now visualize the Sacramento region: the Sacramento Valley, the Delta, and the foothills. No single word can characterize the diverse geography of this area.

The Sacramento Valley, almost featureless except for the Sutter Buttes, is surrounded by rugged and interesting terrain. The Yuba River joins the Feather and then adds the Bear before becoming the Sacramento River in the north. To the west are the coast ranges, which trend northwest–southeast from the coast right up to the valley. The southern border is broken by slough and levee holding the fresh- and salt water in a delicate balance at the confluence of the Sacramento and San Joaquin rivers above San Pablo Bay. The east is filled with the tortured geology of continents in collision. Its river canyons claw their way from their source in the snows of the Sierra Nevada: the North, Middle, and South forks of the American River and the Rubicon, Cosumnes, Mokelumne, and Calaveras rivers all make their mark and add to the physical and historic makeup of the foothills.

URBAN HIKES

Sacramento is known as the City of Trees, and its dozens of neighborhood parks are noted for their majestic arbors. Sacramento's Capitol Park, William Land Park, and the University of California, Davis, Arboretum have excellent trails through magnificent tree displays.

The scars left behind after the gold rush, such as the ones here at
Malakoff Diggins State Historic Park, are slowly fading.

WEST SACRAMENTO VALLEY

Tule elk, bald eagles, and a host of mammals and birds make the dry hills to the west
of the Sacramento Valley their home. The hills run northwest–southeast and edge
right up to the valley about 10 miles west of Interstate 5. The lands that are open to
the public here are often administered jointly by the U.S. Bureau of Land Management and the California Department of Fish and Game. Hunting is regulated in the
Cache Creek Natural Area. Summers are brutally dry in these hills, which can be a real
challenge for hydration. However, Cache Creek flows year-round. It not only has
excellent white-water recreation but also attracts migrating birds. The spring and fall
migrations offer spectacular wildlife-viewing opportunities.

DELTA HIKES

The Sacramento–San Joaquin River Delta drains virtually the entire western slope of
the Sierra Nevada. This inverted delta, one of only a few worldwide, creates a tidal
marshland that is an important resting spot for migrating waterfowl. The recovery of
the Delta region is a fascinating story and can be learned while visiting Grizzly Island
Wildlife Area or the Cosumnes River Preserve. The California Department of Fish
and Game and the Nature Conservancy, as well as other contributing organizations,
have allied to preserve several remaining examples of the once vast riparian forest in
this area.

FOOTHILLS SOUTH

Bounded only by an arbitrary line approximately along US 50 to Tahoe, the southern foothills area has gems that just had to be reached out to. There are no straight lines in the foothills, so driving times would be outlandish if the roads weren't in such beautiful country. It is a stretch to see the Big Trees, but a stretch worthwhile and one not to be found any closer. The dams and reservoirs on the Calaveras and Mokelumne rivers protect against floods, provide reliable drinking water, and offer excellent hiking and other recreational opportunities.

FOOTHILLS NORTH

In an ideal world, all great hikes would be equally distributed for easy access by all. The area bounded by US 50 to the east and CA 99 to the north is the portion of the pie that holds most of the attraction for hikers and other outdoor enthusiasts in the region. Home of the Mother Lode, birthplace of the gold rush, and route of the Emigrant Trail and Pony Express, the foothills between Placerville and Marysville are as exciting a place for day hikes as any in the country. Seven sites hiked here are listed on the National Register of Historic Places. You can discover even more historic sites by taking the route less traveled.

This area's access is arranged largely along the canyons of the American's three forks and the Yuba's south fork. The North Fork of the American is reachable from both I-80 and Foresthill Road, which also provides access to the Middle Fork. The South Fork is reached via CA 49 through either Auburn or Placerville. The Confluence of the North and Middle forks is a focal point of activity in the Auburn State Recreation Area, where many excellent routes were hiked for this book. The South Fork and North Fork are united at the upper end of Folsom Lake State Recreation Area, which can be accessed from both I-80 and US 50. Many of these hikes pass historic mining sites yet are not as challenging as those on the other forks. Hikes in the South Yuba River region can be accessed from Marysville or Nevada City. They also lead to historic locations, including the longest single-span wood-covered bridge in the United States.

RECOMMENDED HIKES

HIKES 1 TO 2.9 MILES

HIKES 3 TO 6 MILES

HIKES MORE THAN 6 MILES

BEST HIKES FOR CHILDREN

BEST HIKES FOR CHILDREN *(continued)*

BEST HIKES FOR SOLITUDE

EASIEST HIKES

FLAT HIKES

FLAT HIKES *(continued)*

HIKES TO RIVERS AND ALONG CREEKS

HIKES GOOD FOR RUNNERS

BEST HIKES FOR DOGS

HIKES WITH HISTORIC SITES OR RELICS

HIKES WITH OLD-GROWTH TREES

LAKE HIKES

MOST DIFFICULT HIKES

MOST SCENIC HIKES

STEEP HIKES

URBAN HIKES

WATERFALL AND CASCADES HIKES

WHEELCHAIR-ACCESSIBLE HIKES

WILDFLOWER HIKES

WILDFLOWER HIKES *(continued)*

WILDLIFE HIKES

INTRODUCTION

Welcome to *60 Hikes within 60 Miles: Sacramento*! If you're new to hiking or even if you're a seasoned trailsmith, take a few minutes to read the following introduction. It explains how this book is organized and how to use it.

HOW TO USE THIS GUIDEBOOK

THE OVERVIEW MAP AND OVERVIEW-MAP KEY

Use the overview map on the inside front cover to assess the exact locations of each hike's primary trailhead. Each hike's number appears on the overview map, on the map key facing the overview map, and in the table of contents. As you flip through the book, a hike's full profile is easy to locate by watching for the hike number at the top of each page. The book is organized by region as indicated in the table of contents. A map legend that details the symbols found on trail maps appears on the inside back cover.

REGIONAL MAPS

The book is divided into regions, and prefacing each regional section is an overview map of that region. The regional maps provide more detail than the overview map, bringing you closer to the hike.

TRAIL MAPS

Each hike contains a detailed map that shows the trailhead, the route, significant features, facilities, and topographic landmarks such as creeks, overlooks, and peaks. The author gathered map data by carrying a Garmin GPSMAP 60CSx GPS unit while hiking. This data was downloaded into DeLorme's digital mapping program Topo USA and processed by expert cartographers to produce the highly accurate maps found in

1

this book. Each trailhead's GPS coordinates are included with each profile (see discussion below).

ELEVATION PROFILES

Corresponding directly to the trail map, each hike contains a detailed elevation profile. The elevation profile provides a quick look at the trail from the side, enabling you to visualize how the trail rises and falls. Key points along the way are labeled. Note the number of feet between each tick mark on the vertical axis (the height scale). To avoid making flat hikes look steep and steep hikes appear flat, height scales are used throughout the book to accurately depict the hike's climbing difficulty.

GPS TRAILHEAD COORDINATES

To collect accurate map data, each trail was hiked with a handheld Garmin GPSMAP 60CSx GPS unit. Data collected was then downloaded and plotted onto a digital U.S. Geographical Survey (USGS) topo map. In addition to rendering a highly specific trail outline, this book also includes the GPS coordinates for each trailhead in two formats: latitude–longitude and Universal Transverse Mercator (UTM). Latitude–longitude coordinates tell you where you are by locating a point west (latitude) of the 0° meridian line that passes through Greenwich, England, and north or south of the 0° (longitude) line that belts the earth, aka the equator.

Topographic maps show latitude–longitude as well as UTM grid lines. Known as UTM coordinates, the numbers index a specific point using a grid method. The survey datum used to arrive at the coordinates in this book is WGS84 (versus NAD27 or WGS83). For readers who own a GPS unit, whether handheld or on board a vehicle, the latitude–longitude or UTM coordinates provided on the first page of each hike may be entered into the GPS unit. Just make sure your GPS unit is set to navigate using WGS84 data. Now you can navigate directly to the trailhead.

Most trailheads, which begin in parking areas, can be reached by car, but some hikes still require a short walk to reach the trailhead from a parking area. In those cases, a handheld unit is necessary to continue the GPS navigation process. That said, however, readers can easily access all trailheads in this book by using the directions given, the overview map, and the trail map, which shows at least one major road leading into the area. But for those who enjoy using the latest GPS technology to navigate, the necessary data has been provided. A brief explanation of the UTM coordinates from Hike 46, Green Valley Trail (page 239), follows:

UTM Zone (WGS84) 10S

Easting: 0691415

Northing: 4336186

The UTM zone number **10** refers to one of the 60 vertical zones of the Universal Transverse Mercator projection. Each zone is 6 degrees wide. The UTM zone letter S refers to one of the 20 horizontal zones that span from 80 degrees south to 84 degrees north. The easting number **0691415** indicates in meters how far east or west a point is from the central meridian of the zone. Increasing easting coordinates on a topo map or on your GPS screen indicate that you are moving east, while decreasing easting coordinates indicate that you are moving west. The northing number **4336186** references in meters how far you are from the equator. Above and below the equator, increasing northing coordinates indicate you are traveling north; decreasing northing coordinates indicate you are traveling south. To learn more about how to enhance your outdoor experiences with GPS technology, refer to Russell Helms's GPS *Outdoors: A Practical Guide for Outdoor Enthusiasts* (Menasha Ridge Press).

HIKE DESCRIPTIONS

Each hike contains seven key items: an In Brief description of the trail, a Key At-a-Glance Information box, directions to the trail, trailhead coordinates, a trail map, an elevation profile, and a trail description. Many hike profiles also include notes on nearby activities. Combined, the maps and information provide a clear method to assess each trail from the comfort of your favorite reading chair.

IN BRIEF

A "taste of the trail." Think of this section as a snapshot focused on the historical landmarks, beautiful vistas, and other sights you may encounter on the hike.

KEY AT-A-GLANCE INFORMATION

The information in these boxes gives you a quick idea of the statistics and specifics of each hike.

LENGTH The length of the trail from start to finish (total distance traveled). There may be options to shorten or extend the hikes, but the mileage corresponds to the described hike. Consult the description to help decide how to customize the hike for your ability or time constraints.

CONFIGURATION A description of what the trail might look like from overhead. Trails can be loops, out-and-backs (trails on which one enters and leaves along the same path), figure eights, or a combination of shapes.

DIFFICULTY This is a highly subjective matter, and it is tempting to stick with the tried-and-true one-to-five scale and let the reader guess what it means. In conversations with other hikers, equipment manufacturers, guides, clients, and my children, I have been able to successfully employ common terminology for describing trail effort.

> *Cakewalk* Level ground; effortless, short, shaded; almost a catered affair.

> *Easy* Like an A-ticket ride. No real sweat. Just fun.

> *Moderate* Now you sweat some. Uphill, downhill, navigate.

> *Challenging* Long; uphill, downhill, navigate; a workout.

> *Difficult* Vertical exposure; elevation gain/loss; scrambling; route finding; long or remote.

WATER REQUIRED How much hydration (in liters) you'll need to bring along.

SCENERY A short summary of the attractions offered by the hike and what to expect in terms of plant life, wildlife, natural wonders, and historic features.

EXPOSURE A quick check of how much sun you can expect on your shoulders during the hike.

TRAIL TRAFFIC Indicates how busy the trail might be on an average day. Trail traffic, of course, varies from day to day and season to season. Weekend days typically see the most visitors. Other trail users that may be encountered on the trail are also noted.

TRAIL SURFACE Indicates whether the trail surface is paved, rocky, gravel, dirt, boardwalk, or a mixture of elements.

HIKING TIME The length of time it takes to hike the trail. A slow but steady hiker will average 2 to 3 miles an hour, depending on the terrain.

SEASON Time(s) of year when the hike is accessible.

ACCESS A notation of any fees or permits that may be needed to access the trail or park at the trailhead. A list of parks and recreation areas that charge fees is available at the California State Parks Web site, **www.parks.ca.gov.** An annual day-use permit can be obtained at park offices (when they're staffed) or online at the Web site. City and county parks typically do not require any permits or fees.

MAPS Here, you'll find a list of maps that show the trail topography, including USGS topo maps and local trail maps. The Auburn State Recreation Area has a map that clearly identifies each of its 50 trails. In addition, the Tahoe National Forest map shows a number of trails and trailhead access points.

WHEELCHAIR TRAVERSABLE Indicates whether all or part of the hike can be enjoyed by persons with disabilities.

FACILITIES What you can expect in terms of restrooms and water at the trailhead or nearby.

DRIVING DISTANCE Listed in miles.

SPECIAL COMMENTS Any extra details that don't fit into the categories above.

DIRECTIONS

Used in conjunction with the overview map, the driving directions will help you locate each trailhead. Once at the trailhead, park only in designated areas.

GPS TRAILHEAD COORDINATES

The trailhead coordinates can be used in addition to the driving directions if you enter the coordinates into your GPS unit before you set out. See page 2 for more information on GPS coordinates.

DESCRIPTION

The trail description is the heart of each hike. Here, the author summarizes the trail's essence and highlights any special traits the hike has to offer. The route is clearly outlined, including any landmarks, side trips, and possible alternate routes along the way. Ultimately, the hike description will help you choose which hikes are best for you.

NEARBY ACTIVITIES

Look here for information on nearby activities or points of interest. This includes parks, museums, restaurants, or even a brew pub where you can get a well-deserved beer after a long hike. (Note that not every hike has a listing.)

WEATHER

Sacramento sits in the middle of the Central Valley, almost midway between the Sierra Nevada and Coast ranges. It has a Mediterranean climate that brings warm days and cool nights in the spring and summer along with cool, wet winters as shown in the table of temperature averages and extremes. In short, Sacramento has a climate that is very hiker friendly.

Sacramento Valley, however, has more than one face when it comes to the weather you may encounter on any particular day. Located near sea level in the middle of a geologic bathtub, Sacramento itself succumbs to very hot summer days when temperatures exceed 90°F for more than 60 days from June through September. In winter, the rain and fog return the moisture lost in the valley, while the snowstorms that coat the sierra sometimes dip into the foothills.

Spring and autumn are the colorful seasons in the valley and the foothills. Spring in the Sacramento Valley and the foothills is an explosion of color with wildflowers and trees blooming and budding everywhere that water soaks the soil. Trails that cross creeks and streams should be approached with some planning and caution during the spring runoff. Wet rocks are slippery and running water is often stronger than hikers realize before it is too late. Hike with a partner or use trekking poles at creek crossings at this time of year.

Average Temperature/Precipitation by Month: Sacramento

Month	Avg. High	Avg. Low	Mean	Avg. Precip.
January	55°F	41°F	48°F	4.18 in.
February	62°F	45°F	54°F	3.77 in.
March	67°F	47°F	57°F	3.15 in.
April	74°F	50°F	62°F	1.17 in.
May	82°F	54°F	68°F	0.60 in.
June	89°F	58°F	74°F	0.18 in.

Average Temperature/Precipitation by Month: Sacramento (continued)

Month	Avg. High	Avg. Low	Mean	Avg. Precip.
July	94°F	61°F	77°F	0.05 in.
August	93°F	61°F	77°F	0.05 in.
September	89°F	59°F	74°F	0.37 in.
October	79°F	54°F	66°F	1.00 in.
November	64°F	46°F	55°F	2.59 in.
December	55°F	40°F	48°F	2.76 in.

These hot days in the valley that are so important for crops mellow somewhat as one climbs into the foothills of the Sierra Nevada. However, as the sun ascends and extends its rays into these foothill canyons and drainages, they too become ovenlike as the summer days grow. Temperatures exceeding 100°F are not uncommon either in the valley or in the foothill canyons. This seasonal heat wave can really temper your choice of trails to hike. The slow-moving pools found on the forks of the American River are excellent destination points on a summer hike.

Looking at the precipitation chart, you can see that these same four months garner as little moisture as they do cool days. This makes summer hiking a bit more demanding and forces hikers to think carefully about their water needs for the day. Hydrate yourself thoroughly prior to your hike and be sure to carry enough water to replenish your lost body fluids.

Your hiking experience will change with the seasons. Streams that flowed with gusto in the spring are not guaranteed to be visible in midsummer. Even the picturesque falls you want to hike to may not be much more than a trickle in midsummer. Nevertheless, wildlife is still all about. Deer are in velvet, and the remaining water sources can be great places to observe in the early morning and evening.

Autumn is, of course, a multicolored extravaganza in the foothills, where the native trees and plants—oak, ash, sycamore, redbud, maple, toyon, willow, cottonwood, and others—change from green to red and gold. Not to be outdone, the Sacramento Valley is awash with colors of both native and ornamental trees and plants. Combined with moderate temperatures and infrequent rainfall, autumn is a very popular time of year to hike.

You can expect mild temperatures in the winter, when this area realizes the majority of its rainfall. Winter months, when the highs are generally in the 50s and 60s and the lows are rarely under 40, may be ideal for difficult hikes that might otherwise sap your strength in the summer. In this season, the Sacramento region receives the majority of its rainfall—that is, almost 75 percent of its annual precipitation—in just four months. The positive side is that this water charges all of the drainages, creeks, and rivers with the raw material for real hiking wonders: cascades, waterfalls, wildflowers, and wildlife. The only downside is that some foothills trails turn rather sticky after a soaking rain.

Every hike in this book but two is walkable at any time of year. Both exceptions are in Calaveras Big Trees State Park. The South Loop Trails at Big Trees State Park is closed when snows block the road leading to the grove. However, the North Loop Trail is converted to a cross-country-skiing trail when snowfall conditions permit. No other trails described in this book are closed unless the trailhead is temporarily inaccessible. On occasion, Foresthill Road closes at China Wall after a snowstorm in the foothill region. A few of the unpaved and unimproved trailhead access roads such as Drivers Flat Road, Ponderosa Way, Elliott Ranch Road, and Yankee Jim's Road are extremely difficult to navigate after it rains.

WATER

How much is enough? Well, one simple physiological fact should persuade you to err on the side of excess when deciding how much water to pack: a hiker working hard in 90°F heat needs approximately 10 quarts of fluid per day. That's 2.5 gallons—12 large water bottles or 16 small ones. In other words, pack one or two bottles even for short hikes.

Some hikers and backpackers hit the trail prepared to purify water found along the route. This method, while less dangerous than drinking it untreated, comes with risks. Purifiers with ceramic filters are the safest. Many hikers pack the slightly distasteful tetraglycine-hydroperiodide tablets to debug water (sold under the names Potable Aqua, Coughlan's, and others).

Probably the most common waterborne "bug" that hikers face is giardia, which may not hit until one to four weeks after ingestion. It will have you living in the bathroom, passing noxious rotten-egg gas, vomiting, and shivering with chills. Other parasites to worry about include E. coli and cryptosporidium, both of which are harder to kill than giardia.

For most people, the pleasures of hiking make carrying water a relatively minor price to pay to remain healthy. If you're tempted to drink "found water," do so only if you understand the risks involved. Better yet, hydrate before your hike, carry (and drink) six ounces of water for every mile you plan to hike, and hydrate after the hike.

ESSENTIAL EQUIPMENT

One of the first rules of hiking is to be prepared for anything. The simplest way to be prepared is to carry the essentials. In addition to carrying the items listed below, you need to know how to use them, especially navigation items. Always consider worst-case scenarios such as getting lost, hiking back in the dark, broken gear (for example, a broken hip strap on your pack or a water filter getting plugged), twisting an ankle, or a brutal thunderstorm. The items listed below don't cost a lot of money, don't take up much room in a pack, and don't weigh much, but they might just save your life.

MAP AND COMPASS: trail or topographic map, simple compass, the route description, and the knowledge to use these

WATER: full bottles plus extra or water treatment tablets or purifying filter

FOOD: nutrition bars, snacks, or meals for the day, plus extra; always try to return with some food

FIRE: matches, lighter, fire starter, or stove with full fuel bottle/canister

LIGHT: headlamp with fresh batteries

SUN PROTECTION: hat, sunglasses, sunscreen, lip balm

EXTRA CLOTHING: insulation layer, gloves, raingear, socks, soft-shell jacket

FIRST-AID KIT: with fresh supplies, instructions, and the knowledge to use them

EMERGENCY TOOLS: signal whistle, signal mirror, knife, multitool, cord

SHELTER: a space blanket or Siltarp can provide immediate sun or rain protection for accident victims

TREKKING POLES: third leg, monopod, shelter pole, cougar and bear defense, poison-oak deflector, general poking and irritating

This list is fully weather and trip dependent. If you hike in Capitol Park in the spring, you will require virtually none of this gear. However, if you hike on the Stevens Trail in the fall, you might need and use every bit of it. This list will help you structure and plan for the requirements of each trip. The only item on the list that the author has not yet used is the whistle.

No matter where you go, it is a good idea to consider other, *nonessential,* gear that could add to your experience, comfort, or general pleasure on the trail.

GEAR AND CLOTHING RECOMMENDATIONS

It should be as easy as throwing on a pair of cutoffs and T-shirt, but it simply isn't. Depending on the difficulty, length, location, and season, your individual clothing and equipment needs will change.

This is a list of the gear and clothing that the author wore or carried on these hikes. The items listed as essential equipment are also carried on every hike.

GAITERS: almost essential, they keep dirt, sticks, seeds, and other crud from getting inside boots; good protection against poison oak

SHORTS: cargo pockets are a fashion plus for collecting leaves, rocks, lizard tails, feathers

WICKING T-SHIRT: a good base layer or outerwear in summer

WICKING UNDERWEAR: cotton feels great until it gets sweaty

SOCKS AND LINERS: two pairs of socks are a sure way to protect against blisters

LIGHTWEIGHT LONG-SLEEVED SHIRT: to protect your arms when the sun is blistering down at lunchtime

BANDANNA: great mosquito swatter, brow wiper, impromptu hat

BOOTS: lightweight hiking *boots* are recommended for every natural trail; lightweight hiking *shoes* rarely stand up to the trail

TREKKING POLES: lightweight with shock absorbers; invaluable on steep hills

DAY PACK: 30- to 40-liter pack (depending on how many books are carried)

NUTRITION BARS: convenient, nutritious, and so tasty

TRIPOD: compact and flexible for a variety of surfaces

BINOCULARS: 8 x 21, compact size

CAMERA

SIT PAD

FIELD GUIDES: paper and pencil

GPS DEVICE and extra batteries

SPECIMEN BAGS: gallon- and quart-sized, resealable

FIRST-AID KIT

A typical first-aid kit may contain more items than you might think necessary. These are just the basics. Prepackaged kits in waterproof bags (Atwater Carey and Adventure Medical make a variety of kits) are available. Even though there are quite a few items listed here, they pack down into a small space:

Ace bandages or Spenco joint wraps

Antibiotic ointment (Neosporin or the generic equivalent)

Aspirin or acetaminophen

Band-Aids

Benadryl or the generic equivalent, diphenhydramine (in case of allergic reactions)

Butterfly-closure bandages

Epinephrine in a prefilled syringe (for people known to have severe allergic reactions to such things as bee stings)

Gauze (one roll)

Gauze compress pads (a half-dozen 4- by 4-inch pads)

Hydrogen peroxide or iodine

Insect repellent

Matches or pocket lighter

Moleskin/Spenco Second Skin

Sunscreen

Whistle (it's more effective in signaling rescuers than your voice)

HIKING WITH CHILDREN

No one is too young for a hike in the outdoors. Be mindful, though. Flat, short, and shaded trails are best with an infant. Toddlers who have not quite mastered walking can still tag along, riding on an adult's back in a child carrier. Use common sense to judge a child's capacity to hike a particular trail, and always assume that the child will tire quickly and need to be carried.

When packing for the hike, remember the child's needs as well as your own. Make sure children are adequately clothed for the weather, have proper shoes, and are protected from the sun with sunscreen. Kids dehydrate quickly, so make sure you have plenty of fluid for everyone. A list of hikes suitable for children is provided on page xv.

GENERAL SAFETY

To some potential mountain enthusiasts, the steep slopes and deep canyons seem perilous. It is the fear of the unknown that causes some anxiety. No doubt, potentially dangerous situations can occur outdoors, but as long as you use sound judgment and prepare yourself before hitting the trail, you'll be much safer in the woods or mountains than in most urban areas of the country. It is better to look at a backcountry hike as a fascinating chance to discover the unknown rather than a chance for potential disaster. Here are a few tips to help make your trip safer and easier.

- **ALWAYS CARRY FOOD AND WATER,** whether you are planning to go overnight or not. Food will give you energy, help keep you warm, and sustain you in an emergency until help arrives. You never know if you will have a stream nearby when you become thirsty. Bring potable water or treat water before drinking it from a stream. Boil or filter all found water before drinking it.

- **STAY ON DESIGNATED TRAILS.** Most hikers get lost when they leave the path. Even on the most clearly marked trails, there is usually a point where you have to stop and consider which direction to head. If you become disoriented, don't panic. As soon as you think you may be off-track, stop, assess your current direction, and then retrace your steps back to the point where you went awry. Using map, compass, and this book, and keeping in mind what you have passed thus far, reorient yourself and trust your judgment on which way to continue. If you become absolutely unsure of how to continue, return to your vehicle the way you came in. Should you become completely lost and have no idea how to return to the trailhead, remaining in place along the trail and waiting for help is most often the best option for adults and always the best option for children.

- **BE ESPECIALLY CAREFUL WHEN CROSSING STREAMS.** Whether you are fording the stream or crossing on a log, make every step count. If you have any doubt about maintaining your balance on a foot log, go ahead and ford the stream instead. When fording a stream, use a trekking pole or stout stick for balance and face upstream as you cross. If a stream seems too deep to ford, turn back. Whatever is on the other side is not worth risking your life.

- **BE CAREFUL AT OVERLOOKS.** While these areas may provide spectacular views, they are potentially hazardous. Stay back from the edge of outcrops and be absolutely sure of your footing; a misstep can mean a nasty and possibly fatal fall.

• **STANDING DEAD TREES AND STORM-DAMAGED LIVING TREES POSE A REAL HAZARD** to hikers and tent campers. These trees may have loose or broken limbs that could fall at any time. When choosing a spot to rest or a backcountry campsite, look up.

• **KNOW THE SYMPTOMS OF HYPOTHERMIA.** Shivering and forgetfulness are the two most common indicators of this insidious killer. Hypothermia can occur at any elevation, even in the summer, especially when the hiker is wearing lightweight cotton clothing. If symptoms arise, get the victim shelter, hot liquids, and dry clothes or a dry sleeping bag.

• **BRING YOUR BRAIN.** A cool, calculating mind is the single most important piece of equipment you'll ever need on the trail. Think before you act. Watch your step. Plan ahead. Avoiding accidents before they happen is the best recipe for a rewarding and relaxing hike.

• **ASK QUESTIONS.** Forest and park employees are there to help. It's a lot easier to gain advice beforehand and avoid a mishap away from civilization when it's too late to amend an error. Use your head out there, and treat the place as if it were your own backyard.

ANIMAL AND PLANT HAZARDS

MOUNTAIN LIONS

Mountain lions are important members of the natural community and may be found in this area. Although these animals are seldom seen, they can be unpredictable and have been known to attack humans without warning. It is best to hike with another person and to keep children close when hiking. If you should encounter a mountain lion, wave your arms overhead and make plenty of noise to frighten it away.

These, or words to their effect, are often seen at trailheads or recreation area entrances throughout the Sacramento region. Mountain lions are a real and potential danger on most of the trails described in the foothill area.

Also known as cougars, pumas, or panthers, mountain lions are everywhere in California and are most abundant where there is a supply of deer and ground cover. They are tan-coated, have black-tipped ears and tail, weigh between 75 and 150 pounds, and are about seven feet long from nose to tail.

Never approach a mountain lion. If confronted, do anything to make yourself appear larger: raise your outspread arms, wave trekking poles or tree limbs, gather other hikers (especially children) next to you. Act threatening but allow the animal a path to escape. Avoid bending over or turning your back on mountain lions. Do not run. Make noise, yell, and throw rocks or anything that can be had without bending over.

If you are attacked, try to remain standing, as lions will try to bite the neck or head. Always try to fight back. In 1994, a lone runner was attacked and killed as she jogged on a trail near Auburn. In 2006, a woman successfully used a ball-point pen to fight off the mountain lion that was attacking her husband. Both of them survived the ordeal thanks to her quick action.

CALIFORNIA BLACK BEARS

With the possible exception of mountain lions, most animals will be scared of you and will not be a threat as long as you respect the animal's space. California has a large population of black bears, which are actually cinnamon to dark-brown colored. The threat from black bears is that they are very intelligent and they are always searching for large quantities of food. Despite weighing between 200 and 500 pounds, black bears can run up to 30 miles an hour.

Bears want your food. Take all precautions to keep food items under your control. Do not leave food out and unattended. If a bear is eating your food or shredding your pack in search of your snacks, do not attempt to retrieve any of your food items. In the bear's mind, it is now the bear's food. Let the bear have it. Perhaps you can walk away with just a great story.

If you do encounter a black bear on the trail, do not run. Make eye contact but do not stare. Pick up small children to keep them from running. If a bear approaches, make yourself appear larger by spreading your arms or holding your jacket open. Make as much threatening noise as you can by yelling or banging gear together. If a bear is after you and not your food, throw rocks or sticks and make every attempt to fight back.

TICKS

Ticks like to hang out in the brush that grows along trails. Hot summer months seem to explode their numbers, but you should be tick-aware during all months of the year. Ticks, which are arthropods and not insects, need a host to feast on to reproduce. The ticks that light onto you while hiking will be very small, some-times so tiny that you won't be able to spot them. Primarily of two varieties, deer ticks and dog ticks, both need a few hours of actual attachment before they can transmit any disease they may harbor. Ticks may settle in shoes, socks, and hats and may take several hours to actually latch on. The best strategy is to visually check every half hour or so while hiking, do a thorough check before you get in the car, and when you take a posthike shower, do an even more thorough check of your entire body. Ticks that haven't attached are easily removed, but not easily killed. If you pick off a tick in the woods, just toss it aside. If you find one on your body at home, dispatch it and then send it down the toilet. For ticks that have embedded, removal with tweezers is best.

SNAKES

Rattlesnakes, as well as other species of snakes, are important members of the natural community. They will not attack, but if disturbed or cornered, they will defend themselves. Rattlesnakes will usually warn you with the "buzz" of their rattle.

RATTLESNAKE

The only pit viper native to Northern California, the Northern Pacific rattlesnake, makes its home in the foot-hills around Sacramento, so some caution is required when you travel in the snake's habi-tat. Rattlesnakes like to rest on warm rocks and in small spaces, often moving in and out of warmth to maintain body temperature. Be careful when you are stepping over logs or boulders. Do not place your foot in a spot that you cannot see. Watch where you place your hands when scrambling. Snakebites occur most often when the snake is inadvertently touched by a human.

Rattlesnakes eat rodents, lizards, squirrels, rabbits, and sometimes birds. They do not eat humans. The Northern Pacific rattlesnake is most active in the spring and hunts at dawn, dusk, or night. Mating occurs in the spring and young are born in the fall. Rattlers are rather shy and will usually move out of your way before you are aware of the snake.

If you encounter a rattlesnake, consider how lucky you are to see this beauti-ful snake. They cannot hurl themselves at you to strike, but if you get within the distance of their body length, about five feet, you are within their strike zone. Do not try to touch or move the snake. Give rattlesnakes distance and respect. Step back. Take a picture. Walk away with another great story.

It is unlawful to kill or harm rattlesnakes or any other wildlife in California state parks.

POISON OAK

Recognizing poison oak and avoiding contact with it is the most effective way to prevent the painful, itchy rashes asso-ciated with this plant. In the Southwest, poison oak occurs as either a vine or shrub, with three shiny identical leaflets. Urushiol, the oil in the sap of this plant, is responsible for the rash. Usually within 12 to 14 hours of exposure (but some-times much later), raised lines and/or blisters will appear, accompanied by a terrible itch. Refrain from scratching

POISON OAK

because bacteria under fingernails can cause infection and you will spread the rash to other parts of your body. Wash and dry the rash thoroughly, applying calamine lotion or other product to help dry the rash. If itching or blistering is severe, seek medical attention. Remember that oil-contaminated clothes, pets, or hiking gear can easily cause an irritating rash on you or someone else, so wash not only any exposed parts of your body but also clothes, gear, and pets.

MOSQUITOES

You will encounter mosquitoes on most of the hikes described in this book. Although it's not a common occurrence, individuals can become infected with the West Nile virus by being bitten by an infected mosquito. Culex mosquitoes, the primary varieties that can transmit West Nile virus to humans, thrive in urban rather than natural areas. They lay their eggs in stagnant water and can breed in any standing water that remains for more than five days. Most people infected with West Nile virus have no symptoms of illness, but some may become ill, usually 3 to 15 days after being bitten.

In the Sacramento area, spring and summer are thought to be the highest risk periods for West Nile virus. At this time of year—and anytime you expect mosquitoes to be buzzing around—you may want to wear long sleeves, long pants, and socks. Loose-fitting, light-colored clothing is best. Spray clothing with insect repellent. Remember to follow the instructions on the repellent and to take extra care with children.

TIPS FOR ENJOYING THE SACRAMENTO REGION

Before you go, visit the various Web sites. This will help you get oriented to the region's roads, features, and attractions. Detailed maps of the specific parks or recreation areas are available from the Web, stores, or the agencies themselves (see "Managing Agencies" at the end of this book). They will really help you get around the forest's backcountry. In addition, the following tips will make your visit enjoyable and more rewarding.

- **Investigate different areas of the region. The Delta offers flat hikes with huge wildlife populations. Western Sacramento Valley cloaks its dry hills with golden fields splattered with oak. The southern foothills' broad and rolling hills conceal reservoirs and lakes for Bay Area residents. The northern foothills are a wild, steep jumble of geologic catastrophes displaying the remnants of the region's mining legacy**

- **Take your time along the trails. Pace yourself. The foothills are filled with wonders both big and small. Don't rush past a tiny salamander to get to that overlook. Stop and smell the wildflowers. Peer into the clear rivers for trout. Don't miss the trees for the forest. Shorter hikes allow you to stop and linger more than long hikes. Something about staring at the front end of a 10-mile trek naturally pushes you to speed up. That said, take close notice of the elevation maps that accompany each hike. If you see many ups and down over** large altitude changes, you'll obviously need more time. Inevitably you'll finish some of the "hike times" long before or after what is suggested. Nevertheless, leave yourself plenty of time for those moments when you simply feel like stopping and taking it all in.

• We can't always schedule our free time when we want, but try to hike during the week and avoid the traditional holidays if possible. Trails that are packed in the spring and fall are often clear during the hottest months of summer. If you are hiking on a busy day, go early in the morning; it'll enhance your chances of seeing wildlife. The trails really clear out during rainy times; however, don't hike during a thunderstorm.

TOPO MAPS

The maps in this book have been produced with great care and, used with the hiking directions, will direct you to the trail and help you stay on course. However, you will find superior detail and valuable information in the USGS's 7.5-minute-series topographic maps. Topo maps are available online in many locations. TerraServer, a well-known free service, is at **terraserver.microsoft.com**; another free service with fast click-and-drag browsing is **TopoZone**, at **www.topozone .com**. You can view and print topos of the entire United States from both Web sites and view aerial photographs of the same area at TerraServer. Several online services such as **www.trails.com** charge annual fees for additional features such as shaded relief, which makes the topography stand out more. If you expect to print out many topo maps each year, it might be worth paying for shaded-relief topo maps. The downside to USGS topos is that most of them are outdated, having been created 20 to 30 years ago. But they still provide excellent topographic detail.

Digital topographic-map programs such as DeLorme's Topo USA enable you to review topo maps of the entire United States on your PC. Gathered while hiking with a GPS unit, GPS data can be downloaded onto the software, letting you plot your own hikes.

If you're new to hiking, you might be wondering, "What's a topographic map?" In short, a topo indicates not only linear distance but elevation as well, using contour lines. Contour lines spread across the map like dozens of intricate spiderwebs. Each line represents a particular elevation, and at the base of each topo, a contour's interval designation is given. If the contour interval is 20 feet, then the distance between each contour line is 20 feet. Follow five contour lines up on the same map, and the elevation has increased by 100 feet.

Let's assume that the 7.5-minute-series topo reads "Contour Interval 40 feet," that the short trail we'll be hiking is 2 inches in length on the map, and that it crosses five contour lines from beginning to end. What do we know? Well, because the linear scale of this series is 2,000 feet to the inch (roughly 2.75 inches representing 1 mile), we know that our trail is approximately four-fifths of a mile long (2 inches are 4,000 feet). But we also know we'll be climbing or descending 200 vertical feet (five contour lines are 40 feet each) over that distance. And the elevation designations written on occasional contour lines will tell us if we're heading up or down.

In addition to the sources listed in Appendix B, topos are available at major universities and some public libraries, where you might try photocopying the ones you need to avoid the cost of buying them. But if you want your own and can't find them locally, visit the USGS Web site, **topomaps.usgs.gov.**

BACKCOUNTRY ADVICE

Some hikes in this book on BLM land and in national forests let you camp along the way or at the destination. A permit is not required before entering the backcountry to camp. However, you should practice low-impact camping. Adhere to the adages "Pack it in, pack it out," and "Take only pictures, leave only footprints." Practice Leave No Trace camping ethics while in the backcountry; basic information on how to do so can be found at **www.lnt.org.**

Open fires are permitted except during dry times when the Forest Service may issue a fire ban. Backpacking stoves are strongly encouraged and fires are discouraged. You are required to protect your food from bears and other animals to minimize human impact on wildlife and to avoid their introduction to and dependence on human food. Wildlife learns to associate backpacks and backpackers with easy food sources, thereby influencing their behavior. Bear-proof canisters or odor-sealing bags will help prevent advertising your food's location. Hanging a bear bag is no longer considered effective against California black bears and is now discouraged.

Solid human waste must be buried in a hole at least 3 inches deep and at least 200 feet away from trails and water sources; a trowel is basic backpacking equipment.

Following the above guidelines will increase your chances for a pleasant, safe, and low-impact interaction between humans and nature. Forest and park regulations can change over time; contact the appropriate managing agency to confirm the status of any regulations before you enter the backcountry.

TRAIL ETIQUETTE

Whether you're on a city, county, state, or national park trail, always remember that great care and resources (from nature as well as from your tax dollars) have gone into creating these trails. Treat trails, wildlife, and fellow hikers with respect.

- **Hike on open trails only. Respect trail and road closures (ask if not sure), avoid possible trespassing on private land, and obtain all permits and authorization as required. Also, leave gates as you found them or as marked.**

- **Leave only footprints. Be sensitive to the ground beneath you. This also means staying on the existing trail and not blazing any new trails. Be sure to pack out what you pack in. No one likes to see the trash someone else has left behind.**

- Never spook animals. An unannounced approach, a sudden movement, or a loud noise startles most animals. A surprised animal can be dangerous to you, to others, and to themselves. Give them plenty of space.

- Plan ahead. Know your equipment, your ability, and the area in which you are hiking—and prepare accordingly. Be self-sufficient at all times; carry necessary supplies for changes in weather or other conditions. A well-executed trip is satisfying to you and to others.

- Be courteous to other hikers, bikers, equestrians, and others you encounter on the trails.

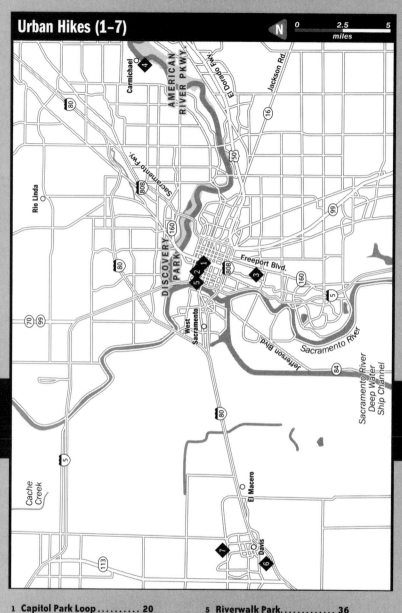

URBAN HIKES

01 CAPITOL PARK LOOP

KEY AT-A-GLANCE INFORMATION

LENGTH: 1.5 miles
CONFIGURATION: Loop
DIFFICULTY: Cakewalk
WATER REQUIRED: 1 liter
SCENERY: Arboretum, statuary, monuments, memorials
EXPOSURE: Some sun, some shade
TRAIL TRAFFIC: Moderate
TRAIL SURFACE: Paved walkways
HIKING TIME: 2 hours
SEASON: Year-round
ACCESS: No fees or permits
MAPS: USGS Sacramento East; park-brochure map
WHEELCHAIR TRAVERSABLE: Yes, if you access trail at 11th and L streets
FACILITIES: On- and off-street parking; water fountains; benches
DRIVING DISTANCE: 1 mile
SPECIAL COMMENTS: This route can be walked in any direction, depending on the interests of the hiker or location of your parking space.

IN BRIEF

The California State Capitol Park is one of the most outstanding capitol grounds to be found in any state. You can meander aimlessly through the dozen or so memorials, which are spread among hundreds of trees, bushes, and flowers from around the world in this 40-acre Victorian-style garden.

DESCRIPTION

Capitol Park can be accessed from any point along its 12-city-block length, and so it seems natural to start closest to where you park. The starting point of this hike is on the north side steps at 11th Street. You can get a pamphlet at the State Capitol Museum, which offers a good map and an informative description of the park's many features.

Several major plantings, or "beautifications," were undertaken between the park's inception in 1869 and the most recent beautification in 1951, when the capitol annex was built. Rather than plantings having been added to the park, only memorials have been erected since the 1950s. Some of the oldest trees, the "heritage" plantings, have succumbed to age or storms. The very prominent tulip tree, which stands right before the center of the north

---

Capitol Park Loop
UTM Zone (WGS84) 10S
Easting: 0631243
Northing: 4270940
Latitude: N 38° 34' 38"
Longitude: W 121° 29' 35"

Directions ————————————————————→

From Interstate 5 North in downtown Sacramento, exit at J Street and drive 12 blocks to 15th Street, where you will turn right. Drive two blocks to L Street and take another right. Parking is available at metered spaces on L Street. Or drive to Ninth Street, turn left, and make another left on N Street, where there is more metered parking. There are also several covered garages nearby.

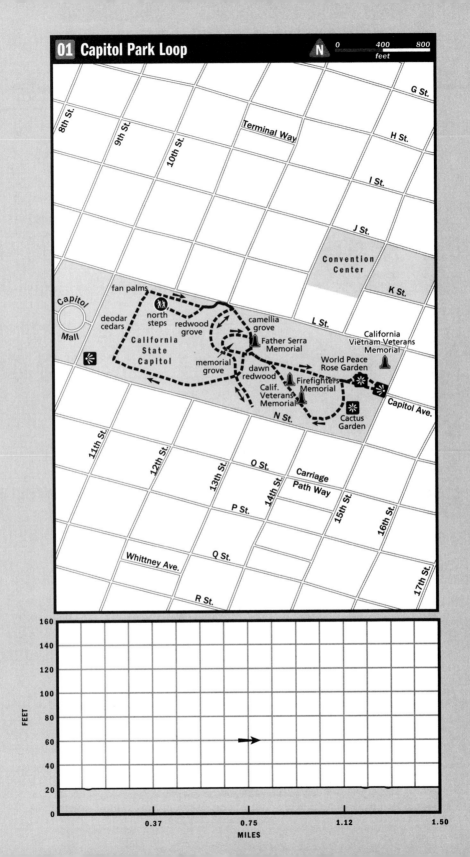

The Cactus Garden features plants donated by schoolchildren in 1914.

facade of the capitol, is currently being dismantled.

The sidewalks that encircle the park are lined with palms, and the walkways throughout the park are lined with trees; both paths are designed for the easiest and most complete access to the park's features. Paths are not always at right angles, so the park has a very natural appearance.

There is no one specific direction for visitors to travel through this park. If you turn right from the starting point, you will see a line of coast redwoods, original plantings from the 1872 beautification. A grove of coast redwood and giant sequoia is planted on the north side of the capitol, just to the east of the security entrance. One of the trees in this grove is called the "moon tree" by park staff because the seed was carried on an Apollo lunar mission and then planted on its return. The tree is not signed, however.

As you angle toward L Street, you will see the sole Italian stone pine remaining from the original planting in 1872. Turn right at 12th Street and head to the east entrance of the capitol, where you have some excellent photo opportunities. From here, walk east on the central promenade, where there are memorials and commemorative gardens on either side of you.

Next, walk to the 15th Street end of the park, where you will have some excellent photo opportunities of the capitol. The World Peace Rose Garden features a fragrant and colorful garden with benches dedicated by notable women who are themselves dedicated to peace.

The California Vietnam Veterans Memorial is adjacent to the rose garden. Its striking theme features stylized ammunition and starkly contrasting white limestone that holds black granite panels bearing the names of missing or dead California veterans of that war. The inside of the circular monument features reliefs and sculptures representing various aspects of armed service in Southeast Asia. The centerpiece of the memorial is a life-size bronze statue of a 19-year-old soldier.

The Firefighters Memorial is also made of granite and bronze and dramatically depicts the dangers facing firefighters in action. These two sculptures were added in 2002. Out toward N Street is the California Veterans Memorial, which is dedicated to all Californians who have served in the armed forces. Its use of photography and stone is unique.

An Indian grinding rock is to the west before you reach another coast redwood–giant sequoia grove with a comfortable bench encouraging rest and contemplation. Make your way north again, where the Spanish-American War Memorial, the Civil War Memorial, and the Liberty Bell Memorial are grouped among flowers and trees. An example of the dawn redwood, the only deciduous redwood species, is here. From the interior of China, it was long thought to be extinct.

The life-size monument featuring Father Junipero Serra is prominently featured in front of the colorful camellia grove. Standing beneath a lamppost shaped like a shepherd's crook, Father Serra's bronze statue looks down on a bronze relief map of California mounted on a black marble pedestal.

You can wander around the inside perimeter sidewalk on the west side of the capitol, where a row of deodar cedars flanks the walkway for two city blocks. The corner is a good spot from which to take some pictures.

Walking along these pathways on a weekend morning is a real pleasure at Capitol Park, where you can find both natural and man-made art. The architecture is classic and unimposing. The gardens and groves, with their thousands of flowers, bushes, and trees, are just waiting for you to view, smell, touch, photograph, and wander among.

NEARBY ACTIVITIES

Old Sacramento features original buildings and excellent restorations, along with dining and entertainment. Hike 2 in this book (see next page) guides you through the streets of Old Sacramento Historic State Park.

02 OLD SACRAMENTO STATE HISTORIC PARK

KEY AT-A-GLANCE INFORMATION

LENGTH: 1.75 miles
CONFIGURATION: Loops
DIFFICULTY: Cakewalk
WATER REQUIRED: None
SCENERY: Restored 19th-century buildings
EXPOSURE: Shade inside every door
TRAIL TRAFFIC: Busy
TRAIL SURFACE: Cobblestone pavement, wooden sidewalk
HIKING TIME: 1–2 hours
SEASON: Year-round
ACCESS: Always open; no fees or permits
MAPS: USGS Sacramento West
WHEELCHAIR TRAVERSABLE: Yes
FACILITIES: All amenities are available here.
DRIVING DISTANCE: 1 mile
SPECIAL COMMENTS: Brochure with street map available at www.oldsacramento.com

IN BRIEF

In the middle of the 19th century, Old Sacramento was a pioneer post, a glint-in-the-eye trading town with decent growth prospects. When the discovery of gold was announced, the nonnative population of California rose from fewer than 15,000 in 1848 to more than 100,000 by 1850, and then exceeded 250,000 by 1852. Old Sacramento bore the brunt of that growth explosion and, surviving repeated floods and fires, quickly became a noted transportation and terminus and communication hub, and the enduring center of California's government.

DESCRIPTION

The golden glimmer of the sun-drenched Tower Bridge almost forces you to turn in to Old Sacramento to escape the glare. Once you find yourself on Front Street, a quick look around tells you that you are in another era.

The cobblestone streets and wooden sidewalks of Old Sacramento are as appealing as you might expect, inviting its 5 million annual visitors to stroll . . . and stroll some more. With more than 50 reconstructed 19th-century buildings, the entire 1850s business district lies within the park's limits and was named a National Historic Landmark in 1965.

Old Sacramento State Historic Park

UTM Zone (WGS84) 10S

Easting: 0630080

Northing: 4271344

Latitude: N 38° 37' 51"

Longitude: W 121° 30' 23"

Directions ⟶

Old Sacramento is downtown and can be reached via Interstate 5's J Street exit. Follow the signs for covered, street, or open-lot parking. Enter Old Sacramento at Third and I streets or at Capitol Mall and Front Street.

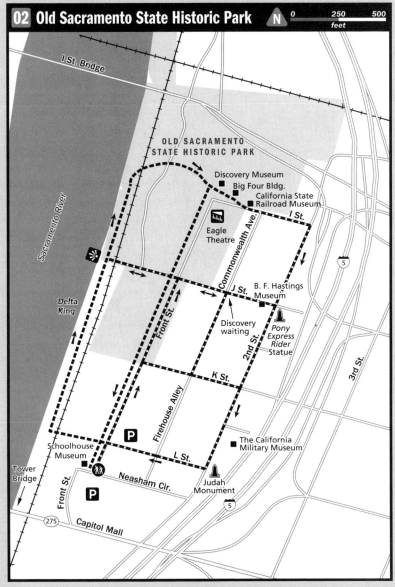

N 0   250   500
feet

I St. Bridge

OLD SACRAMENTO
STATE HISTORIC PARK

Sacramento River

Discovery Museum
Big Four Bldg.
California State
Railroad Museum
I St.

Eagle
Theatre

Commonwealth Ave.

5

J St. B. F. Hastings
Museum

Delta
King

Front St.

Discovery
waiting

Pony
Express
Rider
Statue

2nd St.

3rd St.

K St.

Firehouse Alley

The California
Military Museum

P

Schoolhouse
Museum

L St.

Tower
Bridge

Front St.

Neasham Cir.

Judah
Monument

P

5

275

Capitol Mall

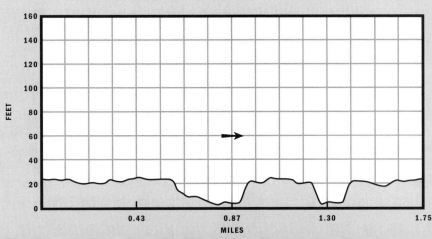

The Pony Express Rider portrays Sacramento's frenzied growth.

The Sacramento Schoolhouse Museum is a natural starting point for your walk among these restored historic buildings. Stroll through the Waterfront Park on your way to the market, where the activity of vendors recalls that of the original waterfront. While John Sutter was going about setting up an agricultural empire, Sam Brannan was doing business with the steady tide of business people arriving by riverboat.

The waterfront was the center of activity in Sacramento. Riverboat fans will enjoy the close-up views of the *Delta King* riverboat, which can be seen between the market and the railroad station. Look across the street from the passenger station to see the historic Eagle Theatre. It was the first theater to be opened in California, in 1849, and it was the first theater in California to be closed by flooding, in 1850.

Across the street from the freight station is the Booth Building, which housed wholesale dry goods and groceries. It appears that in the 20 years since John Sutter settled here, pioneers had transitioned from hunting rabbits for dinner to buying groceries at the store.

You will probably see or hear old steam trains traveling back and forth along the spur tracks heading past the station platforms and the Discovery Museum into the California State Railroad Museum. Trains operate on a 6-mile round-trip route for a 40-minute excursion on the Sacramento River levees. Volunteers from around Sacramento maintain and operate the trains, which run on weekends from April through September. They will gladly interrupt their tasks to answer questions.

Pass a cluster of picnic tables huddled under the massive sycamore tree shading the front of the Discovery Museum. The entrance is just beyond the branches' reach. If you are walking between the two museums on I Street, notice the historic Big Four Building, which housed the offices of the Central Pacific Railroad and the Huntington and Hopkins Store. The entrance to the California State Railroad Museum is just past the Big Four Building. When you exit there, look across the street at the patio dining area below the street. You are looking down on what was once the ground or street level before the city was raised 12 feet in 1862 to thwart further destruction caused by flooding.

On the left is the famous *Pony Express Rider* statue by Thomas Holland, one of the most popular items on display. This 3,800-pound bronze casting stands 15 feet tall and accurately portrays the rider and horse, according to contemporary accounts, which include Mark Twain's commentary on the rider's clothing. However, riders wore skullcaps more often than the hat depicted.

The western terminus of the Pony Express was across the street in the historic B. F. Hastings Building, which has housed a number of illustrious tenants. Built immediately after the fire of 1852, it once contained the Wells Fargo office and the California Supreme Court. It was also the western terminus for the transcontinental telegraph. Today it houses the Old Sacramento Historic State Park Visitor Center and the Wells Fargo Museum.

Pass the tall, narrow, brightly painted Sacramento Engine Company No. 3 (unless you are ready for an excellent meal), and look for the sculpture on the left. Theodore Judah's remembrance, detailed here in this intricately carved rock, can scarcely reflect the monumentality of his great achievement—engineering the Central Pacific Railroad's route across the Sierra Nevada Mountains.

Wander up and down the streets and sidewalks of Old Sacramento to see more historic buildings. The Lady Adams Building, the oldest in the city, houses a popular costume and variety shop. The Union Hotel, rebuilt with brick after the 1852 fire, was a fine hostelry in its day.

Sidewalk vendors ply their trade in front of the saloons, hotels, restaurants, and an assortment of shops that occupy the rest of the buildings composing Old Sacramento. Regardless of its occupant, the building itself is sure to have a story or secret for you to discover.

NEARBY ACTIVITIES

Walk across the river on the Tower Bridge to West Sacramento's Riverwalk, which is described in Hike 5 (page 36). Head east down the Capitol Mall to Capitol Park, also described in Hike 1.

03 WILLIAM LAND PARK TRAIL

KEY AT-A-GLANCE INFORMATION

LENGTH: 3 miles
CONFIGURATION: Out-and-back
DIFFICULTY: Cakewalk
WATER REQUIRED: 1 liter
SCENERY: Tree-filled city park
EXPOSURE: Shaded
TRAIL TRAFFIC: Moderate
TRAIL SURFACE: Sand and gravel
HIKING TIME: 1 hour
SEASON: Year-round, sunrise–sunset
ACCESS: No fees or permits
MAPS: USGS Sacramento East, Sacramento West; park map at www.cityofsacramento.org/parksandrecreation/parks/sites/land_map
FACILITIES: Restrooms, parking, phone, water
WHEELCHAIR TRAVERSABLE: Yes
DRIVING DISTANCE: 2 miles
SPECIAL COMMENTS: Land Park, with its varied features, has an active, family-oriented atmosphere.

IN BRIEF

This biking and jogging track leads through a grand old city park and is a wonderful place to hike among the native and ornamental trees, which border some wonderfully architected homes. Parking is near Fairytale Town. The route begins in front of the zoo, winds along the fishing pond and the golf course, and then leads on to circumnavigate the ball fields.

DESCRIPTION

When you need a place to hike that is close to home and still has a natural look and feel to it, William Land Park is the place to visit. Most people think of children's attractions when Land Park is mentioned. While the zoo and Fairytale Town are great attractions, there are a host of other attractions in this 146-acre park, such as a nine-hole golf course; fields for soccer, baseball, and softball; fishing ponds; and basketball courts. The clean, broad jogging and walking track winds among all of these.

William Land Park was added to Sacramento's park system with the purchase this land in 1918. The park's namesake, a former Sacramento mayor and hotel owner, William Land, willed the City of Sacramento $250,000 for "recreation sport for children and a pleasure ground for the poor." Although the city

---

William Land Park Trail
UTM Zone (WGS84) 10S
Easting: 0630540
Northing: 4266769
Latitude: N 38° 32' 23"
Longitude: W 121° 30' 07"

Directions ⟶

From downtown Sacramento at J Street and Interstate 5, drive 1.6 miles south on I-5 to the Sutterville Road exit. Take Sutterville Road east 0.4 miles and turn left on Land Park Drive. Take the first right turn to park next to Fairytale Town. The sand-and-gravel trail begins across from the zoo entrance at 15th Avenue and Land Park Drive.

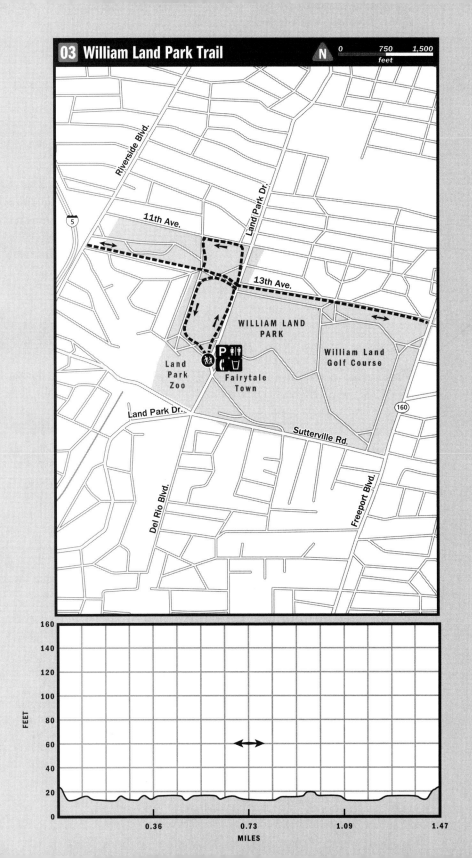

N

0   750   1,500
feet

Riverside Blvd.

11th Ave.

Land Park Dr.

5

13th Ave.

WILLIAM LAND PARK

William Land Golf Course

Land Park Zoo

P

Fairytale Town

Land Park Dr.

Sutterville Rd.

160

Del Rio Blvd.

Freeport Blvd.

160

40

60

80

100

120

140

160

20

0

FEET

0.36   0.73   1.09   1.47

MILES

had decided on this property for the park, Mr. Land's niece opposed the site's purchase and declared that her uncle had never liked the location. The zoo was opened in 1927 and Fairytale Town was opened in 1959.

At the sign declaring BEGIN BIKE LANE, just across from the zoo entrance, you will usually see a few daily athletes stretching and warming up as they ready themselves for a workout. This is where your 3-mile route begins as well.

Walk under the Douglas firs, foothill pines, and coast redwoods as you head north past the amphitheater. Pass the fishing pond, where you will hear whoops and cries of delight as youngsters reel in their first perch. You may hear other sorts of shouts as you pass golfers critiquing their latest shot.

There is a great deal of flexibility in how each individual completes this route, but the described track continues straight north across 13th Avenue on the way to looping around the baseball field at the top of Doc Oliver Park. Take a left on 11th Avenue and walk under the shade of the valley oaks and sycamore along there.

Turn left in order to continue south on sycamore-lined 13th Street as it rounds the ball fields before you bear right onto 13th Avenue. This street section is 0.3 miles long and takes you to Riverside Boulevard, where you will make a U-turn. Backtrack past the south end of Doc Oliver fields and continue along 13th Avenue 0.5 miles to Freeport Boulevard and back.

The promenade along 13th Avenue is made to seem so much larger by the towering cottonwood and sycamore trees in the park. Valley oaks, with their spreading limbs inviting strollers to enter their shade, dot the margin of the golf course. Houses lining the avenues around the park have added to the natural tone here, being surrounded by ornamental trees and shrubs.

Now that you have walked the two "arms" of the hike, cross Land Park Drive and walk to 13th Street. Then turn south on 13th Street and walk the 0.25 miles to 15th Avenue, where you will cross the street to your starting point.

NEARBY ACTIVITIES

Nine holes of golf can be arranged here by contacting the pro at William Land Park Golf Course, 1701 Sutterville Road, Sacramento, CA 95822; (916) 277-1207.

EFFIE YEAW NATURE CENTER TRAILS **04**

IN BRIEF

This 77-acre nature preserve offers a glimpse of the once-vast riparian and oak woodlands, shrub lands, meadows, and aquatic habitats along the American River. Deer, squirrels, wild turkeys, rabbits, snakes, hawks, owls, woodpeckers, songbirds, and waterfowl add to the adventure of the three self-guided walking trails.

DESCRIPTION

The Effie Yeaw Nature Center captures a time when Maidu Nisenan people camped along this area each summer, enjoying the plentiful food in this riparian habitat that once extended 5 miles on either side of the American River. Deer, rabbit, squirrel, fox, turkey, fowl, crayfish, and salmon, and plentiful valley oaks, willows, sedges, and reeds—all of the essential ingredients for Native American life—could be found where you now walk.

In the 1950s and 1960s, Effie Yeaw— a teacher, conservationist, and environmental educator—began leading natural and cultural history walks in this area formerly known as Deterding Woods.

Directions ⟶

From downtown Sacramento, take US 50 east 5 miles to the Watt Avenue North exit. Follow Watt Avenue north 0.8 miles to Fair Oaks Avenue. Turn right on Fair Oaks and drive 4 miles to Van Alstine (El Camino to the left). Turn right on Van Alstine and in 0.3 miles, turn left on California. Go 0.2 miles to Tarshes Drive, where you will turn right at the Ancil Hoffman Park sign. Drive 0.4 miles along Tarshes Drive to the entrance kiosk and then 0.2 miles to San Lorenzo Way; then turn left and head 0.1 mile to the nature center parking lot. The trailheads are on either side of the nature center.

KEY AT-A-GLANCE INFORMATION

LENGTH: 0.75–2.5 miles
CONFIGURATION: 3 loop trails
DIFFICULTY: Cakewalk
WATER REQUIRED: 1 liter
SCENERY: Riparian zone along American River
EXPOSURE: Shaded along 75% of trail
TRAIL TRAFFIC: Varied, depending on the day of the week
TRAIL SURFACE: Pebble and duff; river cobble and sand
HIKING TIME: 0.5–2 hours
SEASON: Open November–January, 9:30 a.m.–4 p.m.; February–October, 9 a.m.–5 p.m.; closed Thanksgiving, Christmas Day, and New Year's Day
ACCESS: No fees or permits
MAPS: USGS Carmichael; maps of the nature trails are available online and at the nature center.
FACILITIES: Restrooms, picnic tables, outdoor theatre, gift shop
WHEELCHAIR TRAVERSABLE: Yes, from the parking lot up to the nature center and possibly along parts of River History Trail. Trails are bumpy, slippery, and muddy in spots.
DRIVING DISTANCE: 7 miles
SPECIAL COMMENTS: See longer note at end of Description.

Effie Yeaw Nature Center Trails

UTM Zone (WGS84) 10S
Easting: 0646982
Northing: 4275671
Latitude: N 38° 37' 02"
Longitude: W 121° 18' 42"

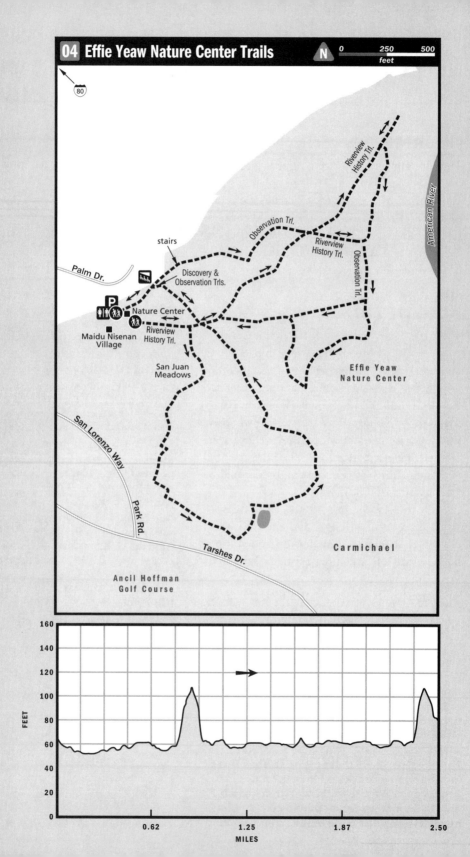

Protected wildlife thrives in the nature center's sanctuary.

Yeaw raised interest in preserving the lands along the river and worked with the Sacramento County Parks Department to develop the concept of a parkway along the river that would include these grounds. Most importantly, her vision helped stimulate the formation of the Save the American River Association (SARA) and establishment of the American River Parkway.

As you walk from the parking lot to the nature center, pause and read the interpretive signs for the native California species displayed here. Look to your right at the Maidu Nisenan summer village, where you will see authentic examples of a tule shelter, grinding rock, acorn granary, and fire pit, plus a shade shelter.

Pick up a free map of the nature preserve trails inside the center. You have a choice of three trails, which start in two different spots: The Observation Trail and Discovery Trail begin at a trailhead behind the center. The Riverview History Trail begins (and the Discovery Trail ends) near the huge walnut tree to the left of the picnic tables next to the Maidu village.

The interpretive signs on these trails are among the best in any park system. Each consecutively numbered sign has a symbol which indicates the trail, drawings or pictures, and complete descriptions—all etched into a durable metal sign.

The Discovery Trail, the Observation Trail, and the Riverview History Trail have common starting points, common ending points, and parts of the trail in common—but not all in the same way. If it sounds confusing, relax. These trails are delightful and well signed. So while you might easily get off one route and onto another, there is no fear of becoming "temporarily mislocated."

Step back out of the nature center, turn left, and walk around the building. Pass the Himalayan blackberries on your right, then pass the small outdoor theatre, and your trailhead is another ten feet.

This is a dual trailhead—straight ahead for the Observation Trail and right for the Discovery Trail. The Observation Trail both starts and ends here. The Discovery Trail starts here but ends at the start of the Riverview History Trail.

Ahead, on the Observation Trail, you will start out with a nicely shaded, winding, duff-covered trail that leads to a bench atop the only stairs on the trails. Look at the moss covering the north side of the trees in this damp valley-oak grove. Momentarily, the trail will open up and join the Riverview History Trail for a brief bit of full sunshine. In this open area, the native grasses and sedges proliferated after floods.

Pay close attention as you approach the river. The Observation Trail makes a turn to the right, and the Riverview History Trail turns to the left 10 feet farther along. Take the Observation Trail, heading south on this duff trail and ignoring the first trail that comes in from the right. Although that trail from the right will reconnect with this trail and lead back to the center, the Observation Trail continues ahead. Look to the left at the moonscape of large river cobble and boulders. This spectacular scene is just part of the original land granted to John Sutter.

Make a right onto the next trail and plunge into a thick copse of live oak, where you can feel the air temperature drop. Sample more blackberries if there are any. The undergrowth is so lush and the foliage so thick that it is difficult to hear or see others, which affords a nice sense of solitude; take a break at the bench where the trail turns briefly north.

A small meadow ringed by live oak offers a nice spot for deer to browse. The trail crosses Riverview History Trail but soon turns toward the nature center, so do not let the deer capture your attention at this junction. A short uphill section returns you to the trailhead and the start of Discovery Trail.

On Discovery Trail, you will descend gently alongside Himalayan blackberries, past giant—fallen and decomposing—valley oak, alongside Dutchman's pipevine, all of which provides habitat for beetles, ground squirrels, hummingbirds, and woodpeckers.

As you look to your right, you will see deer lounging near the trail and around the margin of San Juan Meadows. The meadow is defined by huge valley oaks. These prototypically spreading oaks are found only in California and are the largest species of oak in North America. Deer and rabbit are plentiful here, and the opportunities for outstanding wildlife photos are abundant. But stay on the trails—particularly in this area. As in most parks, this one also posts cautions about poison oak and even has interpretive signs pointing it out along this section of the trail.

Turkeys are abundant in this area and you will notice their signs everywhere if you do not slip on or trip over them first. And they roost in trees! Enjoy the sandy, winding trail as you read the signs on the way to the nature pond. A clean bench there makes a great perch to observe bugs, reptiles, and birds.

After winding through sedge-filled groves of live oak and western redbud, the trail begins to turn to sand and river cobble. At the junction with the Riverview History Trail, turn left. Walk past your initial crossing with this trail and head west along the San Juan Meadows. The Discovery Trail ends where the Riverview History Trail begins—at the huge, two-toned walnut tree.

Now at the beginning of the Riverview History Trail, you have seen and crossed several parts of it. The trail, made of river cobble and sand, is partly service road and is therefore potholed in spots. On this, the most openly exposed of all the trails, walk straight; the trails you walked earlier cross your path. You will angle toward the American River. Beautiful modern homes on the cliffs above you stand in stark contrast to the quiet as you approach the river. You will take a much smaller footpath off to the right, angling another 50 feet toward the river. If you happen to miss this turn, you will find a bench about 100 feet ahead. Turn there and come back to this trail alongside the river.

Head south along the trail and try to imagine the view without the remains of gold dredging. A bench ahead on your right is a great spot for that and for bird watching.

At the next signed junction to the right, you will turn and retrace your steps from the Observation Trail as the Riverview History Trail now joins with it for the return to the nature center.

Note: The Effie Yeaw Nature Center (inside Ancil Hoffman County Park, 2850 San Lorenzo Way, Carmichael, California; [916] 489-4918) offers programs for all ages every Saturday and Sunday at 1:30 p.m. Visit the center's Web site, **www.effieyeaw.org,** for details, a calendar, and maps.

NEARBY ACTIVITIES

Folsom State Recreation Area has a 90-mile network of multiuse trails that includes the Pioneer Express Trail (Hike 28, page 153) as well as a 21-mile segment of the American Discovery Trail, the nation's first coast-to-coast nonmotorized recreation trail.

05 RIVERWALK PARK

KEY AT-A-GLANCE INFORMATION

LENGTH: 1.07 miles

CONFIGURATION: Semi-loop

DIFFICULTY: Easy

WATER REQUIRED: 1 liter

SCENERY: Sacramento riverfront

EXPOSURE: Completely exposed to sun

TRAIL TRAFFIC: Moderate

TRAIL SURFACE: Paved sidewalks and pathways

HIKING TIME: 30 minutes

SEASON: Year-round

ACCESS: No fees or permits

MAPS: USGS Sacramento West

WHEELCHAIR TRAVERSABLE: Yes

FACILITIES: Picnic areas, pit toilets

DRIVING DISTANCE: 1 mile

SPECIAL COMMENTS: Garage and metered street parking; work is under way to extend Riverwalk's landscaped walkway and grounds past E Street to the I Street Bridge, as mapped here.

IN BRIEF

West Sacramento's Riverwalk Park offers a fresh perspective on the Sacramento River at the embarcadero. There are shade trees lining the riverbank where you can picnic and watch boat traffic. The promenade will ultimately reach from the Lighthouse Marina to the locks at the Port of Sacramento. The walk currently runs from the Tower Bridge to a block south of the I Street Bridge. Pass the Grand Staircase and the renowned Ziggurat Building on your way to crossing the railroad bridge as you return to Old Sacramento.

DESCRIPTION

The most convenient, and most interesting, place to park is on the cobbled streets of Old Sacramento. Whether you use the garage or metered parking on the street, walk out to the Tower Bridge, which you will cross to reach the Riverwalk arch. Alternatively, there is a pedestrian access point to Riverwalk in the cul-de-sac at the end of Second Avenue on the north side of the Ziggurat Building.

Look east and you will be met with an excellent view of the white dome of the capitol, sitting handsomely above its surrounding trees. A right turn places you squarely in front of the Tower Bridge—gleaming gold at

---

Riverwalk Park

UTM Zone (WGS84) 10S

Easting: 0629803

Northing: 4271360

Latitude: N 38° 34' 52"

Longitude: W 121° 30' 35"

Directions

From Interstate 5 North in downtown Sacramento, take the Old Sacramento exit onto J Street, then head toward the Tower Bridge. Turn right into Old Town Sacramento and park. Walk across the Tower Bridge and turn right beneath the Riverwalk archway, which is your trailhead.

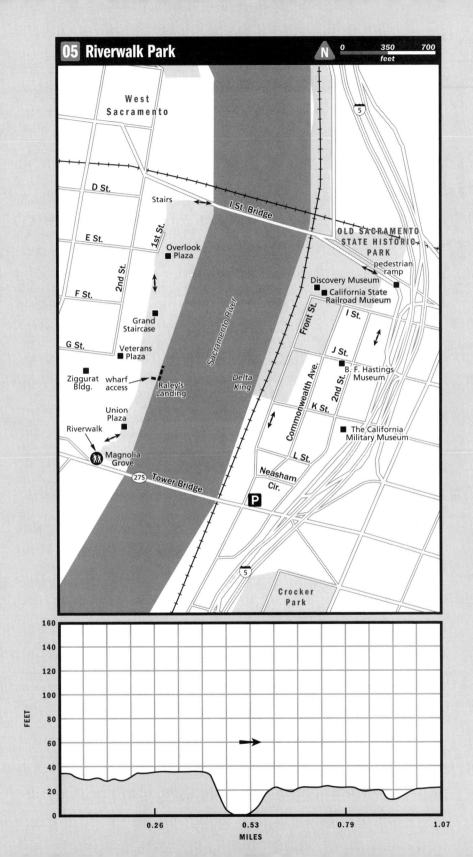

N

0   350   700
feet

West
Sacramento

D St.

Stairs

I St. Bridge

1st St.

Overlook
Plaza

OLD SACRAMENTO
STATE HISTORIC
PARK

E St.

2nd St.

pedestrian
ramp

Discovery Museum

California State
Railroad Museum

F St.

Front St.

I St.

Grand
Staircase

Sacramento River

J St.

G St.

Veterans
Plaza

B. F. Hastings
Museum

2nd St.

Ziggurat
Bldg.

wharf
access

Raley's
Landing

Delta
King

Commonwealth Ave.

K St.

The California
Military Museum

Union
Plaza

Riverwalk

L St.

Magnolia
Grove

Neasham
Cir.

275   Tower Bridge

P

5

Crocker
Park

160

140

120

100

FEET

80

60

40

20

0

0.26   0.53   0.79   1.07

MILES

Cross Tower Bridge from Old Sacramento to Riverwalk's arched entry.

any time of day but shining brightest at sunrise. The bridge's gold paint pays homage to the mineral that made their boat landing at Sacramento a turning point in the lives of so many following the spring of 1848.

Built in 1935 for less than $1 million, the Tower Bridge originally accommodated trolleys in the middle of four traffic lanes. Pedestrians have always been able to walk across the 737-foot bridge on its outside walkways. Walk to the west and look up under the arched trusses. The 200-foot center span and the equipment used to lift it weigh more than 5 million pounds.

Once on the West Sacramento side of the river, turn right at the brick-paved entry to the Riverwalk. The Flemish settler known as John Schwartz settled West Sacramento in the 1840s. He and his brother founded salmon fisheries, along with drying, pickling, and other seafood operations along the river's shores. They later sold land to the McDowell family; when Mr. McDowell was killed in a bar fight, his widow subdivided her land, which became known as the Town of Washington and was later renamed Broderick.

At about the same time, a hopeful but unlucky gold miner named Mike Bryte retreated from the foothills and took up dairy farming on the west banks of the Sacramento. The community known as Bryte was established after his farm was subdivided. The communities of Broderick and Bryte, also called East Yolo, eventually became incorporated as the town of West Sacramento.

From the arched entrance, walk toward the river. The first set of steps, decorated with a derrick, is Union Square, which is dedicated to the port laborers who had worked here and at the Port of Sacramento in the early days. An iron anchor chain borders the promenade to the north. Below you, just past the picnic area and the trees along the shore, are a water-taxi stop and a fishing pier.

Through a break in the sycamore, you can see the *Delta King* moored on the opposite bank, below the train depot in Old Sacramento. Bird's-eye view drawings from 1849 show a river port active with ships of all types on both shores. Most maritime commerce today is handled in the deep-water Port of Sacramento. Now a local landmark, the Ziggurat Building is the largest office building in West Sacramento and is known not only for its unique terraced design but also for its use of seismic dampers. The Ziggurat Building overlooks the Raley's Landing boat wharf. A wooden boardwalk provides access to the wharf through the giant cottonwoods; there are picnic tables on the lawn on either side of the boardwalk.

Pass the simple Veterans Plaza just before the Grand Staircase, which fans out down to the picnic areas. Just opposite E Street are another overlook and a plaza that offer great vistas of Sacramento's skyline and the Sacramento River, along with views of waterfowl and shorebirds.

Continue north to the I Street Bridge, which you will cross to reach Old Sacramento. This double-decker bridge is one of two built in 1911. The original 1911 bridge at M Street is no longer there, but the one at I Street remains. Stroll across the Sacramento River for an excellent view. The Amtrak Capital Corridor rumbles beneath you, and you will swear the whole bridge is going to shake apart.

The sidewalk exits onto the circular ramp leading into Old Sacramento. Wind along Second Street and turn up J Street. You can explore the below-grade courtyard filled with columns at the corner of J and Commonwealth. Finally, continue up to Front Street and back to your car.

NEARBY ACTIVITIES

The Discovery Museum and the California State Railroad Museum are on I Street next to the Big Four Building in Old Sacramento. The Museum is open daily (except Thanksgiving, Christmas and New Year's Day) from 10 a.m. to 5 p.m. Effective January 1, 2006: $8 adults; $3 youths ages 6 to 17; children ages 5 and under are free. More information is online at **www.csrmf.org.**

For information regarding Old Sacramento, a brochure is available online at **www.oldsacramento.com.**

06 UC DAVIS ARBORETUM TRAIL

KEY AT-A-GLANCE INFORMATION

LENGTH: 3.5 miles
CONFIGURATION: Loop
DIFFICULTY: Cakewalk
WATER REQUIRED: 1 liter
SCENERY: Flora from around the world
EXPOSURE: Mostly shaded
TRAIL TRAFFIC: Light
TRAIL SURFACE: Asphalt, pebble, and sand
HIKING TIME: 2 hours, plus lingering time
SEASON: Year-round
ACCESS: No fees or permits
MAPS: USGS Merritt, Davis
WHEELCHAIR TRAVERSABLE: Yes
FACILITIES: Water fountains and restrooms in various locations near the trail. See UC Davis Arboretum map for exact locations.
DRIVING DISTANCE: 14 miles
SPECIAL COMMENTS: This hike is not only beautiful and enjoyable but accessible and educational, too.

- -

UC Davis Arboretum Trail
UTM Zone (WGS84) 10S
Easting: 0608159
Northing: 4265533
Latitude: N 38° 31' 53"
Longitude: W 121° 45' 32"

IN BRIEF

More than 4,000 plants and flowers are on display at the University of California, Davis, Arboretum in 18 collections and gardens. If you want to learn about the flora in California's biozones, a few hours among these magnificent gardens and collections will satisfy your interest.

DESCRIPTION

The UC Davis Arboretum Trail winds peacefully along an interstate highway and city streets. On this hike, you start out by walking southwest through fragrant lavender, rosemary, and other herbs growing on both sides of the Mediterranean Collection along Putah Creek Lagoon.

When Putah Creek's channel was diverted in the 1870s, what remained was this abandoned oxbow—the old north channel—which dried up over the years and became the sole depression among otherwise flat farmland. From its beginnings as an actual farm for horticultural

- -

Directions ⟶

From Interstate 5 in downtown Sacramento, drive 13 miles west on I-80 to Davis. Exit I-80 at UC Davis (Exit 71), and turn right on Old Davis Road. Continue straight ahead onto California Avenue and make the next left onto La Rue Road. Turn left on Putah Creek Lodge Road and then right into the parking area. Parking is also available in Lots 47 and 48 on La Rue Road and costs $6; you can use a credit card or $1 bills. Parking is limited on weekdays, but on weekends it is free and more broadly available. The trail described here starts at the Putah Creek Lodge footbridge. You can begin your hike from any point along the path, but this hike begins at the Mediterranean collection at the footbridge on the side of the creek opposite the Putah Creek Lodge.

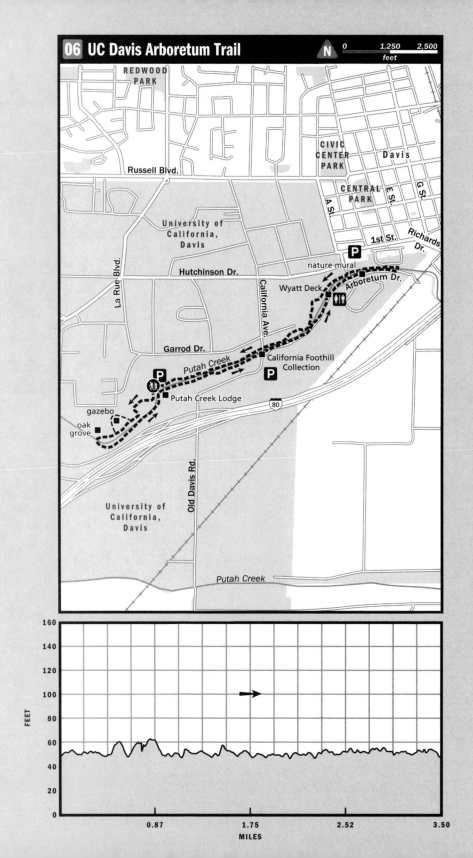

N

0   1,250   2,500
feet

REDWOOD
PARK

Russell Blvd.

CIVIC
CENTER
PARK

D a v i s

CENTRAL
PARK

A St.

E St.

G St.

University of
California,
Davis

1st St.

Richards
Dr.

P

nature mural

Hutchinson Dr.

Wyatt Deck

Arboretum Dr.

California Ave.

Garrod Dr.

California Foothill
Collection

Putah Creek

P

P

80

Putah Creek Lodge

gazebo

oak
grove

La Rue Blvd.

Old Davis Rd.

University of
California,
Davis

Putah Creek

160

140

120

100

80

60

40

20

0

FEET

0.87   1.75   2.52   3.50

MILES

> The Redwood Grove hosts picnic tables for a quiet repast.

instruction in World War I until 1936, the arboretum area became the collection point for an abundance of unwanted materials. The arboretum was founded February 29 of that same year, when students, faculty, and administrators joined in their traditional "leap day campus-improvement project." This included the arboretum's "first planting," which comprised many of the trees seen along the south shore from Wyatt Deck to the California Avenue Bridge.

The design and placement of the arboretum included plants native to California that have low water requirements, and protected the magnificent 400-year-old valley oaks (*Quercus lobata*) growing in the California Foothill Collection. Caretakers of the arboretum have adhered to the principle of using the natural landform whenever possible. The larger ponds at the south end of the arboretum were sculpted, but you may not notice this as you walk around the vine-covered gazebo and its fragrant white-flower garden. The oak grove to the far right is popular for catching shade on hot summer days.

The plants lining the trail represent those specifically native to the various regions of California and, more generally, to the regions of the world where a Mediterranean climate predominates. You will find gardens and collections in this 100-acre arboretum that represent areas such as South Africa, Australia, or South America; also, specific plants are grouped by type, as in the oak groves, the redwood grove, and the acacia collection, and there are demonstration gardens and horticultural theme gardens, like the white-flower garden.

As you might expect, you are never far from shade on this trail, but a broad-brimmed hat will help keep you cool as you browse around at the boathouse, where an early-California garden displays plants found in the state before the gold rush. There really are no empty spaces—understory trees and bushes, grasses and flowers seem to occupy the terrain and line the creekside path.

Pass to the right of Putah Creek Lodge, with its inviting fire pit and seating area, through the South American Collection with its lush Cuyamaca cypress, and then into the dense, cool shade of the acacia grove. As you walk around the little side trails and groves, take notice of the soil underfoot on these bordered trails. The silt and plant debris deposited alongside this former channel were the ingredients that created the rich sandy loam that is so beneficial to all of the plants here. Towering Torrey pines and spreading California sycamore suddenly dwarf any understory plants, but California poppies can be counted on for color.

There are very few surprising turns on this trail, and all are clearly marked. Aleppo pine, buckeye, and California box elder lead into the valley-oak grove as you head toward the Mondavi Center for the Performing Arts. The California Foothill Collection features live oak, toyon, mesa oak, gray pine, and a streamside covered with wild grapes, in addition to a five-foot-diameter valley oak.

Flowers and shrubs accompany you past Marak Hall Drive, and native Californian plants fill the side gardens just ahead of Wyatt Deck and the redwood grove. California fuchsia, dwarf coyote bush, Torrey pine and Santa Cruz ironwood, Catalina Island mountain mahogany, Canary Island pine and sand mesa manzanita, shooting star, and penstemon are all part of this impressively colorful display.

Leap Day 1941 saw the planting of the redwood trees in this grove. Because they are not native to the valley, these coast redwoods were hand-watered by energetic students, who are responsible for the trees' maturing into the grove you see today. This is the spot to stop and take notes and pictures and have a drink or a snack. The picnic tables offer solitude within these giant trees.

Art and nature are as important as the gardens to the arboretum. The huge, colorful, and oversize nature lesson that is found in the tunnel-wall mural is an example of that partnership. Take the left fork after this tunnel and enter the Australian collection. Your turnaround takes you to the other side of the creek, onto a dirt path just opposite the mural tunnel. Meander through the North Coast Collection opposite the redwood grove. Your dirt path will return to asphalt at the next footbridge. Formosan redwood, soquel coast redwood, and egg-shaped sculptures precede the desert collection, with its sunny patch of blossoming prickly-pear cactus and looming agave plant.

Gray pine, Oaxaca pine, Chinese juniper, and a long line of redbud lead into the South American Collection and back to the trailhead.

NEARBY ACTIVITIES

Group tours can be arranged with 30 days' notice by calling (530) 752-4880.

07 DAVIS-COVELL GREENBELT

KEY AT-A-GLANCE INFORMATION

LENGTH: 2.7 miles

CONFIGURATION: Loop

DIFFICULTY: Cakewalk

WATER REQUIRED: 0.5 liters

SCENERY: Urban green space with wildlife-viewing platforms

EXPOSURE: Plenty of sun and shade

TRAIL TRAFFIC: Moderate but not crowded

TRAIL SURFACE: Asphalt pavement

HIKING TIME: 1.5 hours

SEASON: Year-round

ACCESS: No fees or permits

MAPS: USGS Davis, Merritt

FACILITIES: Restrooms here and at Northstar Park

WHEELCHAIR TRAVERSABLE: Yes

DRIVING DISTANCE: 15 miles

SPECIAL COMMENTS: This hike features playgrounds, lawn sculptures, and a nature walk.

Davis–Covell Greenbelt

UTM Zone (WGS84) 10S

Easting: 0609110

Northing: 4268722

Latitude: N 38° 33' 36"

Longitude: W 121° 44' 51"

IN BRIEF

The Davis–Covell Greenbelt links the Davis Community Park and Northstar Park while it weaves through neighborhoods and their playgrounds. The well-lit asphalt path has location signs and easy access to all the adjacent communities.

DESCRIPTION

The Davis–Covell Greenbelt is a wonderful path to walk and includes a surprising diversity of interesting sights. The described hike begins at the pedestrian overpass at the north end of the Davis Community Park. There is an alternative starting point, also with parking and restrooms, at Northstar Park, which is located at the north end of the greenbelt. If you are arriving on foot, almost every side street along the path accesses the greenbelt, which winds through the surrounding communities.

Once across the bridge, the trail splits at the first playground. You will be returning along the path to the left. Walk straight, generally north northwest, along the greenbelt as it meanders through Covell Park. The names of the streets you pass all have a Spanish

Directions

From Interstate 5 in downtown Sacramento, drive west on I-80 to the Russell Boulevard exit in Davis. Follow Russell Boulevard under the railroad overpass and bear slightly right at First Street, where Russell Boulevard becomes E Street. Turn right at Fourth Street and then left on F Street, one block later. Continue north on F Street ten blocks to West Covell Boulevard. Turn left on West Covell Boulevard and then left into the parking lot just before the pedestrian overpass. Your trailhead is at the end of the overpass.

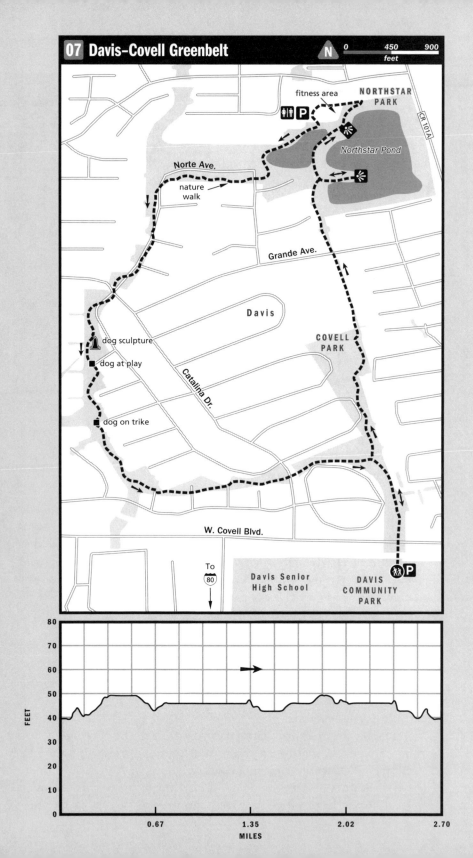

The Hugest Tongue in Davis Contest was a draw.

theme, and nearly every street has an entrance to the greenbelt. Within the first half mile, you will see tennis courts, benches, barbecue grills, swings, slides, merry-go-rounds, and other leisure amenities.

Continue past the empty field to your left and cross Grande Avenue. A fence to your right marks the border of the Northstar Park wetland area. A variety of waterfowl inhabit this small pond, and, from the sounds of it, so does a bevy of frogs. A nicely architected viewing platform extends into the wetland, allowing you to observe the wildlife. Egrets, herons, Canada geese, mallards, and coots comprise just a partial list of birds that live or visit here. An identically designed, but much smaller, viewpoint is located just 500 feet down the path on these tiny, wooded islands.

Pass the aerating pond to the left of the path and walk toward Anderson Road, where you will turn left. A fitness and warm-up area sits on the path's left just 100 feet past the smaller viewpoint. This is a good reason for beginning an exercise run at the Northstar Park and using the parking lot on the west side of the Tandem Properties building.

Continuing on the described path takes you through the parking lot, past the restrooms on the left, southward toward your trailhead. You will once again pass the aerating pond, with the playing fields of Northstar Park to your right.

There is a nature walk on your right just after the playing fields. An informational kiosk lists a huge variety of trees, shrubs, and flowers to be found here and also along the path. Walk west along the gravel path through the shady nature area and make sure to look up as you pass under the welded arbors.

Exiting the nature walk, turn to the south again along this pleasant walk. Within a few minutes, you will cross Catalina Drive and reach another of the small parks along the walk. Eucalyptus trees tower over the path as you enter Greenbelt Area #10. You may not have expected artwork to be among the interesting things you would be seeing on this walk Rendered in bronze and natural stone, several clever installations liven the pathway. Keep a lookout for a turkey-chasing dog along here. As you pass Ecuador Place, you may notice another friendly dog ready to share his water with your pup. And as you watch out for bicycles along the path, be on the alert for happy tricycle riders around Estrella Place.

The route described here continues straight south. But if you want to wander further to the west, turn right and walk through the tunnel under Anderson Road when the trail ends, just one block farther west you can pick up an alternate trail back to the north. Your path continues through signed greenbelt areas with playgrounds, Frisbee fields, picnic tables, and benches before crossing Catalina Drive and reentering Covell Park to the east. At the playground, you will take the path to the right and head toward the pedestrian overpass where you began your walk.

NEARBY ACTIVITIES

Before you get on the interstate, stop in for a burger at Redrum Burgers, at the intersection of Olive Drive and Russell Boulevard. When Murder Burger, a straightforward burger-and-beer joint expanded to Rocklin, residents objected to the violent nature of the name, and so a renaming contest was held wherein Redrum was conceived. It continues to be known for its wide variety of beers and low-fat-beef burgers (ask about the Zoom).

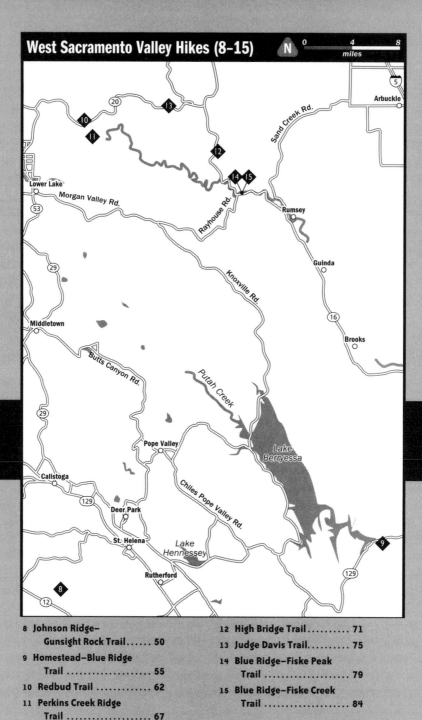

N 0   4   8
miles

Arbuckle

20   13

10

11

Lower Lake

Morgan Valley Rd.

53

Sand Creek Rd.

12

14 15

Rayhouse Rd.

Rumsey

Guinda

29

Knoxville Rd.

16

Middletown

Brooks

Butts Canyon Rd.

Putah Creek

Pope Valley

Lake
Berryessa

Calistoga

29

129

Deer Park

Chiles Pope Valley Rd.

St. Helena

Lake
Hennessey

Rutherford

9

129

8

12

WEST SACRAMENTO VALLEY HIKES

08 JOHNSON RIDGE– GUNSIGHT ROCK TRAIL

KEY AT-A-GLANCE INFORMATION

LENGTH: 9.2 miles
CONFIGURATION: Out-and-back
DIFFICULTY: Challenging
WATER REQUIRED: 3 liters
SCENERY: Foothill woodland, wildflowers, broad vistas
EXPOSURE: Mostly shaded, but some southern exposure
TRAIL TRAFFIC: Light
TRAIL SURFACE: Dirt and duff, dirt and rock
HIKING TIME: 5–6 hours
SEASON: Year-round, 8 a.m.–sunset
ACCESS: $5 fee
MAPS: USGS Kenwood; park trail map at trailhead
WHEELCHAIR TRAVERSABLE: No
FACILITIES: Parking area has water, toilet, maps, pay station, and informational kiosks.
DRIVING DISTANCE: 82 miles
SPECIAL COMMENTS: Awesome view of Sonoma Valley from the aptly named Gunsight Rock

---

Johnson Ridge–
Gunsight Rock Trail
UTM Zone (WGS84) 10S
Easting: 0537149
Northing: 4256081
Latitude: N 38° 27' 08"
Longitude: W 122° 34' 27"

IN BRIEF

There is no other vista overlooking the Sonoma Valley that is as broad as the one that you have from atop Gunsight Rock. Hikers can reach this lookout on an easier trail; in fact, this route is used by those training to climb Mount Shasta. Wildlife, wildflowers, and wild views en route to the summit make this one wild hike.

DESCRIPTION

Drop $5 into the self-register pay station, check out the maps and natural history information on the kiosks, pick up an area trail map from the dispenser, and stretch a bit, then take off along the pole-fence next to the road. Fifty feet up, under a live oak, is the trailhead. Here a sign indicates distances to various destinations and gives some safety rules.

Directions ———————————————→

From the intersection with Interstate 5, drive west on US 50, which will soon merge with Interstate 80 West. Drive 45.5 miles to the CA 12 West exit toward Napa/Sonoma (Jameson Canyon Road). Head 5.4 miles west on Jameson Canyon Road. Stay right on CA 12 West, driving 1.4 miles, then keep left on CA 12 West for 2.6 miles. Turn left at the traffic light onto CA 12/121S and drive west 9.3 miles. About a mile and a half after you cross the railroad tracks, turn right onto CA 116 heading north toward Glen Ellen and Kenwood. Drive 8 miles (note that in a mile and a half the road becomes Arnold Drive) to Madrone Road, and turn right. Drive 1 mile over to Sonoma Highway and turn left. Drive 8.2 miles on the Sonoma Highway to Pythian Road on the right next to the St. Francis Winery. Drive 0.2 miles to where Los Guilucos Road bears left and Pythian Road bears right. A marker at the junction informs you that the park and trailhead are 1 mile ahead.

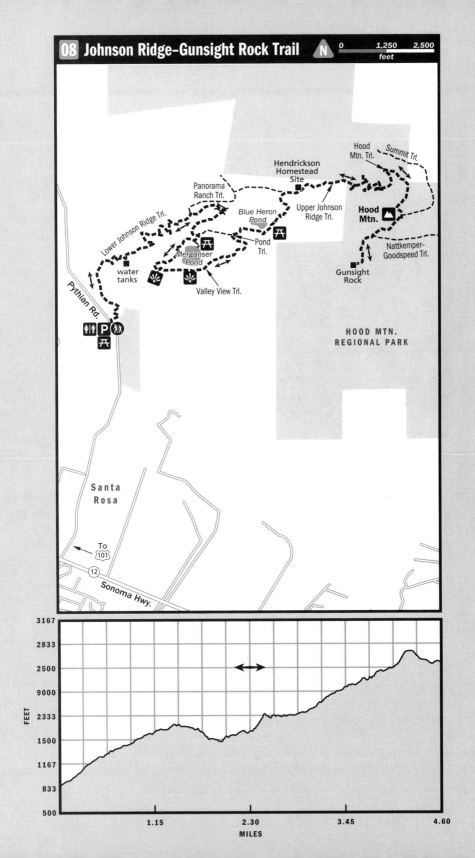

N

0   1,250   2,500
feet

Hood
Mtn. Trl.   Summit Trl.

Hendrickson
Homestead
Site

Panorama
Ranch Trl.

**Hood
Mtn.**

Blue Heron
Pond

Upper Johnson
Ridge Trl.

Lower Johnson Ridge Trl.

Pond
Trl.

Nattkemper-
Goodspeed Trl.

Merganser
Pond

water
tanks

Gunsight
Rock

Valley View Trl.

**HOOD MTN.
REGIONAL PARK**

Pythian Rd.

Santa
Rosa

To
101

12

Sonoma Hwy.

FEET				
3167				
2833				
2500				
9000				
2333				
1500				
1167				
833				
500				

1.15   2.30   3.45   4.60
MILES

The aptly named Gunsight Rock

The Hood Mountain Regional Park and Open Space Preserve stretches from the Santa Rosa Creek to the summit of Hood Mountain at the crest of the Mayacamas Mountains. It connects with Sugarloaf State Park on the east and has a 1,200-acre addition to the north. Your 4.5-mile trail gains 1,750 feet from the trailhead to a spot on Hood Mountain.

This route combines six excellent trails to create a trek that mirrors the Bay Area Ridge Trail on the park map. You will start out on the Lower Johnson Ridge Trail and then join the Pond and Valley View trails and finally the Upper Johnson Ridge Trail to reach the Hood Mountain Trail and the Gunsight Rock Trail.

Walk along the board fence to your right and cross the open space on a gravel path, winding around the huge live oak. Throughout the park, look for six-by-six-inch wooden posts bearing trail names and directional arrows. You are currently on the Lower Johnson Ridge Trail, which passes the second house and climbs up to meet the road, where the park boundary is.

Tighten your bootlaces. As the PLEASE DISMOUNT sign suggests, the next 0.3 miles are seriously steep. Shaded by madrone, live oak, sycamore, and Douglas fir, the path—and your uphill grind—end when you reach the gated residence on the right. Your trail is 100 feet on the left, beyond the gate. Under the shade of bay-laurel trees, hike the switchbacks past boulders and then snake past three wooden water tanks. The pipes leading from the spring to the tanks border your trail to the right. Walk along the left side of the road, then cross to the right along a gravel path next to a park-boundary fence. Walk up the road, with boulders to your left, and turn right at the next trail marker. The posts can sometimes blend with their surroundings, but all the trail junctions are marked on this route. Live oak and madrone have shaded this rock-and-dirt trail from the trailhead on, and occasional manzanita crowds the junctions. A few switchbacks lead to the next junction.

This junction calls for you to turn right and head toward Valley View Trail. A turn to the left would lead you away, on Panorama Ranch Trail. So take a right on Valley View Trail as it climbs a bit to reach the 1-mile mark on your hike. Cross a culvert over a small runoff, and then continue heading uphill on the right-hand trail as it turns to a gravel causeway that crosses a hillside meadow thick with Santa Barbara sedge, accented by blue-and-yellow, purple-and-white, and green-and-silver flowers mobbed by bees and butterflies.

As you step across the rock culverts of two more drainages on the way to Hood Creek, you will see a jumble of downed trees that speaks of the torrents and winds that can rip through this canyon. Cross the bridge over Hood Creek, then head up to the right toward Pond Trail. The sound of the cascades to your right fades as you move away from the creek and start descending on a single-track.

Avoid the old trail to the left; your trail winds along in total shade. Head around a knob from the north side to the south on this rocky section, with the creek to your right. At a junction, the Pond Trail heads both left and right. Heading left takes you about 1,500 feet over, to the Blue Heron Pond. But this shortcut misses the Valley View Trail.

So take the right fork downhill toward the Valley View Trail, then continue downhill, where you will see a NO sign off to your left just as you reach Merganser Pond. If you want to picnic, you can walk up the road about 500 feet past the NO sign, where there is a table at the pond's edge. Your route keeps on going along the Valley View Trail past the fenced culvert to your right. Another Valley View Trail sign is up ahead; where you will turn left and walk past the pond with a view of Merganser Island on your left.

A huge outcrop of rock imposes itself on the opposite side of the pond as you walk through the grass on the double-track. At the end of the pond, walk to the right, down the trail and past a rock outcrop. You are now on the Valley View Trail as it descends under Douglas fir and bay laurels. Start skirting the hill and then turn southeast up a 150-foot road to a wonderful vista point overlooking the valley at exactly the 2-mile point. Wind uphill again to a shady spot, where you will have another nice vista if you climb to the trail's right a bit.

Descend to another broad vista point, descend some more and then climb on a broad double-track with a steep slope to your left. After 2.5 miles, the trail flattens a bit at the junction where you head right on Pond Trail on the way to Upper Johnson Ridge Trail. On your left is small Blue Heron Pond; a picnic area sits just past the pond's southern end. The road remains flat as you pass over another culvert with water cascading across it.

The next junction sees Orchard Meadow Trail going off to the left where you head to the right on the Upper Johnson Ridge Trail. A scant 200 feet ahead on the left is the fenced-off Hendrickson homestead site for which the county is conducting a historical survey in order to best preserve and present the site.

A long uphill stretch of double-track leads you to a junction with the Knight's Retreat Trail, which heads off to the right in front of you. The Upper Johnson Ridge Trail turns left under the shade of live oak, sycamore, and bay laurel. Foothill pine and manzanita crowd the trail as you switchback up some 300 feet to the junction with the Hood Mountain Trail. As you near the junction, cypress trees begin to appear as well.

Now, well exposed to the sun, you reach the Hood Mountain Trail, which leads 0.3 miles up to the summit of Hood Mountain. This ranch road leads southward to a broad, flat area at the summit. It can be combined with the Panorama Ranch Trail for a loop route, or it can be taken all the way here from the Los Alamos Road trailhead.

This section is so steep that it may seem like an unpaved version of the third of a mile you climbed at the outset. The leaves, duff, and pebbles on this section make this steep trail slippery. Watch your footing on both the uphill and the return (no sudden stops going downhill).

After you catch your breath at the summit, look around as you enter this broad clearing. To your left is a trail sign for the Summit Trail. This does not lead to the summit. It is the trail that descends to Azalea Creek alongside the Hood Mountain Trail. Look across the clearing and you will see a trail marker for the Gunsight Rock Trail and Sugarloaf Ridge State Park. The summit is located past the break in the manzanita to the left of the trail marker. A summit register is hidden in a red coffee can to the left of the rocks.

After marking your summit, descend on the rocky Gunsight Rock Trail and squeeze through the volcanic rock outcropping before coming to the junction with the Nattkemper–Goodspeed Trail to Sugarloaf State Park. Gunsight Rock Trail turns right here; walk the final 0.1 mile to the overlook.

It is not too hard to understand how the trail got its name. Climb up the left- or right-hand boulders by easing around to the front of the rock. The vultures take off from their perches below you and soar up and around your lofty seat while you look out over the Sonoma Valley landscape. Orchards, hills, vineyards, and fields are spread out below and before you. Your vista includes three state parks, famous wineries, and the valleys and towns in which they lie, from Napa to Santa Rosa.

After the pictures are finished, turn back and retrace your steps 4.6 miles to the trailhead. Water is available at the trailhead, so stay hydrated and safe.

NEARBY ACTIVITIES

Kenwood, Agua Caliente, Glen Ellen, and Oakmont are open year-round and have excellent wineries and tasting rooms.

Jack London State Historic Park, Annadel State Park, and Sugarloaf Mountain State Park have excellent hiking trails and are all within 10 miles to the east, south, and west of the St. Francis Winery.

HOMESTEAD-BLUE RIDGE TRAIL   09

IN BRIEF

Offering adventurous day hikers spectacular views of Lake Berryessa from the solitude of a ridgeline trail, this informative and physically demanding hike is hard to surpass. Start out the morning walking along a seasonal canyon stream on a self-guided interpretive trail that culminates at an abandoned homestead site. Then tighten your laces as you ascend the "monster stairs" to a ridgeline trail where what was once ocean floor now stands on its side. This loop takes hikers through seven habitat zones, or biozones, which support a vast array of fauna and flora.

DESCRIPTION

Every hiker has yearned for the trail that seems like an all-you-can-eat buffet for the naturalist. Set in the Stebbins Cold Canyon Reserve, the Homestead–Blue Ridge Trail offers it up. The Homestead Trail is an easy hike along an interpretive trail. In a short time, you will learn about trees, shrubs, flowers, reptiles, amphibians, insects, and rocks. At about 1 mile, you will encounter the abandoned Vlahos Homestead overlooking Cold Canyon Creek.

Directions ⟶

From the junction of the Capital City Freeway and Interstate 80 West, drive 10 miles to CR 113 North. Take CR 113 two exits to reach the Russell Road exit. Turn left and drive another 12 miles to Winters.

Continue straight on CR 128 toward Lake Berryessa. Pass the Pleasants Valley Road at 4.5 miles, and continue another 4.5 miles to a bridge across Putah Creek. Cross the bridge and park in the second, smaller parking area on the right 0.2 miles after the bridge. The trailhead is directly across the road.

KEY AT-A-GLANCE INFORMATION

LENGTH: 5.1 miles
CONFIGURATION: Loop
DIFFICULTY: Challenging
WATER REQUIRED: 2–3 liters
SCENERY: Ranges from idyllic canyon streams to spectacular views of Lake Berryessa
EXPOSURE: Mostly shaded trail with some brief exposure
TRAIL TRAFFIC: Light, with only 5,000 visitors annually
TRAIL SURFACE: Sand and rock, dirt and duff
HIKING TIME: 4–5 hours
SEASON: Year-round, sunrise–sunset
ACCESS: No fees or permits
MAPS: USGS Monticello Dam, Mount Vaca
FACILITIES: None
WHEELCHAIR TRAVERSABLE: No
DRIVING DISTANCE: 36 miles
SPECIAL COMMENTS: While information states that dogs are permitted, this hike is unsuitable for dogs. Details on all aspects of the reserve can be found at nrs.ucdavis.edu/stebbins/technical/hiking.htm.

Homestead–
Blue Ridge Trail
UTM Zone (WGS84) 10S
Easting: 0578733
Northing: 4262658
Latitude: N 38° 30' 31"
Longitude: W 122° 05' 49"

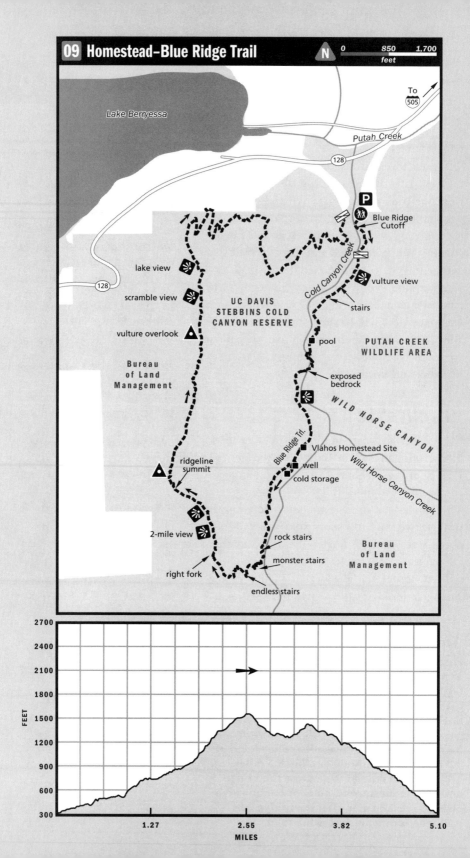

09 Homestead–Blue Ridge Trail

N

0   850   1,700
feet

Lake Berryessa

To 505

Putah Creek

128

P

Blue Ridge Cutoff

lake view

scramble view

vulture overlook

Cold Canyon Creek

vulture view

stairs

UC DAVIS STEBBINS COLD CANYON RESERVE

pool

PUTAH CREEK WILDLIFE AREA

Bureau of Land Management

exposed bedrock

WILD HORSE CANYON

Blue Ridge Trl.

Vlahos Homestead Site

well

cold storage

Wild Horse Canyon Creek

ridgeline summit

2-mile view

rock stairs

monster stairs

Bureau of Land Management

right fork

endless stairs

2700

2400

2100

1800

1500

1200

900

600

300

FEET

1.27   2.55   3.82   5.10

MILES

Vista point over Lake Berryessa

Ascending Blue Ridge Trail after the homestead site will take you through grassland, woodland, chaparral, and lower montane zones up to a newly maintained ridge-top trail. The Coast Range was formed by the deposition of coastal sediment falling to the ocean floor more than 160 million years ago; these layers of sand, clay, and silt eventually solidified into rock. That metamorphic rock—with layers still visible—was uplifted by the collision of the Pacific and North American plates. And those uplifted rocks have been further eroded and their sediments sent out to sea again. At present, they are highly visible in the middle of your trail, near the apex of the hike.

The Stebbins Cold Canyon Reserve is part of the University of California Natural Reserve System and is managed by UC Davis. This means there are wonderful resources for naturalists—amateur and professional alike—available at the UCD NRS Web site (**nrs.ucdavis.edu/stebbins.html**). In-depth species lists and geologic information are provided to enhance your hike.

Step through the opening in the gate across the road from the parking area and you will see an informational sign with a trail map immediately on your left. The trail offers distance markers every 0.25 miles to help you track your location. This combination of trails is a long, narrow loop of about 2 miles, per long leg generally running south–north with the canyons.

Follow the cautions in the front matter regarding poison oak, rattlesnakes, and mountain lions because all are prevalent in the entire reserve. Watch your

The Coast Ranges consist mostly of upended ancient seafloor.

footing on the rock-speckled trails. They are both slippery when wet and easy to stumble over.

Immediately, the trail forks, the left fork heading uphill on Pleasants Ridge Trail. The Homestead Trail begins down the right fork, across some landslide debris, and then past the right-turn cutoff over to the Blue Ridge Trail. You continue to the left, stepping over rocks that do not appear to be normal river cobble; in fact, it is debris from a 1995 mudslide. As you hike this trail, there are visible signs of slumping in the surrounding hills.

Another green gate signals the area boundaries and provides another permanent trail map to study. A sign-in register bordered by toyon stands ready for you to log your visit. The sand-and-rock trail diverges left at some coyote brush, with the creek on the right.

As you gain a bit of elevation along this manzanita-shaded trail, look up to the right to view the distinctive V of the turkey vulture as they circle in front of the rocky ridge (which you will later hike). The trail continues south, gaining about 20 feet above the creek; a series of stairs will help you across a 1982 land slump. You cannot help but notice the energetic croaking of frogs along this section that is shaded by bay laurel, manzanita, and live oak.

Get used to the word *stairs*, because they are the preferred (for sound soil management practices) "elevation assist" in the reserve. When you reach more stairs, turn and take in the view of the Coast Range as it disappears into the

Central Valley. Now, climb 18 steps, and in ten yards descend 15 steps. After a half mile, as you continue to ascend the drainage, you can see the scar made by seasonal runoff.

Pause next to gentle cascades and pools among the spicebush plant after taking any one of the short side trails over to the creek. Some of the pools have been created by rock and cobble dams. These pools support a diverse community of aquatic insects, amphibians, and mammals.

Boulder-hop across the stream at the trail, but be careful not to get tangled in the brush on the opposite side. In another 250 feet, you will have a rare opportunity to see some exposed bedrock along the stream to your left. Your trail alternates from rocky to sandy now as foothill pine becomes the predominant large tree. Just after you cross a little bridge, around 0.75 miles along, a large cottonwood stands right in the middle of the creek.

Stairs will help you through some steep spots along here; the live oak and the foothill pine provide nice shade, and the dense mat of moss and ferns helps keep you cool. The trail narrows and slithers uphill, but the sunlight never makes it through this tunnel of brush. Emerging at about 1 mile, you are greeted with a wonderful view up the canyon and the sight of an exemplar foothill pine, whose needles shimmer green and silver in the sunlight.

Walk through the space in the fence that says NO ENTRY and head toward the large clearing in front of you. Slightly ahead and to the right are the remains of the Vlahos Homestead. From atop the stone foundations, you can look out at Cold Canyon Creek and off to the confluence with Wild Horse Creek. Can you imagine a house sited here with goats corralled in the flat area in front of you? Just down the path are the remains of a well and a retaining wall or building foundation. Past the well, down the path to the left and across the drainage, is the cold storage shed. Built of cemented stone into a hillside and covered with limbs and dirt, this room would have stayed quite cool. If you cross for a closer look, be aware that there is a beehive in the fork of the tree on the left, immediately next to the cold storage.

Retreating back to the well site, ascend the right-hand trail as it crosses the drainage farther uphill. You are now on the Blue Ridge Trail. As you approach 1.25 miles along the shaded trail, try to spot the witch's butter—the bright-orange fungus on downed pine limbs. You may also try to keep an eye open for signs on the ground of roosting turkeys. With so many species in this reserve, you are sure to see signs of many, but some are more obvious than others. On or next to the trail, look for signs of weasels and coyote in addition to raccoon and skunk.

Toyon will continue providing shade as you approach about six steps in the rock. After clambering over these giant steps, notice the moss-covered boulders surrounded by white alder. In another few paces, you'll come upon—you can hardly avoid—a huge, impressive madrone that is actually two individual trees, each with trunks about 16 inches in diameter. A few more monster stairs will warm you up for the approximately 180 more to come over the next half mile (but who's counting?).

As you approach the ridge, the trail will be squeezed by chaparral, but after your last ten steps, you will level out among scrub oak and ceanothus. Take the right fork, climbing somewhat rapidly and, as you near a high spot around the 2-mile point, turn to the northwest for a wonderful view of Lake Berryessa through the clearing.

Brush closes in against the rocky trail on the way to the next high clearing. There are some rocks on the left side of the trail that can provide a nice off-the-trail viewpoint to cool your feet. Or, you may want to continue on this easy dirt trail section to the next summit, at around 1,500 feet. Watch along here for surprising displays of larkspur and Indian paintbrush.

Ahead, toward a beautiful overlook, you will be stopped by what appears to be a dead end. The brush is close in and there appears to be no way forward, only retreat. Turn to your left and clamber over the boulder you are facing. Now you will see your clear trail continuing. Before you leave this spot, take a look below to your right. Do you see that distinctive V again? The turkey vultures will circle above and below you, their heads always down, their eyes always scanning, their wings almost motionless. Listen quietly as one passes just overhead, and hear its silent glide.

A great spot for pictures and snacks is just ahead as boulders provide an overlook for you to dangle your legs while leaning back against the rocks. Leaving this beautiful overlook, your rock-and-dirt trail descends slightly to the east side of the ridge. The trail continues to be easily distinguished, but a short stretch does wander along the ridgeline atop boulders.

Rocky and slightly steep as it exits the ridge's north end, your trail will level out about the time you are shaded and cooled by some large manzanita. The hills to your east are momentarily going to come into view. The manzanita will continue to crowd your northward trail. Just before the trail emerges from the brush, tread cautiously across the left side of a rock jumble. After a bit of exposure, you are back in the shade.

When you cross the next boulder patch, the trail will exit ahead to the right. Initially, walk around to the left of the rocks and cross the boulders; the trail will seem obvious as you look to the north. The next summit point along the dirt trail is at 2.75 miles. Right after this spot, you will run into some leg-stretching boulder stairs. It is a bit tight along here, so do not let your pack catch on the brush.

Looking ahead, your trail becomes wide and obvious and climbs slightly but steadily. Look down at the line in the center of the trail. On closer inspection, that line is not one but hundreds of alternating light and dark strata of the ancient (160-million-year-old) sediments compressed to just inches thick per millennia. The sediments—silt, sand, and clay—fell to the ocean floor and have been altered by heat and pressure, tilted up by the collision of the Pacific and North American plates, and eroded again by the power of water—and your boots.

There is a bit of a scramble on the south side of this next summit. As you skirt the summit and exit the north end, go around the big boulder, using it as a handhold. When around the boulder, turn left, not straight. A freshly maintained trail picks up here, where you will head downhill. Watch the first three steps—they are tall.

At the 3.25-mile point, you will see a large boulder on your left. This spot marks Blue Ridge Trail's best view of Lake Berryessa. It is well worth carrying the camera for the pictures here. Your trail continues to the north, gently trending downhill. It levels out just before a trail-restoration zone. This newly constructed portion of the trail enters a copse of trees, which breaks briefly giving you a view of the uplifted rock that anchors the Monticello Dam across Putah Creek.

This trail was reconstructed by crews from the California Department of Forestry and Fire Protection Delta Conservation Camp and staff members from the University of California, Davis, Natural Reserve System. In 2000, to make the trail safer and more accessible, some 200 of the wooden steps were carried in and set in place by hand.

Just as you pass the manzanita that seems to grow out of a boulder in the newly dug trail, look ahead to the right to see your destination—just in time as the shadow of another vulture crosses your path. As you descend to the gate at the end of the trail, you can enjoy the butterflies on the larkspur. The gate, another informational sign, and a register are at the 4.75-mile mark. Walk ahead to the road, then go about 100 yards right, to the parking lot across the road.

10 REDBUD TRAIL

KEY AT-A-GLANCE INFORMATION

LENGTH: 15.5 miles

CONFIGURATION: Out-and-back

DIFFICULTY: Challenging

WATER REQUIRED: 3–4 liters

SCENERY: In spring, the wildflowers are magnificent. Broad, open meadows are ringed by oak and pine.

EXPOSURE: More exposed than shaded

TRAIL TRAFFIC: Light

TRAIL SURFACE: Dirt and duff, gravel and dirt

HIKING TIME: 8.5 hours

SEASON: Year-round

ACCESS: No fees. This area is open to hunting. Check www.blm.gov/ca/st/en/fo/ukiah.cachecreek.html for hunting dates.

MAPS: USGS Lower Lake, Wilson Valley

FACILITIES: Pit toilet, trash receptacles, and picnic tables available at trailhead

WHEELCHAIR TRAVERSABLE: No

DRIVING DISTANCE: 84 miles

SPECIAL COMMENTS: Extraordinary wildlife viewing

IN BRIEF

Redbud Trail offers the hiker a beautiful trail, an opportunity to observe wildlife, and seclusion along a moderate trail surrounded by wildflowers. You will ascend the hillside above the North Fork of Cache Creek, heading south. Walk along the ridge, heading east, and descend to a crossing of the nascent Cache Creek at Baton Flat; climb farther to gain a ridge paralleling the Peninsula, a ridge separating the North Fork and Cache Creek, while heading south again. Descend the hill to Wilson Valley and ford the wide and aptly named Rocky Creek just above Cache Creek. Walk to the end of Wilson Valley and Cache Creek or stop at any point to watch the wildlife.

DESCRIPTION

Redbud Trail takes advantage of both State of California and Bureau of Land Management lands to create an easy entry for wildlife viewers and wilderness hikers into a primitive area where the habitat is managed for wildlife and plants. Located in the northwest corner of the 70,000-acre Cache Creek Natural Area, the Redbud Trail allows hikers to access an area that supports two extraordinary species: tule elk and bald eagles.

Redbud Trail

UTM Zone (WGS84) 1oS

Easting: 0539875

Northing: 4315436

Latitude: N 38° 59' 13"

Longitude: W 122° 32' 22"

Directions

From Arco Arena, drive north 53 miles on Interstate 5 to Williams, where you will take the CA 20 West exit (#577). Drive 31 miles, to the crossing with the North Fork of Cache Creek. About 0.2 miles after the bridge, turn left at the BLM sign, drive 0.1 mile, and park in the spacious gravel lot. A pit toilet, trash receptacles, interpretive signs, and picnic tables are nice conveniences at the trailhead.

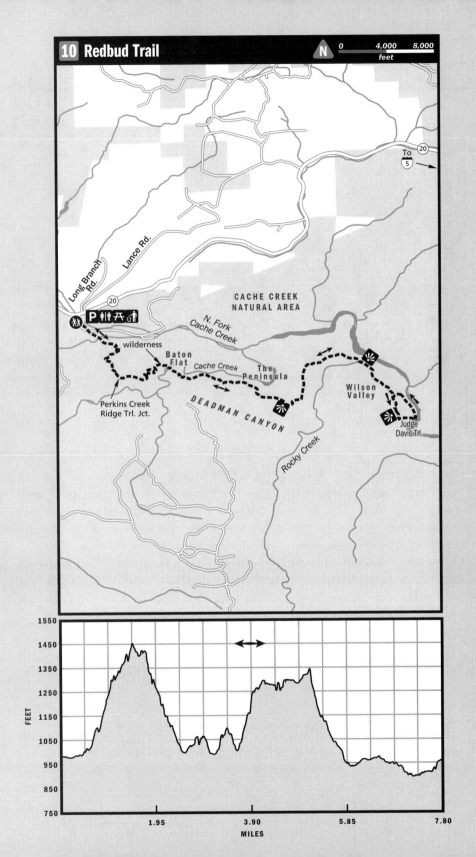

Cache Creek runs through Baton Flat.

Your trail, almost 8 miles long if you walk to the end of Wilson Valley, winds along the North Fork of Cache Creek through a riparian zone—live oak, alder, cottonwood, grass, and sedge—which supports an abundant community of wildlife. Wild turkey, black-tailed deer, black bear, and one of the few free-roaming herds of tule elk make this area home and share it with migrating waterfowl, upland birds, and the magnificent bald eagle, which winters here.

The Cache Creek Natural Area also exhibits a display of wildflower color and scent that makes a visit here an experience to anticipate. Your trailhead starts at the parking lot just to the left of the pit toilets. The sign will direct you left, away from the gravel road, to a trail that passes the information kiosk and picnic table, crosses the creek, and heads southeast across the meadow.

Follow the trail sign as you begin an uphill trek to Perkins Creek Ridge. First, cross a seasonal stream that can be up to 50 feet wide when in season. As you walk through live oak, manzanita, foothill pine, buck brush, and alder, you will be escorted by a squadron of tiger swallowtails moving from one nectar feast to another.

The smaller flora and fauna are—counterintuitively—far easier to see. The butterflies and moths flutter all around you; the alligator lizards, tree frogs, and common king snakes scurry under your feet; and the blue wally baskets, yellow pretty face, white globe tulips, and purple irises just sit there looking good. The larger flora—spreading blue oak, smooth-barked manzanita, and fragrant buck brush—provide shade for hikers and other mammals.

Observing the larger fauna, such as elk, deer, and turkey, is a bit trickier, despite their size. On this hike, carrying a pair of compact binoculars will help. You will greatly increase your chances of sighting wildlife if you hike at dawn or at dusk. Otherwise, just find a spot that looks across a meadow or down on the creek and wait patiently. The meadows are full of tracks, laydowns, and other signs of large mammals.

Water or a treatment/filtering method is needed on this hike, especially in the summer months. Do not ignore sunscreen, and be aware that this hike has plenty of poison oak on it.

After walking through a very mature, spacious manzanita grove, you will have a nice vista of Al Slides and the Peninsula. Your trail climbs some easy switchbacks through manzanita and oak groves. At about 1.5 miles, you will emerge into a pleasant grove of blue oak atop a knoll. Look directly in front of you here; a trail sign indicates that Perkins Creek Ridge Trail heads right and your trail heads left (east).

Look down to the slow pools of Cache Creek on your right just before they enter the rapids and Deadman Canyon some 300 feet below. Use-trails off to the right reveal the paths taken down to the pools. Just about the time you are seriously considering a swim down there, your trail begins a gentle downhill to Baton Flat. As you wind down past blue oak and foothill pine, the trail's smooth surface is interrupted only by the foothill pine's cones. Heft a fresh one and compare it with the core left by squirrels, and you will see why these squirrels are sometimes mistaken for elk.

Shortly after passing a sign indicating entry into designated wilderness, your trail crosses the algae-laden rocks in Cache Creek. Frogs, lizards, and snakes are all common in this creekside area. Look carefully before you step because some spend their downtime in the middle of the trail. On the other side, your trail is a distinct double-track in a parklike area.

At the next fork, a trail sign will direct you uphill to the right. On a path winding in and out of lupines, irises, and yellow-star tulips, you ascend to cross one creek, drop down to Cache Creek again, and ascend again to oak-covered hillsides. Roughly paralleling the creek below, your trail through the trees will be interrupted by large meadows extending uphill from the margin of the creek. There are excellent wildlife-viewing opportunities from these spots.

Trail markers guide your way across a small stream with milky-looking water—or clear water in a milky-looking streambed; then the trail really turns scuddy and becomes an uphill slog next to a rutted-out four-wheel-drive road. Blue wally baskets are the only joy that this short stretch brings.

Notice the amount of rock debris strewn in this area. Large outcrops of rock are scattered, with one monolith appearing completely out of place on the left side. A blizzard of yellow poppies engulfs the trail as you top out in a moist, grassy spot that sports a couple of seasonal runoffs protected by culverts. Look for Chinese houses adorning the trailside here.

Head toward a huge blue oak on a four-wheel-drive road around 4.4 miles into the hike, and prepare for another viewing opportunity before you emerge from the forest cover. The oak up in the middle of the meadow is a common laydown for black-tailed deer and tule elk. Turkey hens move through the grass, head high and scanning the terrain, with their brood stumbling along behind. Blue-eyed grass and paper onions are everywhere among the grasses. Indeed, the foxtail varieties will remind you of the gaiters that protect your socks and boots from collecting seeds and pebbles along the trail. That thought is interrupted by a California quail within feet of you that starts up at 90 miles an hour.

At the end of this open area, around 4.5 miles, your rock-and-dirt trail widens, thanks to excellent treatment by trail crews. The walk through this chaparral, free of poison oak, reveals an abundance of other mammal "signs," so watch where you step. As this section of the trail heads uphill, it becomes somewhat indistinct and appears to end. Keep walking straight, then left. You can see a copse of oak in the middle distance. It looks like a nice place for a shady respite, but before you know it, the trail has bypassed it.

Your downhill trail, with its rocky slope to the right, flanks a hilltop of dense chaparral. Descending a grassy slope sprinkled with dark-purple larkspur, the distinct trail heads directly toward two tall foothill pines, which mark the beginning of more double-track.

The map says "Rocky Creek." It is hard to imagine that it could be named anything else. Short, tumultuous, and untamed Rocky Creek empties its liquid load into Cache Creek just below your crossing. As you cross this wide stream, the dry gravels along its margins will reveal clusters of white whorl lupine.

Turn southeast as you enter Wilson Valley; the trail climbs slightly. When you arrive at the next stream crossing, your choice will depend on the time of year. A jumble of trails or shortcuts confuses the situation somewhat, but you can take one of them southeast to the creek and walk along the lower side of the meadow. In wetter months, you can head about 150 feet southwest and cross a small stream, allowing you to skirt the upper edge of the meadow and enjoy a view down to the creek.

In late April, a late-staying pair of bald eagles was nesting in the foothill pine at the far south end of Wilson Valley. Lingering to take advantage of the solitude and plentiful food in Cache Creek, this pair would soon be ready to continue its northward migration. Take care not to harass the birds—especially when they are nesting. Approaching no closer than 500 feet to their nesting spot is a responsible approach. Your telephoto lens or binoculars will give you an excellent view without stressing the raptors.

If your destination is Cache Creek, you have arrived. If you continue across the creek, you can join the Judge Davis Trail. Follow your tracks and take your memories back to the trailhead.

PERKINS CREEK RIDGE TRAIL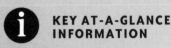

IN BRIEF

Hiking this trail in the winter, spring, or fall is highly recommended because this is a hot, exposed route that can be blistering during the late summer. The wildflowers and green grasses are so spectacular in the spring that they eclipse the beauty of the woodland and chaparral. However, in the summer, the blue oaks and foothill pines contrast with the sun-browned stems and seeds to yield a unique beauty best enjoyed early in the day. This route follows the Redbud Trail to its junction with the Perkins Creek Ridge Trail, about 1 mile from the trailhead, where it turns southwest and begins ascending and descending along the ridge to a final vista of Clear Lake.

DESCRIPTION

The initial 1.5 miles of this hike follow the Redbud Trail (see previous profile) from its trailhead up to the point of the junction with the Perkins Creek Ridge Trail.

Head southeast across the large meadow, which is filled with pretty face, wally baskets, and poppies in the spring; then cross a normally dry 50-foot stream before you enter a woodland of blue oak, manzanita, foothill pine, and toyon. Switchback to the southwest

KEY AT-A-GLANCE INFORMATION

LENGTH: 12.3 miles
CONFIGURATION: Out-and-back
DIFFICULTY: Challenging
WATER REQUIRED: 4–5 liters
SCENERY: Foothill woodland and chaparral with ridge-top views
EXPOSURE: Barely a mile of trail is shaded; wear a hat and sunscreen.
TRAIL TRAFFIC: Light
TRAIL SURFACE: Dirt and rock
HIKING TIME: 6–8 hours
SEASON: Year-round
ACCESS: No fees or permits
MAPS: USGS Lower Lake
WHEELCHAIR TRAVERSABLE: No
FACILITIES: Pit toilets, interpretive kiosk, trash receptacles, and picnic table at spacious trailhead parking lot
DRIVING DISTANCE: 84 miles
SPECIAL COMMENTS: Great views are the rewards for those hikers who ascend and descend this chaparral-covered ridge. There is no drinking water at the trailhead.

Directions

From Arco Arena, drive 53 miles north on Interstate 5 to Williams, where you will take the CA 20 West exit (#577). Drive 31 miles on CA 20 to the crossing of the North Fork of Cache Creek. When you are 0.2 miles past the bridge, turn left at the BLM sign, drive 0.1 mile, and park in the spacious gravel lot. A pit toilet, trash receptacles, interpretive signs, and picnic tables are welcome conveniences.

Perkins Creek
Ridge Trail
UTM Zone (WGS84) 10S
Easting: 0540745
Northing: 4314082
Latitude: N 38° 58' 29"
Longitude: W 122° 31' 46"

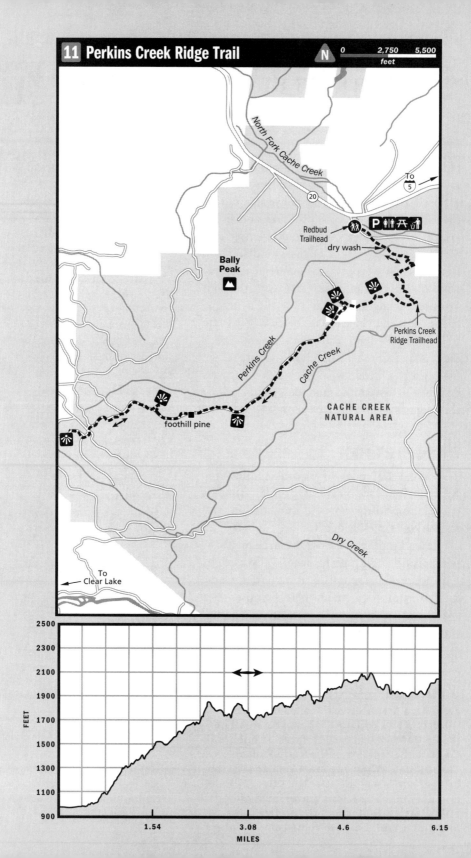

Mount Konocti over Clear Lake

through a stand of mature white-leaf manzanita bushes and then head southeast as blue oaks become the dominant flora, with foothill pines adding colorful accents above the oaks' dark leaves. The berries of the manzanita, which is the Spanish word for "little apple," become ripe and red in late summer, adding more color.

After gaining about 500 feet, you reach the signed junction at the top of an oak-laden hill. Notice the sign facing backward at your left shoulder as you near the top; it directs your return to the trailhead. This is a pleasant point to catch your breath and take pictures of Deadman's Canyon and Baton Flat down below. The scattered blue oak make this shaded and breezy spot a welcome respite after your first 45 minutes of hiking.

After resting and checking maps, turn right, to the southwest, and head up a short, steep hill through the thickening chamise bushes. Often called grease-wood, chamise is the dominant shrub in these chaparral-covered hills. After another short, steep hill, you will reach a very steep hill. You can circumnavigate this hill by taking the trail to the left. Alternatively, you can hustle up the steep pitch and take some pictures from this excellent vantage point.

As you walk along, you will surely notice, and perhaps try to avoid, the signs of a few of the more territorial animals in Cache Creek. Footprints of turkeys and quail are clustered randomly in the dust, where it looks as if a happy hour was held. Raccoon, coyote, and even mountain lion signs are evident. With the forage diminishing in the late summer, eating requires animals to do a bit more traveling, and so game trails intersect your route constantly.

At this point, you are about 150 feet above the junction, and you will ascend some 600 more feet over the next few miles. However, you will also descend frequently. At many of the high points on the ridge, you will notice a trail leading off to the side, at the base of the slope. These are wonderful energy-saving trails that generally contour around the hill. The junctions are all fairly evident.

In the next mile of this dirt-covered trail, you will notice—perhaps when you slip on their small acorns—that the blue oaks have become the more dominant species of flora. By late summer, the blue oak has reached its full complement of foliage, so it presents a nicely rounded blue-green profile against the golden dried grasses. In contrast, the gray-green of the foothill pine dazzles in the bright sun in the canyon below and on the ridge above the trail. For the next 40 minutes or so, you can see down to Cache Creek on the left. Bally Peak is about a mile off to the north. Chamise still crowds the trail, which continues southwest following the ridge up and down.

You can just begin to see Clear Lake in the distance by the time you have reached the 4-mile point. Trails are clearly visible against the chaparral, which also includes bush monkeyflower and buck brush. From a knoll with a solitary foothill pine, you can see trails in all directions. Some of these—OHV trails used by the Bureau of Land Management and the California Department of Fish and Game— head northwest. Continue along the ridge another 1.5 miles to the southwest.

If you are buzzed by vultures every now and then, it's because they're sizing you up for later. Take heart just about when the chamise is joined by the tiny-leaved scrub oak. An OHV road makes a U-turn at a flat spot about ten minutes before you reach your destination. Although it is up a hill, you will find it easily because X marks the spot. Off to the northwest and 200 feet above you sits the rocky knob of Quackenbush Mountain, a couple of foothill pines on its side. Clear Lake is about 600 feet below to your west, glinting in the sun.

From this serene viewpoint, game trails and laydowns are visible on the slopes below you. Apparently, deer and tule elk seek solitude in the same areas that hikers do. The breeze is refreshing and the view is excellent, but there is a distinct lack of shade at this spot, which encourages you to hasten into the shade of the oaks back down the trail. Retrace your steps to the trailhead.

NEARBY ACTIVITIES

Cache Creek is popular among kayakers and rafters of all skill levels. All-inclusive package trips are available from a number of travel companies in the area. Whitewater Adventures in Sacramento can be contacted at (800) 977-4837 or online at **www.gotwhitewater.com**; contact Cache Creek Whitewater River Trips of Rumsey by phone at (800) 796-3091 or through its Web site, **www.cachecanyon.com**.

HIGH BRIDGE TRAIL

IN BRIEF

You will see magnificent groves of blue oaks, vistas of distant hills, and fields full of grasses and wildflowers, but you will not see a bridge on this trail. This hike climbs 700 feet in about 3 miles on a new dirt trail that is graded for a practically effortless ascent. If you climb to the ridge early enough, you will have a great perch from which to focus your binoculars on the wildlife at Bear Creek.

DESCRIPTION

Your trailhead is to the left of the steel-cable gate marked TRAIL. It winds down to cross Bear Creek on the mineral-encrusted boulders lining its banks. Turn sharply left at the bottom of the hill around the old fire rings, and follow the sandy path about 75 feet through the willows to the rocky cobble at the creek. Choose the path across that keeps you driest. Upstream about 50 feet may be the easiest.

Once across the creek, step up onto the conglomerate of rocks and turn again to the southwest. You will see the path ahead leading up the spur of a ridge. Rejoin the path, and you will gain some elevation over the creek as you walk around this sparsely treed

KEY AT-A-GLANCE INFORMATION

LENGTH: 5.64 miles
CONFIGURATION: Out-and-back
DIFFICULTY: Moderate
WATER REQUIRED: 2–3 liters
SCENERY: Hillsides of blue oak and wildflowers
EXPOSURE: There is not much shade despite all the trees.
TRAIL TRAFFIC: Light
TRAIL SURFACE: Dirt
HIKING TIME: 3 hours
SEASON: Year-round
ACCESS: No fees or permits
MAPS: USGS Glasscock Mountain; trail map available at www.blm .gov/ca/st/en/fo/ukiah/cachecreek
WHEELCHAIR TRAVERSABLE: No
FACILITIES: Parking area, pit toilet, picnic tables
DRIVING DISTANCE: 77.5 miles
SPECIAL COMMENTS: Great hike for children; start early on summer days.

Directions

From Interstate 5 near Arco Arena, drive 55 miles north to CA 20 in Williams. Drive 18 miles west on CA 20 to the junction with CA 16. Turn south and drive to the trailhead parking lot, which is 4.5 miles ahead on the right. It is an unmarked turn-in, immediately after the second bridge over Bear Creek, and has ample parking, a pit toilet, and two picnic tables. The trailhead is in the southwest corner of the parking area.

High Bridge Trail
UTM Zone (WGS84) 10S
Easting: 0556871
Northing: 4312166
Latitude: N 38° 57' 23"
Longitude: W 122° 20' 37"

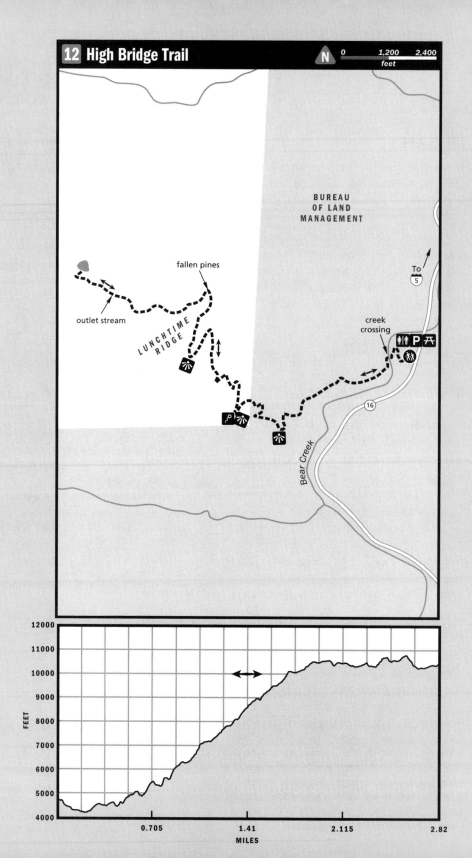

The view south toward Brophy Canyon

hillside and enter a ravine, which will allow you to cross the confluence of two drainages.

After just 100 feet of upward travel, you are rewarded with an exceptionally striking view of the creek and valley to the south. But this is not in fact the best view. Climb to the next vista, and the one after that. Make certain to take your camera along when you hike this picturesque trail. In fact, sunrise and sunset on the blue-oak-studded hillsides are spectacular.

The trail sometimes becomes slightly narrow, but for the most part it is wide enough to walk along with children at your side. There is no point on this trail that would prove difficult for children over 4 years of age. The pond at the end of the hike has a sufficient stock of frogs, turtles, and birds to interest everyone. Look for signs of mammalian visitors along the margins of the pond. Tree frogs and pond turtles slip quickly into the muddy water when you approach. You will see raccoon and coyote footprints along with the tracks of deer and birds of all types.

On the way to the pond, you may find yourself thinking only of the sound of the wind through the trees. In fact, this trail will lull you into actually enjoying an uphill hike. The BLM trail designers and builders deserve kudos for this easy route into the wilderness.

A quartet of stout manzanita presents a rare change in the tree foliage as the trail meanders through the grasses. After about 2 miles of hiking, you will

Blue oaks fill the hillsides above Bear Creek.

have reached roughly 1,500 feet elevation. If you look uphill and around you, the blue oaks seem to have flowed downhill from the ridge summit, almost blanketing the slope down to the creek. However scarce the foothill pines are on this slope, they are just as prolific on the facing slope as the oaks are on this one.

Now descend slightly toward a switchback in the crux of a ravine marked by two foothill pines, lying opposed and parallel to each other across it. From this last switchback, which heads southwest, the trail will slowly resume a northwest heading for slightly less than 0.5 miles up to your destination.

The trail crosses an outlet stream just beneath the pond. Climb to the left and around to the ranch road. A lone oak at the far end of the pond on the east side may provide shade for your pondside picnic. Another rest spot with a good view is atop the rocks to the right after you pass the twin downed pines on your return.

JUDGE DAVIS TRAIL

IN BRIEF

Judge Davis must have been as straight as an arrow, as this hike title implies. His route to the creek used to be so fast and straight that it has been modified to make the uphill and downhill more knee-friendly and environmentally sound. The views from above Wilson Valley are spectacular.

DESCRIPTION

Cache Creek Natural Area covers more than 70,000 acres of public lands open to mixed use. A variety of wildlife is supported in this area, which includes lush riparian forest along the creeks, hillside blue-oak woodlands, foothill woodland forest, and dense chaparral.

In particular, the Wilson Valley on Cache Creek—your destination—is a haven for both wildlife and plant life. Bald eagle, tule elk, wild turkey, coyote, mountain lion, bear, black-tailed deer, and jackrabbit all thrive on the wide variety of grasses, berries, and aquatic life in this secluded area.

From your trail you can overlook the entire habitat and its inhabitants all at once. Early morning and evening are prime viewing hours, whether you are up above or down along the creek. Waterfowl use this as an

KEY AT-A-GLANCE INFORMATION

LENGTH: 11.5 miles
CONFIGURATION: Out-and-back
DIFFICULTY: Challenging
WATER REQUIRED: 2–3 liters
SCENERY: Panoramic views of Wilson Valley and Cache Creek
EXPOSURE: Some welcome shade from blue-oak groves; trail is 75% exposed.
TRAIL TRAFFIC: Enjoy your solitude.
TRAIL SURFACE: Dirt and duff, dirt and rock, grass
HIKING TIME: 6 hours
SEASON: Year-round, sunrise–sunset
ACCESS: No permits required; check www.dfg.ca.gov/lands/wa/region2 for hunting dates.
MAPS: USGS Wilson Valley, Wilbur Springs; local maps available at www.blm.gov/ca/st/en/fo/ukiah/cachecreek.html
FACILITIES: Pit toilets and parking at trailhead
WHEELCHAIR TRAVERSABLE: No
DRIVING DISTANCE: 75 miles
SPECIAL COMMENTS: Easiest route into Cache Creek; superb wildlife viewing

Directions

From Interstate 5 near Arco Arena, drive 55 miles north to CA 20 in Williams. Travel 22.6 miles west on CA 20. Watch for the Colusa–Lake county line. The parking lot for the trailhead is exactly 0.1 mile ahead on the left. Park in the lot to the right of the pit toilet. Your trailhead starts between the two large posts here. Note: Do not confuse this with the gated trail that starts to the left of the pit toilet.

Judge Davis Trail
UTM Zone (WGS84) 10S
Easting: 0550571
Northing: 4317891
Latitude: N 39° 00' 30"
Longitude: W 122° 24' 57"

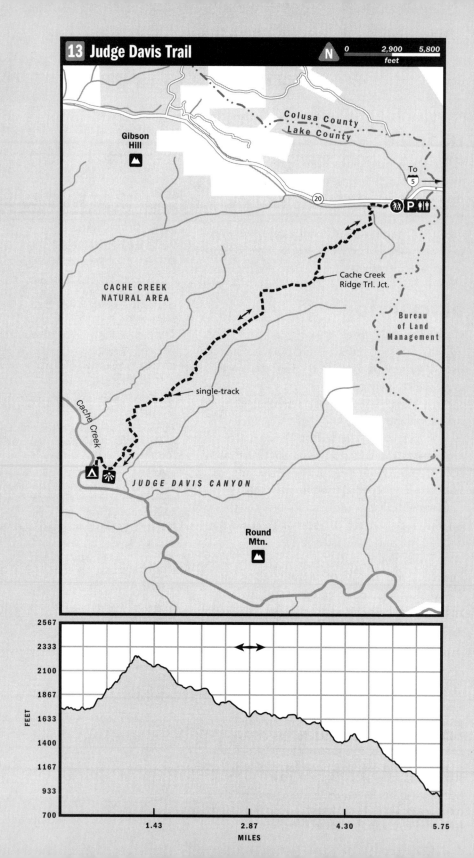

13 **Judge Davis Trail**

N   0   2,900   5,800
     feet

Gibson
Hill

Colusa County
Lake County

To
5

20

CACHE CREEK
NATURAL AREA

Cache Creek
Ridge Trl. Jct.

Bureau
of Land
Management

single-track

Cache Creek

JUDGE DAVIS CANYON

Round
Mtn.

FEET	
2567	
2333	
2100	
1867	
1633	
1400	
1167	
933	
700	

1.43   2.87   4.30   5.75
MILES

Pure stands of chamise are common chapparal features.

important rest spot along their annual migration. The free-roaming herd of tule elk, which browses the grasslands and chaparral, often seeks out the cool shade of the creek in the summer.

Start your hike in the parking lot to the right of the pit toilet, where a pair of stout posts stand astride a dirt single-track that heads west, somewhat paralleling the road to the right. In a few hundred feet, follow the trail as it turns away from the road at a creek running through an oak-speckled hillside. Even after rain, your crossing of this creek upcoming in a few minutes will be easy.

In this wet area, wildflowers jump out at you: larkspurs, lupines, Chinese houses, wally baskets, clover, and irises adorn the trailside and streamside banks. The next mile will boost your elevation from about 1,700 to about 2,200 feet—heading up the side of a slope to meet the ridgeline. After that, the trail will largely head downhill to the creek. Blue-oak limbs adorned with moss add a brilliant yet diffuse glow around the trees as you stride this easy, uphill walk.

In 0.5 miles, the entire slope takes on a parklike appearance, covered with a stand of blue oak. This well-crafted trail meanders through it, taking your mind off the fact that it is all uphill. You will emerge from the cool shade after exactly 1 mile. The exposure remains southerly and sunny for the rest of the hike, with periodic respite found among stands of blue oak. The primary vegetation along the trail is chaparral—mostly yerba santa and manzanita.

Looking off to the southwest, your trail appears as a distinct tan line through the green chaparral. Other trails are visible, but yours takes a definite tack southwest. The first trail junction enters from the right—heading off to the north—and should be ignored. Continue left and slightly downhill, past the burned gateposts and their downed gate, to the only signed junction on this trail.

The signpost, 1.5 miles from the trailhead, indicates that Cache Creek Ridge Trail leads off to the left. Almost as an afterthought, a handwritten sign has been posted to indicate that the Judge Davis Trail—marked with an arrow—leads off to the right. Neat or not, that's the way to go.

There are no trails intersecting the Judge Davis Trail other than Cache Creek Ridge Trail, which you just passed, so you won't have to make any navigational decisions. This wide trail has been well maintained and, in several places, has been redesigned to make the trail more manageable and less prone to erosion. Keep a watchful eye for downed wood, which has been placed across the trail to block it off. Over the next 2 miles, there will be three trail "reroutes."

Chaparral, the dominant biozone along your trail, consists of many species of shrubs: manzanita, rabbit brush, buck brush, sagebrush, Ceanothus, tobacco brush, Scotch broom, greasewood, and at least a dozen others that fall into this broad category. The dominant chaparral shrub along your trail is greasewood, which comprises pure stands in some areas, denying access to other plants and large mammals. These areas support large numbers of smaller mammals and reptiles. Don't be surprised by a fat lizard drowsing beside the trail or the occasional garter snake lounging in the middle of these dense shrubs.

You can depend on a few well-placed stands of blue oak for shade. But keep a sharp eye out for the trail, which, upon entering the trees, becomes a grassy single-track and remains so until it reaches the creek.

When you are 0.25 miles above the creek, vistas of Wilson Valley below will start to open up. Just before the trail makes its final descent to the creek, you will reach a fairly flat, open space in the trees. This 100-foot area has a perch overlooking the creek, the meadow, and a bald eagle nest straight ahead. If you arrive at dawn or dusk with binoculars and an hour to sit, your chance of observing wildlife will be greatly enhanced. If you don't have the patience or time, take a photo or two before descending to the creek on a winding single-track.

At creek level, you will emerge right next to a tall foothill pine, which has a distinctive huge branch that curves in the opposite direction to the rest. Use this as your marker of the correct trail for your return.

The trail ends at a broad, flat area next to the creek. Other hikers have camped beside the creek here, as evidenced by the rock-enclosed fire ring and paths leading to the creek. Although it looks possible to cross Cache Creek near this spot, you will have to do so later in the season because spring runoff poses real risks.

When you are well rested and ready to face the uphill return, remember to thank the trail crews for their work in "moderating" the trail along the way. After taking farewell photos of Wilson Valley, you will look forward to entering the shade of oaks, about 1 mile from the trailhead.

BLUE RIDGE-FISKE PEAK TRAIL

IN BRIEF

Tighten your bootlaces and clean the camera lens for the hike to Fiske Peak. This is a well-maintained trail that ascends steadily through a lush foothill woodland forest to the peak of vertically uplifted ocean floor—revealing views from the coast range to the central valley.

DESCRIPTION

If any entirely uphill hike can be enjoyed, it is this one. Your hike begins on a shaded path at the yellow gate on CR 40. Descend and cross the low-water bridge that straddles Cache Creek. River rafters are required to portage here and so they take the opportunity for a lunch break right at the trailhead. After crossing the creek, walk uphill and watch for a sign about 200 feet on the left, indicating the trailhead's location. Make a U-turn to the left and walk to the yellow gate; step through on the left and follow the double-track over toward the rafters' picnic grounds.

A sign on your right marks the trailhead and advises you of the distances to several points: Blue Ridge (3 miles), Fiske Peak (4 miles), and Fiske Creek Road (8.5 miles). Check your packs for loose fasteners, and

KEY AT-A-GLANCE INFORMATION

LENGTH: 8.6 miles

CONFIGURATION: Out-and-back, up-and-down

DIFFICULTY: Difficult

WATER REQUIRED: 3–4 liters

SCENERY: Coast mountains and valleys; foothill woodland; huge wooded vista from several vantage points along trail and summit

EXPOSURE: Surprisingly shaded on most of the trail

TRAIL TRAFFIC: Leave the river crowds behind at the trailhead.

TRAIL SURFACE: Dirt and duff

HIKING TIME: 7 hours

SEASON: Year-round, sunrise–sunset

ACCESS: No fees or permits

MAPS: USGS Glasscock Mountain. Area-specific maps can be found at the BLM Web site, www.blm.gov/ca/st/en/fo/ukiah/cachecreek.

FACILITIES: Pit toilet at the trailhead parking lot

WHEELCHAIR TRAVERSABLE: No

DRIVING DISTANCE: 91 miles

SPECIAL COMMENTS: Hydrate before you begin hiking; carry water in your pack. Streams are seasonal.

Directions

From Sacramento, drive 55 miles north on Interstate 5 to CA 20 in Williams. Follow CA 20 west and south 18 miles to Wilbur Springs, where you will turn south on CA 16. Take it 8.9 miles to old CR 40. Your landmark is the campground located 0.7 miles before the turnout on the right. A day-use parking lot may be open. Otherwise, you may park under the trees along old CR 40. After situating your car at the parking area, walk to the yellow gate that stands across the old CR 40.

Blue Ridge–Fiske Peak Trail

UTM Zone (WGS84) 10S

Easting: 0560091

Northing: 4307009

Latitude: N 38° 54' 35"

Longitude: W 122° 18' 24"

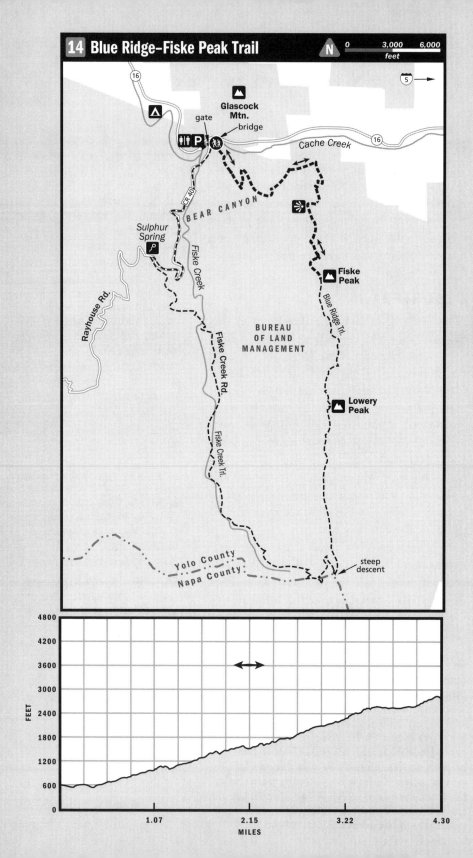

14 Blue Ridge–Fiske Peak Trail

N   0   3,000   6,000
feet

5 →

16

Glascock Mtn.

gate

bridge

Cache Creek   16

P

C.R. 40?

BEAR CANYON

Sulphur
Spring

Fiske Creek

Fiske Peak

Blue Ridge Trl.

Rayhouse Rd.

BUREAU
OF LAND
MANAGEMENT

Fiske Creek Rd.

Lowery
Peak

Fiske Creek Trl.

Yolo County
Napa County

steep
descent

FEET

4800
4200
3600
3000
2400
1800
1200
600
0

1.07   2.15   3.22   4.30

MILES

Cache Creek Canyon

turn right, uphill, into a foothill-pine and live-oak forest that surrounds the single-track. You will ascend quickly on the dirt-and-duff trail as the creek veers off to the left.

This splendid trail winds through a manzanita grove where foothill pines loom overhead and young grasses beneath. Unfairly, this well-groomed trail is filthy with poison oak. In an ironic twist, the poisonous plant is decorated with beautiful Indian pink, Indian warrior, and Indian paintbrush. But resist the temptation to wade in for a closer look: on this hike, there will be few, if any, water sources to wash off the itch-inducing oils.

You'll next encounter a few minutes of gentle contouring, some gentle ascents, some monster uphills, and finally a stream to cross as you head into another uphill covered with fiddlenecks and blue dicks.

In a few minutes, you will reach the 1-mile mark, just about at the point where you are able to look back down Still Gulch—the canyon you have just ascended. If you are here in the spring, you will see redbud trees highlighting the hillside whenever you emerge from cover to glimpse them.

The geological features of this area are primarily sedimentary and metamorphic rock. At this moment you are walking on flat sandstone and mudstone, alluvial deposits that long ago slumped to the seafloor and then were scraped up again as plates collided. Some deposits were deeper, older, and more dramatically inclined, as in the case of the metamorphic rock vertically oriented and exposed at Cache Creek. Notice that the plates here are horizontal. At other points in the hike, these strata will be oriented at various angles.

As you survey the surrounding hills, you may pick up on other ways the hills have been formed. As the incline becomes steeper, material on top loses its grip

A Western fence lizard warms itself on a rock.

and slumps to a lower elevation. Look at the hillsides above the highway directly below you, and you can see evidence of hill formation due to slumping.

If you are early enough in the season, you can linger around the next stream crossing, captivated by the sound of the water cascading gently above and below your crossing point. Shooting stars have been added to the displays of Indian pink, Indian warrior, and Indian paintbrush. You never have to wait long to hear the sound of hummingbirds as they take long draughts from each plant.

After 1.5 miles, the vista of the creek below and of the surrounding hillsides is matched only by the much closer splash of yellow poppy and rabbit brush. Turn your back on the creek below and continue ascending. The trail makes no unexpected direction changes other than to enter and exit ravines. When boulders in the trail block your path 2.2 miles along, climb over them. You may notice that the cool areas along the trail support a variety of mosses and ferns, including California maiden-hair fern and bracken fern. The views are plentiful as you walk in and out of the shade of huge, spreading manzanitas.

Shortly after some switchbacks at 2.5 miles, you will see a signpost on the right indicating that you are now at the 2,000-foot elevation point. This is a welcome sign on a hike that is more up than out. You will be impressed by the maintenance crews' handiwork as the trail widens out through the next set of switchbacks. Now you can be a bit less worried about being crowded by poison oak.

Look for a huge outcropping on the right with a hollow beneath it. You have hiked about 3 miles at this point. The shade of a large foothill pine at the 3.25-mile point provides a nice spot for you to rest before you ascend another 150 feet to the ridge. Continue across the outcroppings and the fire-scorched manzanita. Fence lizards skitter out of your way as you approach an intersection with a sharp peak visible to your right and more uphill trail to your left.

You will want to continue on the trail to your left, but first gaze out from the peak ahead of you on the right. A use-trail and some hunters' campsites are hidden in the brush as you make your way uphill to the peak at 2,631 feet. This is a great spot for lunch; the warmth of the sun and rocks balances the steady, chill winds that support a squadron of turkey vultures purposefully gliding by, eye-to-eye with you for a momentous instant.

Your trail to Fiske Peak—easily seen from this high vantage point—heads south and continues gaining elevation along a series of short uphill efforts until you reach a flat area at 2,850 feet. In front of you is a rectangular patch of grass about 10 feet by 15 feet. Before entering that grassy area, the trail turns left and, ten feet later, turns left again for the final steps up to the USGS marker on 2,868-foot Fiske Peak. A glass jar holds the peak-baggers' log, which you should sign and read: you've earned it.

From this peak you can visually grasp the earth-building process by observing the arrangement of the mountains in this coast range: a series of north–south ridgelines interrupted by valleys that lie along earthquake fault lines. A look over the east side of the ridgeline reveals the Cache Creek Valley and the town of Rumsey.

If this hike has satisfied your sense of adventure and properly tired you, then make a U-turn to retrace your steps downhill. If, somehow, the heat has not affected you or you have a gluttonous appetite for trail miles and great views, then follow the trail south along the Blue Ridge through the grassy patch, a trek described in the next hike—the Blue Ridge–Fiske Creek Trail, Hike 15 (see following page).

NEARBY ACTIVITIES

The Cache Creek Natural Area has several new trails which have been developed by the BLM. One excellent new trail is the High Bridge Trail (Hike 12, page 71), which begins at the turnout on the west side of the CA 16 4.5 miles south of CA 20.

Cache Creek Regional Park Campground is located on CA 16 0.7 miles north of CR 40. RV and tent sites are available for a fee.

15 BLUE RIDGE-FISKE CREEK TRAIL

KEY AT-A-GLANCE INFORMATION

LENGTH: 17.5 miles

CONFIGURATION: Loop

DIFFICULTY: Difficult

WATER REQUIRED: 4–5 liters in summer

SCENERY: Huge views; foothill and riparian woodland; chaparral

EXPOSURE: Largely shaded, but the walk south is exposed; use sunscreen before reaching vista point.

TRAIL TRAFFIC: Light. A hiking partner is a desirable accessory here. Footprints are rare along the ridge.

TRAIL SURFACE: Varies from dirt-and-duff single-track to rock-and-gravel four-wheeel-drive road

HIKING TIME: 10–12 hours, if you linger in all the right places

SEASON: Year-round, sunrise–sunset

ACCESS: No fees or permits; hunting allowed in area

MAPS: USGS Glasscock Mountain, Knoxville. Maps at www.blm.gov/ca/st/en/fo/ukiah/cachecreek.html

FACILITIES: Pit toilet at the trailhead parking lot; camping nearby.

WHEELCHAIR TRAVERSABLE: No

DRIVING DISTANCE: 91 miles

SPECIAL COMMENTS: This hike is arduous due to its elevation gain and loss and its overall length. There is considerable exposure to the sun, as well as steep terrain. The magnificent views reward every step hiked.

Blue Ridge–Fiske Creek Trail

UTM Zone (WGS84) 10S

Easting: 0560091

Northing: 4307009

Latitude: N 38° 54' 35"

Longitude: W 122° 18' 24"

IN BRIEF

After you climb through foothill woodlands to reach Fiske Peak, a walk along the ridge through chaparral and then a descent to Fiske Creek's riparian woodland sounds like a great idea. This long trail will help condition you for more-serious treks. And while the snow melts in the Sierra, you can enjoy the wildflower displays here.

DESCRIPTION

Follow the trail from the yellow gate at CR 40 to the Blue Ridge Trailhead and the route to Fiske Peak.

After checking in at the summit, turn around, facing south, and it will appear the obvious trail is straight ahead—but that trail goes nowhere fast. Instead, take a look down from the peak to see your trail leading off to the west, skirting the burned chaparral on the flat summit before circling south again. To find your way, walk back to the grassy patch, turn left there, and walk through it to pick up the track you just observed.

Once you have the trail, follow it as it finally turns straight south across a burned

---

Directions ————————➤

From Sacramento, drive north on Interstate 5 approximately 54 miles to CA 20 in Williams. Follow CA 20, which heads west then south, approximately 19 miles to Wilbur Springs, where you will turn south on CA 16, which you will take 8.9 miles to old County Road 40. Your landmark is the campground that is 0.7 miles before the turnout, on the right. If the day-use parking lot is closed, you may park under the trees along old CR 40. After parking, walk to the yellow gate across old CR 40.

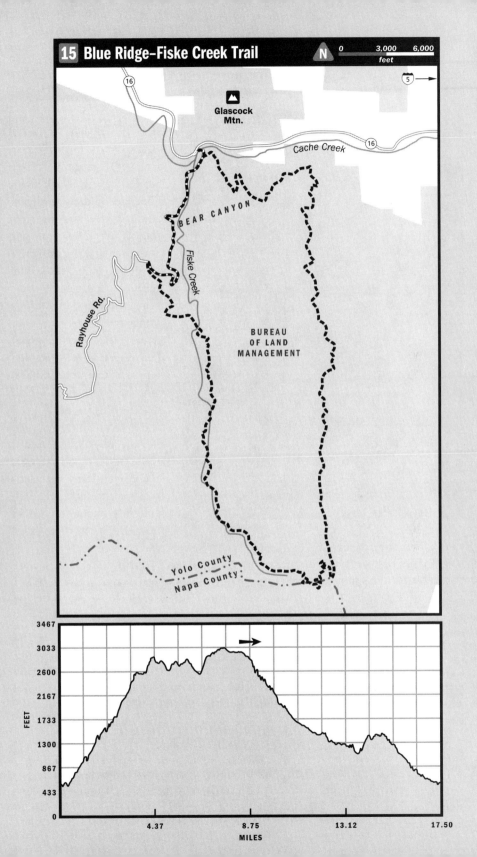

The stairs cut into the slope facilitate a safe descent.

area down into a broad saddle. The wind will whip across the ridgeline along here as you walk through a burned-out boulder farm. Often rocky and narrow, your trail takes on the character of a use-trail.

The only skills you need for finding the route along the ridge and down along the creek are diligence and attentiveness. The trail may *seem* to disappear a time or two, but it ends up being right where you expect it to be.

Ascend the other side of the saddle along the edge of the ridgeline on the west side. When the trail seems to be at its least distinct, you will encounter rocks lining the path, rocks piled into a duck, or an elevation marker—all will help you stay on course.

In and out, or down and up, another saddle leads to the 3,038-foot Lowery Peak. The trail quality improves significantly as you bottom out in the saddle— the head of Rumsey Canyon—and ascend to Lowery Peak. Over the next 500 feet, you will have a wide, albeit rocky, trail to the summit. Take a well-deserved moment to sign the register, take pictures, drink water, or watch the vultures soar along the ridgeline below you.

As you head along, your trail will turn to gentle grass—just enough grass to attract California quail and their abruptly startling takeoffs. Continue straight across this open, boulder-strewn area. The trail is dim along here, but you really can't go off to either direction.

Your next turn comes 1.2 miles from Lowery Peak. At the 9-mile point, look carefully for a signpost no longer supporting a sign. This is the point at which you get the answer to "How am I going to get down from here?"

The trail disappears over the right side with the help of some primitive steps in the face of this ridge. Switchback down this tight trail, past cascades of lupine and poppy, toward the fire road visible just below.

The sign at the fire road (9.3 miles into your hike) informs hikers going the other way that Blue Ridge is 0.5 miles off, and Cache Creek 8.5 miles away. With a wide, grassy road in front of you, enjoy a nice, gentle descent along Fiske Creek Road.

A nascent Fiske Creek begins as a trickle alongside the road, and within 0.75 miles is channeled through a culvert under the road, where you should start looking among the bushes to the right for a trail sign. Your odometer at the culvert is 11.25 miles.

Fiske Creek Road heads uphill to the left. Your trail leads to the right, past the sign reading FISKE CREEK TRAIL–CR 40, 4 MILES. Walk through the opening in the gate onto a dirt, duff, and grass trail with dense lupine at your knees and scattered redbud trees all around.

Evidence of fire scars the live oak where you make a couple of creek crossings. A sign indicating Hank's Creek hangs in the trees near the creek on your left. In a few moments, your trail will emerge into a hillside of valley oak on a path littered with lupine and blue-eyed grass.

For the next few miles, your trail will cross the creek several times, allowing you to observe the opposite hillside of the canyon at regular intervals. You will notice how the vegetation changes according to which direction the hillside faces. On one slope, there are regularly spaced valley oaks with broad, grassy areas beneath them; on the opposite, foothill pine, live oak, and manzanita tend to thrive, with occasional redbuds visible. Some creek crossings are choked with willows, but none of the crossings is difficult.

On the east slope, you will rise above the creek and walk through a grove of majestic valley oak decorated with shooting stars and lupine. Returning to your northward trail along the creek, fire-scarred manzanita looms over the trail as foothill pine towers above, stretching out over the creek. The charred skeletons of foothill pine caricature their former beauty.

You may notice the bedrock beneath your feet as you cross the creek to ascend the west slope on a double-track high above the creek. You will leave the creek for the 1.5 miles to Sulphur Spring. First, you encounter an uphill grind into and out of a ravine that could not be breached at the creek level.

The trail remains distinct through groves of valley oak as you continue northward. When you pass through a broad, flat area of oak, with Fiske Creek far below, look for a signed gate and a CR 40 marker. Your destination is approximately 2.5 miles north.

Head downhill, turning south after about 0.5 miles, and continue to follow the old county road as it turns north. You will hear the croaking of tree frogs growing louder as you approach the creek again. Cross the ravine at Bear Canyon and continue north. The barn that you could see from the trail vistas on this morning's climb should be coming into closer view on your left within another mile. Take the small footbridge to cross Fiske Creek, step across a cattle guard, and then cross the low-water bridge spanning Cache Creek.

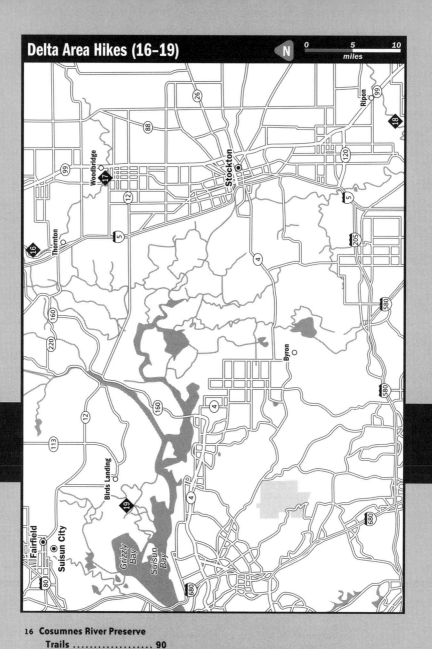

N

0   5   10
miles

26

88

Ripon 99

18

Woodbridge

99

17

120

Stockton

12

5

Thornton

16

5

205

4

160

580

220

Byron

580

12

160

4

113

580

Birds Landing

19

4

Fairfield

Suisun City

680

Grizzly Bay

Suisun Bay

680

80

DELTA AREA HIKES

16 COSUMNES RIVER PRESERVE TRAILS

KEY AT-A-GLANCE INFORMATION

LENGTH: 4.1 miles
CONFIGURATION: Connected loops
DIFFICULTY: Easy
WATER REQUIRED: 0.5 liters
SCENERY: Open savanna and riparian woodland
EXPOSURE: Bright in the meadows
TRAIL TRAFFIC: Light
TRAIL SURFACE: Grass or dirt trail; concrete sidewalk
HIKING TIME: 2 hours
SEASON: Year-round, sunrise–sunset
ACCESS: No fees or permits
MAPS: USGS Bruceville
FACILITIES: Pit toilets in the parking lots on both sides of Franklin Road
SPECIAL COMMENTS: Excellent hands-on displays are included in the visitor center exhibits.
WHEELCHAIR TRAVERSABLE: Yes; the Wetlands Trail is a level sidewalk with observation platforms.
DRIVING DISTANCE: 22 miles

IN BRIEF

The River and Wetlands Walks at the Cosumnes River Preserve showcase the plant and wildlife communities of the largest free-flowing river entering the Great Central Valley. Close to town and accessible to all, these trails offer tranquility, beauty, and a sense of what the area once looked like to settlers.

DESCRIPTION

The trails at the preserve guide hikers through two of the Central Valley's diminishing plant communities. Here, hikers can stroll through a riparian forest, past a freshwater marsh and vernal pools, and along annual grasslands at a leisurely pace.

The Cosumnes River Preserve is managed by the Nature Conservancy, the U.S. Bureau of Land Management, Ducks Unlimited, the California Department of Fish and Game, the State Lands Commission, the California Department of Water Resources, Sacramento County, and private landowners.

If your party includes children, the visitor center should be your first stop: let them acquaint themselves with the plants and wildlife they are about to see. Hands-on displays encourage everybody to touch, feel, and learn

---

Cosumnes River
Preserve Trails

UTM Zone (WGS84) 10S

Easting: 0636511

Northing: 4236478

Latitude: N 38° 15' 57"

Longitude: W 121° 26' 22"

Directions ⟶

From Interstate 5 in Sacramento, drive south 20 miles to the Twin Cities Road exit. Turn east, driving 1 mile to make a right onto Franklin Boulevard south. In 0.4 miles, you will see the Cosumnes River Preserve sign on the right. The visitor center is located on the left, another 1.2 miles down Franklin Boulevard. The trailheads are located next to the visitor center on the left.

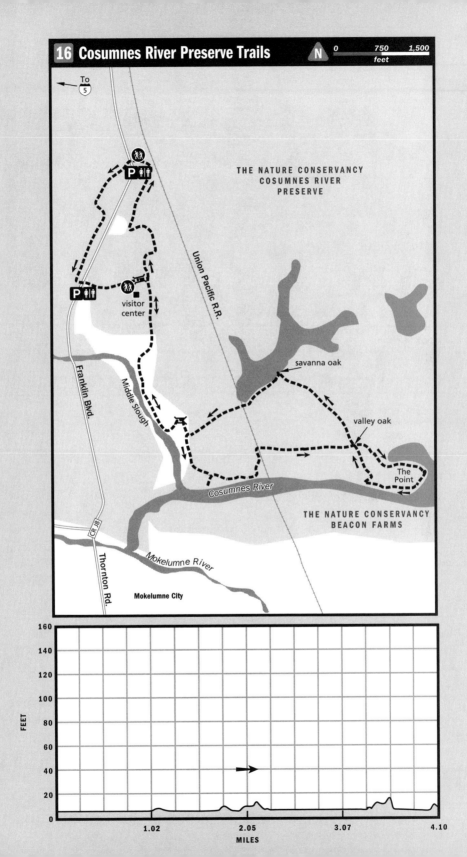

N

0   750   1,500
feet

To
5

THE NATURE CONSERVANCY
COSUMNES RIVER
PRESERVE

Union Pacific R.R.

visitor
center

savanna oak

valley oak

Franklin Blvd.

Middle Slough

The
Point

Cosumnes River

THE NATURE CONSERVANCY
BEACON FARMS

CR 18

Thornton Rd.

Mokelumne River

Mokelumne City

160

140

120

100

80

FEET

60

40

20

0

1.02   2.05   3.07   4.10
MILES

Savanna and oaks

about the elements of this unique and diminishing environment. Pick up trail maps and interpretive information for the area. The visitor center is staffed by volunteers, who also conduct guided tours. Call ahead for details and hours of operation.

The annual grasses and flowers surrounding the visitor center hint at the flora along the trails. Trailheads for both trails are located to the left of the visitor center at the top of a wooden ramp that descends to Willow Slough. The benches and observation points at each end of the bridge are nice spots to reflect on the posted interpretive material and touch-signs.

When you cross the bridge, you have two choices. One is to turn left onto the concrete sidewalk of the Lost Slough Wetlands Walk. Lost Slough Wetlands Walk is 1 mile long and shares the trailhead with the Cosumnes River Walk. Wetlands Walk can be started at the parking lot across Franklin Boulevard as well.

The trail described here turns right onto the Cosumnes River Walk, following its dirt path south along Middle Slough. A warning sign at the trail's start relates the danger mountain lions pose to humans. For more information on this very serious hazard, read the mountain lion warning in the front of this book.

This dirt trail can be flooded at times, but when dry it is smooth, soft, wide, and shaded. Himalayan blackberries line the path on the left, and songbirds exercise both lungs and wings. Flashes of color and whistles follow you along as you pass by each of the interpretive-sign markers.

The trail has been planned so that hikers are treated to a bit of everything the preserve has to offer. Well marked at every turn, the path even allows for whimsical side trips or loops to let you see all its features.

The marshland to the east of the trail was restored through the efforts of Ducks Unlimited. Mallard ducks and egrets, red-wing blackbirds, and even slow pond turtles move among the tall grasses and reeds. Make a left turn and head to the footbridge on the marsh's south side. Another 200 feet along, head up the wooden step to your right.

A boulevard of majestic valley oaks shades your way as you walk toward the river to the south and then head east along it, listening to acorn woodpeckers. These beautiful trees shaded the Miwok people, who used the Santa Barbara sedges as material for their intricate baskets which they used to cook the abundant acorns.

The scent of the wild California rose becomes stronger as you approach the Cosumnes 0.5 miles above its mouth at the Mokelumne River. The Cosumnes flows about 80 miles from its source high in the El Dorado National Forest to join the Sacramento–San Joaquin Delta. The river and sloughs here are subject to the same tidal forces as those in the San Francisco Bay. It is the spawning grounds of Chinook salmon, and is home to muskrat, beaver, mink, and river otter.

Now it's time to turn north before passing under the railroad trestle. A pair of interpretive signs tells of the work involved in identifying and managing nonnative species. Your grassy trail is exposed as you parallel the Union Pacific tracks. As soon as you turn under the tracks, you will see that the extra sun is worth it.

Immense valley oaks are the highlight of this grassland savanna. The color surrounding you depends on the season, but the lush grasses, wildflowers, and oaks are a backdrop for wonderful memories.

Continue walking east across this vast meadow. At the next trail crossing, you may turn right or go straight, as this route describes. The nesting boxes in the trees are for wood ducks. Kites soaring and spotted towhees scrambling underfoot are hints of the 200 identified species of birds that visit or live here. House finches and sandhill cranes, swans, ducks, geese, and coots flock to this wetland annually.

Complete this mini-loop by walking south and west past The Point, where you may enjoy a rest on the benches placed here as part of a Boy Scout project. Then it's on to a lonesome live oak, where you will turn left and head northwest to the oak-marked junction you passed earlier.

Continue northwest across the meadow toward a grand savanna oak at the edge of a tule marsh. Linger in the shade here and take a moment to use your binoculars while under cover. You won't have to wait long to observe several species from this cool spot.

Now head southwest to follow the trail signs under the tracks and across an old double-track, and then make a right at the wooden stairs that you

The great egret patiently hunts frogs and fish.

ascended previously. Cross the bridge, turn left, and follow the path back to the visitor center.

When you reach the concrete sidewalk, you have traveled 3.1 miles. The Lost Slough Wetlands Walk is 1 mile long. Within 200 feet, an observation point and benches entice you to rest. The trail continues to the right, past the native ryegrasses.

After crossing the bridge, you will see the uniform growth of the grove of valley oaks planted as acorns in 1988. Brush your hand lightly across the fennel to release more of its fragrant scent as you pass. Butterflies are all over this and other blossoms along the path.

An observation point is conveniently located along the slough just before the trail crosses the road. Another viewing area extends from the parking lot into the wetland on the other side of Franklin Boulevard. There are interpretive signs in the parking lot. The ponds to your right are wet year-round, although they grow and shrink. Another observation deck awaits at the southernmost end of this section of the walk. Cross Franklin Boulevard to return to the visitor center.

NEARBY ACTIVITIES

Excellent home-style meals are prepared at Giusti's, which is next to the Walnut Grove Marina. Drive 2 miles south on I-5 to Walnut Grove Road. Drive west to the second bridge and turn right for good food and good company.

LODI LAKE NATURE TRAIL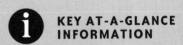

IN BRIEF

The nature trail joins the exercise trail to form a pleasant loop that lets hikers experience the wonderful sights, sounds, and scents to be found in the Mokelumne River riparian area.

DESCRIPTION

Rarely does a small town take such care to preserve an important ecological area such as the city of Lodi has done with this 58-acre nature area. You know this place is special as soon as you see the murals at the trailhead. Walk straight ahead on the asphalt-paved pathway, the Nature Trail, which will take you generally northeast 0.5 miles. In fact, you could turn around at that point, satisfied that you have seen most of what the park has to offer; but this hike continues on the exercise trail to make a loop around the park and along the former river channel.

Walk past the outdoor theater that is set amid a grove of majestic coast redwoods. They may be the most obvious of the trees that are not native to the Central Valley, but they are not the only nonnative species. The Himalayan blackberry (not a foreign handheld device) and black locust (not an insect)

KEY AT-A-GLANCE INFORMATION

LENGTH: 2.5 miles

CONFIGURATION: Loops

DIFFICULTY: Cakewalk

WATER REQUIRED: 0.5 liters

SCENERY: Riparian area with nice views of the Mokelumne River

EXPOSURE: Shaded trail; little exposure

TRAIL TRAFFIC: Light on weekday afternoons

TRAIL SURFACE: Asphalt and packed dirt

HIKING TIME: 1.5 hours

SEASON: Year-round, sunrise–sunset

ACCESS: $5 fee

MAPS: USGS Lodi North

FACILITIES: Restrooms near swimming area

WHEELCHAIR TRAVERSABLE: Yes, on the paved nature trail

DRIVING DISTANCE: 34 miles

SPECIAL COMMENTS: Docent-guided tours can be arranged by contacting Lodi Lake Park, 1101 West Turner Road, Lodi, CA, 95242, (209) 333-6742. Bicycles are not allowed on the trails, and dogs must be leashed. Your canine hiking partner may appreciate a run at the dog fields over near the swimming area.

Directions

Starting out from the intersection with Capital City Freeway, drive 32 miles south on CA 99 to Lodi. Leave the highway at West Turner Road, Exit 267a. Turn left on West Turner and drive 1.7 miles to the park entrance on the right, on Laurel Avenue. This is directly opposite Superburger Drive-In. Drive down the lane and turn right when the large oak in the road causes you to slow down, and park inside the gate. The trailhead is directly adjacent to the lot.

Lodi Lake Nature Trail
UTM Zone (WGS84) 10S
Easting: 0649665
Northing: 4223671
Latitude: N 38° 00' 53"
Longitude: W 121° 17' 31"

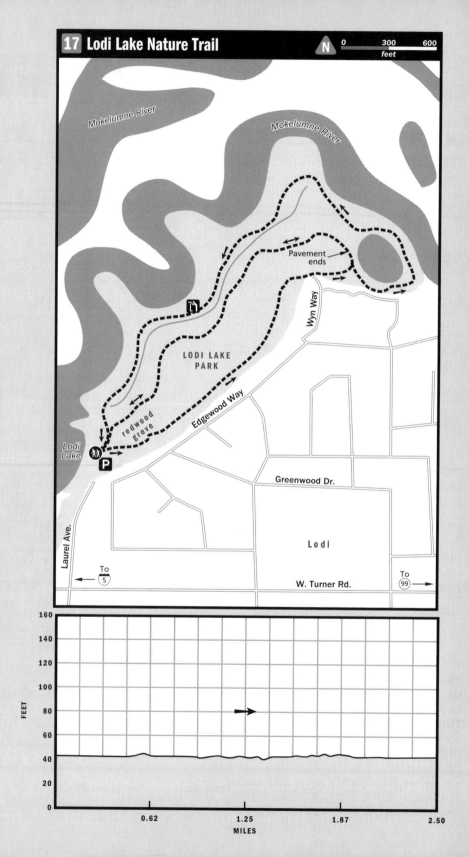

17 Lodi Lake Nature Trail

N

0   300   600
feet

Mokelumne River

Mokelumne River

Pavement ends

Wyn Way

LODI LAKE PARK

redwood grove

Edgewood Way

Lodi Lake

P

Greenwood Dr.

Lodi

Laurel Ave.

To 5

To 99

W. Turner Rd.

160
140
120
100
80
60
40
20
0

FEET

0.62   1.25   1.87   2.50

MILES

Blackberries abound on the
Lodi Lake Nature Trail.

are also introduced species that have adapted well to the sandy loam of the valley's riparian environment.

The grasslands that you soon pass display both native and nonnative species. There are informational placards in the ground that have suffered some flood damage, but they are generally well placed. Markers attached to the trees seem to last longer.

Valley oaks stand like huge, ponderous ancestors of the area, but even they look up to the noisy foliage of the cottonwoods. When the explorer John C. Fremont came through here in 1844, he made special comment about the musical rustlings of the leaves of the cottonwoods and oaks. Just about the time you are thinking about relaxing while listening to the trees yourself, nice benches will start appearing like poppies.

Casual trails lead off to the water's edge or across the area between trails, but the Nature Trail continues on the pavement until a substantial, yellow, metal post. Continue past the post and your dirt-and-duff trail will lead left around a small pond, which is excellent for spotting frogs, turtles, mallards, and wood ducks amid the dozen birds hiding in the understory and sprinting along the pond's edge. As you exit the pond area, you will walk past the tree dedicated to the anonymous "E"—perhaps indicating an invitation to eat the mountain of blackberries along here.

The cattails and their resident frogs line the trail as it traces a small creek formed by river water that has soaked the ground. Hummingbirds and a variety of understory-dwelling songbirds and dozens of little brown birds join the frogs just after you pass the viewing platform.

Back at the trailhead, this half of the trail and loop has covered about 1.5 miles. If you want, continue around to the other half of the exercise trail

A pond turtle shares its perch with a pair of mallards.

and walk with the outdoor theater and redwood grove on your left. There is some exposure along here, where your trail runs close to the neighborhood. The unexpected feature of this hike is not that it is so quiet along the trail, but that it is so noisy—but just noisy with sounds of the trees, wind, and animals.

At 1.9 miles, you will plunge back into the woods once again just before the path joins the nature trail at the yellow post. Turn left here and follow the nature trail back to the trailhead and the parking lot.

NEARBY ACTIVITIES

The Discovery Center natural history museum has excellent displays. Located near the dog fields and picnic area at the far end of the parking lot, it is open Saturdays between Memorial Day and Labor Day, and admission is free.

RIVER BEND-MAJESTIC OAKS LOOP TRAIL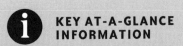

IN BRIEF

These easy trails loop through the magnificent valley oaks and towering cottonwoods of this rare riparian forest. A hike through this forest draped with wild grapevines and filled with the song of various birds will be remembered even by children for a long time. Excellent interpretive signage also makes this hike an educational trip for adults as well as children.

DESCRIPTION

Only about 5 percent of California's original Central Valley riparian forest remains. Located on the Stanislaus River, the Caswell Memorial State Park (MSP) has preserved an impressive expanse of woodland, 258 acres of this rare California ecosystem that once stretched for miles toward the mountains.

If you begin at the restrooms, your trailhead is at the end of the walkway leading west past the picnic tables and the seating area. An informational kiosk at the trailhead displays a general map of the park, along with descriptions of the flora and fauna one might encounter in this park.

Directions

From the intersection of the Capital City Freeway and CA 99 South, drive 58 miles south toward Stockton on CA 99. Just past CA 120, exit at Austin Road, cross the railroad tracks, and drive south 5.1 miles on Austin Road, cruising through orchards to reach the Caswell Memorial State Park entrance. The entry kiosk is 100 feet ahead. After paying your entry fee and picking up a map, drive 0.4 miles to the end of the shaded road. Turn left into the parking lot. Restrooms are at the east end of the lot, and the trailhead is toward the west end, near the information kiosk.

KEY AT-A-GLANCE INFORMATION

LENGTH: 3 miles
CONFIGURATION: Loop
DIFFICULTY: Easy
WATER REQUIRED: 1 liter
SCENERY: Riparian forest
EXPOSURE: Shaded trail
TRAIL TRAFFIC: Light
TRAIL SURFACE: Duff and dirt
HIKING TIME: 1.5 hours
SEASON: Year-round, 8 a.m.–sunset
ACCESS: $6 fee
MAPS: USGS Ripon; local map at entry kiosk
WHEELCHAIR TRAVERSABLE: Access on Grey Fox and part of River Bend Trail
FACILITIES: Trailhead toilets and water; picnic tables; camping
DRIVING DISTANCE: 63.5 miles
SPECIAL COMMENTS: This is a great trail for children on a hot day. The trail is wide, shaded, and surrounded by wonderful plants and animals.

River Bend–Majestic Oaks Loop Trail

UTM Zone (WGS84) 10S

Easting: 0660115

Northing: 4173386

Latitude: N 37° 41' 37"

Longitude: W 121° 11' 02"

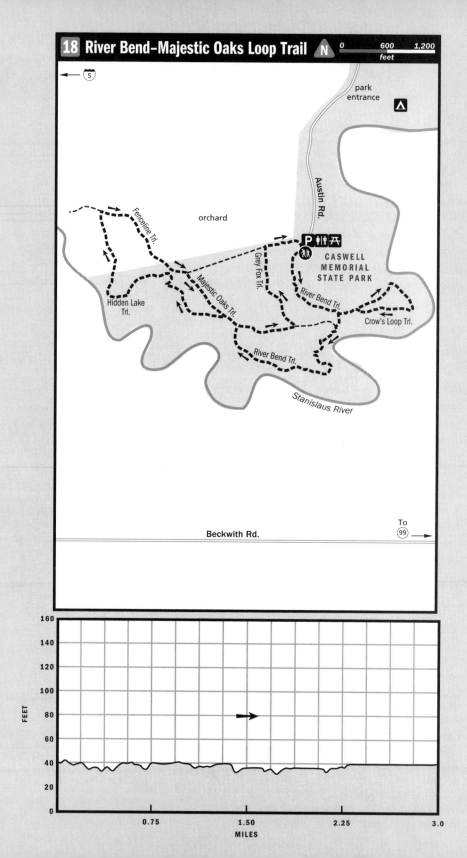

N

0   600   1,200
feet

5 ←

park
entrance

orchard

Fenceline Trl.

Austin Rd.

Grey Fox Trl.

Majestic Oaks Trl.

Hidden Lake
Trl.

CASWELL
MEMORIAL
STATE PARK

River Bend Trl.

Crow's Loop Trl.

River Bend Trl.

Stanislaus River

To
99 →

Beckwith Rd.

160

140

120

100

80

60

40

20

0

FEET

0.75   1.50   2.25   3.0

MILES

Black oaks shade this well-placed causeway.

Hikers in wheelchairs can access the first 0.25 miles of the River Bend Trail. Connect to the Grey Fox Trail for a 0.7-mile loop. These trails are made of smooth, packed dirt, not paved, so those in wheelchairs may need some assistance along both the trails.

Past the signs for the trailhead, towering valley oaks and cottonwoods cast shade across the trail, and any light that might sneak in is caught by the curtain of wild grapevines draped from the trees. Immediately after they are made, the sounds of owls calling and woodpeckers hammering are muffled. Your footsteps are almost silent as you proceed along this dirt-and-duff trail on the way to the next interpretive sign.

Rather than just listing the species of this riparian habitat, the signs in Caswell MSP relate a natural scenario in terms that are easy for children to remember. You will pass an area close to the river, where a sign cautions hikers to stay back from the eroding bank. After that, the trail is wide and there is not too much poison oak.

Head into the Crow's Loop Trail by taking the next two left turns. Blackberries and sedges both thrive in this floodplain, growing amid the poison oak. There are some nice vistas of the river here as long as you stay on the trail. Although it is not as manicured as the interpretive section, this 0.4-mile loop gives one some insight into the variety of this ecosystem's wildlife. Raccoons, foxes, skunks, weasels, and squirrels have all left evidence of their passing. Most of the smaller mammals, such as the riparian brush rabbit and the riparian wood rat, take up residence in the thick understory and rarely venture farther than 50 feet from their burrow or nest. And for good reason. Sitting at the bottom of the food chain, they are meals for raptors such as great horned owls, osprey, and

A hidden gem at the end of an orchard road

Swainson's hawks; they are also on the menu of all the mammals listed above; and, they are even taken by snakes. No wonder they live in seclusion.

When you are halfway around the loop, valley oaks will fill the sky above your trail and block the horizon. Pass through a grove of young sycamores to finish this loop. Take the same two left forks you passed previously to return to the River Bend Trail. Every intersection in this park is marked with a brown wooden post signed with trail names and directional arrows, so you should have no worries about becoming disoriented in this thickly forested park.

In about 100 feet, you will stay on River Bend Trail by turning left at the intersection with the Grey Fox Trail. Follow the River Bend Trail with the river on your left as you head south. As you walk in and out of the shade, your path is interrupted by a horizontal oak that offers no options other than scrambling through its broken limbs and over its trunk as the blackberries on the other side beckon and the wild rose perfumes the air. The poison oak reminds you to watch what you grab.

There are plenty of side trails over to the edge of the Stanislaus River. Here you can watch for the occasional turtle as it suns itself on a stick poking out of the mud bank. The trail remains a wide double-track despite the overgrowth of sedges. More frequently now, cottonwoods tower 75 feet over your track. You are totally shaded for the next five to ten minutes on even the sunniest day. Look down for a bit to spot the next two turns. Take a left at the intersection that puts you on Majestic Oaks Trail. (Straight ahead would take you to the parking lot.) Walk just 100 feet and take another left back onto River Bend Trail.

Geese can be heard arguing over on the river as you walk through the wild grapevines, but you'll be unable to see past the greenery to the water. Continue to the junction with Hidden Lake Trail. Make a left on this trail, heading southwest. (From this point, you can reach the Fenceline Trail by walking 50 feet ahead.) As you walk along Hidden Lake Trail (it could have been called the Active Raccoon Trail for the plentiful markings of these nocturnal mammals), you will encounter another fallen oak where a trail enters from the right. Signed as the Mosquito Trail, it does not appear on the park map. Our route goes forward in search of Hidden Lake.

Perhaps there is a lake hidden in the thick forest that this trail skirts, but light does not penetrate far enough to reveal any sort of secret fishing spot here. Regardless, the trail is soft, the shade is cool, and the wild rose is relaxing. Notice that some small areas of the forest have been thinned by burning; the Yokut people did the same thing when they lived in this area. Look for green or brown narrow fiber tubes standing in these thinned areas: they protect valley oak seedlings as they gain a foothold in the forest. Hike onward to a right turn at Fenceline Trail, where Rabbit's Run Trail leads off to the left, then hike along Fenceline Trail about 0.25 miles. The duff-covered road is bordered by the orchard to your left and valley oaks to your right. You can see many more of the seedling tubes here as you approach a junction with River Bend Trail. Continue on to your left and pass a wood-chipping area. In a moment, you will take a right onto Majestic Oaks Trail. Aside from the huge valley oaks with their spreading canopies, there are numerous seedlings planted and protected here for future generations to enjoy.

Pass the next two intersections; they are both part of the River Bend Trail. Your task is to take in the vast numbers of valley oaks that grow here. They are magnificent and will be here for a while, thanks to the care of this park and the Caswell family.

Turn north on Gray Fox Trail, where the interpretive signage continues. Blackberries and roses on one side and grapes overhead bound your trail an hour into the hike. When you reach the fence line, turn right toward the parking lot. The corner of the orchard is to your left, and the trail enters the parking lot at the northwest corner.

19 GRIZZLY ISLAND WILDLIFE AREA TRAIL

KEY AT-A-GLANCE INFORMATION

LENGTH: 4.5 miles

CONFIGURATION: Balloon

DIFFICULTY: Easy

WATER REQUIRED: 1 liter

SCENERY: Delta marshland

EXPOSURE: Fully exposed to sun and wind. Ear protection, hat, windbreaker, and gloves may be needed any time of year. The temperature here will be several degrees lower than in the valley.

TRAIL TRAFFIC: Minimal

TRAIL SURFACE: Dirt and grass

HIKING TIME: 2 hours

SEASON: Feb.–July, sunrise–sunset

ACCESS: $2.50 admission; free with one of several state permits. Open for hunting seasons; call ahead for hiking dates. Check with the Department of Fish and Game for closures and permit details.

MAPS: USGS Honker Bay; area map in office or at www.dfg.ca.gov/lands/wa/region3/grizzlyisland.html

FACILITIES: Pit toilet at trailhead

WHEELCHAIR TRAVERSABLE: No

DRIVING DISTANCE: 57 miles

SPECIAL COMMENTS: This is an unsigned route on levee roads. Levee roads may lead to dead ends or small adventures. Do not leave the levee roads, even for short distances.

Grizzly Island
Wildlife Area Trail

UTM Zone (WGS84) 10S

Easting: 0593076

Northing: 4218698

Latitude: N 38° 06' 40"

Longitude: W 121° 56' 17"

IN BRIEF

Carved out of the Suisun Marsh, the largest contiguous saltwater marsh on the West Coast, the Grizzly Island Wildlife Area offers an abundance of wildlife and botanical diversity. This short hike lets hikers walk slowly enough to quietly observe amphibians, reptiles, and fish; waterfowl, songbirds, and raptors; and burrowing mammals, grazing mammals, and predatory mammals. At any given moment along this trail, the alert hiker will be able to spot easily identified specimens, whether turtles, frogs, otters, or skunks. Your challenge is to not miss the next three while identifying the first; there are that many species to see.

DESCRIPTION

The informative kiosks at the DFG Field Office provide a good overview. Inside the office

---

Directions ⟶

Drive 38 miles west on Interstate 80 to CA 12 East (Exit 43) in Suisun City. Follow CA 12, Rio Vista Road, 3.8 miles to Grizzly Island Road, where you will turn south. This turn is directly across from the shopping center at Sunset Avenue. As you drive south around the Potrero Hills, you may notice an immediate change of scenery from valley to delta. About 5.5 miles from your turn south onto Grizzly Island Road, you will make a right turn across the bridge and boat-launch ramps at Montezuma Slough; the transition is unmistakable. Another 3.5 miles and you will be greeted by signs requesting you register at the DFG office. After registering and looking at the displays inside, continue 5.6 miles straight ahead on the gravel-and-dirt road (bear left whenever given a choice) until you see the towering eucalyptus tree at the signed parking lot 3. There is plenty of parking here and a portable toilet but no water.

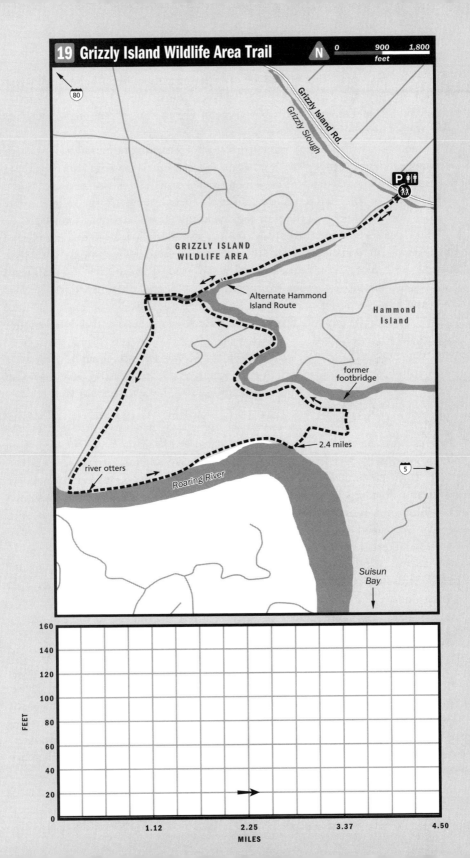

19 Grizzly Island Wildlife Area Trail

N

0   900   1,800
feet

80

Grizzly Island Rd.

Grizzly Slough

P

GRIZZLY ISLAND
WILDLIFE AREA

Alternate Hammond
Island Route

Hammond
Island

former
footbridge

2.4 miles

5

river otters

Roaring River

Suisun
Bay

160
140
120
100
80
60
40
20
0

FEET

1.12   2.25   3.37   4.50

MILES

there are more displays that hint at the diversity of wildlife here. The Suisin Marsh Natural History Association Web site, **www.suisunwildlife.org,** includes lists of species found on Grizzly Island that you can use for quick reference. Such lists make it easy to recall all you have viewed.

Binoculars will help the patient hiker spot a surprising number of species. Morning and late afternoon are best because most animals tend not to move during the heat of the day. Hikers will need a hat with a brim, sunglasses, sunscreen, and a wind jacket or soft shell top. Light gloves also help, even when the valley is quite warm. Insects abound, and the trail is uneven, thanks to burrowing mammals.

Starting at the large eucalyptus tree at the parking lot, cross the gravel road to the wooden footbridge. Stop along the bridge and take a moment to look around. You may have spotted several raptors while driving to the trailhead. You will see harriers swooping from field to field, kites hovering just above their prey, and hawks soaring even higher. For no apparent reason, an entire flock of mallards, egrets, or any of a dozen other waterfowl may churn the water and air to get somewhere else fast.

Walk across the bridge, heading toward Mount Diablo, about 15 miles due south from the trailhead eucalyptus. Legend holds that Grizzly Island was so named because bears from Mount Diablo used to make an annual trek to feast on the island's blackberries.

At the end of the bridge, zig to the right and then zag to the left on the obvious levee road, heading southwest toward the Roaring River. At 0.6 miles, a levee road will enter from the left. (You can take an alternate route from this point. Turn left and follow this road, taking two left turns to get back to the trailhead.) This hike continues 0.2 miles farther down the trail to another junction. Your choices are to cross the canal and turn left, make a U-turn to the left, or turn left over the culvert pipe and continue on the dirt tracks.

The hike described here turns left over the pipe and heads slightly southwest on the dirt tracks. Mount Diablo, off to the southeast, can act as your guide. More directly east are the large wind turbines that harness the constant gusts to busily churn out electricity. It is common to spot tule elk in the highlands around the island. They were successfully reintroduced to the marshes in the late 1970s.

Along this short stretch of dirt trail, travel may be difficult in wet weather. Take the next left 0.7 miles, noticing the steep edges of the slough. In midday, none were active, but the signs of river otter and their slides were everywhere. Tracks and signs of other mammals were also frozen in the muddy margins of the sloughs and shallow ditches. Sometimes our own senses provide us all the clues we need to identify a mammal. Very close encounters with very active skunks are a real possibility. Let your nose be your guide in turning away whenever the odor intensifies. These trails are choked with tall grasses and weeds or have grass-constricted margins that can conceal any manner of creatures. Keep a sharp lookout for a T-intersection just before you walk into the slough.

Windswept delta-levee road

Another left turn and another 0.7 miles—to the east this time. Your left-turn marker is the point at which you are directly south of the trailhead eucalyptus. So far, you have traveled 2.4 miles. It is just a short walk north to another T-intersection; take a right there. When a pheasant cock takes flight along here, try to stay on the trail and in your boots. They go from 0 to 60 right underfoot.

Navigation is easy, and you can see your trailhead, so spend some time crawling along the margins of the slough, where the amphibians and reptiles spend their days. Western pond turtles enjoy warming in the sun along a log or on a muddy bank. The two-tone green Pacific tree frog may surprise you with its voice but if you are sharp enough to spot one, you will see that its call far outweighs its body.

Turn left at the next intersection and then make another left before you run into the water at the dilapidated footbridge. You will now be heading generally northwest. Your winding trail parallels the trail along the opposite shore of Hammond Island. (That is the alternate trail that was mentioned above.)

Your next intersection is a repeat of your confusing first turn. Cross over the culvert and turn right, toward your trailhead tree. If you prefer a longer hike from this point, in just 0.2 miles you can turn right to follow the margins of Hammond Island, circumnavigating it back to the trailhead parking lot. Just turn left twice and you will be back at the trailhead with more stories.

Western pond turtle lying low

The great thing about Grizzly Island is its concentration of wildlife and its network of levee roads, all of which are open to hikers. And, remember, dead ends are just a reason to enjoy your trail twice.

NEARBY ACTIVITIES

Nearby Rush Ranch is a 2,070-acre open space which protects important brackish tidal marshes. For details on its many offerings, including hiking, see its Web site, **www.rushranch.org.**

The Delta region has several preserves and parks with interpretive nature trails. The Cosumnes River Preserve (Hike 16, page 90) and Caswell Memorial State Park (Hike 18, page 99) both have excellent interpretive trails.

Foothills South Hikes (20–24)

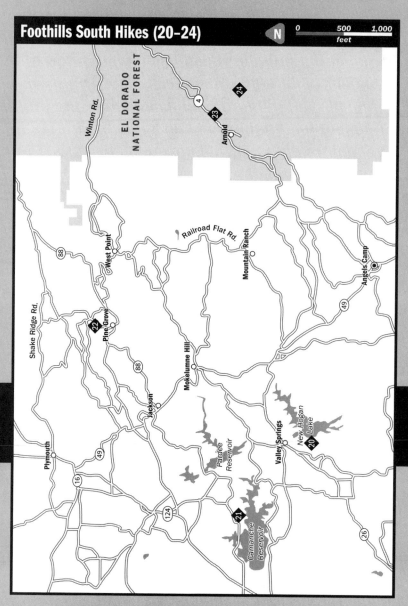

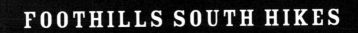

FOOTHILLS SOUTH HIKES

20 RIVER OF SKULLS TRAIL

KEY AT-A-GLANCE INFORMATION

LENGTH: 1 mile

CONFIGURATION: Loop

DIFFICULTY: Cakewalk

WATER REQUIRED: 1 liter

SCENERY: Riparian and foothill woodland

EXPOSURE: Mostly shaded trail

TRAIL TRAFFIC: Light

TRAIL SURFACE: Dirt and duff

HIKING TIME: 1 hour

SEASON: Year-round, sunrise–sunset

ACCESS: No fees or permits

MAPS: USGS **Valley Springs; New Hogan Lake Trail map**

WHEELCHAIR TRAVERSABLE: No

FACILITIES: Pit toilet, parking area

DRIVING DISTANCE: 62 miles

SPECIAL COMMENTS: Pick up a trail map and interpretive trail booklet at the headquarters building before driving to the trailhead. Turn left at the sign 0.4 miles south of Valley Springs and follow the signs to the headquarters. You can reach the trailhead from here by turning left at the end of the parking lot onto Silver Rapids Road, and then turning left onto Hogan Dam Road after 1.2 miles.

River of Skulls Trail

UTM Zone (WGS84) 10S

Easting: 0690716

Northing: 4224542

Latitude: N 38° 00' 53"

Longitude: W 120° 49' 24"

IN BRIEF

In about an hour, you can walk through two of the valley's important ecosystems—foothill woodland and increasingly vanishing riparian forest. The entire family can learn about the major flora while cruising along this mile-long rock-lined path.

DESCRIPTION

Nature trails are wonderful vehicles for learning about natural history and are fun places to hike. River of Skulls Trail is an important part of the riparian conservation effort. Less than 5 percent of the original riparian area in the Sacramento Valley and foothills remains today. This trail is fun and informative for hikers of all ages.

Although the name of the trail repulses some, children seem naturally drawn to it for just that reason. *Calaveras* is the Spanish word for "skulls." Apparently, the large number of human skulls found along the lower reaches of the river were the inspiration for the river's name. Regardless of the name, this trail has been excellently laid out to make the most of a small area's diverse flora.

Directions

From the junction of US 50 East and CA 99 South, drive 31 miles south on CA 99 to the Victor Street (CA 12) exit in Lodi. Then drive 5 miles east on CA 12, where it will join CA 88 for 7 miles. Continue 15 more miles on CA 12 east to the town of Valley Springs. Turn right onto CA 26, drive 3 miles south to Silver Rapids Road, and turn left. In 1.5 miles, turn right onto Hogan Dam Road. Cross the bridge over the Calaveras River, and immediately turn left into the equestrian parking lot at the Monte Vista Day Use Area. The trailhead is on the left at the far end of the parking area.

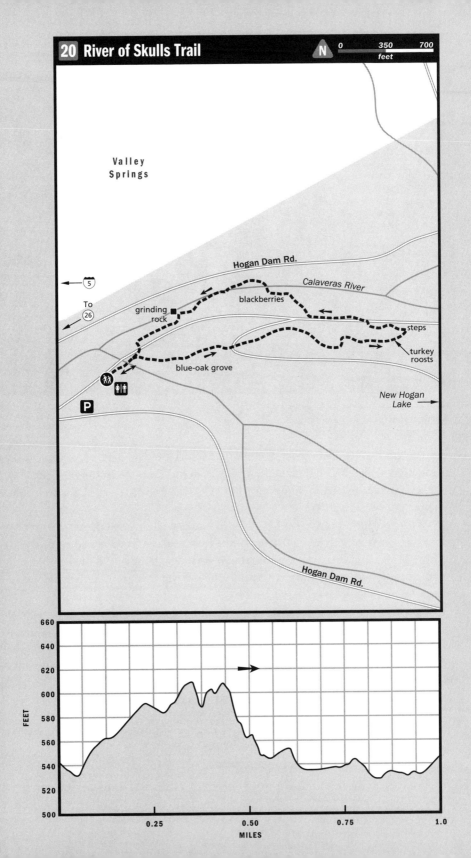

A perfect spot for an impromptu classroom

The trail covers two ecosystems. The first half of the path encompasses the upland area, which highlights the foothill woodland flora. Then the trail descends to the river, where riparian flora flourishes. That the two are so close is not uncommon in Central California.

With your interpretive trail booklet in hand, walk over to the northeast corner of the parking lot, where posts mark the trailhead. Follow the wide gravel path over the bridge and then bear right as the next trail sign indicates. Bear right again and then follow the rock-bordered trail to the left, up to a group of benches at the beginning of a blue-oak grove.

The dominant hardwood of the upland area is blue oak. Its small acorns were gathered by the Miwok, the Native Americans who occupied this area for thousands of years before settlers arrived en masse during the gold-rush era. You will see a variety of oaks on this trail. Besides the blue oak, there are also valley oak, black oak, and live oak. All of these supplied large quantities of acorns, which were an important staple to the Miwok. As you identify each of these trees, notice the size differences of their acorns and leaves.

The upland area is also noted for its chaparral, which consists, in this area, of chamise and buck brush. These offered the Miwok a good area in which to hunt for deer and rabbit. Walk beneath the dying foothill pine's one massive limb that reaches out and down to the ground. Colorful in any season, there is plenty of poison oak here to keep you on the trail as you continue along under foothill pine and live oak.

The trail emerges onto a wildflower-encrusted hillside after you pass the knoll above you to the right. Reenter the shade of pine, toyon, and manzanita as the trail continues eastward. Manzanita, Spanish for "little apple," was another food source of the Miwok, who used the red berries for tea and stored the dried berries for winter.

There are several turkey roosts among the black oak and its large pointy-lobed leaves. As you walk toward a set of steep steps, look trailside for feathers. Carefully avoid the poison oak as you examine the different types of feathers discarded here by preening turkeys.

From the bench at the stairs, you can hear the rushing of the water as it exits the dam about 1,000 unseen feet from your position. Continue down the steps, where you will see black oak, elderberry, toyon, coffeeberry, and valley oak. Another nice grouping of benches offers a great place to sit in the shade and read about what you have seen so far. Head west on the trail and skirt the base of the short slope that you traversed moments earlier.

The trail crosses a dirt-and-gravel road on its way to the river. There is never any doubt about which way to travel on this well-marked route. The trail does become rockier as you near the river, which grows louder despite the thick trees lining its banks.

Riparian trees and bushes close in tightly on the trail, which often looks like nothing more than a break in the vegetation. Blackberries grow in profusion here, and there are signs that other berry lovers, including birds, skunks, and raccoons, have stopped by for a snack. A large buckeye on the opposite shore leans out over the river and nearly touches the trail as you walk by. Another huge buckeye actually has half its large trunk in the water and half on the shore. Several small clearings allow access to the swiftly flowing river to the west. Fremont cottonwood trees comprise an important part of the riparian zone and can grow to heights of a hundred feet.

As the trail moves away from the river, it passes over ancient sedimentary rock, formerly ocean floor, which has been upended and now forms much of the exposed bedrock in this complex geological area. As you near the trail's end, notice a small rock outcrop, nearly covered by brush, which has a few Miwok grinding holes in it. These mortars were used to pound the acorns that were so highly prized. Even in ancient times, food processing was done on site, just as it is today.

In another minute, you will arrive back at the bridge leading to the trailhead.

NEARBY ACTIVITIES

If you want a bonus trail, follow the 8-mile Equestrian Trail. It is sunny, with only a little shade, but it is an interesting hike, with huge wildflower displays and plenty of fishing opportunities. The trailhead is across the parking lot next to the toilet.

There are also excellent hike-and-bike trails that begin near the headquarters parking lot but can also be accessed from many of the campgrounds along the way. The bike trail has sections rated for all skill levels from easy to difficult.

21 CHINA GULCH TRAIL

KEY AT-A-GLANCE INFORMATION

LENGTH: 11 miles
CONFIGURATION: Out-and-back
DIFFICULTY: Challenging
WATER REQUIRED: 3–4 liters
SCENERY: Blue oak and open grassland meadows overlooking lake
EXPOSURE: Exposed to the sun for most of the route
TRAIL TRAFFIC: Light
TRAIL SURFACE: Dirt and gravel
HIKING TIME: 4 hours
SEASON: Year-round, sunrise–sunset
ACCESS: $9 fee
MAPS: USGS Wallace; EBMUD trail map available at entry kiosk
WHEELCHAIR TRAVERSABLE: No
FACILITIES: Parking lot with two pit toilets and trash receptacles; water available at trailhead
DRIVING DISTANCE: 46 miles
SPECIAL COMMENTS: The blue-oak-studded meadows are overflowing with wildflowers in spring. No dogs permitted. Unless you are hiking in the spring or early summer, water is unavailable on this trail after the trailhead.

China Gulch Trail
UTM Zone (WGS84) 10S
Easting: 0680151
Northing: 4234238
Latitude: N 38° 14' 17"
Longitude: W 120° 56' 29"

IN BRIEF

This hike takes wildflower lovers through vast meadows of colorful blossoms every spring. The rolling hills are sprinkled with handsome blue oaks that contrast with the light-blue sky. This equestrian and hiking trail is easy to follow, but it is exposed to the sun all day. A hat is a must on this hike.

DESCRIPTION

The China Gulch Trail is an equestrian trail that traces the north lakeshore past China Gulch to the area of Lancha Plana and then returns to the equestrian assembly area. Your track takes advantage of the wide horse route as it meanders around, over, and down small hills and knobs, all decorated with uniformly spaced blue oaks and alive with colorful wildflowers in spring.

Once you have parked, find the trail, which begins at the north end of the staging area, and start by walking north on the gravel road next to the board fence. When you round the first curve, a sign-in kiosk, which is the

Directions

From the junction with US 50, drive 25 miles south on CA 99, past Galt, to the Liberty Road exit. Drive 12.5 miles east on Liberty Road to the junction with CA 88. Continue straight across on Liberty, which will become North Camanche Parkway, driving another 7.5 miles. After the village of Camanche, turn right onto Camanche Road; the entry kiosk is about a mile on. To reach the trailhead, follow the road to the left after the kiosk, and the sign will point to the trail, which is about 0.2 miles ahead, to the left of the mobile-home park. The trailhead is reached from the north end of the equestrian staging area.

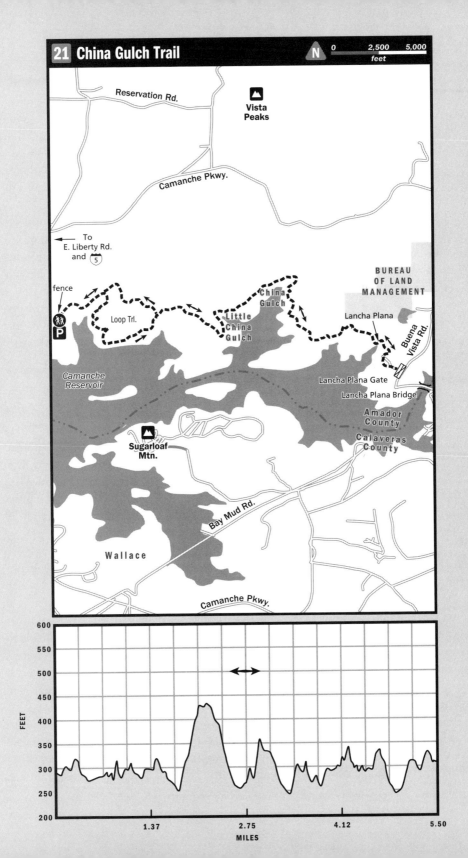

official trailhead for the China Gulch Trail, comes into view on the other side of a gated fence. Make sure to close the gate across the trail after you pass through.

If you picked up a trail map at the entry kiosk, you will see a narrow-gauge trail leading to the south and then looping back to join the main trail. Your route follows this extra loop. However, if you feel like taking only a short trail, you can return to the trailhead after rejoining the main trail, and your trek will have covered just 3 miles. The described hike goes outbound via the loop trail and returns via the main road, making an 11-mile round-trip.

Your first scenic vista pops into view within 0.25 miles of the trailhead. When you finish taking pictures here, you may notice one of the first few watering stations for horses over on the right. Descending this larkspur- and buttercup-lined road northeast, you might stop, turn around, and take in the broad, blue-oak meadow on both sides of the upcoming drainage.

A trail sign on the right indicates the loop trail—"narrow gauge" on the map—which approaches the lake for a 1.5-mile diversion before rejoining the main trail. Your route turns southeast at this point and crosses a seasonal drainage. Your direction reverses as you parallel the trail you descended, now visible across the meadow.

The path is covered by horses' hoof prints, which have erased the previous night's wildlife tracks. So if you are on this trail early in the day, pay close attention to the animal tracks in the dust. They were all made overnight. These prints tell little stories about the wildlife here: A cluster of quail prints midtrail that lead off at an angle into the grass might be an interrupted meeting. Raccoon prints that change from a walk to a run, crossing the many large tracks of a trailside turkey convention, followed by a small pillow of down in the grass bring to mind a frantic but brief chase. A careful coyote's prints at the margin of the trail tell of a search for other nocturnal travelers.

Blue oak is certainly the dominant tree species of this open chaparral. No other tree is visible here as you first spot a silent flotilla of houseboats at anchor in the small bay to your west. This trail will generally skirt the knoll, which crests about 100 feet above the trail. As you contour along, you will pass an old fig tree, which, despite being completely toppled, still bears fruit. Reverse direction again and travel east, with the lakeshore on your right. The broad hillside to your left is topped by distinctive blue oaks and is filled with butterflies and bees, mauling every one of the thousands of flowers like ants at a picnic.

As the ridge dwindles out on the east end, cross a seasonal drainage and then angle right, across the wash, where you can see the junction with your original trail. If you are returning to the trailhead, keep left on the wide trail to rejoin your track. Otherwise, keep right, across the meadow. If you embarked on this trail without a hat, this is about the point at which you will start to think about fashioning a *chapeau* from just about anything: kerchief, T-shirt, sandals, maybe a snack wrapper. It is hot and exposed along the entire route.

Trail markers are plentiful here.

Camanche Reservoir, which straddles the San Joaquin, Amador, and Calaveras county lines, fills the lower valleys along the path of the Mokelumne River. While the land in the vicinity of the Mokelumne was being settled during the gold-rush years of 1849 and 1850, Campo Seco and Mokelumne Hill were thriving towns, and even Camanche had a population of up to 1,500 people, who hailed from all over the world. Hydraulic mining moved the course of the river, dried it completely at times, altered its looks, polluted it, and returned enormous monetary profits, until flood control, irrigation, and electricity production became more profitable and important than gold. Developed and operated by the East Bay Metropolitan Utility District (EBMUD), Camanche Reservoir is the largest in its system of lakes in the southern foothills.

There are differing accounts regarding the naming of Camanche. The one thing all agree upon is that its original name was Limerick and that it was subsequently changed to the current misspelled version, either purposely in memory of a town in Iowa or inadvertently after a frustrated postmaster proposed two other names that were rejected. Either way, the town now lies silently beneath the lake's waters.

Turn right and head uphill, where you have a nice vista to the south and east. Another watering trough sits amid the blue oaks and small displays of irises and lilies. Spend the next five minutes walking along the ridgeline toward the southeast. Enter the shade of another blue-oak grove, and the trail heads down. As you descend this long switchback, you will see trail signs directing hikers away from sensitive or revegetated areas.

Blue oaks cover the hillsides.

Enter this next ravine, Little China Gulch on the maps, and then exit it while climbing northeast, with trees to your right, where your trail becomes gravel-covered after it crosses the small drainage. Continue uphill, probably following turkey tracks, and it changes to dirt again. For the first time on this route, a few foothill pines appear on the knoll ahead that separates Little China Gulch from China Gulch.

When you gain about 50 feet, the trail will contour across the face of this hill and then descend again into China Gulch. Just as you begin heading downhill, you'll see the crowns of about a half dozen gray pines sticking out above the blue oak on the hill to your right. A close look reveals another few dozen spread out across the hill.

Cross the rock culvert at China Gulch, where a ranch house looks down on your trail. In wet years the lake sneaks up to this crossing. When it's dry, you can track raccoons as they travel along this dirt trail. Leave China Gulch behind as you ascend the hill and cross another small drainage. In a short distance, live oaks briefly provide shade as you climb up and over another low ridge to Lancha Plana.

A parklike setting awaits you as you enter the signed Lancha Plana. The low-canopied trees grow close enough together to block the sun and keep the grasses from scorching. This is a great spot for a relaxing break. Lancha Plana, meaning "flat boat" in Spanish, was the name of the ford in the Mokelumne River where a

The rolling, forested grassland is typical of the southernmost foothills.

ferry operated in 1850. The ferry is reported to have run at the site of the Lancha Plana Bridge on Buena Vista Road.

Head uphill and cross another small culvert, also signed as Lancha Plana, on your way to the trail's end about 0.5 miles away. A small pond sits atop the next hill. Your trail skirts it to the right and then drops downhill to the right. You'll see an irrigation ditch from the trail. This may be part of the old Poverty Bar Ditch, which the lakes and reservoirs later replaced. You can trace portions of this, or some other irrigation ditch, at various points along your route.

The trail winds around until it comes within sight of Buena Vista Road. The end of this hike is along the road at a gate marked LANCHA PLANA GATE—AC 49. You can walk past this gate down to the trees alongside the lake and then return via your previous route. When you reach the LOOP TRAIL sign on your return, you can retrace your steps exactly onto the 1.5-mile loop, or you can continue straight for 0.8 miles to the staging-area parking lot.

NEARBY ACTIVITIES

The Mokelumne Watershed and Recreation Division maintains 21 miles of hiking, equestrian, and jogging trails. Call (209) 772-8204 for permit information.

22 INDIAN GRINDING ROCK LOOP TRAILS

KEY AT-A-GLANCE INFORMATION

LENGTH: 1.8 miles

CONFIGURATION: Connected loops

DIFFICULTY: Cakewalk

WATER REQUIRED: 1 liter

SCENERY: Foothill woodland and grassland

EXPOSURE: Shady, except at midday

TRAIL TRAFFIC: Moderate

TRAIL SURFACE: Dirt and duff, asphalt

HIKING TIME: 1 hour

SEASON: Year-round, sunrise–sunset

ACCESS: $6 day-use fee

MAPS: USGS Pine Grove; local map in park brochure

WHEELCHAIR TRAVERSABLE: Partly, near grinding rocks and other exhibits

FACILITIES: Restrooms, water, camping

DRIVING DISTANCE: 55 miles

SPECIAL COMMENTS: The Indian Grinding Rock has the most mortar holes of any grinding rock in North America.

Indian Grinding Rock
Loop Trails

UTM Zone (WGS84) 10S

Easting: 0705921

Northing: 4255605

Latitude: N 38° 25' 29"

Longitude: W 120° 38' 27"

IN BRIEF

The trails around the 135-acre Indian Grinding Rock State Historic Park pass exhibits, plants, reconstructions, including a Miwok village and a ceremonial round house, and the famous Indian Grinding Rock, Chaw'se. Having nearly 1,200 mortars on its bedrock limestone, this is the largest number of bedrock mortars anywhere in North America. Still visible next to some of the mortars are 2,000-to-3,000-year-old petroglyphs.

DESCRIPTION

The two trails—the North Trail and the South Nature Trail—can be joined conveniently to create a loop that encompasses all of the park's sights. There is no route finding necessary because all the trails are well marked and easily identified. This loop starts at the trailhead in front of the museum.

Head up the stone steps and walk along the trail as it trends northeast above the parking area. Walking between the road and the entrance drive, you will pass under incense

---

Directions

From downtown Sacramento, drive 3 miles east on US 50 to the Howe Avenue exit toward Rancho Murieta. Drive southeast 18 miles on the Jackson Road to Rancho Murieta, then about 13.5 miles to the CA 49 junction (the second right turn); drive 7 miles south to Sutter Creek and another 4 miles to Jackson. Turn left on CA 88 and drive 8 miles to Pine Grove. Turn left onto Pine Grove–Volcano Road toward Volcano. In about 1 mile, a sign on the left indicates the campground. The park entrance is 0.25 miles past this on the left. The trailhead, marked by a directional arrow, is at the end of the sidewalk that leads into the museum.

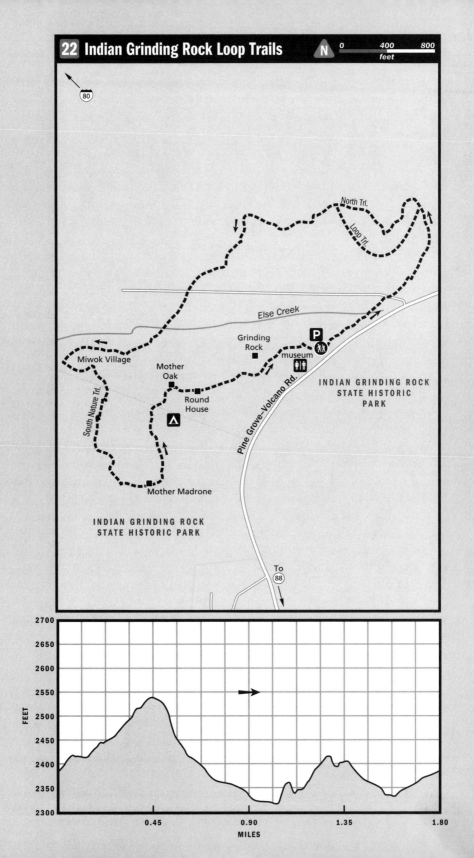

cedars, foothill pines, and live oaks. Some faint-purple brodiaeas add color to the trailside. A footbridge keeps your feet dry as you cross the head of Else Creek, named for one of the original farming families. Look ahead for the hole in the wooden fence, where you will cross the road.

The farmhouse to your right was an original pioneer homestead. In the late 1880s, the land here was sold to Serafino Scapuccino, who protected the grinding-rock area and whose family sold the farm to the state in 1958 to be used as a park. The orchards here provided fruits for miners in Volcano and elsewhere. Continue your northward walk under some huge madrone and white-leaf manzanita.

A junction offers hikers a choice between the lower Loop Trail or the upper North Trail. Both trails feature foothill woodland and grassland ecosystems. Small clearings between manzanita display colorful irises and lupines, and buttercups, monkeyflower, and brodiaea border the trail. Towering overhead are Douglas fir, ponderosa pine, incense cedar, and foothill pine, all mixed in with live oak and black oak. But none of these specimens shines like the majestic valley oak—of which there are huge examples here.

Head slightly uphill on the North Trail, a packed-dirt path that winds in and out of the madrone and pine. The scent of needles baking in the sun fills the air. A grove of live oak provides some cool shade at midday, when the sun breaks through onto the trail just before the Loop Trail rejoins the North Trail.

Meander down some easy switchbacks through the manzanita on this rock-lined section of the trail. Fence lizards are the only critters scurrying about in the heat of the day, and they reveal their every step in the dry duff littering the forest floor. Cross a small runoff stream and head down some improvised steps.

Your trail takes a distinct left turn downhill toward the first valley oaks to come into view. Cross the gravel road, making a slight jog to your right, and continue walking, now through the tall grass bordering a much narrower trail. A sign displays the distance to junctions and park features.

Ahead of you on the right is a grove of valley oaks in which all of the oaks are more than 300 years old. With the support of their enormous trunks, these trees spread majestically across the meadow, creating a shaded parklike setting. A small footbridge helps hikers across Else Creek at the end of the meadow. Incense cedars and native grasses lead hikers up to the Miwok village reconstruction at the junction with the South Nature Trail.

The Miwok settled a broad area between the Cosumnes River to the north and the Calaveras River to the south. Because acorns were a staple food crop, the Miwok were attracted to this area, which has groves of valley oaks and a broad, flat rock on which to grind the nuts into flour. One wonders if the trees were here before the rock was discovered, or if their proliferation was a result of the grinding rock's use.

After inspecting the round cedar-bark houses in the village, turn right onto the South Nature Trail and start looking for interpretive-marker posts—about

Miwok bark houses in front of Chaw'se Museum

three feet tall, brown, numbered, and hard to spot. The interpretive guide for sale in the museum will guide you along.

Towering incense cedar, Douglas fir, ponderosa pine, sugar pine, and valley oak shade your downhill trail as you cross a creek and enter a rather open area right up against fenced-in private property. Blackberry, iris, and columbine grow in this moist, cool area, along with ferns and kit-kit-dizze, which crowd the trailside.

Winding around a bit brings you to a spectacularly large madrone. Fire-scarred and weather-beaten, it is surrounded by iris and lupine. The trail continues north past the trailside bench.

The trail borders the campgrounds to their left and passes a grand incense cedar with an imposing split trunk that reaches eight feet in diameter. Trail markers will keep you on track when you are about to walk into the picnic tables. Jog slightly left and stay close to the fence around the campsites. Watch for signs directing hikers to the park's features. The grandest living feature of the park is the Mother Oak—a 600-year-old valley oak that spreads across the meadow. It is an awesome natural wonder and an imposing presence not found in most parks.

Valley oak also shades the entrance to the ceremonial Round House, which is one of the largest in California. Continue along the walk to the grinding rock itself. The grinding rock is a bedrock formation of marbleized limestone. Having 1,185 individual grinding holes, it is the largest such collection of mortars

The Chaw'se (Grinding Rock) was used for three millennia.

in North America. The rock's use has been dated to 2,000 to 3,000 years ago. Beside some of the mortars are petroglyphs—pictorial representations carved in the stone—which show everyday important objects such as nets, the sun, and man himself. A viewing platform allows for up-close views of the entire rock.

Return to the museum trailhead by walking past the bark houses and the metal sculpture of a Miwok Indian dancer.

NEARBY ACTIVITIES

The Chaw'se Indian Museum next to the trailhead has excellent Miwok displays and natural history exhibits and is especially oriented to children, with many hands-on displays.

BIG TREES NORTH GROVE TRAILS

IN BRIEF

The interpretive trail through the North Grove of Sierra redwood trees offers hikers of all ages and abilities a detailed, up-close, and inside view of these impressive giants. Clearly signed and well designed, the trail through these spectacular trees is a pleasure to hike in almost every month.

DESCRIPTION

Discovered in 1852, these trees have, incredibly, avoided the fate of other groves throughout the state, many of which were destroyed by logging. Your trailhead through these centuries-old trees is signed NORTH GROVE TRAIL, RIVER TRAIL, THREE SENSES TRAIL, GROVE OVERLOOK TRAIL. If you did not pick one up in the visitor center, purchase a guide to the Calaveras North Grove Trail at the trailhead for 50 cents. It contains an excellent map and helpful, informative notes about the area's natural history.

"Wow!" and "That's huge!" are the most common words heard on these trails. And

KEY AT-A-GLANCE INFORMATION

LENGTH: 3 miles
CONFIGURATION: Loops
DIFFICULTY: Cakewalk
WATER REQUIRED: 1 liter
SCENERY: Old-growth forest
EXPOSURE: Totally shaded trail
TRAIL TRAFFIC: Moderate
TRAIL SURFACE: Duff and dirt, boardwalk
HIKING TIME: 1.5–2 hours
SEASON: Year-round, sunrise–sunset
ACCESS: $6 fee
MAPS: USGS **Dorrington**
WHEELCHAIR TRAVERSABLE: The Three Senses Trail
FACILITIES: Visitor center, picnic tables, restrooms, telephone
DRIVING DISTANCE: 91 miles
SPECIAL COMMENTS: This is an excellent interpretive trail among gigantic old-growth trees.

Directions ————————————>

From the junction of US 50 and Capital City Freeway, drive 3.6 miles east on US 50 to the CA 16 exit at Howe Avenue. Take CA 16 (Jackson Highway), 31 miles to CA 49. Turn south toward Jackson and drive 34 miles to Murphys Grade Road in La Honda. Turn left on Murphys Grade Road and continue 7.5 miles to Murphys. Turn left on CA 4 and go 11 miles, heading toward Arnold. The park is on the right, 3 miles past Arnold on CA 4. Stop at the entry kiosk to pay your fee and pick up a map. Bear right, then turn left into the main parking lot. The trailhead is at the far end, on the right, past the restrooms and next to the Warming Hut.

Big Trees
North Grove Trails
UTM Zone (WGS84) 10S
Easting: 0735540
Northing: 4240207
Latitude: N 38° 16' 44"
Longitude: W 120° 18' 25"

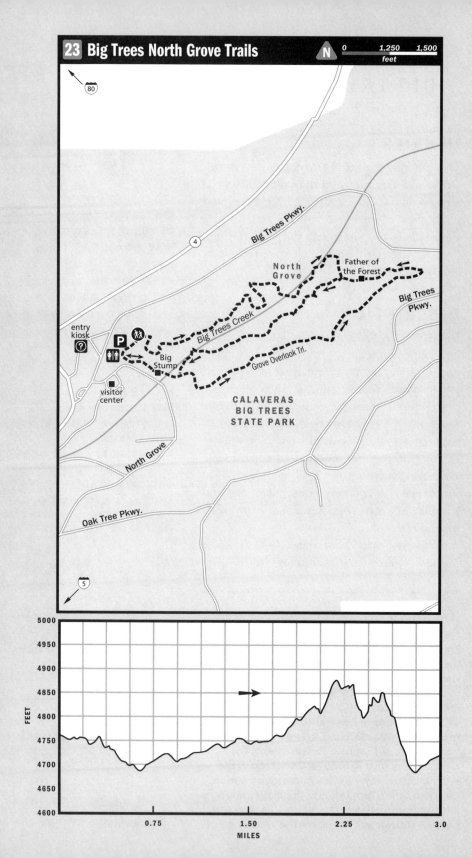

23 **Big Trees North Grove Trails**

N

0   1,250   1,500
                  feet

Crystalline beauty among
old-growth majesty

how could it be otherwise? These trees *are* huge. The loop trails wind around the giant sequoias and other old-growth trees, such as ponderosa pine, white fir, sugar pine, and incense cedar. We are familiar with these trees, but they certainly are an order of magnitude larger due to their having been protected from logging.

This hike takes in two of the trails in the North Grove: the North Grove Big Trees Trail, which is the interpretive loop, and the Grove Overlook Trail. This does require repeating a short segment of the trail—but that is not a drawback, considering the awesome scenery. The interpretive loop is highly recommended if you prefer a shorter hike. The Grove Overlook Trail is not signed and is a bit less tame than the loop.

From the trailhead, you will follow a path that, like the entire trail, is bordered and signed the whole way. Pass the campfire center, with its outdoor theater, on your way to the Big Stump. The Discovery Tree had stood for more than a millennium when this 300-foot Sierra redwood, or giant sequoia as it is also known, was discovered in 1852. One year later, it had been stripped of its bark and toppled, and its stump had been turned into a dance floor and saloon. Interpretive signs and descriptive kiosks ring the Big Stump, where docents or rangers are on hand to answer questions. You can walk up on the stump and get a view of the area, too.

Look for the trail sign just past the downed log of the Discovery Tree; it points you toward the Grove Overlook Trail. Take the right-hand path and ascend slightly. Then turn left and continue an easy, yet steady, slant up the hillside. Douglas squirrels may flash by you along here as they retreat from the activity along the main trail. These squirrels are undoubtedly well fed, judging by the

Gentle pathways weave quietly through the forest.

massive amounts of nuts and seeds evident in this old-growth forest.

The trail is made of the softest duff, part of a deep layer of organic material in which the redwoods spread their roots, keeping them from toppling onto random hikers. The path traverses the hillside through stands of incense cedar, which also has a soft, reddish bark. But even as the view through the trees changes along this trail, the unmistakable red of the giant sequoia glows in the sunlight from the grove. When you look toward the grove from this elevation, you are looking at the midsection of the sequoias.

Although the trail along here is fairly clear, watch out for the cones of the many old-growth sugar pines in this forest. For the most part, there are very few exposed rocks along the trail. Thick duff of tree bark, cones, and needles overlays almost every mineral outcropping. Some of the young redwoods along here play host to woodpeckers, which seem to work their way down trees in search of their next snack. On this quiet, lightly traveled trail, the woodpecker's rapid hammering is muted and muffled by the redwood's soft, fibrous bark.

You will spend so much time looking up that you may miss some of the ground cover, especially the lupine. But you needn't worry about missing a junction or trail directions: They're posted at every point where you might wonder which way to go. In fact, the exact location of the trails was reworked during the summer of 2007, although it appears that the general layout will remain unchanged.

At the end of the overlook trail, turn west, (left) and descend somewhat to the main loop trail. When you rejoin the loop trail, turn left and proceed clockwise along the loop, or head straight to go counterclockwise along the second

The starting point for another E-ticket ride

half of the loop before walking the first half. Either way, you can repeat any of the three legs to return to the trailhead.

Benches are liberally scattered around the grove, not only for resting but also for lining up that difficult photo. Wherever the understory is thick or the terrain uneven, either a wood-lined pathway or a boardwalk will assist you.

This trail has an even more magical appearance in winter, when the crowns of the trees are topped with snow. The trail is passable on foot except after a heavy snowfall, when it is open to cross-country ski travel.

NEARBY ACTIVITIES

If you have time, the South Grove Trail (Hike 24, next page) is another wonderful stroll, with fewer hikers sharing the trail.

Want to get off your feet? Take a swim at the Oak Leaf Spring Picnic Area or the River Picnic Area, on the Parkway about two miles from the South Grove. Information about camping is available through the California State Parks Web site, **www.parks.ca.gov.**

On your way back through Arnold, have a bite at the Grizzly Express, alive and jumping on CA 4.

24 BIG TREES SOUTH GROVE TRAILS

KEY AT-A-GLANCE INFORMATION

LENGTH: 5.4 miles
CONFIGURATION: Out-and-back
DIFFICULTY: Moderate
WATER REQUIRED: 2 liters
SCENERY: Awesome old-growth forest
EXPOSURE: Nothing but shade
TRAIL TRAFFIC: Light
TRAIL SURFACE: Duff and dirt
HIKING TIME: 3 hours
SEASON: May–October, weather permitting
ACCESS: $6 entry fee
MAPS: USGS Stanislaus, Crandall Peak
WHEELCHAIR TRAVERSABLE: No
FACILITIES: Pit toilet and benches in parking area
DRIVING DISTANCE: 91 miles
SPECIAL COMMENTS: Bring a wide-angle lens and a pad to lie on to frame these spectacular giant trees. Dogs are not allowed on the trails.

IN BRIEF

More than 1,000 giant sequoias tower over you and everything else in this natural preserve. The trails lead you through and around more than 100 individual redwood trees, including one of the ten largest trees on Earth.

DESCRIPTION

The South Grove trails lead hikers through a mixed-conifer forest dominated by towering, old-growth ponderosa pine to the grove of giant sequoias that straddle Big Trees Creek. The South Grove is within the Calaveras South Grove Natural Preserve, which contains more than 1,000 of these giant trees. Known commonly as the giant sequoia, the Sierra redwood is a species distinct from the coast redwood. Discovered by settlers in the 1850s, the trees in this grove have been protected since the early 1860s from being disturbed by extractive industries.

The trails in this grove are, in a word, sweet. Duff and dirt are so thick in this preserve that rocks, boulders, and outcrops are rarely seen. This is good for hikers who

Big Trees South Grove Trails

UTM Zone (WGS84) 10S
Easting: 0739081
Northing: 4236721
Latitude: N 38° 14' 48"
Longitude: W 120° 16' 04"

Directions

From the junction of US 50 and Capital City Freeway, drive 3.6 miles to the CA 16 exit at Howe Avenue. Take CA 16 (Jackson Highway) 31 miles to CA 49. Turn south toward Jackson and drive 34 miles to Murphys Grade Road in La Honda. Turn left on Murphys Grade Road, and drive about 7.5 miles to Murphys. Turn left on CA 4, heading 11 miles toward Arnold. The park is on the right, about 3 miles past Arnold on CA 4. Stop at the entry kiosk to pay fees and pick up a map. Signs ahead will direct you to the South Grove.

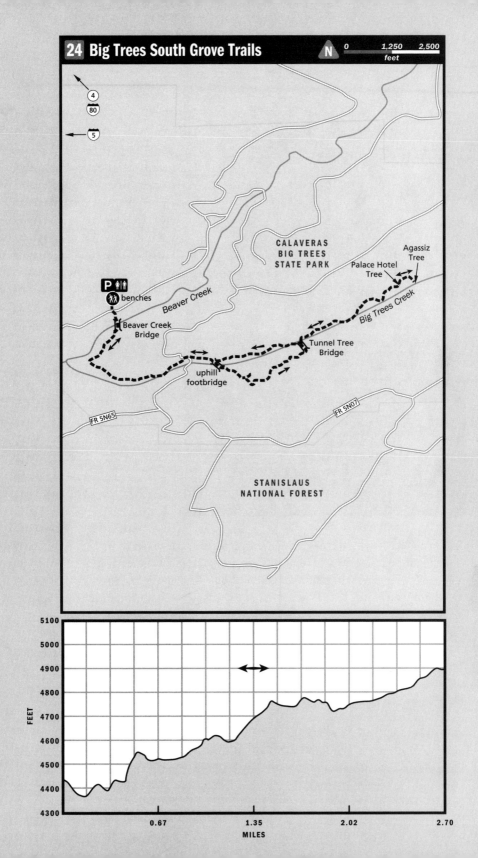

N

0   1,250   2,500
feet

4
80

5

CALAVERAS
BIG TREES
STATE PARK

Agassiz
Tree

Palace Hotel
Tree

P 👫
👥 benches

Beaver Creek

Big Trees Creek

Beaver Creek
Bridge

Tunnel Tree
Bridge

uphill
footbridge

FR 5N65

FR 5N07

STANISLAUS
NATIONAL FOREST

The Agassiz Tree, 25 feet around and 250 feet tall, is named after the famed naturalist.

spend Considerable time looking up at the treetops and do not enjoy tripping over rocks. Highly visible and distinct in all parts of the preserve, the trail winds around noteworthy trees. Although an excited populace felt compelled to name the trees, very few have the kitschy-sounding names that are popular in many caverns. It is recommended that hikers pick up an informational pamphlet and trail map at the visitor center, or download one free. Complete with tree names, the pamphlet is an informative guide and will add to your understanding of the special forest you are visiting.

Start out on the south side of the parking area, opposite the toilets, near the trash receptacles. A clearly signed trailhead marks the start of your trek. An informational kiosk about 100 feet down the trail will tell hikers a bit about the memorial groves that are eternal thank-you notes to the benefactors of this grove. Continue through a small meadow of bunchgrasses and descend to the Beaver Creek Bridge. The trail eases off to one o'clock at the end of the bridge and begins gently gaining elevation. In a matter of moments, you will pass the trailhead for the Bradley Grove Trail, which takes interested hikers to a grove of redwoods that were planted in the 1950s by the preserve's caretaker. You may already be dizzy from looking at these huge trees surrounding the trail. And not one of them is a sequoia.

This entire preserve is full of old-growth trees. These are all familiar trees: ponderosa pine, incense cedar, and white fir. The difference in these trees is that most of them are a few hundred years old. Their size reveals it: These trees are huge. Seeing a ponderosa pine with a trunk more than seven feet wide or a sugar pine with one more than ten feet is not uncommon along this trail. The fir and cedar are similar in size and proportion.

Continue slowly gaining elevation for approximately a mile. When you leave the Beaver Creek drainage, your direction will change from generally southwest to somewhat southeast, now trekking along Big Trees Creek, which empties into Beaver Creek after its approximately 3-mile course. At a junction with a dirt road, cross and bear slightly left on the obvious trail past a blackened stump and a burned-out standing snag. The trail is now sloped at a somewhat gentler angle.

Keep on the lookout for the point at which the trail splits. The sign is difficult to see, but the split is marked by an unusual-looking white fir stump next to its healthy-looking twin. Keep to the right at this split, but first turn and look back into the forest. You may have missed a tree or two, but a glance will reveal the overlooked, distinctive, red-barked goliaths. There will be so many more in the next mile. Even the standing snags, bereft of their bark, are majestic looking.

Big Trees Creek can be heard on your right as you head upstream. In a short while, you will cross a footbridge that slants uphill. Take a left at the end of the bridge and allow yourself a moment to look around. You will likely comment out loud when the redwoods come into view. Look all around. Take a few steps. Stop. Look around again. More trees are visible every time your aspect changes, and it changes with every step. Walking gradually uphill to the southeast, you are surrounded by more than 30 of these massive trees.

The trail is flawless soft duff, but the egg-shaped redwood cones often collect themselves into a cone-puddle, which, when stepped on, has a ball-bearing effect on unwary hikers. The trail is incredibly distinct throughout the preserve. As you walk northeast, you are is somewhat crowded by bush chinquapin and Sierra dogwood. This is the only thing close to a hindrance on this stretch. It would be hard to complain about it for long though: Look around at these trees. Whether they are standing or fallen, dead or alive, with bark or without, they are impressive. When you see a tree down on the ground, look more closely. It might be just a limb from the sequoia 30 feet from you.

Even in death, these trees are spectacular. Fallen trees are neatly cut through to ease your travel along the trail. That is true for the smaller trees like the fir. The downed sequoia, however, is not so accommodating. When your trail reaches a redwood on its side, broken and hollowed out, you will recross Big Trees Creek on a footbridge. Walk around, through, and past this tree. Its immense root system is above ground now. As it decays, it has become home to a variety of plant and animal life—including a redwood growing from the top.

Turn left after the tree and walk about 50 feet to another well-signed junction. Turning left at this point will lead you back to the parking lot. A right turn will take you about 0.5 miles uphill to the end of the trail, where the famed Agassiz Tree is located. Trees that you pause and inspect, perhaps even photograph and discuss, will have a distinctly different appearance on your return trip. One of these trees is about 0.1 mile along on the right. You will certainly notice that it has an uncommonly large amount of burn damage. Indeed, this tree's trunk has burned through completely. Incredibly, this tree has also burned through its top—that is, the place where its top

The track through the bunchgrass leads to the memorial groves and the Beaver Creek Bridge.

used to be—revealing sky where the crown once was. How the crown came off is unknown. Strong winds are probably responsible. However these calamities occurred, the tree remains alive. On your return, you will think you had never seen this tree. From the opposite direction, the crown's disappearance is obvious. But in place of the tree's original chapeau, there are two limbs the size of normally large trees, growing straight up.

Sequoiadendron giganteum has a few unique survival techniques. One is the ability, as you can tell from the scars on every single redwood, to resist fire: Its thick, fibrous bark provides this barrier to fires. "Self-healing" is another tactic which can be observed on one of the upcoming twin trees. As the trail leads around the tree, notice how the bark has grown over the deep fire scar to repair itself. Another survival strategy is that its cones open and its seeds are released following hot, debris-clearing fires.

The trail leads gradually uphill to a broad, flat area with a stand of young fir and redwood. Listen as the Douglas squirrels (chickarees) jabber at you, and then try to figure out what might prompt their verbal tirades. A fir, fallen across the trail, has become a racetrack for gray squirrels that appear to be far too well fed. Walking through the cut in the downed fir reveals a nearly perfectly circular hole to a depth of three feet in place of the tree's heartwood.

Continue a short way to the signed Palace Hotel tree. Its trunk has been burned out so evenly that it makes a nice room; early visitors to the grove were reminded of the San Francisco Hotel. A few hundred feet away is the famed Agassiz Tree, which was named after the renowned zoologist and naturalist. This tree is reported to be one of the ten largest trees in the world. Many of the trees in this grove have been here for as long as 2,000 years.

In the 1940s, the grove was purchased by a logging company and was slated to be harvested, starting with its sugar pine. Like many other groves left to extractive industries, this one came close to ruin. Through the heroic efforts of the Save-the-Redwoods League, the California State Parks, and individuals such as Frederick Law Olmsted and John D. Rockefeller, the grove was purchased for posterity in 1954.

The preserve continues another 2 miles to the northeast. Hikers with good navigational skills are welcome to explore further. The unmaintained use-trail leads past the sign at the Agassiz Tree. This path was not hiked and so is not described here. But if you do decide to explore it, budget plenty of time; Bear in mind that maintained trails are easier to travel and so take less time for equivalent distances.

If you are returning after visiting the Agassiz Tree, retrace your steps to the junction near the tunnel tree but this time, follow the sign toward the parking area. Lustrous copper butterflies dance along the trail's edges as you walk downhill past the Kansas group of trees. Woodpeckers, pounding their beaks at jackhammer speed, make a muffled noise as they look for insects in the soft, fibrous bark. Rejoin the main trail at the junction with the odd stump. The balance of your trail heads largely downhill until the Beaver Creek crossing.

NEARBY ACTIVITIES

The Beaver Creek Picnic Area, which you passed on the parkway to the South Grove, offers great swimming holes in which to cool off.

There are a number of interesting spots to visit in nearby Murphys and Arnold. Stop in at the Snowshoe Brewing Co. on CA 4 in Arnold for several varieties of excellent beers. Details are available at **www.snowshoebrewing.com.**

The Ironstone Vineyards (**www.ironstonevineyards.com**) and the Wild Grape restaurant, both in Murphys, are excellent places to visit for great grapes.

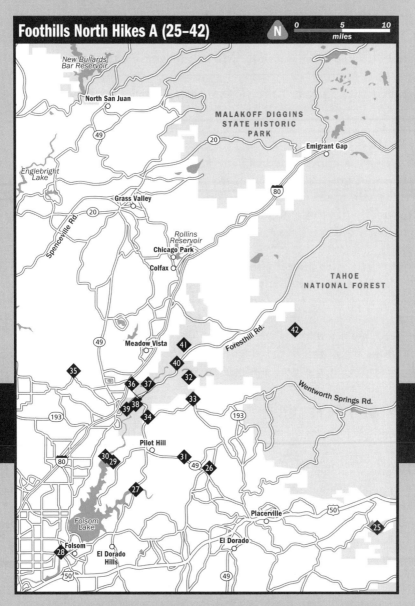

New Bullards
Bar Reservoir

North San Juan

MALAKOFF DIGGINS
STATE HISTORIC
PARK

49

20

Emigrant Gap

Englebright
Lake

80

Grass Valley

20

Spenceville Rd.

Rollins
Reservoir
Chicago Park

TAHOE
NATIONAL FOREST

Colfax

49

Meadow Vista

41

40

Foresthill Rd.

42

35

36 37

32

Wentworth Springs Rd.

193

39 38

33

34

193

Pilot Hill

30

29

31

49 26

80

27

Placerville

50

Folsom
Lake

El Dorado

25

28

Folsom

El Dorado
Hills

50

49

FOOTHILLS NORTH HIKES A

25 JENKINSON LAKE TRAIL

KEY AT-A-GLANCE INFORMATION

LENGTH: 9 miles

CONFIGURATION: Loop

DIFFICULTY: Moderate

WATER REQUIRED: 2–3 liters

SCENERY: Lakeshore trail in foothill woodland; Sierra snow visible from dam

EXPOSURE: Surrounding foothill forest provides shade.

TRAIL TRAFFIC: Light midweek, heavy in summer

TRAIL SURFACE: Dirt and duff, pine needles

HIKING TIME: 4.5 hours

SEASON: Year-round, sunrise–sunset

ACCESS: No fee required

MAPS: USGS Sly Park

FACILITIES: Pit toilets at several points along the trail

WHEELCHAIR TRAVERSABLE: No

DRIVING DISTANCE: 54 miles

SPECIAL COMMENTS: This loop is very populated, and the second half passes through campgrounds and picnic areas.

IN BRIEF

This easy loop is enjoyable any time of year. You hike through Douglas fir and incense cedar forest, where you can seek solitude and visit crystal-clear pools. Continuing along the north shore and past the campgrounds requires a determination to exercise and see new flora.

DESCRIPTION

Jenkinson Lake—formerly Hazel Canyon—was formed by damming the outlet of Hazel Creek and bringing water through a tunnel from a drainage to the south. A popular destination for picnics and family camping, the lake has campsites and picnic tables located on its north side.

Your trail begins at the second dam, on the south side of the lake. Park in the wide dirt patch on the right. The trailhead sign located across the road presents the "tale of the tape": 8 miles around the lake, 3 miles to Park Creek, and 4 miles to Hazel Creek.

Southshore Trail is a multipurpose trail serving hikers, horse riders, and bike riders. With few exceptions, the horse trail is separate from and above the hike-and-bike trail. A number of trails lead off to the lake's edge to reach favorite fishing spots. These trails are usually easily distinguished from the hiking trail proper.

Jenkinson Lake Trail

UTM Zone (WGS84) 10S

Easting: 0712081

Northing: 4287918

Latitude: N 38° 42' 52"

Longitude: W 120° 33' 38"

Directions ———————————————→

From Sacramento, take US 50 east 47.5 miles to Sly Park Road in Pollock Pines. Drive 4.5 miles south on Sly Park Road, passing the entrance to Sly Park Recreation Area, and turn left on Mormon Emigrant Trail, just 0.5 miles past the entrance station. Your trailhead is 1 mile from this turn. Cross Dam 1 and continue to the south end of Dam 2, where you can park on the right side, directly across from the trailhead.

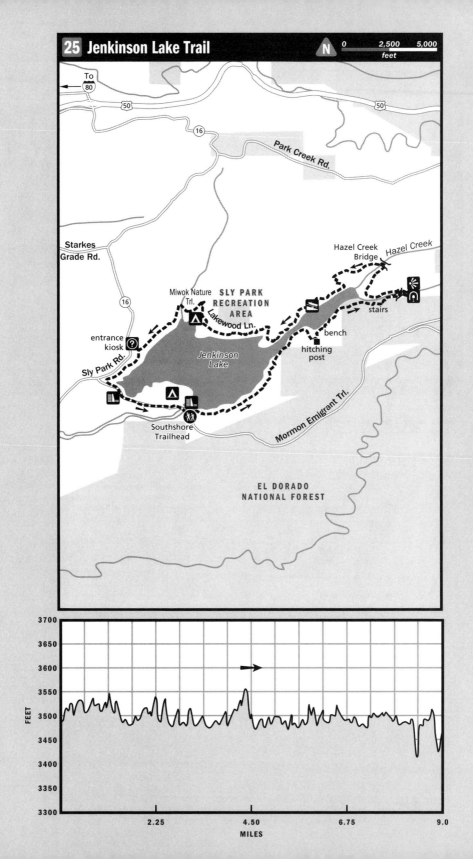

25 Jenkinson Lake Trail

N   0   2,500   5,000
feet

Sierra peaks over Jenkinson Lake

After passing a disused informational kiosk and a lakeside bench or two, your trail heads somewhat downhill and turns left at the large incense cedar, where the horse trail heads uphill to the right.

The terrain on your right rises steeply, lifting the Douglas fir, ponderosa pine, and white fir—giants on level ground—even higher. Black oaks are randomly distributed, but more are toward the lake, surrounded by buttercups.

Shortly after the lake narrows, you will encounter a split: take either track. Turning generally southeast into a secluded cove with a convenient bench, you can sit for a moment to contemplate. You may have company because this bench is the intersection of the horse trail, the hiking trail, and a biking trail. Notice the hitching post and the bike bridge over the puddle. Another nice bench, among trees marked with interpretive signs, overlooks the cove.

The generally flat terrain is interrupted by a brief uphill beneath towering firs. As you approach and then parallel the inlet creek, bikers get a sweet ride down an easy ramp, while hikers descend left down wet stairs. Back down to a broad, flat area, a jumble of driftwood floats against the willow-choked lakeshore. The trail widens here. A bridge appears just as you bear left toward the creek.

The bridge across Sly Park Creek marks the end of your third mile. As you stand on the bridge, you will have two choices to explore. To your right is a trail leading uphill to the outlet of the Bureau of Reclamation tunnel, which diverts water to the lake. To your left is path that leads upstream about 100 feet to a rocky bench on the creek where the waterfall comes directly at you.

After taking a rest or a snack or just a moment to cool your heels in the creek's pool, walk past the kiosk, heading west to circumnavigate the peninsula formed by the ridge dividing the two creeks. It is about 1 mile to the next drainage, Hazel Creek. The dirt-and-pine-needle trail meanders along the shore under a changing canopy. The firs have diminished, and manzanita is flourishing waterside along the open ground. Hikers bear left where horses are directed right.

Cross the road coming in from the right, and continue on the upper side of the road through a ponderosa pine grove. This is a comfortable trail with nothing to break your stride—unless you enjoy kicking pinecones. Stay on the main trail, ignoring trails heading down the bank. Continue straight on the wide four-wheel-drive road as the horse trail joins from the right.

At 4 miles, you will cross the bridge over Hazel Creek at a group campground. A pit toilet stands directly in front of you, about 75 feet after you cross the bridge.

You are at the halfway point. If you do not mind the sudden increase in trail users, continue as described. The hiker is presented with a different aspect of the lake's ecosystem here. Also, the trail is much more "urbanized" from this point. Whether you head forward or back, it's the same distance; you choose.

The trail skirts the shore, along the picnic area, and then continues near the road as it heads west toward the Chimneys Campground. If you want a bit of perspective on the lake, take the horse trail a short way by crossing the road at the pit toilet and ascending the rocky path. When you reach the next campsite, make a short descent to return to the hiking path.

Looking back from your lakeside trail, you can see the chimney ruins. At times, signage is lacking. So, when in doubt, follow the shore and you will soon resume the trail.

The Miwok Nature Center is near Pine Cone Campground. A kiosk on the road has information on the self-guided figure-eight trail. As you pass through a hillside of manzanita, notice that the fire that flowed through here scarred only the uphill side of the trees as it passed.

Follow this trail through the picnic grounds and down to the main marina and launch site. Walk to the far-right corner of the parking lot and resume the trail just after the wheelchair-accessible picnic tables. Before reaching Dam 1, ascend the steps at the Walter Jenkinson Monument and continue on the road across the dam. Your trail is still on the lakeside, just after the chain-link fence. Step up off the road and turn right at the boulder in the trail. Now walk parallel to the road, crossing a driveway that leads to a group campground. At the next campground road, turn left and go 50 feet, then turn right to resume your trail through the woods.

Emerge from the woods at the north end of Dam 2. You should be able to see your car at the trailhead parking area.

26 MONROE RIDGE TRAIL

KEY AT-A-GLANCE INFORMATION

LENGTH: 2.9 miles

CONFIGURATION: Loop

DIFFICULTY: Moderate

WATER REQUIRED: 1–2 liters

SCENERY: Mixed forest cover with lush manzanita, panoramic view of historic gold-mining town

EXPOSURE: Wide trails with forest cover

TRAIL TRAFFIC: Light

TRAIL SURFACE: Forest duff; sandy in spots; mostly smooth and wide

HIKING TIME: 1.5–2 hours at a leisurely pace

SEASON: Year-round, 8 a.m.–sunset

ACCESS: $5 park fee

MAPS: Marshall Gold Discovery State Historical Park brochure and map available on site; USGS **Coloma**

WHEELCHAIR TRAVERSABLE: No

FACILITIES: Generous parking, toilet, and picnic facilities throughout this small park

DRIVING DISTANCE: 49.5 miles

SPECIAL COMMENTS: For more information, call the Marshall Gold Discovery State Historical Park at (530) 622-3470 or visit www.parks .ca.gov. Dogs are not permitted.

Monroe Ridge Trail

UTM Zone (WGS84) 10S

Easting: 0682790

Northing: 4297126

Latitude: N 38° 48' 14"

Longitude: W 120° 53' 41"

IN BRIEF

This pleasant, rolling trail gives hikers a beautiful overview of an area so important to the history of California. The cool, smooth, red skin and waxy leaves of the manzanita color your shaded path to the James Marshall Monument. On your return, you descend the Monument Trail back to the museum.

DESCRIPTION

Stepping onto a path that winds through the forested hills, you also step back to the summer of 1847. Looking down from these formerly ponderosa pine–covered hills, James W. Marshall surveyed the canyon below, gazing at a Miwok Indian encampment called "Culluma," where he found the ideal location for a lumber mill.

By January 1848, having begun construction of a lumber mill the previous fall, James

----

Directions ———————————➤

From its junction with the Capital City freeway in Sacramento, drive 41.2 miles on US 50 east to Placerville and turn left (north) onto Spring Street, at the second traffic signal.

Follow Spring Street 0.1 mile and bear left (north) onto CA 49, Coloma Road. Enjoy this winding road for 7.7 miles to Coloma. Watch for fence posts topped with discarded boots and stray sneakers around 4.6 miles, and then nectarine and pear orchards along the next mile.

You have reached Coloma when you turn right onto Main Street and take a gentle left curve at the old schoolhouse. Another 0.4 miles brings you to the park's visitor center and museum on the left (north), where you can park and/or pay the $5 fee. Trailhead parking is available another 0.4 miles along, on the south side of the highway. The trailhead is directly across road from the parking lot.

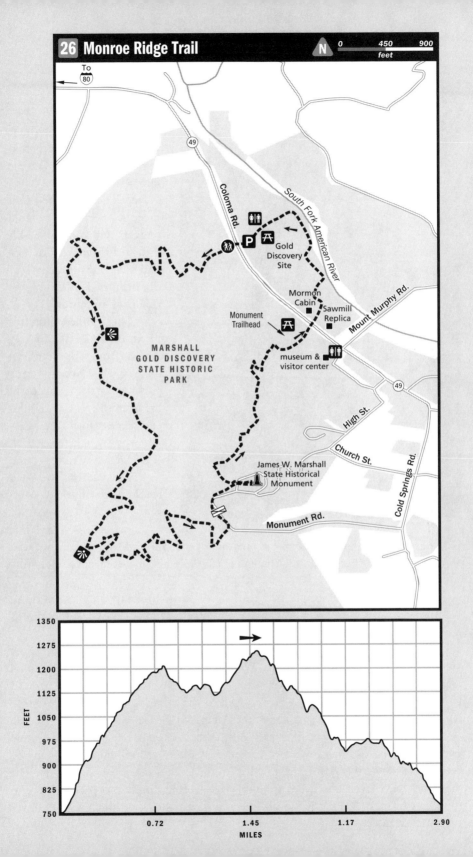

James W. Marshall looks out over Coloma.

Marshall worked daily, troubleshooting the breaking in of the mill. On the morning of the 24th, while inspecting a reworked tailrace, he spotted a few gold nuggets. He announced his find to his workers on site and tucked the nuggets into the brim of his hat for the ride back to Sutter's Fort.

The trailhead for this historical hike is directly across from the southern end of the North Beach parking lot. A convenient break in the fence provides easy access from the parking area. Watch for traffic: It doesn't slow in this area.

Walk across the road to the sign marked MONROE RIDGE TRAIL; MARSHALL MONUMENT 2.3 MILES. The path passes through the original orchard site of the Gooch-Monroe family, freed slaves who settled here in 1849. You can learn more about this fascinating family in the museum.

At about the 150-foot point, a trail sign clearly directs you up to the right, leading you away from the double-track on the left. Do not take the left fork. It's a former fire road in the midst of revegetation and recovery.

The hike's 600-foot elevation gain starts immediately, with a series of short switchbacks up a forested hillside. Well-placed stairs on this well-maintained trail facilitate your ascent. As you progress, the manzanita thickens all around you, but a brief view opens to give a peek to the north at Perry Mountain and Murphy Mountain to the east above the American River.

About 0.75 miles from the trailhead, enter a cheerful clearing with a view overlooking the Coloma town site—from mill site to schoolhouse. This may be one of the views that James Marshall took in as he surveyed his mill site. His view may have been obscured, though, by towering ponderosa pine, which no longer grow here. Enjoy the view while you have a snack or lunch at the convenient picnic table.

Leaving the manzanita break, hike slightly downhill along the ridge while taking in the view. Dense, jade-green manzanita and mixed-pine forest cover the rolling foothills to your south and west. This shady trail remains pleasant and cool throughout the afternoon. Within a few hundred feet, the fire road you encountered at the beginning of the hike again links up to the Monroe Ridge Trail, intersecting it from the left. Continue on your trail to the right, and you will soon be rewarded with another excellent vantage point from which you can view the small town of Lotus. Again, a convenient picnic table offers a fine place to relax.

Continuing along the duff and dirt, within 75 feet or so there will be a trail marker with an arrow pointing toward your most significant waypoint: the Marshall Monument. At the 2-mile point, the trail takes a left at a long-abandoned and overgrown miner's cabin. Pass the gate at the end of the dirt trail, at the Monument Picnic Area parking lot. Continue across the parking lot and follow the signs on the paved path to the James Marshall Monument.

Now 2.3 miles into the hike, you arrive at the site where, in 1885, Andrew Monroe dug James Marshall's grave. This monument was erected in 1890 and was California's first state historic monument. For a nice side trip, walk a few hundred feet farther up the paved path to the Marshall's Cabin Exhibit. Follow the signs there and back to the statue. Next, link up with Monument Trail to descend to the park's visitor center and museum.

While looking up at Marshall's face, turn right and, retracing your steps along the paved path, look for the arbor-covered drinking-water fountains near the park employee residence. Just to your right, along the path, is the signed trailhead for the Monument Trail. This gentle leg ends in 0.6 miles, leaving you adjacent to the park's visitor center.

Watch for quail and deer in this area; both are plentiful. Signs will also warn hikers of rattlesnakes, poison oak, and mountain lions. The trails are plenty wide enough accommodate walking side by side with young children.

A split-rail fence borders the entire trail down to the park's visitor center. Not only does it add charm but it probably provides some measure of safety for the many groups of schoolchildren who visit the park on weekdays. I was safely eyeballed by a six-point buck and two does as I walked past.

The trail crosses one of the many extant mining ditches along the way. Thousands of miles of ditches and flumes were dug to carry water to the placer mining operations and were later used to irrigate orchards and farms. Entire companies were formed solely to dig such ditches—another way to extract gold from the miners. Essentially, more people became wealthy providing services to the miners than became wealthy from mining gold.

As you continue down the sandy, leaf-littered trail, the forest again yields to the town site, and the trail ends overlooking a picnic area where miners once camped. One hundred feet to the southeast is the park's visitor center.

To return to the North Beach parking lot at the Monroe Ridge Trailhead, walk exactly 0.4 miles northwest and cross the road.

Monroe Ridge trailhead

NEARBY ACTIVITIES

The park offers a short, somewhat accessible trail called the Gold Discovery Loop Trail. The sand-and-gravel path winds around several very interesting displays on the museum grounds, including an authentic miner's cabin and a Chinese store. California's first millionaire, Sam Brannan, had a store less than 100 feet from here. Across the road and alongside the river is the most impressive display—a precise replica of Sutter's Sawmill. There are living-history interpretive displays throughout the town. If you are planning to stay a while, the Coloma Resort offers a mile of riverfront camping and river activities.

SWEETWATER TRAIL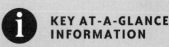

IN BRIEF

This is a hike that you can cruise along on and get a good workout—never really climbing but always on an angle. Following the cool side of Folsom Lake's southern finger, the Sweetwater Trail begins just below the point where the South Fork of the American River meets the waters of the lake.

DESCRIPTION

Your hike starts out under the cover of shade on this multipurpose dirt trail. Little route-finding is necessary, since the south-trending trail is pretty distinct all the way to Sweetwater Creek. You are going to ascend and descend into and out of a few small ravines on the way south.

Foothill pine and live oak afford sparse cover. Stands of manzanita line the trail in places and barely cast any shadows. Before you cross the small runoff creek, stop to count the frogs pinging around the streamside. Blackberries are everywhere . . . except where there is poison oak. And that can be seen easily in the summer because the poison

KEY AT-A-GLANCE INFORMATION

LENGTH: 6.8 miles

CONFIGURATION: Out-and-back

DIFFICULTY: Moderate

WATER REQUIRED: 2 liters

SCENERY: Foothill woodland surrounding picturesque Folsom Lake

EXPOSURE: In and out of sun and shade

TRAIL TRAFFIC: Light

TRAIL SURFACE: Duff and dirt, gravel and sand

HIKING TIME: 3 hours

SEASON: Year-round, sunrise–sunset

ACCESS: $3 parking fee

MAPS: USGS Pilot Hill

WHEELCHAIR TRAVERSABLE: No

FACILITIES: Pit toilet, trash, and pay phone in parking area

DRIVING DISTANCE: 34 miles

SPECIAL COMMENTS: Early-morning hikes around the lake offer chances for bird- and wildlife-viewing.

Directions ⟶

From the junction of US 50 and the Capital City Freeway, drive 24 miles east on US 50 to the El Dorado Hills Boulevard exit. Head north 4 miles, cross Green Valley Road, and then bear right onto Salmon Falls Road. Continue north 5.5 miles on Salmon Falls Road. Watch for the sign on the left, which reads SALMON FALLS–FOLSOM LAKE SRA, just before the Salmon Falls Bridge. Two parking areas for Skunk Hollow straddle the road just past the bridge. The signed trailhead for the Sweetwater Trail is at the south end of the Salmon Falls parking lot, next to the pit toilet.

Sweetwater Trail

UTM Zone (WGS84) 10S

Easting: 0669992

Northing: 4293211

Latitude: N 38° 46' 16"

Longitude: W 121° 02' 35"

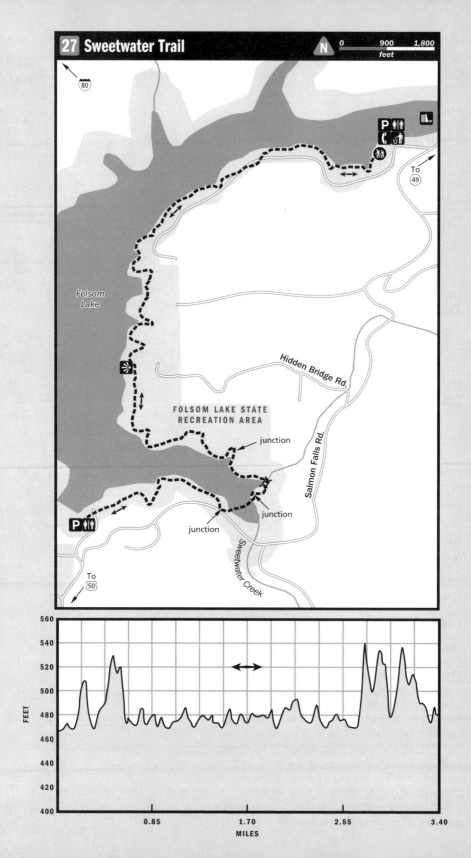

Equestrians can easily follow the fluctuating shoreline.

oak is a beautiful red when everything else is still green or brown. Watch where you wander.

Within 0.25 miles you can turn for a look at the trailhead parking lot and view the secluded upper reaches of the lake. The trail becomes somewhat rocky but not too scuddy. Stone steps help you down the very distinct trail. You walk in shade for the next mile, as you slightly ascend one hillside, descend into a ravine, and then round another small ridge before heading straight south.

Depending on the temperature, you may feel fortunate to be on this side of the lake because the opposite shore appears to be continuously baking in the sun. Manzanita rises to the occasion, keeping you shaded when the trees thin out. The trail now feels more open and less rocky as you approach the 1-mile point.

After you have hiked for about an hour, you will see more chaparral lining the trail. Step across a small stream onto a broad hillside dotted with widely spaced live oaks. Cross a grassy slope while soft breezes waft across the lake to cool you. A vista point lies just ahead as you reach 1.75 miles.

Your trail is now packed dirt. You will see a rocky jumble before a signed junction with a trail that enters from the left. Continue a bit to the right, across the rocky trail. You are following the shoreline, regardless of the water level. As tempting as it looks, shortcutting across this inlet would not be easy. A "black-berry magnet" (any footbridge over a wet spot) is just up ahead a bit, providing an incentive to stay on this trail.

Your trail winds through the trees, and you should still be trending south, walking right up to Sweetwater Creek's junction with Salmon Falls Road and Folsom Lake. A well-defined trail coming from Salmon Falls Road joins your trail from the left as you bear slightly right and now head west.

Continue another 200 feet to a shady valley oak, where there is a three-way junction, which, on our hike, was obstructed by a fallen foothill pine. Angle left and then look a bit right for another trail marker in the middle of the cobble mound. Head toward it and stay on that line, heading west–southwest, as you cross the creek. If you bear north of west, you may miss the trail.

The trail continues about 75 feet past the tree line. To get to it, look for a telephone pole up on Salmon Falls Road. Straight below that, at the tree line, is the trail opening, which is bordered by a foothill pine with two trunks (one skinny, one fat) on the left and a dead tree on the right. Follow this trail as it ascends toward the road. In about 100 feet, take a faint path that leads off to the right through the chaparral.

Walk around the hill, briefly following a north–northwest track. Trails from the ranches above may join yours. Stay about the same distance above the lake as you work your way into and out of the next small ravine. The trail becomes less distinct, more like an informal use-trail, when it turns west to its terminus.

A parking lot with a pit toilet is a convenient turnaround point. The trail sign nestled among the valley oaks points out mileages for destinations to the west: Folsom Point, 15.5 miles; Folsom Dam, 17.5 miles; Brown's Ravine Trail, 17.5 miles. This is a great spot to take a splash before returning to the car at Salmon Falls.

NEARBY ACTIVITIES

The Darrington Bicycle Trail begins at the parking lot on the left as you cross the bridge at Skunk Hollow.

PIONEER EXPRESS TRAIL 28

IN BRIEF

Once the site of intense gold mining and dredging, this former riparian area has been revegetated by the Teichert Corporation in cooperation with California State Parks, allowing native plants to be reestablished and creating an ideal environment for creatures from butterflies to egrets and mud turtles to deer. Your trail wanders across terrain that affords an up-close view of the geology—the ancient river gravels and sands—that beckoned miners of different eras, and ends with a bird's-eye view of Nimbus Dam.

DESCRIPTION

Pioneer Express Trail, which is part of the coast-to-coast American Discovery Trail, runs from Auburn to Sacramento and generally follows

---

Directions ——————————→

From the junction with the Capital City Freeway, drive east on US 50 for 16 miles to the Hazel Avenue exit, then drive north on Hazel Avenue to Madison Avenue. Turn right and drive 3 miles on Madison, which will join with and become Greenback Lane just before the Negro Bar Recreation Area. Turn right at the sign and drive to the entry kiosk, where you may self-register and pay the $7 parking fee. Turn right a few hundred feet past the kiosk and take another right immediately to turn into the boat-launch parking lot; head toward the southwest corner of the parking lot. Drive on and pass the horse-assembly area on the right and continue on to a space in the beach parking lot. Look for an information kiosk at the top of the open field, which is usually occupied by Canada geese, and right on the bike path. Standing with your back to the restroom doors, you can see the kiosk across the field. An overview map and water are available at the kiosk.

KEY AT-A-GLANCE INFORMATION

LENGTH: 9.5 miles

CONFIGURATION: Out-and-back

DIFFICULTY: Moderate

WATER REQUIRED: 2 liters

SCENERY: Excellent views of Lake Natoma and Folsom bridges and Nimbus Dam; revegetated mining site

EXPOSURE: Some shade, some sun; sunscreen advisable

TRAIL TRAFFIC: Light on described route, active on the bike path

TRAIL SURFACE: Duff and dirt, rock and gravel

HIKING TIME: 3.5 hours

SEASON: Year-round, sunrise–sunset

ACCESS: $7 parking fee

MAPS: USGS Folsom; area overview online at www.folsomlakemarina.com/trail_map

WHEELCHAIR TRAVERSABLE: Yes. This route roughly parallels an excellent 2-lane bike path wheelchair users can avail themselves of.

FACILITIES: Toilets at the parking area; water available at the trailhead kiosk

DRIVING DISTANCE: 21 miles

SPECIAL COMMENTS: This hike can be altered easily by hiking the bike trail rather than the Pioneer Express Trail.

Pioneer Express Trail
UTM Zone (WGS84) 1oS
Easting: 0657420
Northing: 4282703
Latitude: N 38° 40' 44"
Longitude: W 121° 11' 24"

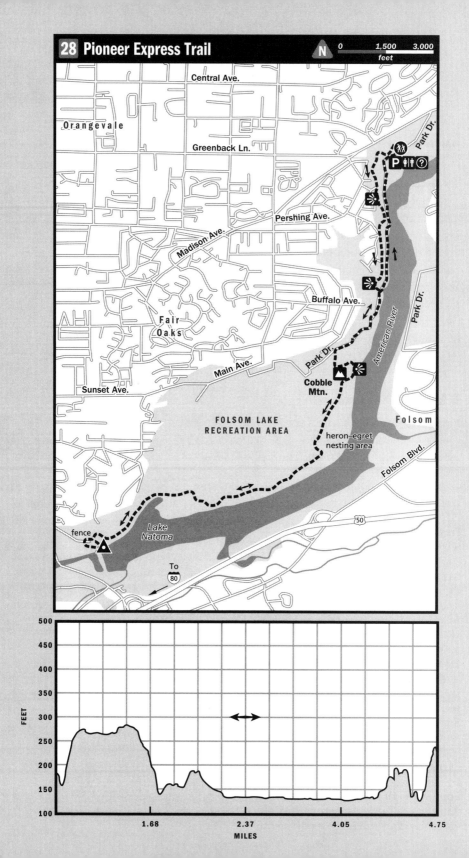

California poppies glow yellow-orange.

the American River. Twenty-one miles of this trail wind through Folsom Lake State Recreation Area (FLSRA). Your trail stretches from the horse-assembly area at the historic Negro Bar downstream to Nimbus Dam at Mississippi Bar.

When you finish reading the information on flora and fauna and fill your water bottles, turn around and look across the bike path for the sign pointing the way to Pioneer Express Trail. At the top of this brief trail stands the Pioneer Express Trail mileage sign. It is the 28.2-mile point, and your hike will take you 4.7 miles to the Nimbus Dam overlook.

If you would like to take the cakewalk version of this hike, stay on the bike path all the way from the kiosk to the dam. It is just as enjoyable a hike as the described route; it does have different vantage points but a bit less solitude.

The Pioneer Express Trail heads southwest and almost immediately joins the bike path. This is a good spot to make your route decision. Turn uphill at the next opportunity to begin the climb to the cliff top—a bit more than a 100-foot ascent will gain you an excellent view of Lake Natoma. Look back over your shoulder to three of Folsom's bridges: Lake Natoma Bridge, Rainbow Bridge, and the historic truss bridge. And what a history the truss bridge has. Designed in 1893 to be used for horse-and-wagon traffic, it was replaced by the Rainbow Bridge in 1917. In 1930 the truss bridge was bought and then sold by the State of California. This bridge gets around: It was moved to Siskiyou County, where it served as a Klamath River crossing until 1998. Then Folsom bought it, and the bridge was returned to the site of its original footings.

Lake Natoma from the Pioneer Express Trail

When you reach the 0.5-mile point, you should have excellent views of all three bridges. There is a protective chain-link fence on your left because the cliffs are sheer, but the views are impressive nonetheless. Walk along the fence line for about 1 mile and then begin to descend. There is an unobstructed viewpoint at the end of the fence. To reach it, stay on the higher trail rather than taking the gently descending trail, which curves around to the right. They join at the base of the hill. On your way down, the trail will cross another at a telephone pole. Continue straight ahead to a small pond, which is well worth a short pause to look for wildlife.

The pond is at a junction of the trail to Snowberry Creek, where the Pioneer Express Trail crosses the bike path as you head toward the river. The trails in the FLSRA are well signed; that is, the signs are both accurate and frequent, so you should not have any difficulty navigating this path. Depending on the time of year, you may have trouble staying on the path—you walk past some huge blackberries. Look for signs of raccoon, opossum, and skunk along here; they love these like a dessert bar.

Walk along to the left of the bike trail, which comes in and out of view for just about 0.5 miles. Your trail will make a U-turn to the left about 500 feet across a tailings pile after you pass a small pond on your left. After that, you will have another, much larger pond on the left as you walk in the shade of live oak and toyon. A large hill, composed entirely of tailings, rises above you to the right. After you ascend this revegetated "hillside," turn to your right for a full view of "cobble mountain."

There is an excellent view of the lake from the prominent, bare area to the east. This spot marks the beginning of Mississippi Bar—an area of intense gold dredging until the late 1880s, and later the site of aggregate mining until the 1980s. Thanks to revegetation efforts, California poppy, larkspur, monkey flower, and lupine are everywhere. Buckeye blossoms fill the air with their sweet scent all along the trail, and native trees like toyon, black oak, foothill pine, and valley oak dot the open areas and hillsides.

The bike path is again in sight as you parallel it for about 0.5 miles before walking beneath the power lines. Follow the trail signs and turn right. You will make a slight jog to the right again when you encounter the sign for the heron–egret nesting area. Continue walking west under the power lines. You will cross and recross the bike path, but the trail will remain obvious, meandering through some ponds as it passes between a power-line pylon and an out-of-place palm tree.

Follow the trail as it crosses the bike path and stays on the right side of it. Pass the turnoff to Snowberry Creek. Then walk across the bridge and head for the grove of buckeye ahead of you on the right. At the base of the overlook hill, you can see the ancient alluvial gravels and sandstones that signaled potential deposits of gold. The trail to the overlook is rocky, slick, and steep. It is also short. At the top of the trail, a walkway through the fence will give you access to the area overlooking the dam.

As an alternative, start your trip from this overlook trailhead and hike to Negro Bar. Or, leave a car here and treat this as a one-way trip with a shuttle.

Retrace your route to the parking lot, but add an easy alternative. At the first pond on the route coming in, stay on the bike path rather than ascending. The exposed portions of the cliff face also illustrate the ancient river deposits and volcanic overlay.

NEARBY ACTIVITIES

The American River Bicycle Path lines both sides of Lake Natoma and will take you from Beal's Point to Sacramento. Complete with solar-powered call boxes, this is rated as one of the best bicycle paths in the country.

29 AVERY'S POND TRAIL

KEY AT-A-GLANCE INFORMATION

LENGTH: 4.1 miles

CONFIGURATION: Out-and-back

DIFFICULTY: Easy

WATER REQUIRED: 1 liter

SCENERY: Foothill forest surrounding lake

EXPOSURE: Shaded, with patches of sun

TRAIL TRAFFIC: Moderate

TRAIL SURFACE: Dirt and duff

HIKING TIME: 2 hours

SEASON: Year-round, sunrise–sunset

ACCESS: $7 parking fee

MAPS: USGS Pilot Hill

FACILITIES: Gravel parking area; picnic tables and pit toilets at boat ramp

WHEELCHAIR TRAVERSABLE: No

DRIVING DISTANCE: 21.3 miles

SPECIAL COMMENTS: Historic North Ditch parallels trail. The Pioneer Express Trail crosses the main road and continues from Rattlesnake Bar to Horseshoe Bar as described in Hike 28 (see previous profile).

Avery's Pond Trail

UTM Zone (WGS84) 10S

Easting: 0665856

Northing: 4298465

Latitude: N 38° 49' 09"

Longitude: W 121° 05' 22"

IN BRIEF

The hike to Avery's Pond is a great adventure for children and parents who want a brief yet interesting hike. This route takes you past Avery's Pond and on past the Newcastle powerhouse at Mormon's Ravine. The trail guides hikers along remnants of the North Fork Ditch, which supplied water to mining camps and towns along the river.

DESCRIPTION

After gold was discovered in the South Fork of the American River in 1848, mining camps sprang up along both the South Fork and the North Fork. The river was worked by men from every corner of the world: England, Scotland, Wales, New York, Virginia, Kentucky, New South Wales, Hawaii, and China. They stayed with their claims, camping right beside their river workplace. The camps turned to towns and, however small or large, these settlements were given names—colorful, descriptive names

---

Directions

From the intersection with Capital City Freeway, drive 15 miles east on Interstate 80 to Loomis, and exit at Horseshoe Bar Road. Turn left at the end of the ramp onto Horseshoe Bar Road; bear left and then take the next left turn onto Horseshoe Bar Road. Continue 3.4 miles to Auburn–Folsom Road. Turn left and drive 2.3 miles to Newcastle Road, where you will turn right and go 1 mile to Rattlesnake Road. Turn right again and follow the road another mile until the pavement ends. Stop and self-register at the entry kiosk. Drive 0.2 miles to the sign for the horse-assembly area and boat launch. Turn left and drive 0.4 miles to the sign for the horse-assembly area, then turn left again, into the gravel parking lot. The signed trailhead is at the northeast end of the lot, in the grass.

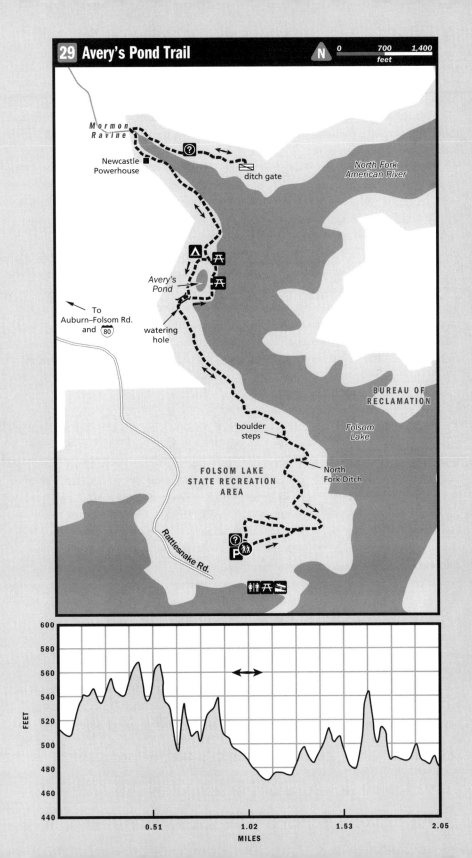

29 Avery's Pond Trail

such as Rattlesnake Bar, Mormon Bar, Mormon Ravine, Oregon Bar, and Manhattan Bar. Some establishments disappeared overnight, but others persisted. In 1865 Rattlesnake Bar was a town of more than 1,000 residents. Avery's Pond and some sights along the way are relics from the gold-mining days along the North Fork of the American River.

Leave the horse-assembly area at the signed trailhead at the northeast end of the parking lot. Your trail starts out as a dirt path that becomes a double-track in short order. When the wide track veers right, stay on the single path that leads left. The double-track will rejoin your path shortly. The meadow you are crossing is filled with wildflowers in the spring. A sign ahead proclaims that you are on the Pioneer Express Trail and indicates the distance to Avery's Pond and Auburn.

After you head generally east for about ten minutes, the trail turns north to meander through live oak and toyon. After 0.25 miles, you will start descending a bit along a deeply rutted section of trail. As you reach a sunny hillside, look to the opposite shore of the lake where the "bathtub rings" in the dirt bespeak the various lake levels over the years. Just as you near 0.5 miles, with the lake in full view, you may be distracted by a turkey or two as they flash by looking very intent on their way to somewhere. Above, foothill pines shade the trail while the manzanita blazes with bright-red berries, which are sticky—like its flowers—and are reported to be edible and sweet.

Walk along in the cool shade of black oak, live oak, and more manzanita until you come to an easy but steep downhill stretch. A large outcrop to your left leans out over the trail. Well protected by poison oak, these are not the rocks one would be enthusiastic about bouldering. The trail is crossed with smaller boulders that serve as stairs to help you clamber down the trail. Your path is now sand and pea gravel and contours along beside the lake about 50 feet above the shoreline. The trail runs right up next to a steep drop to the rocks below just as you see the first signs of the North Fork Ditch. Along here you can see views of the lake as it disappears into the foothills.

Cross a small drainage just before you come upon a large patch of blackberries at about the 1-mile point. The ditch is plainly visible for the next mile. Encrusted with blackberries, the ditch runs to your right. Below you is another section of the concrete wall that comprised part of the ditch. Moisture-loving blackberries are the main ditch plant here, offering themselves to hikers at many points along the trail.

Under a nice cover of shade is a horse-watering trough fed by the spring just on the other side of the bridge at the pond. The wooden bridge crossing the aqueduct was restored in 1994 in an Eagle Scout project. Walk another 175 feet to cross another bridge, which signals your arrival at the pond. Turn right and head toward the lake. Look to the right of the trail and you will see Sierra iris growing among the live oak.

You will find a picnic table about halfway around the pond, next to a lonely live oak tree surrounded by scant vegetation. This spot is totally exposed and might not be the best for a picnic, but the trails that lead to both the lake and

Mormon Ravine at the North Fork of the American River

the pond indicate that this might be a good fishing spot. Be careful: the bank surrounding the pond is steep, and the pond is not suitable for swimming or wading.

For excellent shade while you picnic, there are tables located farther along the pond trail just before the next junction on the left, and also just after it on the right. If you want to circumnavigate the pond, continue left at the next junction and make your way along the north shore of the pond. There is a bit more to see in the vicinity.

About 0.5 miles ahead is a small hydroelectric plant operated by PG&E. To get there, take the right-hand trail at the junction and you will walk roughly parallel to the road you see above you to the left. You will reach the road in a matter of seconds. Take notice of the mountain-lion warning posted on the tree. Follow the road down as it turns to gravel, and then round the bend; you will see the small hydro facility—the Newcastle power plant—ahead. It was built in 1986 and produces electricity for up to 12,000 homes.

As you walk toward the power plant, you can see the point at which the North Fork enters the lake. The powerful stream creates a wide ravine here and drops a jumble of rocks and debris in its wake. Look closely and you will probably see deer feeding amid the willows and sedges growing in this tributary. The South Fork's entrance to the lake near Salmon Falls is 5.5 miles directly southeast of your current position; you can imagine the commerce that occurred between miners on both rivers. According to historical accounts, a bridge was built in 1862 at Rattlesnake Bar that served for almost 100 years, until a truck full of "fertilizer" sparked the bridge's collapse in 1954.

Pass the modern plant now, and follow the trail across another bridge at Mormon Ravine, which is just past the power plant. Turn right and continue through the wooded area above the river. Look below you on the right, and you

Fishing in Folsom Lake is just a few feet away from Avery's Pond.

can plainly see sections of the water ditch. Follow along the trail until, at the 2-mile point, you come to an informational kiosk that highlights the hydro facility and provides some brief history regarding your trail.

The large, open field above you to the left fills with wildflowers each spring. Wally baskets, brodiaea, buttercups, and blue dicks sprinkle the hillside with color. Startle a deer from its afternoon slumber here and see who jumps higher. (Answer: the deer. Repeatedly. But, nice try, anyway.) This trail continues to Auburn, where it begins above the Auburn Dam site. As you look right to the live oak about ten feet off the trail, you may notice a concrete structure. A little investigation uncovers what appears to be a ditch gate, long since disused.

This is a convenient spot to turn around. You have hiked 2 miles, and your small hiking companions are surely ready for refreshments back at the trailhead. Retrace your steps until you come to the pond, and then take the right-hand fork at the junction. Walk through an environmental campsite with a few picnic tables. Just before you cross the bridge at the west end of the pond, look right to see more of the concrete sections of the ditch.

When you near the trailhead, you have a choice. Either retrace your steps exactly from the junction of the single-track and the double-track, or take the fork to the right, startle some more turkeys in the woods, and then emerge at the kiosk adjacent to the trailhead.

RATTLESNAKE BAR–HORSESHOE BAR TRAIL

IN BRIEF

This trail leads hikers up, down, around, and through a slim riparian zone along the fringe of Folsom Lake. The trail is well maintained and lets walkers of all ages forget about the route and watch the flowers, birds, and butterflies. You can easily walk out to the lakeshore at two broad, unshaded bars.

DESCRIPTION

Hiking the Pioneer Express Trail affords choices from among a number of embarkation points along the trail. This hike starts at Rattlesnake Bar, where Folsom Lake nears its upstream boundary and you can select your preferred endpoint, the near side or far side of Horseshoe Bar Road on the other side of the U.

Rattlesnake Bar was covered with hundreds of houses, cabins, and tents in the 1850s

KEY AT-A-GLANCE INFORMATION

LENGTH: 4.7 miles
CONFIGURATION: Out-and-back
DIFFICULTY: Easy
WATER REQUIRED: 1 liter
SCENERY: Great views of Folsom Lake
EXPOSURE: In and out of shade
TRAIL TRAFFIC: Light
TRAIL SURFACE: Sand and dirt
HIKING TIME: 2 hours
SEASON: Year-round, sunrise–sunset
ACCESS: $7 parking fee
MAPS: USGS Pilot Hill
WHEELCHAIR TRAVERSABLE: No
FACILITIES: None at trailhead; toilet at boat ramp
DRIVING DISTANCE: 25 miles
SPECIAL COMMENTS: No water available at trailhead or on trail. Bring an adequate amount of fresh water.

Directions

From Interstate 80 East at the Capital City Freeway, drive 15 miles east on I-80 to Loomis and exit at Horseshoe Bar Road. Turn left at the end of the ramp onto Horseshoe Bar Road; bear left and immediately take the next left turn onto Horseshoe Bar Road. Continue on Horseshoe Bar Road 3.4 miles to Auburn–Folsom Road. Turn left and drive 2.3 miles to Newcastle Road, where you will turn right and follow it 1 mile to Rattlesnake Road. Turn right and follow the road another mile to the pavement end. To the left is the boat-launch area; the right fork leads to your trailhead. Drive slowly over the chuckholed road and keep right about 1,000 feet to reach a large dirt parking lot conveniently located in front of the trailhead. The trailhead sits behind some boulders about ten feet inside the trees opposite the lake. A large sign indicates the mileage and directions on the Pioneer Express Trail.

Rattlesnake Bar–
Horseshoe Bar Trail
UTM Zone (WGS84) 10S
Easting: 0665097
Northing: 4298774
Latitude: N 38° 49' 20"
Longitude: W 121° 05' 53"

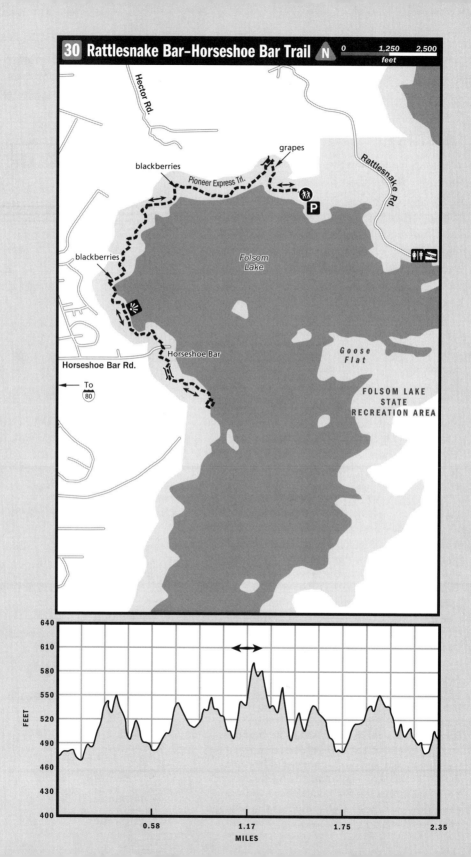

Folsom Lake below Rattlesnake Bar

and was one of several bars connected by trails from the river to the Auburn-to-Sacramento Road. Granite Bar, Whiskey Bar, Horseshoe Bar, and Rattlesnake Bar were all served by this supply route. One formerly successful miner of the Rattlesnake Bar area became infamous as "Rattlesnake Dick" after he robbed several stagecoaches along this pioneer road.

The trailhead is situated behind the boulders at the north end of the parking lot. Watch your step here. This trail is shared with only horseback riders. Start out at the sign indicating your mile point on Pioneer Express Trail, heading west under towering foothill pines, which offer the most wicked hazard: they hurl three-pound, armor-plated and spiked cones from heights of 60 feet right onto the trail below. You may be saved by a well-placed manzanita, but keep your eyes open on windy days, regardless.

The trail is well marked, as it is along its whole length, with signs at every junction, and it has been well maintained, mostly through consistent use. The trail has a comfortable surface of dirt and duff, which blend into sand or hard-packed dirt at times. An immediate opening to your left is a popular gathering ground for flocks of Canada geese.

Head north into and out of a ravine by crossing a footbridge, where live-oak boughs hang over a stream. When you begin to hear the stream on your left, you'll notice grapevines stretching along the trail and hanging from the live oak and cottonwood trees. The grapes start to give way to blackberries around the bridge.

A grassy area below the trail comes into view as you encounter the 45-mile marker, where a trail from the right joins your route just as you descend a bit. A generous expanse of lake comes into view as you walk under the power line and enter a broad, sloping meadow.

Enter the woods again; bush monkeyflower grows beneath the foothill pines. A private-property fence borders the trail on the right for a short distance; several side trails head down to favorite fishing spots on the lake. A footbridge across a stream is a blackberry magnet, and the next stream crossing is no exception. Mmm-mmm, good.

The trail is a bit ditchlike up to the power tower, and then it turns to rock and dirt, making for unsteady footing. Another small stream awaits at the 44.5-mile marker. Just after this 1-mile point and a hill climb, you're rewarded with a nice vista. Toyon and oak still shade your trail. At the crux of the next ravine, your appetite for blackberries is sure to be sated by the fruit on these thick bushes, which are all within easy reach of the trail.

The trail moves closer to the lake, giving you another panoramic vista, with small islands in the view. Descend the short stretch of boulder-strewn path and head through a sandy S-curve before making a slightly longer ascent to the hill-top, where a trail joins yours from the right. Continue downhill and to the right and then uphill on a double-track section of rocky trail to reach a sign marking Horseshoe Bar. To your right are the boulders, blocking street access from the end of Horseshoe Bar Road.

Continue to descend southeast and cross another footbridge near the wind-snapped ponderosa pine. Back on a single-track, you have choice of side trails heading off to the left to access the large bars and their long shorelines.

Now that you have walked a pleasant 2-plus miles, you can linger at the water's edge or explore for more blackberries—jam on a stick—on the hillside above. The Pioneer Express Trail continues 6 more miles to Granite Bay, and beyond that it travels 37 miles to Discovery Park in Sacramento. Your route back retraces your path.

NEARBY ACTIVITIES

Avery's Pond Trail (Hike 29, page 158) is located in the horse-assembly area and leads to the north past the pond all the way to Mormon Ravine.

CRONAN RANCH TRAILS

IN BRIEF

Located in Pilot Hill's Cronan Ranch Regional Trails Park, this hike of connected loops offers a varied terrain of riparian woodland along the South Fork of the American River and the foothill savanna above it. Some open-terrain trails will lead to a movie-set ranch and then loop back to the shade above the river.

DESCRIPTION

Thanks to the collaboration and cooperation of the American River Conservancy, the BLM,

---

Directions ——————————————————➤

Starting at the junction of Interstate 80 east and Capitol City Freeway, drive 24 miles to Auburn. Exit I-80 at Elm Street and turn left at the traffic light. Drive downhill to another traffic light, and turn left again, onto High Street. Continue through the next traffic light and under the railroad crossing, following CA 49 downhill. The Auburn State Recreation Area Headquarters is 1 mile downhill on the left. Continue 1.3 miles down CA 49, passing the ASRA HQ, then make a right turn to cross the river and continue on CA 49 toward Cool. Your trailhead is 11.3 miles from this river crossing. In less than 0.5 miles, you will pass the trailhead for Quarry Road Trail. Pass the quarry at the top of the hill and drive past Cool to Pilot Hill. Look for Pedro Hill Road on your right, 2.3 miles from this trip's trailhead. Taking a right on Pedro Hill Road and then making an immediate left will place you at an alternate trailhead for the same trails. However, this latter trailhead is usually busy with horse riders. So, 2.3 miles farther south on CA 49 will take you to a paved parking area on the right that is equipped with a pit toilet. On the way, you will pass a large new BLM parking area that had not opened as of April 2007. Look for future trailheads here.

KEY AT-A-GLANCE INFORMATION

LENGTH: 10.1 miles

CONFIGURATION: Connected loops

DIFFICULTY: Challenging

WATER REQUIRED: 2–3 liters

SCENERY: South Fork of the American River; foothill woodland and savanna

EXPOSURE: The second half of the hike, from the lunch spot to the ranch and back, is exposed.

TRAIL TRAFFIC: Trails are known mostly to horse riders, but you'll also encounter bikers, joggers, and rafters.

TRAIL SURFACE: Rock and dirt near river; dirt and duff higher up in trees

HIKING TIME: 7 hours

SEASON: Year-round, sunrise–sunset

ACCESS: No fees or permits

MAPS: USGS Coloma; Bureau of Land Management (BLM) Cronan Ranch Regional Trails Park Map available online; find American River Conservancy map at www.arconservancy .org/xoops/uploads/smartsection/ 23_cronangreenwoodtrail07.06.pdf.

FACILITIES: Pit toilet in parking lot

WHEELCHAIR TRAVERSABLE: No

DRIVING DISTANCE: 40 miles

SPECIAL COMMENTS: Made-for-movies ranch site

Cronan Ranch Trails

UTM Zone (WGS84) 10S

Easting: 0678176

Northing: 4299465

Latitude: N 38° 49' 33"

Longitude: W 120° 56' 50"

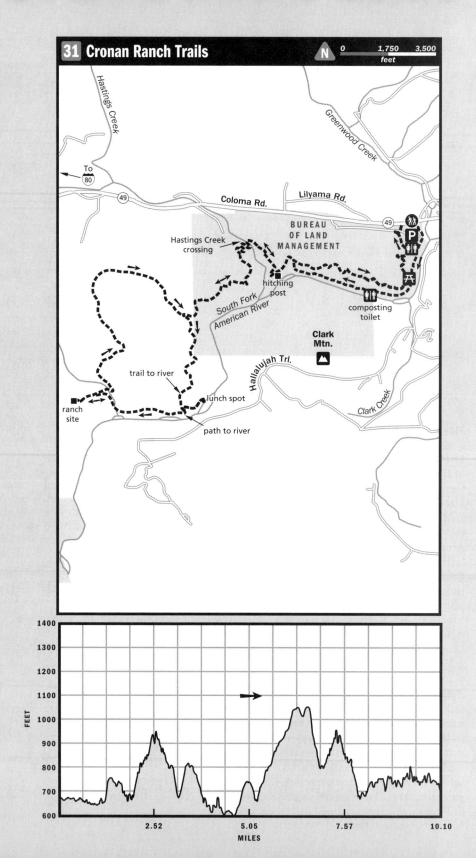

31 Cronan Ranch Trails

N
0   1,750   3,500
feet

To 80

49

Coloma Rd.   Lilyama Rd.

Hastings Creek

Greenwood Creek

49

Hastings Creek crossing

BUREAU OF LAND MANAGEMENT

hitching post

South Fork American River

composting toilet

Clark Mtn.

trail to river

Hallalujah Trl.

Clark Creek

lunch spot

ranch site

path to river

FEET									
1400									
1300									
1200									
1100				→					
1000									
900									
800									
700									
600									

2.52   5.05   7.57   10.10

MILES

The ranch house is part of a larger Western-movie set.

private individuals, and state agencies, the Cronan Ranch Regional Trails Park was added to California's Regional Parks system in 2005 and was expanded in 2006. The trailhead for this hike stands only about 5 air miles downriver from Coloma, the birthplace of the gold rush. Above and below the section of river that borders the ranch, streams, bars, and hillsides, gold miners sought their fortunes throughout the 1850s.

One of the forebears of the Cronan Ranch's owners settled in this area. Like many gold miners, William Bacchi arrived in 1851 or 1852 but, by 1856, had turned from mining to ranching. This part of the Cronan Ranch was purchased by the Central Pacific Railroad in 1887 and then sold to Michael Cronan, who ran cattle on it until 1918. Descendants of William Bacchi retain some portions of the original ranch and sold other portions of it to create this park.

The trails of the ranch tend to run roughly north–south and somewhat parallel to each other along ridges or valleys leading from CA 49 down to the South Fork of the American River. The trail loops that compose this hike will take you through three biozones: riparian forest along the river and Hastings Creek, foothill woodland forest above the river along the hillsides, and foothill savanna.

From the parking lot, walk through the unsigned gate at the trailhead onto a road of broken pavement that heads generally southeast, until you turn off to the right onto a southbound dirt path that takes you closer to the river. When you are walking parallel to the river, you may see signs facing away from the trail. These are signs for the river rafters—usually indicating quiet zones or portages.

South Fork waters run cold until early summer.

Within just 0.5 miles, you'll encounter a picnic table—perfectly sited for watching a group of deer ascending the draw. Net-wrapped tree seedlings that are planted on the river's margins show that deer frequent this spot. After passing the new picnic table, glance into the willows and oaks to see how the floodwaters treated the last table.

Sandy and rocky, this trail is lined by blackberry bushes and poison oak. In the early morning, the abundant mosses that cover the rocks, trees, and trail-sides seem to muffle the river's sound—providing a real sense of solitude.

When you begin to notice manzanita along the trail and the river turns westward, you will have traveled about 0.75 miles. Although the trail surface becomes a bit rougher—cobble and sand—it remains distinct enough for easy route finding. Jog to the left, hop over some boulders, plunge in and out of riverside brush, and, voilà, you will find a trail leading up to a modern composting toilet about 30 feet above the river.

Look for that perfect spot for a snack or water break down on the wide beach below. Or, walk a bit farther downstream to another picnic table set in the shade of spreading live oaks. In fact, the next 0.4 miles offers several side trails that descend to sections of beach along wide, slow stretches of river. At your right shoulder are live oak, foothill pine, and whiteleaf manzanita mixed with white alder and spicebush, shading your often-grassy path. Although the trail moves away from the river, the 1,585-foot peak of Clark Mountain on the opposite shore is rarely out of sight as you walk west.

As you cross another rockfall from the right, you will be pushed up into the blackberries. You may notice the flood debris high up in the trees, but keep your eye on the trail along here. When the trail appears to have run out, it probably has. An intermittent stream enters from the right before a broad, rubble-strewn area. If you see a tree ahead with a triple trunk, stop and go back up the ravine. There is an old, washed-out four-wheel-drive trail alongside it that will help you ascend. It is possible to ascend farther downstream when the trail really does run out, but it is an unnecessary scramble on uncertain terrain.

At the top of the ravine, you will encounter a horse trail, which you will take to the left. At the end of the trees, you could follow the horse trail to the north and west on an exposed route, but this trail turns left back toward the river and views down the canyon. You will pass through an exposed area as you head southwest toward the Hastings Creek ravine. Pass a picnic table and a hitching post just before turning back northeast. The next junction on the left will provide a shady pathway parallel to Hastings Creek. Go left over the next four-wheel-drive road, maintaining a northwest heading for a crossing with an intermittent stream about 0.1 mile before the Hastings Creek crossing.

Approaching the creek crossing among lupine and fiddlenecks, you will see a rock wall on the left and then an obvious but wet crossing at the trail. A tree trunk spans the creek another 50 feet upstream to provide a dry crossing.

Ascend the switchbacks on the opposite hillside to climb about 200 feet above the creek. There are plenty of "horse tracks" along here, so watch your step. After you pass through a grove of incense cedar, you will emerge to a clear view of Clark Mountain above you and, soon after, the South Fork below you.

The next half mile or so will be spent a few hundred feet above the river, contouring through ravines beneath the 1,200-foot peak above you. The next major intersection is both the beginning and end of a large loop that offers two side trips to movie-set locations.

Emerge from a tunnel of oak at a T-intersection at the Down and Up Trail, where you will turn south to continue paralleling the river below. The dirt-and-rock trail will descend a bit to a blackberry patch. Cross the stream and climb southward through the silence. Ignore roads entering your path from the right until about 1,000 feet past a fence line. This four-wheel-drive road crossing your path can be taken down to the river. Descend to the river on this or the next trail to the south, chill your feet in the water, take in the sounds, and then return to this track.

Movie fans may recognize the landscape along this stretch of the river as the background for scenes in *Memoirs of a Geisha*. This is a great spot for a lunch break. You will be sitting right at the river on bedrock greenstone. A short hike around the bottom of this loop will lead you to another movie set: a Western-ranch set (surprise) on a hillside dotted with poppies.

Walk almost 0.5 miles along the river past the "punny" outhouses and picnic tables. Just as you notice the river turning away, to your left, take the obvious four-wheel-drive road to the right. Head north just 0.2 miles, past a junction with a trail to the right (which you will take on your return), to a movie set consisting of a two-room ranch house, a barn and corral, a well, and a chicken coop, all under the shade of a majestic valley oak, and now, a picnic table (not authentic). The history of this site is unclear, but hazy recollections abound in the Auburn area.

Typical Sierra-foothill woodland of mixed conifers and broadleaf trees surrounds the South Fork of the American River.

Return to the intersection with the Hidden Valley Cutoff that you passed earlier. As you ascend the wide trail, Cronan Ranch Road (leading to the movie set) and Long Valley Trail parallel the northward path. As you pass between two stands of oak, look around for evidence of previous gold mining in the road cut. You may also see small herds of deer steeple-chasing each other up the wooded ravines.

After another mile—a total of 6.8 miles—your trail turns southeast toward the river, where you will meet your return track in another 0.6 miles. At the intersection with your intended trail, you will turn left into the shade, heading northeast along and above the river. Return to Hastings Creek and the safe crossing.

After passing the hitching post again, continue through the open to the stand of trees ahead, where you will turn right. This time the return trail stays higher above the river. This easy trail wraps around the hillside, crossing four drainages until it takes you to a convergence of trails above the parking lot.

Some trail closures may be in effect around the parking lot to hasten revegetation. Follow the signs to descend to your car.

NEARBY ACTIVITIES

The Monroe Ridge Trail (Hike 26, page 144) at Marshall Gold Discovery State Historic Park in Coloma gives a bird's-eye view of the South Fork of the American River where James Marshall discovered gold in 1848.

WENDELL T. ROBIE TRAIL

IN BRIEF

Robie Trail begins with blood-pumping switch-backs that boost hikers up above Cherokee Flat and around Summit Hill so they can contour along an historic mining flume with views overlooking the Middle Fork of the American River. Walk past some abandoned mining equipment, hard rock shafts, and dry-stacked walls on this easy-to-follow trail that leads hikers to a cool, shaded crossing of the wide, cobble-strewn Canyon Creek. Bring a picnic and insect repellent to this picturesque spot.

Directions

From its junction with the Capital City Freeway, drive 25 miles on Interstate 80 to Auburn and exit at Elm Street. Turn left on Elm Street, drive downhill, and turn left at the light. Drive 6 miles to Cool, heading beneath the railroad overpass, down the hill on CA 49, and turning right across the CA 49 bridge toward Cool. Turn left in Cool on CA 193 toward Greenwood. Drive 6.2 miles to Sliger Mine Road, where you will turn left. Continue left at the junction with Spanish Dry Diggins Road, and bear left at the Spanish Dry Diggins Cemetery, which is surrounded by a white, wire fence. In 0.3 miles, turn right where Foxglove Lane bears left. From here down, a high-clearance vehicle is advisable but not absolutely necessary. At the next flat spot, look in the bushes on the right for a sign indicating the Cherokee Flat recreation area. You can park here and walk, or continue 0.6 miles downhill to the junction where Sliger Mine Road turns left. Some parking is available on the roadsides nearby.

The trailhead is marked with Western States Trail and Robie Trail stickers on a bullet-riddled marker post that is partially hidden among scrub oak on the right side of the road. Sliger Mine Road turns left, directly away from this marker, and a four-wheel-drive road with a rusted-open gate continues downhill.

KEY AT-A-GLANCE INFORMATION

LENGTH: 8.4 miles
CONFIGURATION: Out-and-back
DIFFICULTY: Moderate
WATER REQUIRED: 3 liters
SCENERY: Grand vistas of the Middle Fork of the American River
EXPOSURE: Nicely shaded trail
TRAIL TRAFFIC: Light
TRAIL SURFACE: Dirt and duff, rock
HIKING TIME: 5–6 hours
SEASON: Year-round, sunrise–sunset
ACCESS: No fees or permits
MAPS: USGS Greenwood; ASRA map
WHEELCHAIR TRAVERSABLE: No
FACILITIES: None
DRIVING DISTANCE: 50 miles
SPECIAL COMMENTS: Part racecourse, part waterway; a hike for solitude

----

Wendell T. Robie Trail
UTM Zone (WGS84) 10S
Easting: 0679314
Northing: 4313285
Latitude: N 38° 57' 00"
Longitude: W 120° 55' 50"

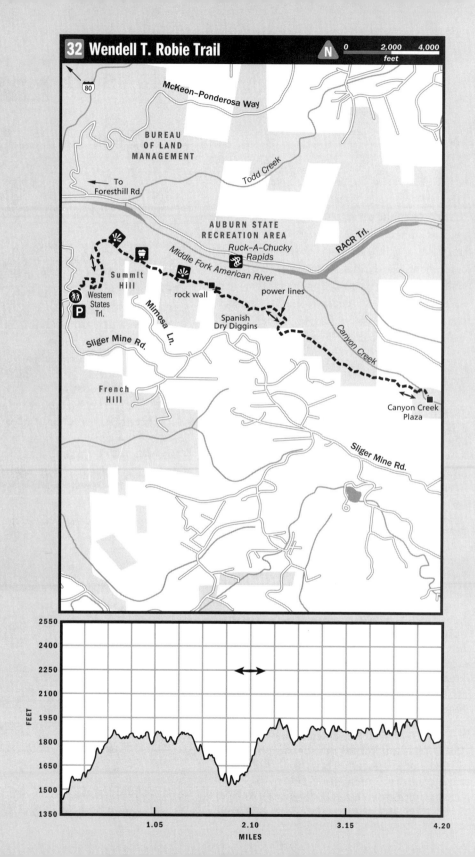

N

0   2,000   4,000
feet

McKeon–Ponderosa Way

BUREAU
OF LAND
MANAGEMENT

Todd Creek

← To
Foresthill Rd.

AUBURN STATE
RECREATION AREA

Ruck-A-Chucky
Rapids

RACR Trl.

Middle Fork American River

Summit
Hill

Western
States
Trl.

P

rock wall

power lines

Spanish
Dry Diggins

Canyon Creek

Sliger Mine Rd.

Mimosa Ln.

French
Hill

Canyon Creek
Plaza

Sliger Mine Rd.

FEET

2550
2400
2250
2100
1950
1800
1650
1500
1350

1.05   2.10   3.15   4.20
MILES

Foxglove in early June

DESCRIPTION

From the trailhead signpost, the trail climbs steeply up three serious switchbacks right away and continues uphill. When the dirt-and-duff trail levels out a bit, you can admire the handiwork of the trail builders whose stonework makes up the fills, walls, and culverts along here. In the early morning, deer can be seen as they depart over boulders and uphill through the thick stands of live oak and huge ponderosa pine. A few more switchbacks lead you past the 21.5-mile trail marker for the Western States Trail.

As you round Summit Hill, the Douglas fir towering overhead throw some cooling shade across your now-flattened trail. The well-worn path opens into a wide vista as you walk along a greenstone outcrop on the right. Poison oak often encroaches, and mosquitoes will frequently accompany you. Wearing long pants or gaiters and using insect repellent will lessen these slight annoyances.

A huge vista point opens up after you have been hiking for about 45 minutes, shortly after your trail changes direction toward the southeast. The roar of the North Fork can be heard from your lookout at this huge outcropping. Downstream lies the site of the Greenwood Bridge, just below Paradise Canyon's junction with the river. Across from your perch is the Ruck-A-Chucky Trail, leading from Drivers Flat Road to Slug Gulch and Fords Bar.

The trail winds slightly downhill for the next 15 minutes or so. On the right is an old mine shaft that was probably for rock used on the trail fills. Animal signs dot the margins and middle of the trail, and squirrel-sized tracks cross and then disappear into the duff. The Robie Trail is memorable for its abundant and unavoidable signs of black bear. More worrisome is the distinctive scent of skunk. Based on intensity of the smell alone, it's likely that skunks are using this small quarry for their den.

Immediately after this stretch, the trail dips slightly, and you can see a trail sign pointing left if you look up into the trees. There is a mileage marker in a hundred paces. Cross a small ravine and pause to look up into the cascades. Dippers, also known as water ouzels, streak in and out of the moss-covered rocks. Another vista point is up ahead on the rock next to the madrone with three trunks. After a moderate descent, you will cross a broad, flat area at a seep in the wall.

As you avoid the poison oak along here, look for discarded mining and ditch-construction equipment on the left. Momentarily, you will be directed around a large outcrop by means of a hand-laid stone wall. This wall, part of the flumeworks built to carry water from Canyon Creek, has withstood the test of time. There is a shaft dug into the outcrop on the right that was evidently the source of the stone for this handcrafted wall. The Ruck-A-Chucky Rapids can be heard churning below here.

Six or seven more switchbacks take you through patches of blackberries, across a creek with some nice cascades, and through some cuts in the rock. There is another small stream in a ravine just after you pass the trail's 23.5-mile marker. The pools above Ruck-A-Chucky can be glimpsed from your trail in the next few minutes. Within five minutes of sighting the pools, you will pass under a trio of power lines that are balanced on a precarious tripod of cut and stripped saplings.

The Middle Fork now changes direction, flowing down from the northeast as your trail remains on a southeast course under tall foothill pine, fragrant buckeye, and cool manzanita. Another creek, amid cool woodland shade, has pleasant cascades, and the water appears to slither across these very slippery rocks. An enormous madrone blocking the trail signals an upcoming junction with an old trail that heads off to the right. You continue on to the left.

Another picturesque stream of water is squeezed out of the greenstone, down a jumble of rocks and boulders, then in to small pools—handy for cooling one's face. Scarlet monkeyflower flares alongside this small oasis of blackberries and fairy lanterns. Within five minutes, your trail will briefly ascend through red columbine. Watch for the path coming in from the right as yours starts to drop. Stay on the descending trail to the left. A trail marker lies just ahead on the right among the purple brodiaea.

Descend this wooded trail, zigzagging across a shallow creek atop very slippery rocks for the next hundred feet or so to the crossing at Canyon Creek. Crossing here offers no advantage to hikers. Exploring upstream on the south side takes you to some sunny, flat areas a few feet from the stream.

Take pictures along these sun-splattered wet rocks to remind yourself of this cool retreat when you get home. To beat the heat on the walk out, dip your hands in and take a face full of cold, clear foothill refreshment. Your hike out retraces your steps.

AMERICAN CANYON– DEAD TRUCK TRAILS

IN BRIEF

American Canyon Trail is an easy route down to the Middle Fork of the American River that lets you explore the streams, waterfalls, and ice-cold pools on the way to Poverty Bar. This route loops back before descending to the river; you'll climb just enough to sweat hard before you walk the gentle route back to your car. Continuing to Poverty Bar is a simple quarter-mile excursion and is described but not mapped.

DESCRIPTION

The trails of the Auburn State Recreation Area (ASRA) take advantage of miners' trails, pioneer roads, newly constructed trails, and some newly discovered mining ditches. This gentle descent into American Canyon takes hikers

---

Directions ⟶

From the junction of Interstate 5 East and Capital City Freeway, drive 24 miles to the Elm Street exit in Auburn. Turn left at the traffic light onto Elm Street. At the bottom of the hill, turn left again onto High Street. Pass beneath the Southern Pacific Railroad trestle as you continue downhill on CA 49. Drive 2.3 miles down the winding highway to the confluence, where you follow the highway as it turns right across the American River toward Cool, where, in 6 miles, you will turn left onto CA 193 toward Georgetown. Drive 5.3 miles, then turn left onto Sweetwater Trail on the north side, which is opposite Pilgrim Court on the south. (This turn is before the village of Greenwood.) Your trailhead is on the right, just at the top of the street, before the gates to Auburn Lake Trails. Parking at the trailhead is limited, but you can park on the shoulder back down the road. The trailhead is signed AMERICAN CANYON TRAIL—THIRD GATE.

KEY AT-A-GLANCE INFORMATION

LENGTH: 5.3 miles

CONFIGURATION: Loop

DIFFICULTY: Moderate

WATER REQUIRED: 2 liters

SCENERY: Falls, streams, cascades, pools, wildflowers, foothill woodlands, birds

EXPOSURE: Mostly shaded

TRAIL TRAFFIC: Light

TRAIL SURFACE: Dirt and duff; dirt and rock

HIKING TIME: 3–4 hours

SEASON: Year-round

ACCESS: No fees or permits

MAPS: USGS Greenwood

FACILITIES: None

WHEELCHAIR TRAVERSABLE: No

DRIVING DISTANCE: 35 miles

SPECIAL COMMENTS: Trail restricted to hikers and horse riders. There is limited parking at the trailhead. Heed the mountain-lion and poison-oak warnings.

American Canyon– Dead Truck Trails

UTM Zone (WGS84) 10S

Easting: 0679727

Northing: 4309213

Latitude: N 38° 54' 48"

Longitude: W 120° 55' 37"

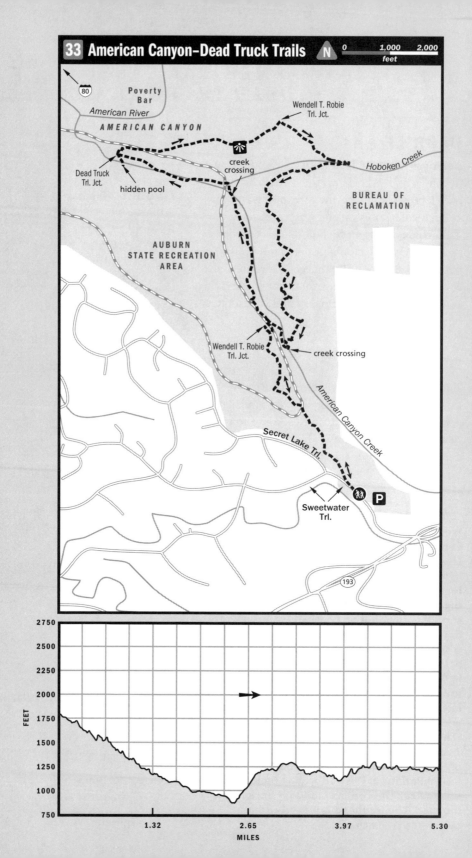

33 American Canyon–Dead Truck Trails

N

0   1,000   2,000
feet

Poverty Bar

80

American River

AMERICAN CANYON

Wendell T. Robie
Trl. Jct.

creek crossing

Hoboken Creek

Dead Truck
Trl. Jct.

hidden pool

BUREAU OF
RECLAMATION

AUBURN
STATE RECREATION
AREA

Wendell T. Robie
Trl. Jct.

creek crossing

American Canyon Creek

Secret Lake Trl.

Sweetwater
Trl.

P

193

FEET

2750
2500
2250
2000
1750
1500
1250
1000
750

1.32   2.65   3.97   5.30

MILES

A hidden gem of the foothills

across two pleasant streams and to a secluded waterfall with a pool carved out of metamorphic bedrock.

The sign at the trailhead lists the mileages to points on this route: Wendell T. Robie Trail (0.8), Western States Trail via American Canyon (2.2), and Sliger Mine Road (3.9).

Hikers start out under a canopy of foothill pine and Douglas fir among live oak, black oak, and buckeye. The trail's descent heightens the steepness of the hillside, dramatized by the tall firs and pines on both sides of the trail. The first trail that joins yours enters from above to the left. It is just a connector from the community uphill.

In the spring, the scent of flowering buckeye follows you down the trail. Later in the summer, the blackberries are sure to delay your hike for a while. As you look to the right, don't be surprised if you meet the gaze of a turkey vulture playing chicken with the treetops. Along this double-track, you will see trees growing horizontally from the hillside before they stretch up toward the sun.

As promised, Wendell T. Robie Trail meets your trail head-on at 0.8 miles, where you will make a U-turn to the right, heading downhill toward Sliger Mine Road. Sliger Mine is reported to have been responsible for half of the $5 million of gold mined in the Greenwood District. From 1848 to 1852, the creeks and canyons in Greenwood District grew to thousands. Although it is difficult to tell now, your destination and areas around it were both the home and workplace of thousands of people as early as 1849. Nature has erased most of the evidence, but you can still see some of it in the form of walls, culverts, and ditches and also platforms and trails.

The next trail junction appears shortly, and you will continue straight ahead as your broad trail narrows. Trail volunteers have made excellent progress pushing back the poison oak along here. Scotch broom, ferns, mosses, and spider-webs dominate the trail now. You are sure to see some firebellies as they make their way across the leaf litter covering the trail. These unflappable California newts are indeed slow but, no, they won't lie still while you take a picture of their bright orange belly. Newts do have toxins in their skin, so it is better not to handle them.

Continue heading north as these cheeky amphibians stare after you. Your next trail junction is a crossing of the American Canyon Creek. Your trail will dip below abundant blackberry bushes as you approach this signed creek crossing. An ASRA sign will let you know your position both here and at the next creek crossing, Hoboken Creek, which is less than 100 feet along the trail. This area is also thick with firebellies—in the water, under rocks, and in the leaves. Watch your step.

Walking above the creek, the single-track is lined with fairy lanterns and larkspur. This dirt-and-duff trail follows wherever the rock outcrops permit it. You emerge from the shade of live oak and manzanita to a hillside fragrant with bush lupine and deep purple larkspur.

A sign verifies your position at Dead Truck Trail—steeply uphill to the right. But here you have choices for a bit more adventure and exploring fun. Look to the left as you face the trail downhill: a side trail angles across the slope beneath you, leading to a real hidden treasure.

Following the downhill trail in front of you, you'll reach the lower section of this creek and then Poverty Bar on the river. Continue along the trail, and you will soon cross to the west side of the creek. Your trail stays just above and ten feet to the side of the creek as it descends by cascade and pool, stair-stepping its way through the forest to the river. A right at the first trail junction will take you down to Poverty Bar.

If you forgo the river, then head down the trail on the slope below you past the sedum-covered boulders, through the popcorn flowers and lupine, down to the sounds of water rushing below. When the pool first comes into view, the creek's waterfalls are still hidden to the left. Descend to the water level to get a good look up into the narrow cascades. Refresh, play, or photograph. Whenever you are ready, ascend to the trail junction above and head up Dead Truck Trail.

Why does the sign say STEEP? A clear example of truth in advertising. But it really isn't terribly steep, or long. No doubt you will be glad when the brief climb is over, though. A beautiful vista point awaits as you top out along the ridge, which grants excellent views to the southeast over Hoboken Creek and up the canyon you originally descended.

The trail intersects the ubiquitous Robie Trail; turn right toward Cool. Losing elevation seems unfair along here; judging from the trail's condition, the horses didn't like it either. Perhaps the mosquitoes will draw your attention away from the ruts. The path crosses one creek's washed-out footbridge before crossing the upended concrete culvert at Hoboken Creek.

AMERICAN CANYON TRAIL
THIRD GATE

WENDELL T. ROBIE TR.	.8 MI.
WESTERN STATES TR.	2.2 MI.
VIA AMERICAN CANYON TRU	
LIGER MINE RD.	3.9 MI.
UCK-A-CHUCKY	6.6 MI.
DRU BARNER PARK	17.7 MI.
MAINE BAR TRAIL	3.1 MI.
BROWNS BAR TR.	7.8 MI.
QUARRY TR.	10.7 MI.
COOL	11.2 MI.
AUBURN	18.9 MI.

Foothills trails are generally well signed.

Your trail is signed now with markers for the Western States Trail. You are about 19 miles from Auburn, according to these signs. The annual horse race—the Western States "100 Miles–One Day" Trail Ride—was founded by Wendell T. Robie in 1955. The Wendell and Inez Robie Foundation currently helps support and maintain the trails and programs for trail users in the Tahoe and foothills areas.

Fairy lanterns and irises line the trail as you enter and exit several small ravines without gaining or losing significant elevation. Keep to the right when you encounter any unsigned trails in the next half mile. When you come to a picturesque glade with a small cascade pooling at the trail crossing, you will head uphill to the right. Your homeward turn comes at an intersection about 500 feet ahead that you passed earlier. Making a left uphill will return you to the trailhead, about 1 mile away. If you are looking down as you trudge uphill, check out the pretty face all over the right bank.

NEARBY ACTIVITIES

Greenwood Pioneer Cemetery is right next to the south side of CA 193 about halfway between Cool and Georgetown. Many of the tombstones here are dated to the gold-rush era.

34 OLMSTEAD LOOP TRAIL

KEY AT-A-GLANCE INFORMATION

LENGTH: 9 miles

CONFIGURATION: Loop

DIFFICULTY: Moderate

WATER REQUIRED: 3 liters

SCENERY: Open meadows full of wildflowers in spring

EXPOSURE: Rarely shaded

TRAIL TRAFFIC: Moderate; heavy on the weekend

TRAIL SURFACE: Dirt

HIKING TIME: 4 hours

SEASON: Year-round, sunrise–sunset

ACCESS: No fees or permits

MAPS: USGS Auburn, Pilot Hill; ASRA map

WHEELCHAIR TRAVERSABLE: No

FACILITIES: Parking area, water, pit toilet, telephone at trailhead

DRIVING DISTANCE: 30 miles

SPECIAL COMMENTS: The trail is extremely muddy and impassable in places after it rains.

IN BRIEF

The Olmstead Loop Trail leads hikers around and through large meadows fringed by live oaks and blackberry thickets. Songbirds, turkeys, and deer are easily observed across the fields of wildflowers.

DESCRIPTION

Behind the fire station in Cool there is an informational kiosk in the parking lot, where, standing under a shady cottonwood, you can study the map and learn about the flora and fauna in this area. Directly west of the kiosk is a pit toilet. To the south, just past the hitching posts, is the trailhead. It is clearly marked as the 0-mile point for the Olmstead Loop Trail. Walk through the pedestrian gate at the corner of the fence.

The Olmstead Loop Trail is a favorite among mountain bikers for good reason. The trail is named in memory of Dan Olmstead, a local bike-shop owner who promoted the creation of multiuse trails and stressed courtesy among trail users. When you arrive at the spacious trailhead parking lot, you will

Olmstead Loop Trail

UTM Zone (WGS84) 10S

Easting: 0671919

Northing: 4306241

Latitude: N 38° 53' 17"

Longitude: W 121° 01' 04"

Directions

From the junction of Interstate 80 and the Capital City Freeway, drive 24 miles on I-80 east to Auburn and exit at Elm Street. Turn left onto Elm Street and take another left at the bottom of the hill. Drive under the railroad overpass and follow CA 49 downhill, turning right to cross the American River. Drive 5 miles to Cool. Turn right on St. Florian Court, which is the first right turn in Cool, before the flashing light and next to the fire station. The trailhead parking lot is behind the fire station. Your signed trailhead is in the southeast corner of the parking lot.

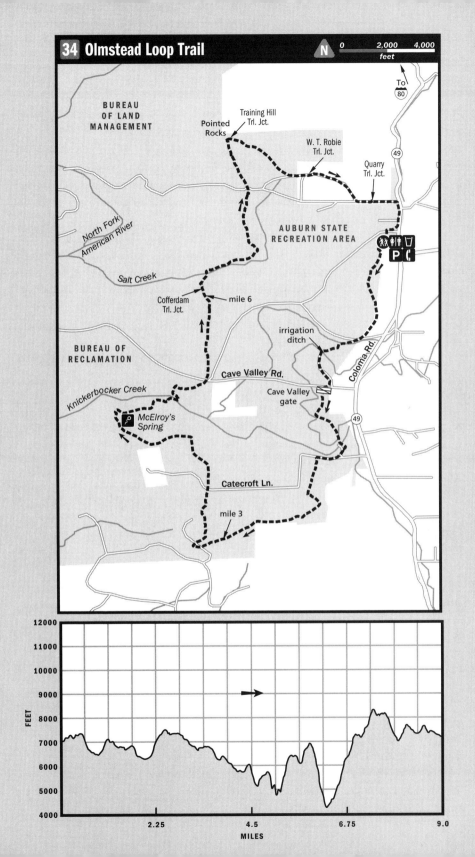

N   0   2,000   4,000
feet

To
80

BUREAU
OF LAND
MANAGEMENT

Training Hill
Trl. Jct.
Pointed
Rocks

W. T. Robie
Trl. Jct.

Quarry
Trl. Jct.

49

North Fork
American River

AUBURN STATE
RECREATION AREA

Salt Creek

Cofferdam
Trl. Jct.

mile 6

irrigation
ditch

Coloma Rd.

BUREAU OF
RECLAMATION

Cave Valley Rd.

Cave Valley
gate

49

Knickerbocker Creek

McElroy's
Spring

Catecroft Ln.

mile 3

12000

11000

10000

9000

8000

FEET

7000

6000

5000

4000

2.25   4.5   6.75   9.0

MILES

see evidence of his work in the hoof prints, bicycle tracks, and boot prints in the dirt.

Although the trail is very well signed, the placement of some of the markers can leave hikers scratching their heads. Right out of the gate, literally, is just such a trail split: The trail sign is smack in the middle of the junction. Take the left fork as the trail roughly parallels the highway, heading south. A trail sign ahead will reinforce your correct choice. Trail signs are so frequent that navigational skills are almost unnecessary. You only have to pay attention so that you do not ignore or miss a few important junctions.

Live oaks dot the huge meadow you are walking past. Your trail, bordered by a fence, passes a few houses on the left. When you near a large metal-roofed horse barn, the trail bears right. The next trail sign is conveniently located beside a blackberry patch full of ripening berries if you arrive in late summer. A second large berry thicket is on your left after you take the right fork at the next split. (Another trail goes around the berries to the left and joins your path again, so you cannot go wrong here.)

Turn right, onto the double-track, and head up the dirt road. An irrigation ditch runs underneath it just before the 1-mile mark. Follow the trail sign up to the right. Shortly, an alternate entrance gate appears on the left. It is marked GATE 156—CAVE VALLEY GATE. Continue past this point, with another trail sign on your right. You will pass Northside Elementary School as you walk uphill. Ignore any side trails that lead off to the right, and walk straight ahead, toward a smaller, open gate. The trail becomes ditchlike and rock-strewn at the gate. Ahead is another trail sign to keep you on track.

Watch the slopes for wildlife, the most visible being the wild turkeys that abound here. Despite their being highly visible in contrast to the golden grasses, they can disappear in exactly the time it takes you to reach for a camera. Wally baskets, brodiaea, and popcorn flowers dot these slopes with color in the spring and early summer. The next trail sign is at the 1.5-mile point. Again, posted right between two trails, this sign is also ambiguous. Take the fork to the left to continue on the correct route.

Your track swings west, bordered on the left by a blackberry-encrusted fence and on the right by blackberry-encrusted earth. Watch for a trail-etiquette sign on the left and a trail sign near that. Turn left at this junction. Raccoons have visited these berry patches and have left plenty of evidence in the middle of the trail. Watch your step.

The long slope in front of you leads past milkweed and buttercup about 100 feet up to a copse of live oak that you will walk through before turning southwest. Your trail crosses a huge meadow and is totally exposed, except for the shade of a single ash, until you reach a large stand of live oak in the distance. Four radio towers off to the left measure your progress as you pass the fence (also on your left). Auburn comes into view about when you reach the corner of the fence. At the stand of oak, a trail sign directs you back to the northeast and 5.8 miles to Cool.

Filled with wildflowers in late spring, the hillsides turn golden brown by late summer.

Finally, the trail has some shade cover. The next 0.75 miles are fairly level, and then you begin to descend a bit. A sweeping turn to the left takes you downhill, now under the cover of tall foothill pines. When you finally encounter these long-needled trees, you have completed half the hike. Walk down a short, rocky stretch and watch for a sign on the right that announces McElroy's Spring. This handwritten posting is attached high up in an oak tree that serves as a corner post for the fence. The spring can be easily spotted by the lush growth to the right of it.

Take a right at the end of the fence (or at the open gate just before it) and begin descending slightly under the cover of pine and fir until you reach Knickerbocker Creek. Enjoy the cool shade beside this stream, where a trail sign among the bushes on the opposite bank marks your fifth mile. Catch your breath here before you begin a fairly steep uphill trudge for the next ten minutes or so. When you emerge from the trees, a grand vista of the terrain you have crossed spreads before you. The trail eases off to the left and crosses paved Cave Valley Road.

To the left, Cave Valley Road leads to the site of the Auburn Dam. To the right, it heads northeast, back to the fire station. Cross the road and continue north 0.5 miles across more open fields, making sure to ignore trails leading off to the left. The foothill pine and live oak are now joined by manzanita stands, which help shade the trail. A signed junction indicates that Cofferdam Trail heads left. You should continue to the right, down to a crossing of Salt Creek, where a large, showy buttonbush crowds the narrow creek's crossing.

Most of the trails in ASRA are multiuse.

Take a drink of water and a deep breath here before you begin an uphill grind that takes 20 minutes or so. Travel about 0.33 miles northeast and then turn north for another 0.33 miles or so to reach flat ground among the oak and pine. The next trail junction is signed and will direct you to the left, just west of north. Your trailhead lies southeast of this point.

The live oaks covering this hillside are spaced exactly far enough apart for their crowns to nearly touch. If you decide to go take some shade, be cautious of poison oak, which commonly appears red on these slopes. Wally baskets and blue dicks add to the color along your trail, which dead-ends at the junction with a double-track. According to the sign on the left, turning that way would lead you to the steep Training Hill Trail more than 1 mile away. Turning right, you have about 1.5 miles to your destination.

Your trail is fully exposed as you descend; watch for trail signs to keep on track. Your trail will swing left a bit, toward the east. As you again head uphill, the Wendell T. Robie Trail joins the Olmstead Loop Trail from the left and then exits to the left in another 100 yards. At the next junction, turn left and walk uphill on a rocky double-track under sparse shade.

The Quarry Trail leads off to the north at a signed junction on your left. Continue uphill until you have a view of the backside of Cool and your original trailhead. Approaching the corner of the fence line, turn right, with the barbed-wire fence at your side. A few minutes more and you are back at the trailhead.

HIDDEN FALLS TRAILS  35

IN BRIEF

Hidden Falls Regional Park, a new addition in Placer County's Placer Legacy Program, is really a model for suburban open-space design and use. The park's 7 miles of trails are available to hikers, bikers, runners, and horseback riders. An accessible trail—the Hidden Gateway Trail—offers excellent views of the 221-acre site. The other paths consist of either loops or out-and-back trails that range from moderate to difficult. The hike described here combines portions of each trail to give the hiker a good workout rewarded by excellent scenery. These trails are well marked, and intersections are somewhat frequent, so being temporarily disoriented should not be a concern on this hike.

DESCRIPTION

Your trail, which starts out near the top of the ridge, descends to Deadman's Creek and then ascends the next ridge to the north before arriving at the pools of Coon Creek. The nicely shaded path takes you along Coon Creek as you make your way west toward Deadman's Falls.

Your trail starts at the information kiosk at the end of the parking lot, where you will see a map of the complete trail system. The

KEY AT-A-GLANCE INFORMATION

LENGTH: 5.1 miles
CONFIGURATION: Connected loops
DIFFICULTY: Moderate
WATER REQUIRED: 2 liters
SCENERY: Riparian and foothill woodland
EXPOSURE: Well-shaded trail most of the way
TRAIL TRAFFIC: Very little
TRAIL SURFACE: Sand and rock; dirt and duff
HIKING TIME: 2–3 hours
SEASON: Year-round, sunrise–sunset
ACCESS: No fees or permits
MAPS: USGS Gold Hill. An excellent color map of all the trails is available online at www.placer.ca.gov/Departments/Facility/parks/hiddenfalls.aspx.
FACILITIES: Restrooms, water fountain, and pay telephone
WHEELCHAIR TRAVERSABLE: Yes. The Hidden Gateway Trail is accessible and begins just 10 feet past the trailhead for this hike.
DRIVING DISTANCE: 32 miles
SPECIAL COMMENTS: Scenic, new trail system on 220 acres being expanded by 960 acres

Directions

From Interstate 80 East and Capitol City Freeway in Sacramento, drive 24 miles to Auburn. Exit CA 49 north toward Grass Valley. Drive north 2.7 miles; turn left onto Atwood Road, which becomes Mount Vernon Road after 1.7 miles. Follow Mount Vernon Road 2.6 miles and turn right on Mears Drive. The Hidden Valley Regional Park entrance sign is up the hill on the right. Turn into the parking lot. The trailhead is to the right of the restrooms.

Hidden Falls Trails
UTM Zone (WGS84) 10S
Easting: 0659081
Northing: 4313838
Latitude: N 38° 57' 32"
Longitude: W 121° 00' 59"

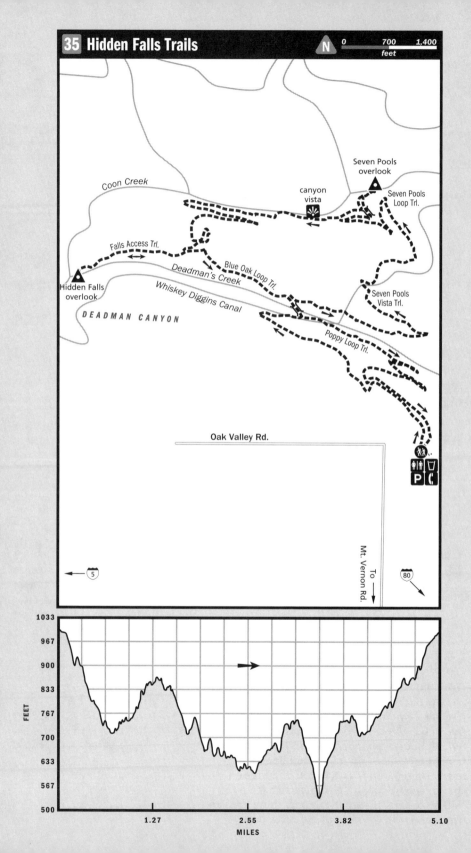

Hidden Falls plunges over cataracts
to Coon Creek below.

restrooms and pay phone
are to your left; walk about
five feet down the sidewalk,
turn right, and descend a
few concrete steps to the
dirt path of Poppy Loop
Trail, and then turn left
and begin walking north.

As you start down
Poppy Loop Trail, the view
to your east is of fenced cattle ranches ringed by foothill woodland forests. This
old four-wheel-drive road
is rather exposed as you
descend to the first U-turn.
The trail you see to the
right is your return route.

On the way down,
though, you will feel a nice
cooling as you enter the
shade of live oak and foothill pine. Within moments
you will begin to hear
Deadman's Creek. Another, more appetizing, sign of the upcoming creek is the
appearance of miner's lettuce on the left side of your trail. Resist the temptation
to pick—it is prohibited—as you head toward the bridge ahead of you.

Crossing the bridge, you are on Pond Turtle Trail. Take this connector 30
feet to the junction with Blue Oak Loop Trail. A sharp right uphill puts you on
the side of the hill under the shade of the foothill woodland understory—toyon
and manzanita. This trail will quickly gain elevation and then level off. To your
left you can see the contours of the hills in the trail cut. Notice the gentle folds
of the rock strata as you pass.

After you round a seasonal runoff ravine from the left, you may begin to
notice more blue oak—much of it speckled with oakmoss lichen. On the right, a
rather large—and horizontal—foothill pine stretches from its roots at the canyon center to its crown tip at the trailside. Signs indicate this tree fell during the
2006 winter. Your trail continues to gain elevation after it swings back to the
north. Walking in the shade, watch for weasel signs, which are usually plumb in
the middle of the trail.

As you level out after 1.4 miles, you will see a signpost (labeled #10) at the junction where you now leave the Blue Oak Loop when it turns left and you continue straight onto the Seven Pools Vista Trail.

Descend a bit to the northeast toward the Seven Pools area. You will not actually reach the pools on this trail. It is the next junction that will get you there. For now, the dirt- and leaf-covered trail seems like the easy part of the hike: gently descending, continuously shaded, quiet enough to hear birds and the stream.

Among the toyon, manzanita, and live oak, the trail will make a U-turn before reaching the Seven Pools area and will then wrap around the hillside, gently descending in and out of a ravine before reaching a well-signed intersection with Seven Pools Loop. Your route turns sharply right, onto Seven Pools Loop, at signpost #11.

Head east, descending just below the previous trail section, getting ever closer to Coon Creek. To help keep your feet dry, use the small bridge that crosses the ravine you walked around earlier. Now head north about 100 yards to a spur trail that leads to a rock outcrop looking over the cascades and into one of the pools.

Return to the Seven Pools Loop, heading west. Notice the bits and chunks of quartz rock along this section of trail. Quartz-bearing gravels attracted miners' attention as the mining ditch along Deadman's Creek reminds us. The large blocks in the creek bottom testify to the general geological makeup of this region: highly fractured blocks and faults, squeezed, uplifted, folded, coated with lava and mudflows, washed, scrubbed, bleached, and left as you find them today. To see a good example, just before reaching the vista ahead on the right, look at the outcrop of rock running from the left on the hill above you, visible as it continues immediately under your feet, and out to your right at the boulder-littered canyon floor.

Shortly after the vista spot, just as the trail turns away from the creek, your path crosses Pond Turtle Trail. This junction is simple: keep walking straight. But, if you want a pleasant spot to sit and have a moment, the creek is right there.

Continuing west on Seven Pools Loop, the trail varies from 5 to 50 feet above the creek bed. Walk past any blocked trails that are marked for trail restoration. The 960-acre ranch to the west is currently being surveyed for additional trails, but vegetation recovery is needed in some areas first.

The Seven Pools Loop will switchback, ascending to the east for 0.2 miles. Turning right at the intersection with Quail Run Trail will send you toward the Falls Access Trail for one of the real highlights of this hike.

As you round the curve of Quail Run Trail, resist the temptation to shortcut the ten feet across to the Falls Access Trail. Restoration of that impromptu trail is in progress and needs cooperation.

Walk another 150 feet around the curve. Just after the contorted black and burgundy madrone, take a right at the junction onto Blue Oak Loop. Walk 75 feet, then turn right onto the Falls Access Trail, heading west.

This is the most difficult section of the route. No horses or bikes are permitted on this trail for good reasons. The Falls Access Trail is the most uneven, least well-established trail in the park. It most closely approximates a typical wilderness use-trail. You will have some rocks and boulders to contend with, and the side trails are obvious enough to avoid. Descending to within 50 feet of Deadman's Creek, you will find nice vista points overlooking some little riffles.

More importantly, this trail ends rather precipitously at the falls overlook, and the footing is quite slippery—so do not rush around that last bend! At least 100 feet before the trail's end, the falls and the viewpoint will be visible. Take moment here to slow your pace. Before you drop down to the overlook, enjoy the view from this upper perch.

In March of 2007, Placer County engineers were surveying to establish a platform overlook and picnic tables in that spot. A platform would be a distinct improvement because there is presently no way to see the entire falls without being in midair. The 35-foot falls flow year-round. It is an impressive cataract that highlights the hike. Just below the falls is the junction with Coon Creek.

Return on this trail to the junction with the Blue Oak Loop, and turn right, heading southeast along the Blue Oak Loop. This section of the trail is flat and shaded. You are heading toward the bridge that ties the Blue Oak Loop with the Poppy Loop Trail.

When you cross the bridge on returning, turn left at the junction with the Poppy Loop Trail to walk along Deadman's Creek and past a massive blackberry patch. Three easy switchbacks lie between the creek and the ridge. Even though you leave the shade of foothill pines and California buckeyes for an open, dry slope, you cannot help but stop and admire the massive mistletoe-blotched valley oak that towers over the trail. Walk another 500 feet to the trailhead, with this giant to your right.

36   LAKE CLEMENTINE TRAIL

KEY AT-A-GLANCE INFORMATION

LENGTH: 4.4 miles

CONFIGURATION: Out-and-back

DIFFICULTY: Easy

WATER REQUIRED: 1–2 liters, depending on season and time of day

SCENERY: River views in a widening canyon lead up to a dammed lake

EXPOSURE: Shaded trail, except during noon hours, in this north–south canyon

TRAIL TRAFFIC: Busy

TRAIL SURFACE: Sand, gravel, river rock, dirt, mud, and pavement

HIKING TIME: 2–3 hours

SEASON: Year-round, sunrise–sunset

ACCESS: No fees or permits

MAPS: USGS Auburn

FACILITIES: Pit toilet at North Fork Dam parking lot. Information kiosks and pit toilets are located about 150 feet south of the trailhead on the west side of Old Foresthill Road, and 200 feet west of the Old Foresthill Bridge on the north side of the road.

WHEELCHAIR TRAVERSABLE: No

DRIVING DISTANCE: 27.5 miles

SPECIAL COMMENTS: This trail is also popular with mountain bikers. Most are courteous and will verbally "beep," but wise hikers will look over their shoulders frequently.

Lake Clementine Trail

UTM Zone (WGS84) 10S

Easting: 0670320

Northing: 4309328

Latitude: N 38° 54' 58"

Longitude: W 121° 02' 07"

IN BRIEF

Lake Clementine Trail features the tallest bridge in California, gold-rush-era bridge remains, exposed Jurassic-period geology, riparian zone and foothill flora, a rock-lined swimming hole, and a tree-lined lake. This easy hike along the North Fork of the American River is largely shaded. A gentle grade offers some exercise along this 2.2-mile hike on a trail shared with runners and mountain bikers. Imagine hiking in Utah's Glen Canyon *before* it was inundated by the Colorado. A similar experience is captured here at the confluence of the North and Middle forks of the American.

DESCRIPTION

The confluence of the North and Middle forks of the American River flows about 15 miles due north of the site where James Marshall first discovered gold on the South Fork of the American River. Since the time of the forty-niners, a dozen bridges have spanned these tributaries. Today, four remain, three of which are used by motor vehicles. They are No Hands Bridge—formerly the Mountain

---

Directions ⟶

Drive 25 miles on Interstate 80 East to Auburn. Take the Elm Avenue exit and turn left at the traffic light. At the bottom of the hill, turn left at the High Street signal. From the railroad track overpass, a block ahead of you, drive 2.2 miles downhill on CA 49. Stay straight as it becomes Old Foresthill Road another 0.3 miles, crossing the bridge to find parking along the road. (You will pass the CA 49 turnoff, which goes east toward Cool and Georgetown.) Parking is allowed on both sides of the road. If you do need to park far from this spot, the trailhead is on the east side of the confluence.

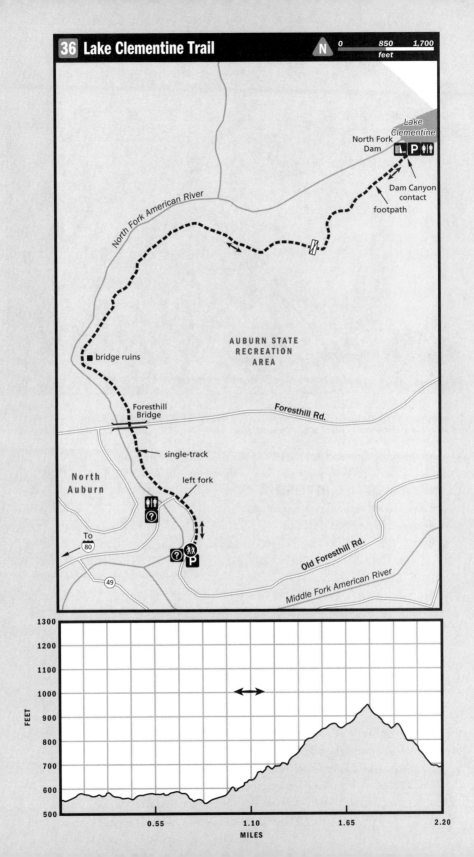

N

0   850   1,700
feet

Lake
Clementine

North Fork
Dam

Dam Canyon
contact
footpath

North Fork American River

AUBURN STATE
RECREATION
AREA

■ bridge ruins

Foresthill
Bridge

Foresthill Rd.

single-track

North
Auburn

left fork

To
80

49

Old Foresthill Rd.

Middle Fork American River

1300

1200

1100

1000

900

800

700

600

500

FEET

0.55   1.10   1.65   2.20

MILES

Seven hundred thirty feet above your riverside trail, the Foresthill Bridge is the tallest in California and the third tallest in the United States.

Quarries RR Bridge and famous for its proximity to the finish of the Tevis Cup Trail Ride, the CA 49 bridge to Cool, Old Foresthill Road Bridge, and the most spectacular of all—Foresthill Bridge.

Lake Clementine Trail begins to the east of the confluence on the southeast side of Old Foresthill Road. The trailhead is marked by a gate signed TRAIL 139. Lined with boulders, this Jeep trail borders the east flank of the North Fork of the American River as it flows past you toward the confluence with the Middle Fork.

Your destination is at the end of a steady uphill amble to Lake Clementine, a lake created by the North Fork Dam, a debris dam built in 1939 by the Army Corps of Engineers. The flows along this fork of the American are not dam-controlled and so, as summer wanes, the waters below you become slower and warmer—making for great swimming opportunities. In late spring, by contrast, the high flow over the North Fork Dam creates a spectacular mist and a thundering rumble.

Walking parallel to the river, look left, to the west side, and you will see Stagecoach Trail, which climbs to join the route of an 1852 toll road known then as Yankee Jim's Turnpike. While you are looking, glance over your shoulder often because mountain bikes can approach quickly.

At about 1,000 feet from the trailhead, we descend the first left fork toward the river's edge. A hundred feet farther, a nice stream crosses from your right. Take a moment to look left, though, to see the first of many bridge remains.

The biozones in this area—riparian and foothill woodland—are easy to tell apart because most of the riparian zone is on your left, and the river and the foothill woodland is on your right, along the canyon walls.

You'll see interior live oak, canyon live oak, madrone, foothill ("digger") pine, and California bay laurel. Watch for the spiky leaves of the toyon and the colorful redbuds interspersed with manzanita and poison oak.

As you look down the slope toward the river, you will pass cottonwoods, willows, valley oaks, and big-leaf maples. If the season is right, you'll find an abundance of blackberries along here.

When the trail turns into a single-track and hugs the river, you have walked a little more than a half mile. Bikers have no place to pass you along here, so be alert. Look up and you will see the concrete pier and roadway of the Foresthill Bridge looming across the canyon. Walk about 500 feet and it will be directly overhead.

It's a record-setting 730 feet above the river, making it the tallest bridge in California and the third tallest in the United States. The bridge, built to carry traffic across the reservoir which would have been created by the Auburn Dam, was finished in 1973.

In the late 1970s, before the construction of the Auburn Dam, seismological risks were revealed and construction plans halted. Downriver from the confluence, a diversion tunnel was built that still stands. The dam's impact is most easily visualized when you look up at the Foresthill Bridge: the water level would have reached just 22 feet below the top of the concrete pier above you.

After hiking 0.8 miles, look along both riverbanks for stone or concrete abutments marking original bridge sites. The concrete abutments were for the steel bridges of the early 20th century. Stone and rock abutments that supported several wooden bridges can be seen upriver within the next 0.3 miles.

Shaded by live oak and manzanita, boulder-lined pools of lazy, clear water lie within view. Stretching for almost a half mile, this portion of the river is known as Clark's Hole. Placer miners made dams of stacked boulders and river cobble, which formed these connected pools. The warm, slow waters are now popular for swimming.

The midday sun at your back can be uncomfortable, and your moderately rolling trail has now turned into a fairly steady uphill exercise. To your right, the canyon wall rises sharply above you. The welcome coolness of ferns and mosses thriving wherever water seeps out of the manzanita-covered hillside helps relieve the heat.

The increasingly loud sound of water signals that you are approaching the North Fork Dam. As the trail turns southeast, you will have a brief view upstream to the dam.

The gravel trail ends at 1.95 miles, at a gate signed 1.4 MILES TO FUEL BREAK ROAD AND CULVERT TRAIL. Follow the paved road as it turns to the left and begins to drop to the dam site and Lake Clementine. In 0.3 miles, a dirt footpath leaves the road and descends left. Those who want a very close look at the dam should

The North Fork Dam above the confluence

take this short spur, which leads to the exact point at which the dam is anchored to the rock of the canyon wall. Along the way to this spot, notice the informal use-trail that descends to the river.

For a tamer look at the dam from a lakeside vantage point, continue along the paved road, turn left into the day-use parking lot, and descend to the lake level.

Retracing your steps will allow you to look for wildlife along the canyon side and flowers along the riverside. There is a long list of both, but you will be able to spot plenty of turkey vultures, squirrels, signs of coyotes, California quails, and scrub jays, along with turkeys and red-tailed hawks. Springtime is a riot of color in this area, with Indian paintbrush, California poppy, lupine, and larkspur among the many flowers. Your hour-long return to the car will be a relaxing walk in one of the foothills' finest hiking regions.

NEARBY ACTIVITIES

Auburn State Recreation Area (ASRA) has more than 50 recognized trails extending hundreds of miles throughout the North Fork and Middle Fork of the American River. Most trails are multiuse trails serving equestrians, mountain bikers, backpackers, and hikers. White-water rafting is very popular on both forks and several commercial raft and kayak outfitters operate from Auburn, Colfax, Cool, and Foresthill.

CONFLUENCE TRAIL

IN BRIEF

A short, gradual climb above the Middle Fork of the American River provides more than exercise. Hikers will be treated to panoramic, upriver views of the Middle Fork, overlooking placer mining and quarrying operations as they were left more than 100 years ago.

DESCRIPTION

The shaded trailhead is below the parking area on the west side of Old Foresthill Road. To reach it, descend from the parking area to the information kiosk and pit toilet. As you walk down toward the river, imagine cooling your feet at the river's edge after your hike.

Begin by walking south along the trail, directly toward the river. The first 500 feet make a sweeping curve from south to east. As you head away from the confluence, the trail begins an easy but steady uphill climb along a single-track.

The trail is sparsely shaded by foothill pine and cool manzanita. The pines can be recognized by their large (six- to ten-inch) globe-shaped cones, which are heavily armored with curved one-inch hooks at the ends of their

KEY AT-A-GLANCE INFORMATION

LENGTH: 3.5 miles
CONFIGURATION: Out-and-back
DIFFICULTY: Easy
WATER REQUIRED: 1 liter
SCENERY: Spectacular panorama of the Middle Fork of the American River
EXPOSURE: Exposed south-facing slope, with some trailside shade
TRAIL TRAFFIC: This is a popular hiking and mountain-biking trail.
TRAIL SURFACE: Dirt and rock
HIKING TIME: 1.5–2 hours
SEASON: Year-round, sunrise–sunset
ACCESS: No fees or permits
MAPS: USGS Auburn
FACILITIES: Pit toilet at the trailhead
WHEELCHAIR TRAVERSABLE: No
DRIVING DISTANCE: 28 miles
SPECIAL COMMENTS: Information kiosks and pit toilets are located at the trailhead on the west side of Old Foresthill Road, and 200 feet west of the Old Foresthill Bridge on the north side of the road.

Directions

Take Interstate 80 East 24 miles to the city of Auburn, then take the Elm Avenue exit and turn left at the traffic light. At the bottom of the hill, turn left at the High Street signal. From the railroad track overpass, a block ahead of you, drive downhill on CA 49 2.2 miles where it becomes Old Foresthill Road, which you will stay on another 0.3 miles, crossing the bridge to find parking along the road. (You will pass the CA 49 turnoff, which goes east toward Cool and Georgetown.) Parking is allowed on both sides of the road.

Confluence Trail
UTM Zone (WGS84) 10S
Easting: 0670274
Northing: 4309236
Latitude: N 38° 54' 55"
Longitude: W 121° 02' 09"

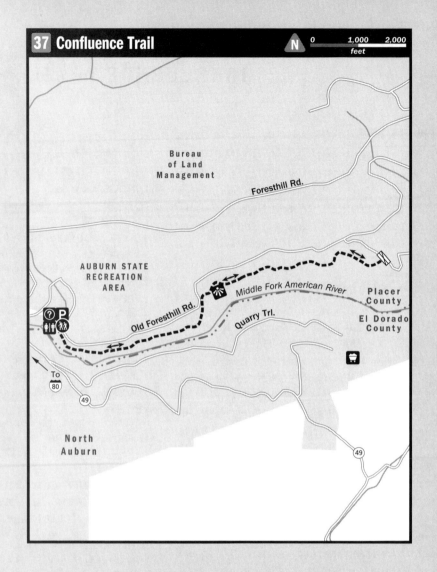

N

0   1,000   2,000
feet

Bureau
of Land
Management

Foresthill Rd.

AUBURN STATE
RECREATION
AREA

Middle Fork American River

Placer
County

El Dorado
County

Old Foresthill Rd.

Quarry Trl.

To
80

49

North
Auburn

49

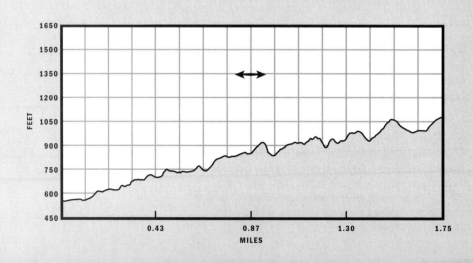

scales—oddly overprotected and showy in comparison to the sparse, uneven growth of the tree itself.

Look to the south side of the middle fork, where the Quarry Trail runs parallel past Louisiana Bar, Warner's Ravine, New York Bar, Murderer's Bar, Mammoth Bar, Murderer's Gulch, Texas Bar, Hoosier Bar, and on. The placer miners named these spots to remind them of home, and the names endure to this day.

Imagine looking down from this point at long, wood-and-canvas sluice boxes lining the river below being worked by hundreds of gold miners. The scene is largely the same as it was in the mid–19th century. But the only thing that moves the rocks now is the river.

Keep your eyes peeled as you look across at Warner Ravine. The trail closely contours along the canyon side, and footing can be slippery at times. You might also look down at the trail and see signs of coyotes, raccoons, and dogs.

On this exposed slope, watch for rattlesnakes, an important part of this ecosystem, seeking some warmth from the afternoon sun. They are shy and will not attack unless disturbed or provoked. Respect them and walk away from rattlesnakes. Do not attempt to touch them or pick them up! It is unlawful to kill rattlesnakes or any other wildlife in the park.

Depending on the time of day, sun can be an issue. Early-morning hikers will enjoy not only a cool trail but also brilliant shows of light and shadow on the opposite hills.

The vehicular Old Foresthill Road follows this path as it rounds the mountain. Although the road is close, one has a hard time hearing any traffic. The trail surface changes from dirt and rock to old, broken pavement.

The hillsides here are exposed and lack the abundance of mosses seen on the North Fork trail. However, the mosses and ferns are replaced on this slope by chaparral flora, which now includes many nonnative grasses and flowers.

After about 0.75 miles, your single-track trail becomes a FWD trail (or fire-suppression trail) that long ago saw its last vehicle. As the path turns east, pause to admire the view upriver from New York Bar below you to Murderer's Bar.

The Mammoth Bar area is reserved on specific days for off-highway-vehicle (OHV) users. Check with the park for the seasonal schedule by calling (530) 885-4527. Established OHV trails may be hiked when not reserved for OHV users.

After 1.75 miles, the trail ends at a gate signed TRAIL #107—EAST GATE and CONFLUENCE TRAIL. Retrace your steps to the trailhead. As you approach the confluence, the refreshing sounds of water will welcome you back.

NEARBY ACTIVITIES

The Confluence Trail is well known to mountain biking enthusiasts. ASRA has hundreds of miles of multiuse trails shared among equestrians, bikers, and hikers. Lake Clementine Trail and Quarry Road Trail in the Confluence area are well-regarded bike trails. The Olmstead Loop Trail in Cool was named in honor of a local bike shop owner and is a favorite among mountain bikers.

38 QUARRY ROAD TRAIL TO AMERICAN CANYON FALLS

KEY AT-A-GLANCE INFORMATION

LENGTH: 14.5 miles

CONFIGURATION: Out-and-back

DIFFICULTY: Challenging

WATER REQUIRED: 3–4 liters

SCENERY: Exceptional views along the Middle Fork and American Canyon Creek

EXPOSURE: Lots of shaded trail, but sunscreen is handy for the long, exposed area.

TRAIL TRAFFIC: Heavy on weekends

TRAIL SURFACE: Gravel and dirt, duff and dirt

HIKING TIME: 6 hours

SEASON: Year-round

ACCESS: No fees or permits

MAPS: USGS Greenwood, Auburn

WHEELCHAIR TRAVERSABLE: No

FACILITIES: Pit toilets and picnic tables along first 1.2 miles

DRIVING DISTANCE: 27 miles

SPECIAL COMMENTS: Take this trail to its destination, or make side trips to the quarry or bars.

Quarry Road Trail to American Canyon Falls

UTM Zone (WGS84) 10S

Easting: 0670404

Northing: 4308804

Latitude: N 38° 54' 41"

Longitude: W 121° 02' 04"

IN BRIEF

Quarry Road Trail is the easiest of walks—for the first 2 miles. Just by adding an idyllic destination, you can turn this simple walk into a challenging adventure. The falls and pool hidden away on American Canyon Creek are worth every step along this historic mining trail.

DESCRIPTION

Your hike starts out at the green gate, next to the informative trail sign, which shows the locations of various facilities along the trail. You will find a toilet and picnic table at 0.2 miles, a picnic table at 0.6 miles, and more picnic tables and toilets at 1.2 miles along. There is no drinking water along this trail.

As you exit the shade of the first bend, look over your shoulder to a nice view of Foresthill Bridge. As you walk along the river toward Warner Ravine and the rapids at New York Bar, your wide trail is lined with fairy lanterns and buttercups in the spring and nicely shaded by live oak and foothill pine year-round. Your trail tells of three periods of history.

- -

Directions ———————————————→

From the junction of Interstate 80 East and the Capital City Freeway, drive 25 miles to the Elm Street exit in Auburn. Turn left at the traffic light, onto Elm Street. At the bottom of the hill, turn left again, onto High Street. Pass beneath the Southern Pacific Railroad trestle as you continue downhill on CA 49. Drive 2.3 miles down the winding highway to the confluence, where you follow the road, making a right turn at the bottom of the hill over the American River, toward Cool. The trailhead parking lot is 0.3 miles uphill on the left. There's plenty of parking in this gravel lot, which adjoins the trailhead.

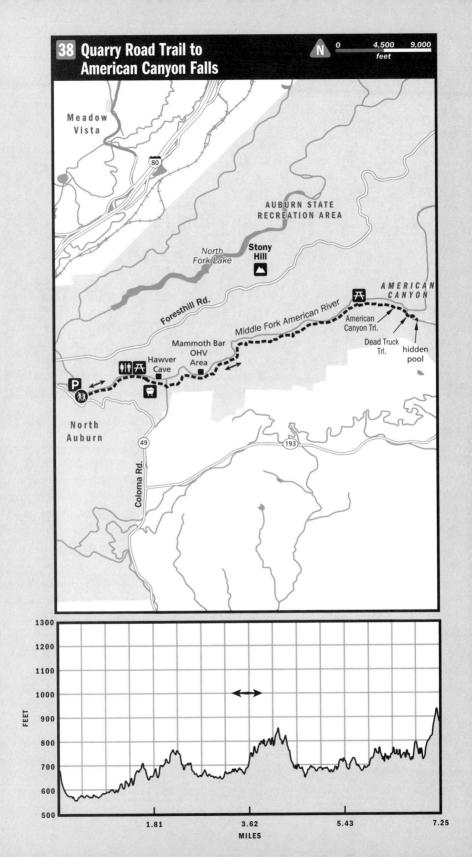

N

0   4,500   9,000
feet

Meadow
Vista

80

AUBURN STATE
RECREATION AREA

North
Fork Lake

Stony
Hill

AMERICAN
CANYON

Foresthill Rd.

Middle Fork American River

American
Canyon Trl.

Dead Truck
Trl.

hidden
pool

Mammoth Bar
OHV
Area

Hawver
Cave

P

North
Auburn

49

193

Coloma Rd.

1300
1200
1100
1000
900
800
700
600
500

FEET

1.81   3.62   5.43   7.25

MILES

Had the Auburn Dam been completed, the water level would have been expected to rise to within 22 feet of the Foresthill Bridge deck.

Most recently, your trail was the track bed for the Mountain Quarries Railroad, which carried limestone from the quarry's loading platform near the gated entrance to Hawver Cave across the famous Mountain Quarries Railroad Bridge ("No Hands Bridge") on its way to Auburn. Built in the early 1900s, the railroad was abandoned and ultimately dismantled during World War II to recycle the rail's steel. You may be able to see some of the leftover ties embedded in the trail before you reach the picnic area below Hawver Cave.

An earlier version of the Quarry Trail was a flume bed. The Confluence area was occupied and worked by nearly 10,000 miners during the gold-rush years. In the late 1850s, individuals banded together to form mining companies—building and operating a 13-mile-long flume-works that was destroyed annually by spring floods. Using canvas and wood, the flume was literally fabricated from scratch each year. The riparian area and the riverbed have been almost entirely reclaimed through natural processes.

It was the process of water dripping through limestone that created the cavernous Hawver Cave. For years, curious settlers found strange animal bones in the cave. In 1906 an Auburn paleontologist named Dr. J. C. Hawver identified many species of animals from the Pleistocene Age, including the mastodon and ground sloth. A few years later, human bones were discovered, leading to the understanding that Native Americans had used the cave as a burial chamber.

Quarrying destroyed the cave, which is now gated. A popular side trail—the PG&E Road Trail—leads 0.6 miles to a quarry overlook. Bypass these side trails if your objective is the falls on American Canyon Creek.

At the next trail junction, a path down to the left will lead you to a spacious picnic area. With three tables beneath pergolas, three toilets, and one enormous view, this is a terrific destination for families with small children. Above the tables stand the blackberry-shrouded remains of the limestone loading-platform foundations.

Hiking up on the right-hand trail at the junction leads you past these concrete blocks and Hawver Cave. Continue straight past the cave entrance and its running stream. There is a nice view of the river from this point. Your trail will be clearly signed at every important junction, and informative signs will pinpoint mileages and trail names.

Continue straight ahead toward Brown's Bar Trail, Maine Bar Trail, and Poverty Bar, which lie 2 to 5 miles ahead. You will pass above Murderer's Bar before coming opposite Mammoth Bar on the far bank. Blackberries and black oak cool and shade you, and swarms of California sisters and yellow tiger swallowtail butterflies descend on pretty face, Indian pink, and larkspur as you hike on to Texas Bar at around 2.7 miles.

The long stretches of exposure are occasionally interrupted by madrone hanging over the trail. Around the pool below the small cascades, you will come to a cool, shady glen that buzzes with activity. Butterflies, bees, and water ouzels dart around in this trailside, air-conditioned rest area. A sound in the brush next to the water draws your attention to the striking black with yellow bands of the king snake as it hustles away beneath the duff. This well-timed pause above Brown's Bar offers welcome rest before you walk toward Maine Bar Trail—about 2 miles ahead with a bit of uphill.

All right. It was a grind, uphill but now the trail is graced by more flowers, the slope above and below steepens, and the dense cover of tall, white firs cloaks you in deep shade as you descend into Wildcat Canyon above Hoosier Bar. Imagine, as you look through the trees, how this area would look with thousands of miners working the river and its streams. Moments after you exit the ravine at Wildcat Canyon, you will need to make a sharp right turn before diving into the river. Your single-track will lead you upstream along the rocky cobble and sand of Hoosier Bar before it climbs above the river and heads to Brushy Mountain Canyon, where there is a pleasant glade in which to cool your heels. Less than 500 yards away is an oak grove shading a picnic table and pit toilet.

Just about the time the picnic site comes into view, you should spot a trail sign on the left. A right turn at this sign is important so that you can take the Maine Bar Trail just 0.1 mile uphill to the American Canyon Trail, where you will again head east. This junction is easy to miss because of the distinct trail beyond the picnic table in front of you, which then leads across the exposed

Philadelphia Bar on an indistinct trail to Poverty Bar. Although this can be a great alternate route, the one described here leads you away from the river into a beautiful side canyon.

Walk uphill 0.1 mile on the upended sedimentary rock to the signed junction with the Western States Trail (WST). American Canyon Trail is 0.9 miles away. This happens to be the worst section of the trail but is entirely worth it as long as you are careful. The trail—actually a soft-dirt-and-duff single-track that feels great underfoot—is choked with poison oak for most of the way to American Canyon. Wearing gaiters or long pants, or carrying trekking poles are about the only ways to ward off these thick plants along here. About halfway along the trail, keep right, heading uphill on the WST at the junction with the trail that descends to Poverty Bar. As the trail steepens farther along, the WST branches to the right, going in and out of a ravine; and you stay on the trail to the left.

Watch for the small cascades as they grow and slice through the greenstone, guiding you uphill into American Canyon. These beautiful pools and cascades lead to a crossing of the American Canyon Creek, just below its confluence with Hoboken Creek. A sign after the crossing identifies this as American Canyon Creek. But your destination, exceeding even this spot in beauty, is just 1,000 feet around the bend.

Head uphill on a rough trail leading to a trail sign marking a junction with the American Canyon Trail and Dead Truck Trail and giving distances to other locations. Look downhill behind you for a use-trail angling across the slope to the hidden creek below. As you approach the sound of rushing water, the creek and then the pool come into range. Crossing bedrock greenstone, the water pools beneath a semicircular bowl carved into the bedrock. Only by descending to the creek and pool level are you able to see up into the waterfall that makes all of the sound.

The crystal-clear water offers hot hikers a great place to completely dunk in and cool off—totally rejuvenating themselves for the hike out. If you do not take the time to swim in this pristine pool, you might look around for California (firebelly) newts (look but don't touch—their slippery skin coating is poisonous to humans) or water ouzels as they motor around this spot. However long you happen to stay here, you are sure to think of this as one of the jewels of the Auburn State Recreation Area.

Your route out to the trailhead requires a slow escape from the lure of the waters; just retrace your path. All of the important intersections and trail junctions are clearly signed.

NEARBY ACTIVITIES

Another excellent route to this waterfall and pool is the American Canyon–Dead Truck Trails (Hike 33, page 177).

ROBIE POINT FIREBREAK TRAIL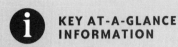

IN BRIEF

You can hike in the Auburn State Recreation Area (ASRA) today on trails that were developed by California natives and pioneers. And the reason you can hike—rather than swim over—them is that the Auburn Dam wasn't built. This reminder of what could have been lost "if" may increase your appetite to see what is over the next hill.

DESCRIPTION

With more than 70 miles of hiking, biking, and horse-riding trails, the Auburn State Recreation Area is a gift for outdoors enthusiasts whose interests vary from fly-fishing to gold panning. Twenty miles of the North Fork and Middle Fork of the American River are covered by ASRA, which is governed by the California State Parks for the U.S. Bureau of Reclamation.

The Robie Point Firebreak Trail guides the hiker through an area filled with the history of what once was, what is, and what once was to be. Heading downhill from the trailhead on broken asphalt, look left and you will see the

**KEY AT-A-GLANCE
INFORMATION**

LENGTH: 5.2 miles
**CONFIGURATION: Out-and-back
with loops**
DIFFICULTY: Easy
WATER REQUIRED: 2 liters
**SCENERY: Foothill woodland;
views of North Fork of the
American River, diversion tunnel,
and Auburn Dam site**
EXPOSURE: In and out of shade
**TRAIL TRAFFIC: This is a multiuse
trail that is regularly used by local
residents.**
TRAIL SURFACE: Dirt and duff, rock
HIKING TIME: 3 hours
SEASON: Year-round
ACCESS: No fees or permits
MAPS: USGS Auburn
WHEELCHAIR TRAVERSABLE: No
FACILITIES: None
DRIVING DISTANCE: 26 miles
**SPECIAL COMMENTS: Heed the
mountain-lion, rattlesnake, and
poison-oak warnings.**

Directions

From the junction of Interstate 80 East and Capital City Freeway, drive 25 miles to the Elm Street exit in Auburn. Turn left at the traffic light onto Elm Street. At the bottom of the hill, turn left again, onto High Street. Pass beneath the Southern Pacific Railroad trestle as you continue downhill on CA 49. Look for the Auburn State Recreation Area sign on the right. The trailhead is 0.2 miles after that sign, also on the right. The number of horseshoes attached to the oak distinguishes this large lot. Your trailhead is at the green gate marked GATE 130—MURPHY'S GATE TO ROBIE POINT.

Robie Point
Firebreak Trail
UTM Zone (WGS84) 10S
Easting: 0668313
Northing: 4307478
Latitude: N 38° 54' 00"
Longitude: W 121° 03' 32"

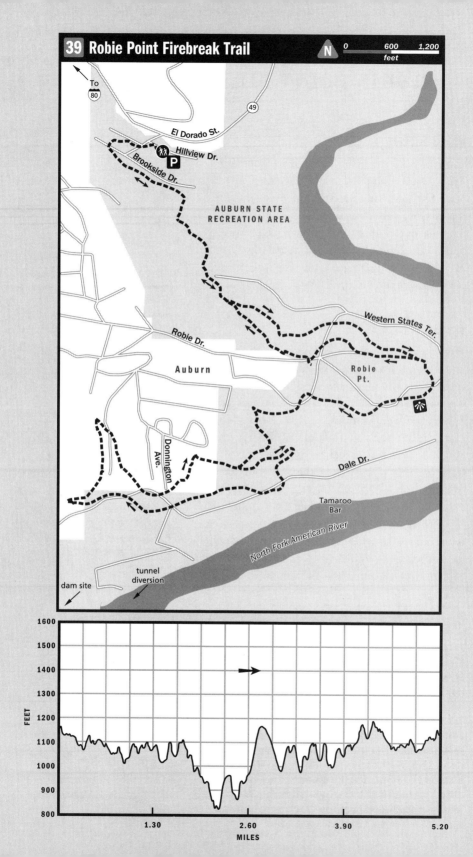

N

0   600   1,200
feet

To 80

49

El Dorado St.

Hillview Dr.

P

Brookside Dr.

AUBURN STATE
RECREATION AREA

Robie Dr.

Western States Ter.

Auburn

Robie
Pt.

Donnington Ave.

Dale Dr.

Tamaroo
Bar

North Fork American River

dam site

tunnel
diversion

FEET

1600
1500
1400
1300
1200
1100
1000
900
800

1.30   2.60   3.90   5.20

MILES

Sweet-smelling buckeye blossoms lure hikers to the foothills in May.

foundation of a hillside homestead just below the trail, which you should take to the right. Your wide path is bounded by lupine, buckeye, and rose. Ignore an old road to the right. Head past the blackberries and meander along the grassy trail. Within 0.25 miles, the sounds of the road diminish as you enter and exit a ravine.

The wide dirt trail heads generally southeast and is occasionally shaded by oak on the hillside above. At about 0.4 miles, turn back toward the confluence for a good view of the Foresthill Bridge, the pylons of which were to be completely submerged by the Auburn Dam reservoir.

A small dirt trail enters your path from the left at 0.7 miles, where you continue heading straight uphill. When a sign says AMERICAN DISCOVERY TRAIL—MILE 2, indicating an uphill track to the right, take the trail to the left. On your return, you will descend to this intersection from Robie Point. Turn around and look down to see the old road cuts and fills of hand-laid stone, which accommodated the track of the Mountain Quarries Railroad. Two of these fills are visible before you reach the point where the ponderosa pines lean over the trail.

As you make your way around the hillside below Robie Point, whiteleaf manzanita will shade you and Indian paintbrush will color the trailside. The path joining yours from the right is the trail you will take on the return to ascend to Robie Point. Shortly, the trail splits, with the Western States Trail (WST) heading right. The only difference is a few feet of elevation: the WST is more level and takes you to the same spot as the other one.

A turkey vulture, common in the foothills, stretches just before takeoff.

Turkey vultures hang out at the vista point beneath Robie Point waiting for the air to warm before taking the leap. From that spot, the entire Auburn Dam construction site comes into view to reveal the terracing, the diversion tunnel, and the western keyway for the dam itself.

The 0.5-mile-long diversion tunnel does not look 30 feet in diameter from this height. It was opened to redirect the waters of the North Fork to allow construction of the dam, which began in the dry riverbed to the right of the tunnel. In 1978 extensive seismic studies revealed the risk to the dam as it was then designed. By the late 1980s, the dam project had been stalled by additional design concerns. The project was later abandoned due to funding concerns. The original riverbed is now being restored, as are the surrounding hillsides and terraces.

Descend, stay on the WST, and ignore trails that enter or leave it. At a distinct fork in the trail, the WST heads right and past a green gate. You will return through this gate, but for now take the left trail, making a U-turn downhill. The trail is rocky and rutted, but there are nice views as you switchback a few times along here. At another obvious intersection, you can take the trail that drops about 400 feet to Tamaroo Bar's rocky beach. However, your route takes the uphill trail to the right toward the telephone poles.

Just past the beginning of the power lines, at about 2.4 miles along, you will encounter a TRAIL CLOSED sign. Just as well, since the trail shortly becomes a paved road. The trail to the right, heading steeply uphill, looks enticing: follow it.

Western Keyway of the proposed Auburn Dam

After a sweat-inducing huff-and-puff hill climb, you enter the cooling shade of a ravine-bound stream. Markers indicate that this is the WST and riders have only 1 mile to go to the finish. Wendell T. Robie was the founder of the Western States "100 Miles–One Day" Trail Ride, and it is in his memory that many trails have been named.

Pass the blackberries along this single-track running through the shade and follow its WST markers to the green gate you eschewed earlier. Now a left turn takes you back the way you came.

When the trail splits after the vista point, take the left fork to go uphill to Robie Point. The trail comes out next to Gate 135, Robie Point to Murphy's Gate–Highway 49, which is on one side of a cul-de-sac; opposite it are Gates 133, Robie Point to Marion Way, and 134, Robie Point to WST. Walk down the trail past Gate 135 to rejoin the double-track you traveled earlier.

Large, yellow-and-black western tiger swallowtail butterflies will outpace you down the trail as they head for the big cone-shaped collection of flowers gracing branches of California buckeye. Other butterflies are also attracted to these sweet-smelling bouquets: Amusingly, the little gray Hairstreaks and California sisters seem to demand aerial battles before they will permit intruders to drink up the nectar.

On your way back to the trailhead, fragrances are brought to you by Chinese houses, lupine, buckeye, California rose, and larkspur. A final plunge into the ravine will cool you off before the short climb to the trailhead.

40 FORESTHILL DIVIDE LOOP TRAIL

KEY AT-A-GLANCE INFORMATION

LENGTH: 10 miles
CONFIGURATION: Loop
DIFFICULTY: Challenging
WATER REQUIRED: 3–4 liters
SCENERY: Foothill woodland forest; spectacular springtime wildflower displays in the open meadows and along trails
EXPOSURE: Shaded more than half the time
TRAIL TRAFFIC: Heavy on weekends
TRAIL SURFACE: Dirt and duff; rock and gravel
HIKING TIME: 5 hours
SEASON: Year-round, sunrise–sunset
ACCESS: No fees or permits
MAPS: USGS Greenwood; ASRA trail map
FACILITIES: Picnic table and pit toilet at the trailhead
WHEELCHAIR TRAVERSABLE: No
DRIVING DISTANCE: 33 miles
SPECIAL COMMENTS: The first half of this trail is bordered by poison oak, which is incredibly thick in places. Watch where you step when you sniff the wildflowers.

IN BRIEF

Meadows with wildflowers galore and easy trails winding through foothill woodland forests provide the backdrop to this easy hike. It is long enough that you will break a sweat, but there is no difficulty in staying on route with minor elevation gain and loss.

DESCRIPTION

This loop's reputation as one of the best all-around hiking trails in the Auburn State Recreation Area is well deserved. Foresthill Divide Loop Trail has a number of access points along the way so hikers can choose to take shorter versions or start from different points. You will start out at the largest of four trailheads on Foresthill Road. Park near Gate 128, Eight Mile Curve, which is your trailhead.

Step over the pass-through and walk straight ahead, with the picnic table to your left, toward the pit toilet and trash receptacles. Your trail is the sand-and-dirt single-track that heads off to the left. It is immediately evident that your trail is shared with nonhikers. Farther along, the trail is generally smooth dirt, duff, or gravel. It does suffer from ruts in some areas, but it has been protected from ruts in other, sensitive areas.

Foresthill Divide
Loop Trail

UTM Zone (WGS84) 10S

Easting: 0677235

Northing: 4315883

Latitude: N 38° 58' 26"

Longitude: W 120° 57' 14"

Directions ———————————————→

From the junction with the Capital City Freeway, drive east on Interstate 80 approximately 25 miles to Auburn and exit at the Auburn Ravine/Foresthill Road exit. Drive 8.3 miles on Foresthill Road to the large parking lot on the left just 0.2 miles after Drivers Flat Road. The trailhead is the gate marked #128—EIGHT MILE CURVE.

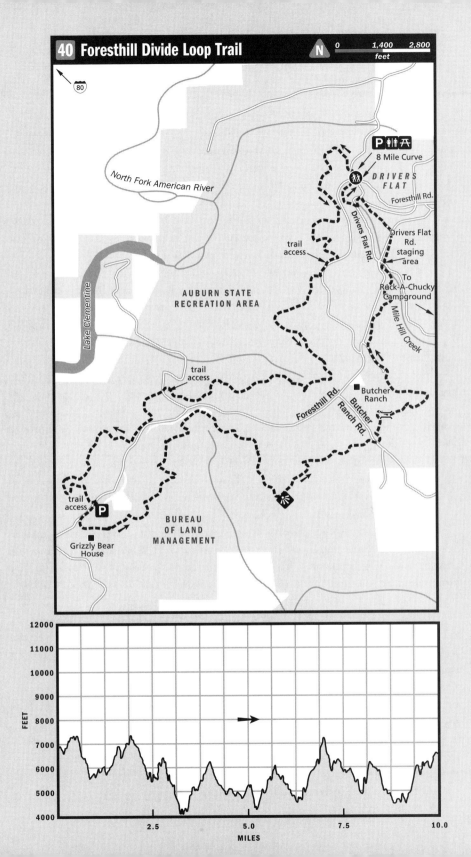

40 Foresthill Divide Loop Trail

N

0   1,400   2,800
feet

80

North Fork American River

8 Mile Curve

DRIVERS FLAT

Foresthill Rd.

Drivers Flat Rd.

Drivers Flat Rd. staging area

trail access

To Ruck-A-Chucky Campground

AUBURN STATE RECREATION AREA

Mile Hill Creek

Lake Clementine

trail access

Butcher Ranch

Foresthill Rd.

Butcher Ranch Rd.

trail access

P

BUREAU OF LAND MANAGEMENT

Grizzly Bear House

FEET

12000
11000
10000
9000
8000
7000
6000
5000
4000

2.5   5.0   7.5   10.0

MILES

A wildflower guide and a pair of light gaiters are excellent gear for this trail. As you head into the forest cover of toyon, foothill pine, live oak, and manzanita, look down to the sides of the trail at the vast swaths of poison oak.

This is somewhat of a cruel irony in that the wildflowers—both beautiful and fragrant—are surrounded by the oily-leafed plant. Staying on the trail will pay off. The flowers you see among the madrone and buckeye—lupine, iris, globe lily, poppy, star tulip, buttercup, blue dicks, pretty face—all appear along the length of your hike.

As your trail heads generally south, you will have occasional views of the North Fork as it flows into Lake Clementine. In midautumn, the display of colors along this trail into the North Fork is spectacular.

Throughout the ASRA, signs warn of the danger of mountain lions. This trail is the same. About the time you read the second warning (the one with bullet holes in it, next to one that says NO SHOOTING), try to sight a couple of very large foothill pines towering above the black oak. Just after these trees, at about 2.2 miles, an open hillside displays its colorful treasures—clover, buttercup, baby lupine, and vetch.

Evidence of bike traffic is fairly noticeable, but some interesting effort has gone into prevention, including caution signs and protection in the form of "tree armor" such as the garbage-can wrapper on a live oak. The trail meanders up and down and in and out of ravines. Additions to the flora now include white fir and the white globe lily—both growing on the uphill side.

Sierra lily and whiteleaf manzanita announce an opening in the forest to reveal a view over Lake Clementine. When the trail breaks out of the trees at about 3.25 miles, the open hillside appears spotted and striped with the blue and violet of blue dicks and lupine.

Continue across the gravel road and walk through the grove of madrone, but stay on the trail. The forest floor surrounding the madrone, and as far as you can see downhill, is poison oak. Do not be alarmed if you happen to hear gunfire from the nearby target range. At the next fork, you will stay to the left, pass a broad, colorful meadow, and then reach Foresthill Road, where you will cross.

Cross the road a bit to the left of your exit, then walk through the fence to the right. Your trail heads southwest to skirt the oak-covered knoll above your left shoulder. The open vista of meadows covered with blue and white flowers waving in the wind is a welcome change of view.

At the next junction with a trail from the right, a sign indicates that you are on the correct trail and that Drivers Flat is 5 miles straight ahead. Over the next mile, glimpse the Middle Fork of the American River 800 feet below.

A trail sign will lead you to the left and down a rocky double-track, which exposes vertically oriented mudstone. You will walk across a few hundred feet of mudstone—approximately 500,000 years of accumulated alluvial deposits—all turned on edge and surrounded by baby lupine, which yields to larger varieties, joined by buttercups.

Fairy lanterns, or globe lilies, decorate early-spring hillsides throughout the foothills.

You will walk in and out of the ravines and feel grateful for the wet areas that sport gatherings of sierra lily. If you lose your way along here, just follow the fragrant ceanothus. Pretty face and sierra iris abound, and a trail sign indicates that you need to descend to the right through more buttercups and lupine and past an enormous valley oak. As the trail turns into rocky single-track, you will reach mile marker 6.

Butterflies are feasting everywhere around this trail and, if you watch the trail closely, you will be able to see caterpillars moving across it. You will occasionally see signs of smaller mammals along the dirt-and-duff trail, where they have feasted on the cones of foothill pines—often leaving surprisingly large piles of cone scales and whittled-down stems.

Within 0.75 miles, you will have an excellent view down into the Middle Fork. You will soon cross some wide-open meadows, which continue to boast a colorful assortment of flowers already seen, and a number of grasses. The trail is now a single-track through the grass.

When you encounter a double-track, turn left onto it. A few hundred feet along, turn right at the trail sign. Cross the bridge in this area, cooled by the boughs of the live oak spreading across the trail. At the next split, the choice is yours. If you turn left at the next trail sign onto a dirt double-track, you will head through some fire-scarred manzanita and downed trees.

Foothill pine, white-leaf manzanita, and sierra iris are common sights on ASRA trails.

Deer prints are all over this area as you pass by a ranch gate that appears to have rusted open. Before the track splits again, you will pass through a copse of live oak. Stay on the single-track that delivers you to the Drivers Flat Road staging area. The road to the right leads to the Ruck-A-Chucky Campground. Walk across the parking area toward the pit toilet. Your trail continues at the sign just past the recycling station.

Sierra irises decorate the flanks of your trail, which passes by two interesting but dead giants. On the left of the trail and perpendicular to it is a newly fallen foothill pine that is just beginning its return to the soil. Compare this to the same species 100 feet along on the right.

Wind your way along the bike trail as it grinds and twists its way up the hill beside Drivers Flat Road. Your trailhead is at the top of the hill and across the road.

NEARBY ACTIVITIES

The Ruck-A-Chucky Rapids Trail (Hike 44, page 230) begins at the base of Drivers Flat Road and leads to picturesque Slug Gulch, where the gold that was pried out of the rocks was "as big as slugs," according to those first to stake their claim.

CODFISH FALLS TRAIL 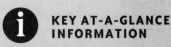 **41**

IN BRIEF

This is either a great hike with a wonderful swim at the end or a fantastic swim with a sweet hike. Either way, this hike leads you to a beautiful 40-foot waterfall with lovely pools beneath smaller cascades. Codfish Falls Trail is an easy trail with interpretive signs along a scenic section of the North Fork of the American River.

DESCRIPTION

You start out for the trailhead by following the wildly curvy, dust-laden Ponderosa Way. Your view to the bottom of the canyon is unimpeded by guardrails as the road hugs the slope. As you approach the river, the bridge across the North Fork comes into view. Yes, you can drive across it, though it is amazing that the bridge is still standing. And it's another good story to tell.

Park next to the river as the signs indicate. Your trailhead is at end of the bridge next to the gate. The trail is visible and skirts the base of the slope to your right as you head downriver. The broad beach to your left is inviting enough as you pass it on the way to the falls. If you have the will to keep walking past this great swimming spot, your sandy trail follows the beach's perimeter and then heads up to a dirt-and-duff trail.

KEY AT-A-GLANCE INFORMATION

LENGTH: 3 miles
CONFIGURATION: Out-and-back
DIFFICULTY: Easy
WATER REQUIRED: 1 liter
SCENERY: Riparian woodland
EXPOSURE: In and out of shade and sun
TRAIL TRAFFIC: Moderate
TRAIL SURFACE: Dirt and duff
HIKING TIME: 1.5–2 hours
SEASON: Year-round, sunrise–sunset
ACCESS: No fees or permits
MAPS: USGS Colfax, Greenwood; ASRA trail map
WHEELCHAIR TRAVERSABLE: No
FACILITIES: Pit toilets and trash receptacles at parking area; pit toilets also located along the trail
DRIVING DISTANCE: 40.5 miles
SPECIAL COMMENTS: The interpretive trail pamphlet was written and illustrated by Heather Mehl as a Colfax High School senior project in 2001.

Directions

From the intersection with the Capital City Freeway, drive 26 miles east on Interstate 80 to the Foresthill Road exit. Cross the Foresthill Bridge and drive 11 miles toward Foresthill. Turn left on Ponderosa Way (bear right at the junction with Eagle Ridge Road). The pavement ends in 0.2 miles. Drive cautiously down this dust-coated road 3.3 miles and cross the bridge to the parking area. (Ponderosa Way can also be reached via Weimar on I-80.)

Codfish Falls Trail
UTM Zone (WGS84) 10S
Easting: 0678357
Northing: 4318824
Latitude: N 39° 00' 00"
Longitude: W 120° 56' 25"

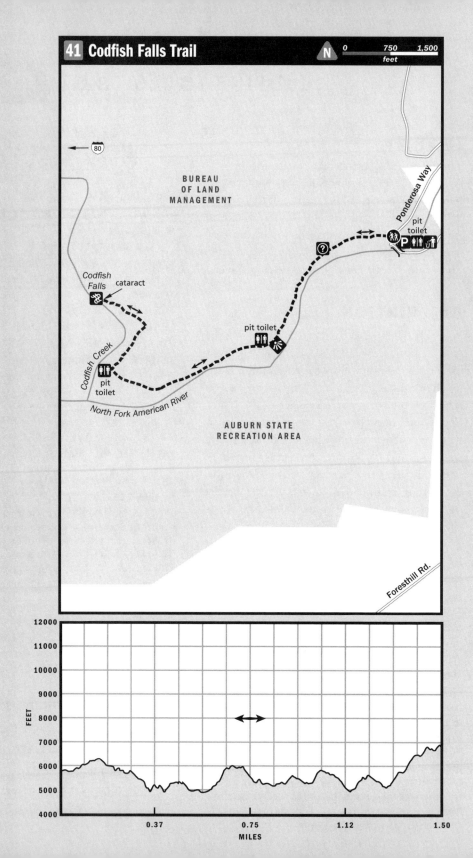

41 **Codfish Falls Trail**

N   0   750   1,500
feet

80

BUREAU
OF LAND
MANAGEMENT

Ponderosa Way

pit
toilet

P   pit
toilet

*Codfish
Falls*   cataract

?

Codfish Creek

pit
toilet

pit toilet

North Fork American River

AUBURN STATE
RECREATION AREA

Foresthill Rd.

12000
11000
10000
9000
8000
7000
6000
5000
4000

FEET

0.37   0.75   1.12   1.50
MILES

The red-berried toyon on your left hides the view for a moment as you pass a hillside of buttercups and wally baskets on your right. In about 1,000 feet you will find a kiosk with, if your timing is right, informative leaflets that describe the flora and fauna to be seen along the trail. Codfish Falls Discovery Trail marks 14 individual points of natural interest over the next 1.2 miles. Refer to the pamphlet for descriptive text and illustrations corresponding to each marker.

Your view of the river comes and goes as the manzanita thins and thickens, alternating with clusters of foothill-pine saplings. The rock-and-dirt trail squirms around a huge shale outcropping as you look down on exposed bedrock in the river channel. Adding to the color surrounding the trail are splotches of red and green poison oak. Although the poison oak is quite pretty, do not admire it too closely. The shooting stars growing a bit farther on may better satisfy your senses.

Buckeye trees scent the trail while tall Douglas firs shade it. Live oak and foothill pine help fill in any hot spots with their own shadows. At a wide vista point, you can look across the river to see the mounds of cobble left over from the dredging operations along here. This spot seems to be popular with animals of the riparian zone. Notice the signs of raccoon and skunk along or in the trail, including several former birds scattered in the kit-kit-dizze and poison oak. The occasional ponderosa pine breaks up the skyline as you continue walking along the river, heading southwest. You may not even notice the pit toilet concealed on the uphill side of the trail. Knock first to give critters time to slither out the side door.

Blocked by a large gravel bar, the river is pushed across to your side of the canyon. The trail, surrounded by manzanita, becomes spiderweb central for a few hundred feet. As you are flailing your arms to clear the silk, look down onto the scour zone, where trees are toppled sideways parallel to the water. Enjoy the next vista from the deep shade of the cool-skinned madrone and towering Douglas fir.

Under cover of black oak, Douglas fir, and foothill pine, your trail begins to turn away from the river and northwest for a few hundred feet. As you approach the 1-mile point, you will see another pit toilet, well hidden among the bay laurel and poison oak, to your left on the river's side of the trail. After turning northward, you will see two fir trees—a large one on the right and a thinner one on the left. About ten feet up in the larger tree is a white-and-blue handwritten sign that reads, DEDICATED TO RUTH MCKEE AND HELEN WAUTERS AND TO ALL OF THOSE WHO SHARE THE JOY OF NATURE, 4-19-94.

Search the ground in this area and you will likely see some type of reptile. A ringneck snake is apt to curl up and display its fearsome red tail as a decoy. These snakes are fairly slow, so you may get to see this more than once. And, you cannot help but hear the tree frogs as you examine this moist, shady area.

The streams may be spilling over their banks as you make your way through blackberry patches and over broken rocks. Cascades to your right make it appear

Placid water pools above the Ponderosa Way Bridge.

that miners reworked the stream's original course. Pools, dams, and rubble piles all seem to indicate that some level of mining activity occurred here.

The stream crossings are easy, although you may get wet feet in early spring. Another stream comes from the right to join Codfish Creek. Almost immediately, a trail on the right ascends and leads you to the top of the falls. From here, you can bushwhack farther up the creek to explore near the Old Vore Mine. In less than 100 feet, you will be at the base of this 45-foot waterfall.

Cascading over bedrock into pools at your feet, the water feeds an abundance of lush greenery. The Indian rhubarb hides everything but the bay laurel. Mosses and ferns cover all the rocks on the periphery of the stream. Depending on the season, you may be able to hop across these refrigerator-sized boulders. Below you are a few small pools that merge into one when the water is rushing. Water ouzels, also known as dippers, peek out to grab at insects that are invisible to hikers. They must be tasty, because the robin-sized birds keep at it quite awhile.

Your trail returns via the beach you saw on the way in. After exploring the falls from top to bottom, you have earned a swim at the trailhead, if you have not had one already.

NEARBY ACTIVITIES

White-water-rafting trips on the Middle Fork often originate in nearby Foresthill. Contact OARS to arrange your own wet adventure at **www.oars.com**.

NORTH FORK MIDDLE FORK AMERICAN RIVER TRAIL

42

IN BRIEF

This trail offers easy access to a beautiful section of the American River. The gravels were worked by miners, and their imprint is faintly visible to this day. You will pass the campsites and debris of former miners and the current camps of present-day gold seekers. Aside from a few dicey spots, the trail is enjoyable all the way to the calm pools below Poor Man's Canyon, where it feels like just you and the river.

DESCRIPTION

The Middle Fork of the American River that flows here, above Oxbow Reservoir, has smoothed over its gold-rush-era scars in the 150 years since the hillsides and streambeds were torn apart by hydraulic mining. The lush vegetation has regrown, and the force of the river has removed most of the waste and silts. The river itself has reclaimed the channels that were given over to sluice, flume, and waterwheel. The Middle Fork was worked by thousands of people living on it to work their individual claims or working as part of a company of others with joint claims.

Your trail begins on the east side of the road at the signed trailhead. The trail heads north, parallel to the road, as it climbs over some talus and boulders of the outcrop above you. Duck behind some manzanita, live oak,

KEY AT-A-GLANCE INFORMATION

LENGTH: 2.2 miles
CONFIGURATION: Out-and-back
DIFFICULTY: Moderate
WATER REQUIRED: 1 liter
SCENERY: Wild and Scenic River canyon, foothill woodland
EXPOSURE: Brief sun exposure
TRAIL TRAFFIC: Light
TRAIL SURFACE: Duff, dirt, and rock
HIKING TIME: 2 hours
SEASON: Year-round
ACCESS: No fees or permits
MAPS: USGS Michigan Bluff; Tahoe National Forest map available at the ranger station in Foresthill
WHEELCHAIR TRAVERSABLE: No
FACILITIES: Limited roadside parking at trailhead, more across bridge
DRIVING DISTANCE: 52 miles
SPECIAL COMMENTS: There are several areas with steep or sheer drops to the side of a narrow trail, and a few areas where some scrambling is required. Trekking poles will be helpful.

Directions

From the junction of the Capital City Freeway and Interstate 80, drive 26 miles east on I-80 to the Foresthill Road exit in Auburn. Then drive 16.7 miles to Foresthill, where you turn right on Mosquito Ridge Road. Go 9.5 miles to the signed trailhead on the left after Circle Bridge, and park on the right.

North Fork Middle Fork American River Trail

UTM Zone (WGS84) 10S
Easting: 0697358
Northing: 4321779
Latitude: N 39° 01' 22"
Longitude: W 120° 43' 12"

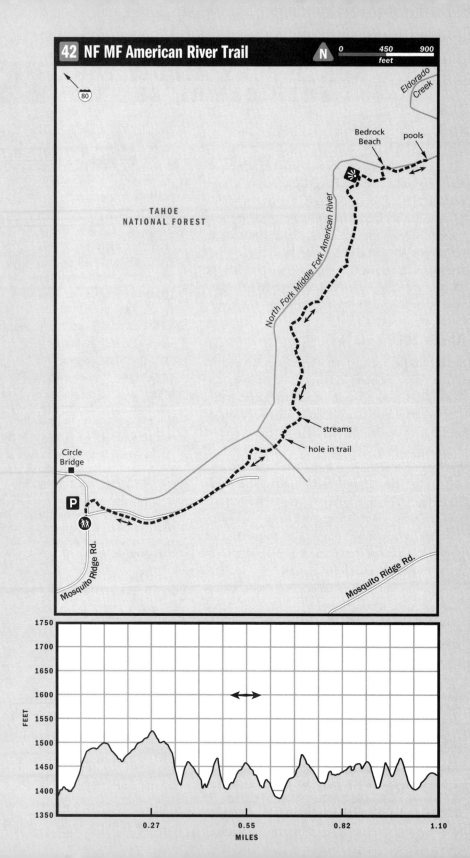

> The North Fork of the Middle Fork has been designated as a Wild and Scenic River.

and Douglas fir on your way around the corner and up past a level spot offering a vista. Your trail turns east with the river, and you can see the miner's camp below on the water. The trail turns again just as you figure out the model of car that settled backward in the trees about 20 feet down the slope.

A steep slope drops off to the left of your trail, which is surrounded by Douglas fir, incense cedar, live oak, and Kellogg black oak. A bay laurel crowds the trail near an imposing, fire-charred ponderosa pine where you walk along this exposed section of slippery dirt- and pebble-covered path. You will ascend just about 100 feet in the first 0.3 miles, and then you will contour along to nearly the trail's end.

The hills surrounding the river are covered with glacial till, most noticeable because it forms the benches 100 feet or so above the river. This geologic characteristic was the feature that drew gold miners to the Sierra Nevada foothills in the first place. Frequent seeps or springs are often good indicators of a glacial past, and you will see them on this trail. And, typically, you will find vegetation abundant in both numbers and varieties, such as here where you have thickly forested hillsides featuring several upper-, mid-, and understory trees and plants.

The trail is often covered with the scree from outcrops of slates, granites, and quartz, which are components of the Shoo Fly Complex. Originally deposited as sediments from alluvial runoff, the rocks of the Shoo Fly Complex were pushed out from the ancient continent, buried, and transformed, then pushed inland, squeezed by tectonic forces, thrust vertically upward, and finally turned 90 degrees, where we find them today. Along the way, molten quartz and granite intruded and now appear as thick gray or white bands.

Just beyond the crossing of the first stream cascading over the trail, at about 0.5 miles, a standing Douglas fir snag has quit standing and it took a large chunk

Down-canyon view of the North Fork of the Middle Fork of the American River

of trail with it when it settled. Negotiate this inconvenience and continue to contour along the hillside. Steep slopes fall away to the left of this narrow trail, so use caution. Although the walking is easy, experience is useful. In addition, trekking poles help one balance on slippery spots. Cascades bounce across the trail in the wet season but should not be difficult to cross. Remember the wet rocks.

The trail is situated on soil that has slumped away from the hillside, sliding down about six feet. This is apparent when you look at the uphill side of the trail along the first 0.25 miles. After a particularly rainy season in the future, this trail will be lowered dramatically as more of the hillside slumps. You will pass outcrops of bedrock slates and sandstones; the trail is littered with their scree and rubble. After 0.5 miles you will walk below a scree-covered slope dotted with bay laurel trees and bushes. Live oak and black oak have shed their leaves here to form a dense mat of duff. Ponderosa pine are scattered across the slope, battling for space with Douglas fir and incense cedar. Amid the trees and bushes lies the colorful tri-leaved poison oak, ubiquitous, if not seemingly mandatory, on all foothill trails.

In the bare dirt sections of the trail along here, you can easily discern the tracks of several mammals, which either wander along the trail briefly, cross it momentarily, mark it as territory, or dine on it. Animal tracks and signs include black bear, fox, coyote, raccoon, deer, skunk, and squirrel.

Cross a rock shelf right after the outcrop. The trail is exposed for about five minutes. When you reach a solitary knobcone pine at 0.9 miles, continue ahead slightly uphill to the right. The knobcone is an easily identifiable pine because it never releases its cones. They stay tucked adjacent to the trunk until the seeds are released—released by fire, which, ironically, destroys the tree, which is not fire-resistant like its Douglas fir neighbors.

When you see a large madrone with two unusual lower limbs—one turns west, and the other turns south—you are near the river overlook. A trail cuts directly through the hillside on the left and leads down to the river. However, you should walk ahead another 75 feet to a prominent lookout, with a great vista of the river's riffles and pools below.

You can descend to the river by walking away from the hearth area to the right, following the cliff side to the river. Steps have been cut in the rock, which makes this an easy descent, if you move cautiously. (Remember those trekking poles?) The steps are often dirt covered and can be slippery.

When you reach river level, climb over the bedrock, back toward the cliff face. Low water levels reveal how the rock has been shaped by the water and how the water has been channeled by the rock. You can judge the river's gradient by looking across the pools upstream from here.

Calm pools await those who scramble upstream on the unmaintained trail toward El Dorado Canyon. Squeeze between the bedrock and a bigleaf maple on the left, and then pass some mining debris. Pipes on the left and a sluice grate on the right, along with drill holes in the rock, testify to the past activity here. Amid boulders the size of a compact car, a rusted steel cable leads down the last ten feet to river level.

Just about 200 feet shy of the mouth of El Dorado Creek on the left at El Dorado Canyon, the large, flat rocks in the center of the river are perfect for viewing the characteristic geology of the Middle Fork. Look over to the other side of the river where you can follow the rock forms right under your feet and on the other side of the canyon. The upturned, folded, blackened, and rotated metamorphic rock has been polished to a shine by the water. It stands like gigantic reams of paper on end, slightly flexed and bowed with quartz and granitic intrusions making it very easy to follow across the chasm as it continues uninterrupted under the water to the south side of the river.

The pools here are slow and cool on hot late-summer afternoons. With rocks to linger on and no rafts coming from above, you may want to relax a while before returning via the trail you came down.

NEARBY ACTIVITIES

This easy trail to the river is an introduction to the majestic beauty in the wild reaches of the Middle Fork. However, 2000 feet above you is the Big Gun Diggings. Hydraulic mining was the man-made disaster that nearly undercut the town of Michigan City and caused it to be moved in 1859. Michigan Bluff, as it is known now, was the embarkation point for pack trains carrying supplies across the rugged canyon to the towns of Deadwood and Last Chance. Hike 45 (page 234) traces the route of this one-time toll road from Michigan Bluff to Deadwood.

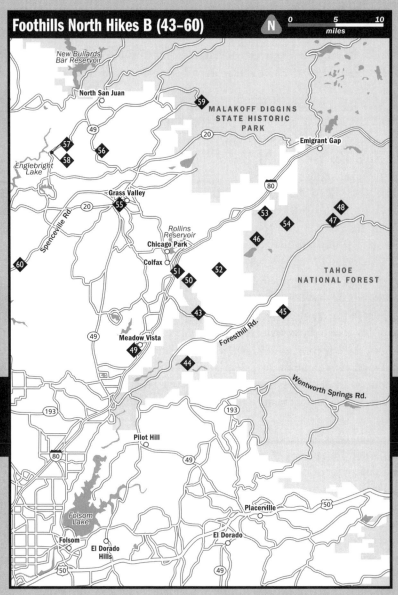

New Bullards
Bar Reservoir

North San Juan

59

MALAKOFF DIGGINS
STATE HISTORIC
PARK

49

20

57

56

Englebright
Lake

58

Emigrant Gap

80

Grass Valley

55

53

48

20

Spenceville Rd.

54

47

Rollins
Reservoir

Chicago Park

46

60

Colfax

51

50

52

TAHOE
NATIONAL FOREST

43

45

49

Meadow Vista

49

Foresthill Rd.

44

Wentworth Springs Rd.

193

193

Pilot Hill

80

49

Placerville

50

Folsom
Lake

Folsom

El Dorado
Hills

El Dorado

50

49

FOOTHILLS NORTH HIKES B

43 YANKEE JIM'S-INDIAN CREEK TRAIL

KEY AT-A-GLANCE INFORMATION

LENGTH: 3 miles
CONFIGURATION: Out-and-back
DIFFICULTY: Moderate
WATER REQUIRED: 2 liters
SCENERY: River vistas and wildflowers
EXPOSURE: Largely shaded trail, exposed on river
TRAIL TRAFFIC: Light
TRAIL SURFACE: Dirt and duff
HIKING TIME: 3 hours
SEASON: Year-round, sunrise–sunset
ACCESS: No fees or permits
MAPS: USGS Colfax
WHEELCHAIR TRAVERSABLE: No
FACILITIES: Toilet and trash receptacles at trailhead
DRIVING DISTANCE: 46 miles
SPECIAL COMMENTS: Plan to swim in the crystal-clear North Fork.

IN BRIEF

This trail leaves the swimmers and boaters behind at the bridge while leading hikers on an easy walk through shaded hillsides awash in colorful wildflower displays. You will be treated to crystal-clear pools on the river, plus secluded pools and a waterfall upstream on Indian Creek.

DESCRIPTION

Wherever you end up parking, make your way to the cables on the east end of the bridge. Some wooden-post stairs leading downhill to the north will take you in the right direction. An information kiosk is to your left. Wander around the old mining-camp foundations and platforms. There were thousands of people working placer deposits here in the 1850s. Old photos show an alarming environmental free-for-all, but it looks as if nature has reclaimed and erased many of the unsightly scenes.

Remember that your path is north, or upriver. You need to cross Shirttail Creek right off the bat. To avoid getting bogged down in the sand and cobble on the sun-drenched river's edge, keep about 100 feet away from the

---

Yankee Jim's–
Indian Creek Trail

UTM Zone (WGS84) 10S
Easting: 0681569
Northing: 4323353
Latitude: N 39° 02' 25"
Longitude: W 120° 54' 7"

Directions ⟶

From Interstate 80 and Capital City Freeway, drive 38 miles toward Colfax to Exit 133. Turn right on Canyon Way and drive 0.7 miles to Yankee Jim's Road. Slowly head downhill 5 miles to the river. Alternatively, drive 26 miles to the Foresthill Road exit in Auburn and then 17 miles to the town of Foresthill. Turn left on Gold Street, which becomes Yankee Jim's Road. Drive 8 miles to the bridge. Parking is available at either end of the bridge. The trailhead is at the bottom of the steps, on the east side of the bridge.

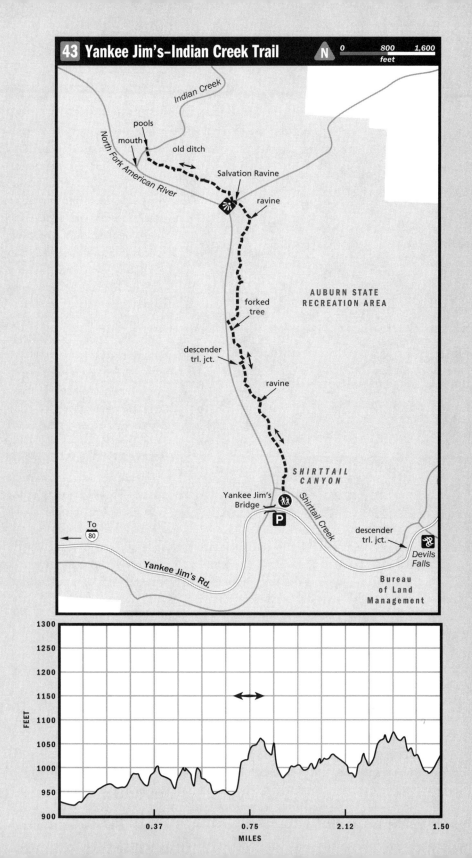

Water ouzels (dippers) feed from behind the cascades of Devil's Falls.

river and mouth of Shirttail Creek. If you do, your path will be fairly clear when you reach the stream. Your crossing location to get to the trail on the other side will depend somewhat on the water level. Boulder-hop carefully, without landing in the blackberry and willows, and make your way to the junction of the trail and Shirttail Creek after you cross.

White-water trips have originated from this crossing for several years. The evidence is seen in the small foundations (with boards covering the basement) that you are walking past right now. These were not for the miners. Continue on the dirt-and-duff trail northward past this bygone toilet-town and duck into the shade of the cool trail. Thistle and brodiaea cluster around the trail as it climbs about 50 feet above the river.

Silky spiderwebs pose the only impediment to travel—the creatures lie in ambush, their webs invisibly traversing the trail exactly at face height. Apparently, wildly waving one's hands around one's head is the recommended antidote for "taking a silk hit." Press on. These adventures will just distract you from watching for rattlesnakes warming themselves on the trail. Fortunately, the slopes above and below are very steep, and the trail is very narrow in many sections, so you will be watching your step anyway.

Enter a small, steep, rock-filled ravine and step across the stream's slippery rocks. Keep right at any trails that descend to the river. The described route leads you right to it.

Protected from the sun by moss-covered live oak, the trail becomes little more than a single-track, wide enough for two boots side by side, with fairly steep drops to the left that are somewhat exposed. Poison oak lines the trail here as you walk beneath the toyon and a laurel tree. Adding nicely to the color of the forest floor, poison oak is often quite red, even in the summer. The color change, in the case of poison oak, is triggered more by heat than by any other factors. Avoid contact with any part of the plant, and wash any affected body part with lots of water as soon as possible.

After walking a total of 30 minutes, you will pass through a forked tree. The next half mile is rolling, generally heading north. The moss-covered branches of live oaks along here take on a fuzzy aura in the splattered sunlight. You can create some spectacular pictures along this section of the river. The opposite slope is bathed in light, which makes the line demarcating the scour zone and the vegetated slope above it very distinct.

Shortly, two ravines and their streams interrupt your path on the way to Indian Creek. The first is a poison oak–bound ravine containing a jumble of rocks. Salvation Ravine appears next, with boulders the size of a small refrigerator. Walk across this ravine and climb a bit at the next jumble of boulders. The hillside you are approaching is covered with clarkia. A riot of purple, lavender, and white welcomes you into the open sun as you head down toward the river. The distinct trail narrows as it reenters tree cover.

Your trail will descend to the bedrock of the river at the mouth of Indian Creek. This is a fine spot to swim or enjoy a picnic. Upstream are a few smaller pools and a waterfall in wetter years. Bush monkeyflower and Indian paintbrush are splotched here and there at this small confluence. The bumblebees have laid claim to this patch and work it tenaciously. Above the creek on its south side are the remains of an old ditch. Hand-laid rock walls directed water around the snout of this ridge that sits north of Salvation Ravine. The ditch is difficult to follow only because it is so overgrown with poison oak, but it appears to connect to Indian Creek just above where the waterfalls would be located.

Descend from that mess across a mound of talus (or tailings) that is totally covered with wild grapes. Be alert for snakes here. A small king snake appeared but declined photo opportunities, preferring to slither under a rock.

Spend some time exploring upstream in the creek. Its secluded pools and many rocks make for an enjoyable adventure. The pools at the river are just right for wading and cooling off. The river is narrow enough that you can test the beaches on both sides. The trail continues for a short bit on the other side of the creek. There are reports that this trail, at one time, continued upstream, where it joined with Windy Point Trail. Perhaps some further exploration will bear that out. Otherwise, retrace your steps to Yankee Jim's Bridge.

NEARBY ACTIVITIES

Kayaks and rafts leave from the east side of Yankee Jim's Bridge. Hike a half mile uphill along Yankee Jim's Road to Devils Falls. A descending trail leads to pools on Shirttail Creek. A rope hanging into the creek will help you out of the water on these slippery rocks.

44 RUCK-A-CHUCKY RAPIDS TRAIL

KEY AT-A-GLANCE INFORMATION

LENGTH: 6 miles

CONFIGURATION: Out-and-back

DIFFICULTY: Moderate

WATER REQUIRED: 3 liters

SCENERY: Middle Fork canyon and rapids

EXPOSURE: Very sunny

TRAIL TRAFFIC: Moderate

TRAIL SURFACE: Dirt and rock

HIKING TIME: 4–5 hours, depending on fishing time

SEASON: Year-round

ACCESS: No fees or permits

MAPS: USGS Greenwood, Georgetown

WHEELCHAIR TRAVERSABLE: No

FACILITIES: Day-use parking facility with picnic table, toilet, and trash receptacle

DRIVING DISTANCE: 40 miles

SPECIAL COMMENTS: High-clearance vehicles are best but not required for descending Drivers Flat Road.
  Paradise Canyon, right at the trailhead, is certainly worth exploring; head upstream as far as the small waterfalls. Kayaks and rafts are put in at the Greenwood Bridge ruins and Ruck-A-Chucky Campground.

Ruck-A-Chucky
Rapids Trail

UTM Zone (WGS84) 10S

Easting: 0680048

Northing: 4314507

Latitude: N 38° 57' 39"

Longitude: W 120° 55' 19"

IN BRIEF

This trail takes hikers past the churning rapids of the Middle Fork of the American River under cover of a foothill woodland forest. The trail is largely level, staying above the river until about a mile before Ford's Bar. Stop at Slug Gulch to explore, or continue along to fish or swim in the pools leading up to Ford's Bar.

DESCRIPTION

The trip really starts up on Drivers Flat Road as you crawl down the slope—hugging the inside of every curve. But, assuming you arrived safely at the trailhead, you can rest easy because this hike is no sweat. There are long, exposed stretches where you will be hot but you will not have to worry about lengthy hills to grind up or navigation problems to solve. There are gold-mining relics and sites along the way, so put your wandering shoes on and head upstream.

The Middle Fork plows through and over the solid bedrock about 100 feet below you as you start out. Since you have just passed the wreckage of the Greenwood Bridge, which

---

Directions ———————————▶

From the junction of Interstate 80 and Capital City Freeway, drive 26 miles east on I-80 toward Auburn to the Foresthill Road exit. Turn right and drive 8 miles, crossing the Foresthill Bridge, to Drivers Flat Road on the right at Eight Mile Curve. Drive slowly down this 5-mile road to the river, passing Ruck-A-Chucky Campground, crossing two forded streams, and passing the day-use parking area and the Greenwood Bridge relics. Park next to the gate marked GATE 101—RUCK-A-CHUCKY FALLS, which is at the end of the road. The trailhead is located at the gate.

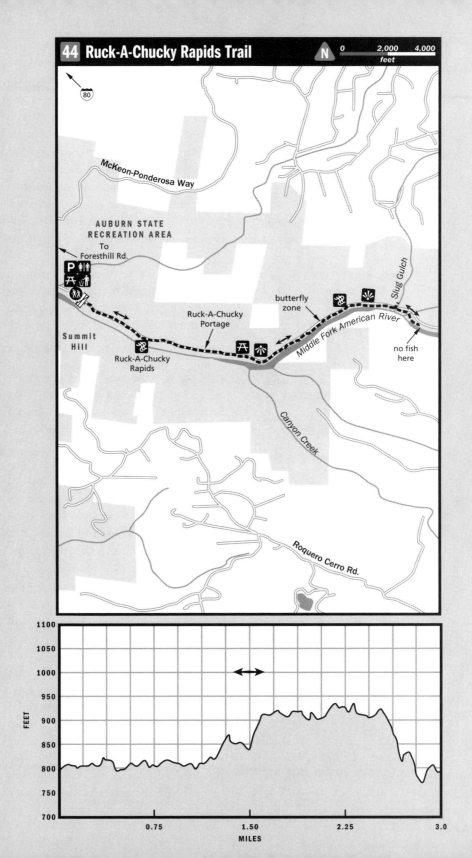

44 Ruck-A-Chucky Rapids Trail

N

0   2,000   4,000
feet

80

McKeon-Ponderosa Way

AUBURN STATE
RECREATION AREA

To
Foresthill Rd.

Summit
Hill

Ruck-A-Chucky
Rapids

Ruck-A-Chucky
Portage

butterfly
zone

Slug Gulch

Middle Fork American River

no fish
here

Canyon Creek

Roquero Cerro Rd.

was one of the casualties of the flooding after the Hell Hole Dam failed, you may have some idea of the power that water has as it sweeps downstream. Look at your trail occasionally and imagine how the sand came to be up there.

Your trail is a double-track that runs along the Western States Trail route from Lake Tahoe to Auburn. For the first mile, your trail ascends or maintains elevation above the river. A few Class III and IV rapids provide drama in the river scene beneath you. From a distance you can hear the roar of Ruck-A-Chucky Rapids—portaged by everyone on the river. Where a stand of live oak to your right suddenly stops, look below to see the portage trail around Ruck-A-Chucky Falls. The trail drops straight down to it—or up from it—right at the live oak.

The trail descends slightly closer to the river while another trail drops all the way down to a conveniently located picnic table and the river just below it. Walk past the picnic table, and the trail becomes a single-track as a beautiful pool appears in the river ahead. The air along here is filled in spring with the fragrance of the flowering buckeye, which grows among the shady, cool, smooth-barked madrone.

The oak trees along the trail are festooned with the vines of wild grapes, inviting you to dally and snack in the late summer. In the early summer, huge flows of bush monkeyflower sweep down the slopes and crossing the trail on their way to the river. Bumblebees and California sisters butterflies are working over the patches fairly methodically, missing not a single blossom.

Ruck-A-Chucky Trail continues downhill a bit along a rocky patch. The river below is shallower, clearly exposing all sizes of cobble and gravel. If you did not fill up on grapes, the blackberries are plentiful on both sides of the trail.

The trail continues to be distinct and well maintained through this second mile. Notice the copious amounts of sand on the path and the occasional cluster of debris in the trees. Imagine the power of the river that caused that debris and sand to land in the branches of trees and on the trail some 50 feet above the water!

Still on a single-track, drop down next to the river through this foothill woodland community. Foothill pine, madrone, toyon, live oak, manzanita, and laurel abound on these hillsides. Sedges line the trail, and canyon or sawtooth ferns cling to moist seeps along the slope above you. Grapevines hang from moist outcroppings or manzanita bushes above you. The trail becomes a butterfly zone among the thick blackberries. You will enter and quickly exit a small ravine, with some pleasant cascades above you. Next to you, the river narrows and turns east.

The trail remains sandy and sticks close to the river, which appears to be only two feet deep and a hundred feet wide now. Boulders the size of a small apartment line the river as you continue along the now-rocky trail. Watching the trail as it becomes chunkier is hard to do because the wildflowers are thick along here. brodiaea, monkeyflower, penstemon, wandering daisy, and more grapes and blackberries greet you at Slug Gulch where miners were reported to have found gold nuggets as large as slugs in the early days of the gold rush.

Ruck-A-Chucky Rapids

The waters in Slug Gulch spill across polished greenstone before tumbling over broken rocks on the way to the river. Climb up the side and over the bedrock, which sits under the cascade, to reach a plateau that hundreds of miners before you have worked. To the left, hand-laid walls are clear evidence of the terra forming that miners undertook to move around the streambed. Walls, trails, platforms, and waterwheel pools are crammed into this tight ravine.

Climb to the upriver side of the creek, where a huge display of rockwork covers the hillside. Explore the paths and try to ascertain whether method or madness governed this construction. A huge clue to this area's attraction lies in the rock, which is deeply ingrained with veins of white, ore-bearing quartz—still visible along the ravine's walls. The pools of the stream are great for cooling your heels after touring the mining operations. When you feel rested and ready for more trail or fish, descend to the path, and continue another 0.5 miles to 1 mile—the choice is yours.

Broad, rocky bars line the river from here to Ford's Bar. Swimming in these calm pools is exhilarating—mostly because of the zero-degree water, and the hot sun feels great and dries anything in minutes. Make sure you have a hat before lazing on these bars. The sun also *bakes* anything—heads especially—in those few minutes. If you are planning on fishing, this is a superb spot to relax while you wet a line. If you plan on actually *catching* fish, there may be better spots, but that just means another hike. Ah, well.

If you missed any photo opportunities on the way in, the river's orientation and changing light will give the scene an entirely different aspect as you return to the trailhead via your original route.

45 MICHIGAN BLUFF-DEADWOOD TRAIL

KEY AT-A-GLANCE INFORMATION

LENGTH: 11.5 miles
CONFIGURATION: Out-and-back
DIFFICULTY: Difficult
WATER REQUIRED: 3–4 liters
SCENERY: Some views of forested canyons
EXPOSURE: Mostly shaded trail
TRAIL TRAFFIC: Rare
TRAIL SURFACE: Dirt and duff, dirt and rock
HIKING TIME: 5–7 hours
SEASON: Year-round, sunrise–sunset
ACCESS: No fees or permits
MAPS: USGS Michigan Bluff
FACILITIES: None
WHEELCHAIR TRAVERSABLE: No
DRIVING DISTANCE: 48 miles
SPECIAL COMMENTS: 7,400' of elevation gain and loss will determine who is in shape and who needs flatter trails.

Michigan Bluff–
Deadwood Trail

UTM Zone (WGS84) 10S
Easting: 0696059
Northing: 4323764
Latitude: N 39° 02' 27"
Longitude: W 120° 44' 04"

IN BRIEF

The Michigan Bluff to Last Chance Trail is on the National Register of Historic Places. Following the supply route to the mining town of Deadwood may not bring you wealth, but it will give you a real sense of accomplishment.

DESCRIPTION

Beginning in the town where Leland Stanford once tended his store, this trail connected the 19th-century mining towns of Michigan Bluff, Deadwood, and Last Chance and was their chief supply route. The markers at the trailhead will give you a good overview into the area's history. The road just to the right of the markers, Turkey Hill Road, is where you embark on today's hike.

Follow the arrow for the Western States Trail (WST) about 0.25 miles past houses and corrals to the actual beginning of the trail. The post on the right will be marked as the Western States Trail and American Discovery Trail (ADT). The WST leads from Lake Tahoe to Auburn and is the course for the annual Western States Endurance Run (100 miles in one day), held at the end of June. The ADT covers 6,800 miles in all, from Point Reyes on the Pacific Ocean to Delaware Bay on the Atlantic.

Directions

From its junction with the Capital City Freeway, drive 27 miles east on Interstate 80 to Auburn and exit at Foresthill Road. Drive 21.7 miles to Baker Ranch and turn right, onto Michigan Bluff Road. Drive slowly 3 miles along this winding, madrone-lined road. Keep right, passing Chicken Hawk Road and High Street. Drive to the end of Michigan Bluff Road and park on the right side of the street, across from the trail markers.

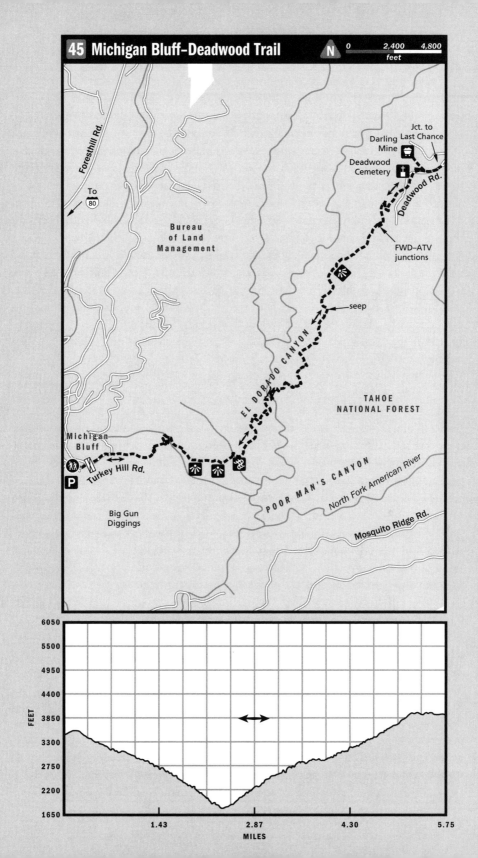

Four hikers were encountered on this normally unpopulated trail: one, from Hawaii, had come to compete in the endurance race; the others, part of a team, were headed for the Atlantic as part of a tour to promote physical fitness.

Head right at the marker post, which you might have noticed also indicates Forest Trail 16E10. There is no mistaking the amount of use this trail has received, judging by the trail's wear at the outset. Although the trail is unshaded for the initial descent, dense manzanita begins to cast shadows on the path when you're about 15 minutes or 0.75 miles along. A few switchbacks introduce you to the zig-zag method of climbing and descending. There will be two sets of switchbacks on the way down and two more on the way up (likewise for the return trip).

Elegant purple brodiaea colors the trail sides where you look down to avoid rocks. The canopy is formed by live oak, white fir, and foothill pine. Within the first 25 minutes, you will have hit your fifth switchback or so (but who's counting, anyway?). Saint-John's-wort leads you into a ravine where the cottonwood has edged out the laurel for prime position—right in the middle of the stream. Continue up to the right across the stream and down mosquito alley. This trail might be called the quartz-and-slate trail for the abundance of both.

A huge knob of quartz shines alongside the trail where you can stand to look southeast at Mosquito Ridge Road, descending on the opposite canyon. Look around on the slope behind you and you may notice the source of that hunk of quartz. Make sure your pack is all zipped before you bend over to examine other rocks. Freeze-dried meals have been seen on the downhill slope where a hiker interested in something on the ground dropped them. The slopes above and below the trail are steep and covered with large outcroppings of quartz.

The arching limbs of laurel, foothill pine, and live oak deliver shade, with manzanita offering its cool touch to hot travelers. Another vista point just ahead gives a broader view of the canyon below. Within the next 0.25 miles, a creek snakes down a ravine to splash against the slate rocks before sliding across the hand-laid slate culvert. Exit this ravine and descend into quartz alley. Here, Douglas firs tower over you and block out the hot sun.

You will head basically northeast for the remainder of this leg to Deadwood. A few intersections over the next mile or so are easy to negotiate, all involving walking straight across a winding four-wheel-drive road that crosses and recrosses your path. Each intersection is marked with a trail marker: WS and 16E10 are stamped into all markers.

Finally, you will arrive at a pleasant stream to cool off in or around. Here in El Dorado Canyon are picturesque pools of water and small cascades gliding across mossy boulders before disappearing under the bridge. California sister butterflies dart around with others while dippers fly into and behind the smallest cascades in search of insects. Rest and cool off while you can. The next ride up the switchbacks starts again just as soon as you cross the bridge.

At the second switchback, it appears that the trail should continue straight, but it actually does a left U-turn to continue up the hill on more switchbacks. The trail is very distinct along here, and so hikers should have no trouble picking

Rest and refill water bottles at this shaded crossing in El Dorado Canyon before a long ascent to Deadwood.

trail from nontrail. The rocky jumbles on the right appear to have been used as dams placed to move the streambed around. A nicely laid wall lines the rocky trail as you ascend. After 3.5 miles, a laurel tree with three trunks next to the trail seems like a great place to catch your breath.

Now you can start exploring a bit on this duff-and-dirt trail. The steep uphill slope to your right gives clues about what happens along here. If you have noticed the scat, the sign of a bear sliding downhill with duff piling up under its front paws as it tries to stop before falling onto the trail, should not be unexpected. Don't let the heavy cover of organic matter stop you from looking around for more secrets along the trail. Footprints and scat reveal what was here and when. Other clues will tell you about these animals' habits. The trails that are convenient for hiking are used by most animals for personal advertising. Their scratching spots and scat piles are everywhere along the trail.

Continue uphill past the wild grapes—if possible. The vines cover the rocks after the switchbacks. A joint in the rock provides a path for water to seep out of the hillside. At just such a seep, hikers have created a small pool by damming the runoff with rocks. Refresh yourself after those last switchbacks and make sure the pool is left intact for others.

Leveling out now, ponderosa pine, Douglas fir, and incense cedar occupy the hillside. The broad, open feeling is welcome, but grasses and abundant poison oak crowd the trail. However, the path remains quite distinct and visible. Continue up the east fork of the canyon until you come to another open vista. Now

Crystal-clear pools in shady
El Dorado Creek

you can look at the terrain you have been ascending and appreciate the task that the pioneers faced. A foraging bear has broken into a fallen snag for ants and grubs. Beneath it, in the trail, are the tracks of a deer and a squirrel.

After about 4.5 miles of hiking, you are about to climb the last set of five or so switchbacks to Deadwood. Continue to ascend a long uphill grade to your destination. A junction with four-wheel-drive and off-highway-vehicle trails will interrupt your path before you arrive at the Deadwood site. Ascend the trail just a bit more. At the top of the trail, a large gateway announces Deadwood Cemetery. Head up a short hill and into the small, fenced, overgrown cemetery.

Two monuments pay homage to the pioneers of Deadwood and are dedicated to their pioneering roles as settlers in Placer County. One is a small plaque on a stone, placed here by the Native Sons of the Golden West in 1987. A larger monument was placed here more recently by friends of Drucilla Barner, the first woman to win the Tevis Cup race. This marble monument lists the pioneer families and individuals interred in this cemetery. The dryer lying beside the fence had no inscription.

Nothing of Deadwood seems to be left. USGS maps show mine locations surrounding the area. Investigation of the Lloyd and Darling mines area yielded no additional information. However, the open hilltop is a good environment for flowers. Gay penstemon, buttercups, Indian paintbrush, scarlet gilia, iris, lily, and Indian pink all grow around this former mining camp.

After you have explored what mine sites you can find, turn around and follow the same route home. Four sets of switchbacks and an equal number of watering spots will see you back to the trailhead.

GREEN VALLEY TRAIL 46

IN BRIEF

One of the most famous of the early mining camps happened to be in one of the most beautiful settings in the Sierra Nevada foothills. The trail to Green Valley, which sits at the widest point of the North Fork Canyon,

---

Directions

From the junction with the Capitol City Freeway, take Interstate 80 east 26 miles to the Foresthill Road exit in Auburn. From Auburn, drive 17 miles to Foresthill, then continue 8.4 miles until you see the sign for Sugar Pine Reservoir. Turn left on Forest Road 10. Drive 7.8 miles on FR 10 and stay on this road until you turn onto a dirt road ahead. On the way, you will pass the OHV assembly area (to your right) and cross the Sugar Pine Dam. When you see signs for the campgrounds (Shirttail Creek, Manzanita, and Giant Gap), continue about 100 feet farther to what looks like a dirt pullout on the right.

A road sign on the right at the pullout says, IOWA HILL, 5; COLFAX, 14; PRIMITIVE ROAD AHEAD NOT RECOMMENDED FOR TRAILERS OR LARGE VEHICLES. A sign that has fallen behind some trees says, WILDLIFE MITIGATION ZONE. Turn right onto this dirt road. This is one end of Elliott Ranch Road, FR 26. The trailhead parking is 2.2 miles from this point here at the paved road. Drive slowly past the open gate at 0.75 miles. Avoid side roads and keep to the right at a junction 1.05 miles from the paved road. The trailhead parking is 1.1 miles ahead. Drive downhill, heading slowly across the water bars, and then ascend a bit. A sign on the right up the hill will say that the trailhead is 0.25 miles to the left.

There is parking here for two cars but no water here or at the trailhead. Walk up to the junction of several forest roads and keep to the left for a few hundred feet. There is no Green Valley Trail sign, but there are signs indicating that this is a part of the Wild and Scenic River system, USFS trail, equestrian trail, and hiking trail.

KEY AT-A-GLANCE INFORMATION

LENGTH: 6.2 miles
CONFIGURATION: Out-and-back
DIFFICULTY: Challenging
WATER REQUIRED: 4–5 liters, depending on season
SCENERY: Wild and scenic North Fork of the American River
EXPOSURE: This is a forested trail with brief sun exposure.
TRAIL TRAFFIC: Light
TRAIL SURFACE: Dirt, duff, rock
HIKING TIME: 6 hours
SEASON: Year-round, weather permitting
ACCESS: No fees or permits
MAPS: USGS Dutch Flat; Tahoe National Forest map
WHEELCHAIR TRAVERSABLE: No
FACILITIES: Parking pullout
DRIVING DISTANCE: 63.5 miles
SPECIAL COMMENTS: You will need a high-clearance or four-wheel-drive vehicle to reach the trailhead parking area.

Green Valley Trail
UTM Zone (WGS84) 10S
Easting: 0691415
Northing: 4336186
Latitude: N 39° 00' 55"
Longitude: W 120° 47' 05"

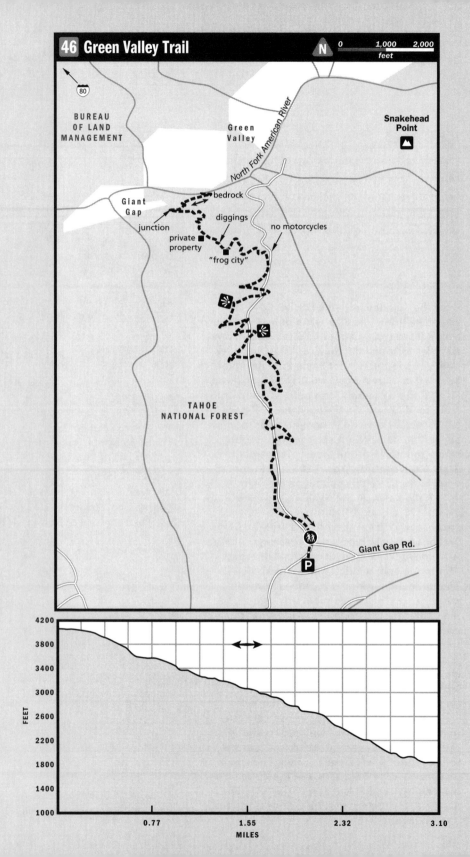

46 Green Valley Trail

N

0   1,000   2,000
feet

BUREAU
OF LAND
MANAGEMENT

Green
Valley

North Fork American River

Snakehead
Point

Giant
Gap

junction

bedrock

diggings

no motorcycles

private
property

"frog city"

TAHOE
NATIONAL FOREST

Giant Gap Rd.

P

Lovers Leap stands over Giant Gap downstream from Green Valley.

descends the ridge via newly created switchbacks that drop 2,300 feet to the river and end at a rocky beach between Giant Gap and Green Valley. Vistas of Lovers Leap and Iron Point on the north rim are rare but impressive.

DESCRIPTION

If you feel like you have turned the family SUV into Nellie Belle after reaching the trailhead parking area, rest assured that the dust will eventually wash off. Gather up your gear, including hiking stick, camera, and water filter (or several full bottles), and start out for the trailhead. In ten minutes you will find signs for everything but the trail's name.

March straight through the opening and keep your footing on the needle- and leaf-covered trail. Black oak, incense cedar, Douglas fir, and ponderosa pine surround the trailhead, closing in as you descend this wide trail. The trees here are similar in size to those in sequoia groves farther east. On the left are ponderosa pine and Douglas fir, with diameters of four to five feet. Incense cedars tower over and out of sight on this densely forested slope.

If you carried lots of snacks with you, try to remember if you left any of them in your car. Before you have traveled a half mile, bear signs and tracks can be found all over the trail. Small tracks are worse than big ones, and these are all small—two prints equaling one size-nine boot. Look for places where some of the larger, decaying logs have been ripped open by bears hungry for grubs as their mother instructs the cubs on dining spots. Claw marks are easy to find in the soft, de-barked wood. Cubs also learn that any snack left in a car is fair game.

Bigleaf maples add a splash of light green as the sun hits them. Deer tracks follow a narrow chute where the trail follows along a downed ponderosa pine.

The bears are not alone: the trail is a game highway, with lots of tracks. A huge Douglas fir root acts as a helpful step when the forest becomes slightly darker. All around are scales that intrepid squirrels have ripped from pinecones. This adds to the duff layer by the bushel. These squirrels must be huge.

At about the 1-mile point, a gap opens in the trees to reveal a view upriver toward Blue Canyon to the east. A few switchbacks traverse the forested slope now dotted with live oak. Another vista down the trail allows views across the canyon to Lovers Leap. You emerge into a grove of bay laurel and manzanita bushes as you descend the point of this ridge above Giant Gap Gulch to the west.

When you reach the 2-mile point, highlighted by the bullet-riddled NO MOTORCYCLES sign, you will have another excellent view over to that huge knob of rock, Lovers Leap. A cruddy hundred yards of steep rock and dirt follow, and then you are back into forest cover. After about five more minutes of hiking, you can cool your face and hands in the small pool at the bottom of the seep coming from the uphill side of the trail. Watch what you scoop up in your hands though. The water pocket is full of tree frogs.

Miners extended their reach about 350 feet uphill, at least as far up as your current position as you cross a mining ditch, pass cabin platforms, and begin to notice abandoned equipment. In a few minutes, the trail becomes more of a run-off watercourse than a footpath. As the conglomerate rocks fade and the manzanita blends with lupine, look for a large green sign on the left, placed there by the neighboring property owner. Follow the warnings and the big helpful arrow and proceed down the trail.

After a couple of switchbacks, you will make a left turn at the miner's luck bucket. It may still have coins and a shovelhead in it when you pass. Switchback down toward the river as you pass through the diggings. A batch of sierra iris colors your trail at a junction, where you descend to the right.

Once down on the water, you can scramble downriver for just over a mile to Giant Gap, where the canyon narrows. The gap results from the gigantic block of greenstone that stands out, nearly closing off the canyon just past Lovers Leap. This narrow gap stands in sharp contrast to the Green Valley, a few thousand feet upstream, where the canyon is at its widest.

You also have the option of crossing the river, if possible, to explore the operations that supported a large mining camp. The trails in Green Valley are reported to be unmaintained, indistinct, and unsigned. They are also on private land: care must be taken to respect those property rights.

After you explore, swim, snack, photograph, or nap, prepare some water and head up the trail behind you. The maintenance on this far-flung trail is impressive: The switchbacks maintain grade most of the time. Brush has been cleared back from the trail, where needed. In addition, deadfall has mostly been cut through.

MUMFORD BAR TRAIL

IN BRIEF

About 150 years ago, miners reached farther east and higher up into the Sierra Nevada foothills to mine the untapped gravels bearing rich loads of gold. The Mumford Bar Trail leads present-day explorers in search of the riches of wild and scenic places. Both groups have found their treasures here on the North Fork of the American River. Mumford's cabin and idyllic pools await your discovery at the bottom of this evenly graded trail.

DESCRIPTION

Your adventure to the North Fork of the American River begins at the trailhead campground adjacent to Foresthill Road. Shaded by Douglas fir and ponderosa pine, the parking area accommodates several cars and has a pit toilet, campsites, and fire rings. There is no clean water at the trailhead. The closest access to supplies is in Foresthill, 15 miles away.

Begin your hike at the parking-area sign, which says, MUMFORD BAR TRAIL CLOSED TO MOTOR TRAFFIC ½ MILE AHEAD. The four-wheel-drive road you are following begins on and leads through a forested area that was (fortunately) left unburned in the 1960 Volcano fire that burned much of the Foresthill Divide. As you walk north toward the trailhead, you may wonder why anyone would drive farther than that last sign on this road. It is only a 20-minute

KEY AT-A-GLANCE INFORMATION

LENGTH: 8.4 miles

CONFIGURATION: Out-and-back

DIFFICULTY: Challenging

WATER REQUIRED: 4–6 liters, depending on season

SCENERY: Foothill woodland; Wild and Scenic River

EXPOSURE: 90% of trail shaded

TRAIL TRAFFIC: Light

TRAIL SURFACE: Dirt, duff, rock

HIKING TIME: 4.5–5.5 hours

SEASON: Year-round, weather permitting

ACCESS: No fees or permits

MAPS: USGS Westville, Duncan Peak; Tahoe National Forest map (available at the Ranger Station in Foresthill)

WHEELCHAIR TRAVERSABLE: No

FACILITIES: Camping; pit toilet available at trailhead parking area

DRIVING DISTANCE: 58.4 miles

SPECIAL COMMENTS: There is no fresh water available at the trailhead. Explore upstream by following the description for the American River–Beacroft Trail (Hike 48, page 248).

Directions

From the junction of Capital City Freeway and Interstate 80, drive east 26 miles on I-80 to the Foresthill Road exit in Auburn. Drive 17 miles to Foresthill, and then continue 15.4 miles to the signed trailhead parking and camping area on the left side of Foresthill Road.

Mumford Bar Trail

UTM Zone (WGS84) 10S

Easting: 0704591

Northing: 4339650

Latitude: N 39° 10' 55"

Longitude: W 120° 37' 52"

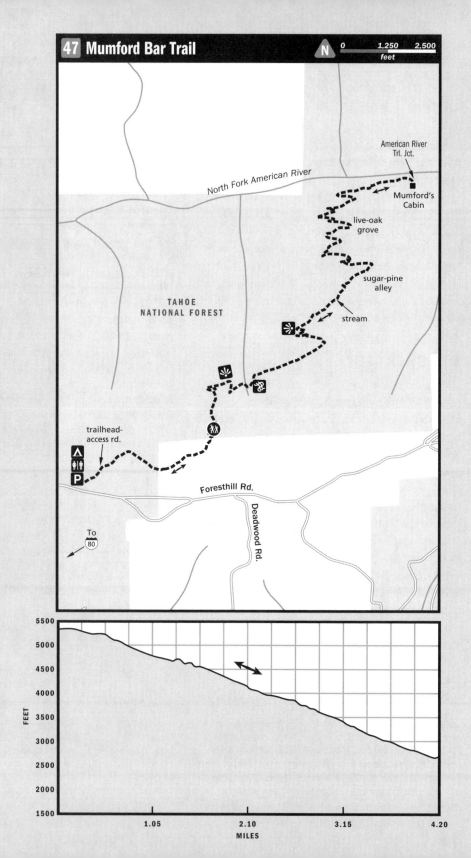

The North Fork of the American River runs over bedrock at Mumford Bar.

walk, but tire tracks along the way show the power of motorized determination.

Despite the trail's looking entirely like a footpath, you will find a conveniently wide turnaround in a clearing at the 0.45-mile point. There is no trailhead here— despite what the sign at the parking area said—just a wide spot beneath a towering Douglas fir and equally tall incense cedar. Push on through the dogwood and laurel as the track appears again to become a footpath before widening enough for intrepid four-wheel-drives. Your trailhead is 0.25 miles farther down the road at an even wider turnaround. The trailhead is on the far left of the circle at a signboard with a cluster of signs—none of which indicate Mumford Bar Trail.

There are two trails to the left of this signboard. Ignore the older trail to the far left, and head down the trail that hooks around to the right behind the signs. Look down to your right as you descend below the signs, and you will see a brass survey marker placed here by the BLM in 1965.

Your trail down is going to lead across three ridges and intermediate ravines. It is an evenly graded route all the way to the river, with plenty of switchbacks to smooth out the steep sections. This 4-mile hike drops almost 2,700 feet, from about 5,450 feet at Foresthill Divide to 2,750 feet at the river.

Descend on the cushiony duff, built up over years of fire suppression, as the trail begins its switchbacks through a forest of huge ponderosa pine, Douglas fir, sugar pine, and incense cedar. Downed trees seem as impressive as those still standing; however, they certainly create more difficult obstacles. The lush vegetation beneath these conifers includes live oak and black oak, along with bay laurel, bigleaf maple, and sierra dogwood.

Continue trending northeast along this long section of forested trail until you come to a vista point about 0.6 miles past the trailhead at a ridge point at

Vista points are rare on these densely forested slopes in the North Fork canyon.

4,730 feet. Sun exposure is somewhat rare, even at the ridgeline. For the most part, your trail is shaded by four magnificent species of tall trees, which are proliferating on the steep slopes above and below you. When you do get a glimpse through the trees upriver, you should be able to see Sugar Pine Point and Snow Mountain up the North Fork Canyon away to the east.

Cross a ravine where rainwater cascades across the trail from above and falls steeply away toward the river. Your trail alternates from rock, to duff, then to dirt and so on. You should be able to clearly see the footprints of small mammals such as skunk and raccoon in the trail when it turns to dirt. A squirrel track may be right next to a deer print, a fox's next to a weasel's. A bear's distinctive print can usually be seen at several points where the bear crossed and recrossed the trail, sometimes just wandering along the trail especially if it is a cub.

Outcrops of the metamorphic bedrock intrude on the trail, belying its suboceanic origin. Formerly alluvial outwash sediments at the margin of the continent, the load became too heavy to support itself and slid to the ocean floor, where it was transformed by heat and pressure into the slates we see now. Before you are able to see them, however, these layers of rock were fractured, folded, deformed, and thrust upward vertically through a series of tectonic collisions and mountain-building events. Further plate movement has rotated these strata, and molten rock has intruded, leaving behind bands of granite and veins of quartz. Finally, a series of glaciations deposited glacial till from mountains upriver and upslope into the ancient ravines, which you are crossing today.

The benches or terraces that held the valuable gold-bearing gravels were those same ancient ravines that had been filled in with cobble, rubble, and till by the advancing glaciers. The terraces you observe and walk along in the North Fork canyon display two distinguishing characteristics of glacial valleys: they are lush and their varied vegetation is fed by numerous springs.

As you travel downhill, look at the vegetation with an eye to how different it is from that in other areas of the foothills. The trees, while normally large, are more on the order of those seen in the scattered stands of giant sequoia and their associated fauna. Stands of black oak mixed with laurel and dogwood add broad leaves to the duff of needles and cone scales. Mature sugar-pine cones are the size and shape of a well-eaten corncob. When you encounter a squirrel tucking in to one of these foot-long cones, they rarely move away but just keep feasting.

Although the vistas are scarce because of the dense foliage, the light that reaches the trail illuminates an abundance of subjects. Broadleaf maple stands add an almost translucent green glow to the hillside. A large ponderosa pine snag towers above and glows with the silvery-gray patina that no less than a century can bestow. When the switchbacks start to steepen, the trail will seem to darken as oaks and maples shut out the light. Kit-kit-dizze crowds the trail wherever poison oak does not.

In the next 30 minutes, you will descend another 1,000 feet and travel about 1 mile. The trail makes a dozen or so switchbacks and yet seems to maintain its grade. This is a lot of downhill: trekking poles can alleviate a considerable amount of shock, normally absorbed by your knees.

When your trail turns northeast, you will be about 200 feet above the river. The trail has been maintained carefully over the years. Evidence of trail building from many years past can be seen on the ponderosa pine with the old Forest Service blaze—a lowercase *i* cut into the tree's bark. Many more of these are visible on the trail. The trail may be a bit indistinct here as it flattens out and the forest opens up somewhat. Look around for paths heading down to the bar to the west. Follow the trail to the east, along the river, to find the side trail to Mumford's cabin. It is off to the right about 150 feet east of the signed junction with the American River Trail, where it sits on a gravel terrace about 75 feet above the river.

Take advantage of low water in the morning to explore the bar on the other side of the river. The American River Trail, on the south side, heads 7.5 miles to Sailor Bar. You can explore the gold workings here, where the river was moved from its channel by dynamite, waterwheel, and flume. The once denuded hillsides and gravel terraces have been reclaimed somewhat by the river and the vegetation. Remnants of mining equipment and excavation still abound, here for you to discover.

Linger a bit to reenergize yourself for the climb out via Mumford Bar Trail. This is the easiest route back to the Foresthill Divide. For those with extra energy, the American River Trail leads up and down along the river and then makes a huge climb out via the Beacroft Trail.

48 AMERICAN RIVER-BEACROFT TRAIL

 KEY AT-A-GLANCE INFORMATION

LENGTH: 9.8 miles

CONFIGURATION: One-way

DIFFICULTY: Difficult

WATER REQUIRED: 6–8 liters

SCENERY: Wild and Scenic River canyon

EXPOSURE: There are areas of very brief exposure to the sun.

TRAIL TRAFFIC: Light

TRAIL SURFACE: Dirt, duff, rock, scree

HIKING TIME: 7.5–8.5 hours

SEASON: Year-round, weather permitting

ACCESS: No fees or permits

MAPS: USGS Duncan Peak; Tahoe National Forest map

WHEELCHAIR TRAVERSABLE: No

FACILITIES: Pit toilet at Mumford Bar parking area

DRIVING DISTANCE: 58.4 miles

SPECIAL COMMENTS: Continuing to the Beacroft trailhead requires a shuttle trip. Have a car ready at the other end, or return via Mumford Bar Trail.

IN BRIEF

The American River Trail guides adventurous hikers up the wild and scenic North Fork of the American River. Once populated with miners and alive with activity, the river works have been washed away, and only a few traces remain. The mature, lush forest that covers the slopes and canyon sides features trees rivaling those in old-growth forests. Views of the canyon upriver are spectacular.

DESCRIPTION

After they descend to the North Fork at Mumford's Bar, hikers are presented with an easy trail ascending the river as it flows between the walls of this steep-sided canyon. If you stopped at the signed trail junction, you can either cross the river to explore the old trail to Sawtooth Ridge, or you can stay on this side and explore downriver to Italian Bar or upriver to Sailor Flat along American River Trail. The trail leads 7.5 miles to Sailor Flat, where there is a steep trail to the divide. Alternatively, you can follow this description and hike the river trail about 2.75 miles to the junction with the Beacroft Trail, which reaches the divide after climbing for 2.5 miles.

The American River Trail begins at the junction with the Mumford Bar Trail at 2,650

American River–
Beacroft Trail

UTM Zone (WGS84) 10S

Easting: 0705826

Northing: 4341870

Latitude: N 39° 12' 06"

Longitude: W 120° 36' 58"

Directions

From the junction of Capital City Freeway and Interstate 80, drive 26 miles east on I-80 to the Foresthill Road exit in Auburn. Drive 17 miles to Foresthill, and then continue 15.4 miles to the signed trailhead parking and camping area on the left side of Foresthill Road. Follow the Mumford Bar Trail to reach the beginning of American River Trail.

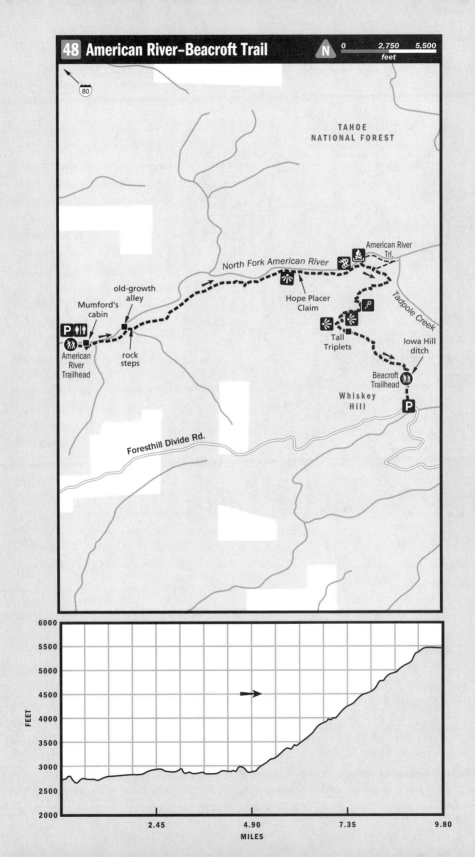

N

0   2,750   5,500
feet

TAHOE
NATIONAL FOREST

American River
Trl.

North Fork American River

old-growth
alley

Mumford's
cabin

Hope Placer
Claim

Tadpole Creek

P

American
River
Trailhead

rock
steps

Tall
Triplets

Iowa Hill
ditch

Beacroft
Trailhead

P

Whiskey
Hill

Foresthill Divide Rd.

FEET

6000
5500
5000
4500
4000
3500
3000
2500
2000

2.45   4.90   7.35   9.80

MILES

feet, and reaches Beacroft Trail at 3,030 feet elevation. The trailhead for the Beacroft Trail is at 5,450 feet above sea level. The 2,400 feet of elevation gain to the divide has many steep spots and is largely without the benefit of long switchbacks.

The gravel terrace holding Mumford's cabin sits about 75 to 100 feet above the river. It is one of the terraces remaining from the last glaciation period, about 12,000 years ago. Mumford's is a square cabin, built from square-hewn logs. The cabin is said to have been renovated . . . when, by whom, and to what extent are all a mystery. Regardless, the cabin looks like it would have been dry and comfortable. Reportedly, Mumford regularly made the hike out for Saturday night dances. One wonders where the dances were held and who dances after a hike like that.

Strike out on the trail heading east from the cabin—the left-hand trail—and cross the stream bounding down the ravine. Climb up the opposite bank, and continue along the fern-bordered trail, which soon crosses another small ravine. Follow the river as its lazy pools stare back at you, beckoning you to abandon the hot trail for a quick dip . . . soon. Here the trees are imposing: Douglas fir, incense cedar, ponderosa pine, sugar pine, dogwood, and laurel.

The trail is crowded with the vigorous growth of understory plants. Fortunately, they hold back the growth of poison oak, which is a constant trailside plant almost everywhere else. The upper-story trees are enormous, and the trail takes you by many of them. A group of three Douglas firs recalls similar groups featured in the sequoia groves of old-growth trees. Keep ducking through the bigleaf maple, laurel, and dogwood while the trail, still somewhat distinct, continues northeast and moves away from the river.

After about 0.5 miles on the trail, climb some rocky steps and cross another stream. The trail is somewhat even now and ascends only slightly. In another ten minutes you will cross a pair of small streams and then weave through the underbrush. Signs of mining activity begin to appear, with small boreholes in the trailside bedrock. While the trail contours along somewhat, the lush vegetation—including downed cedars—makes travel a little harder along here. The river is about a hundred feet below, and you start ascending a bit where a knob looms between you and the river. Continue bushwhacking up and down (especially up), and enjoy the solitude and quiet of the bigleaf maple, black oak, and laurel. At noon you will find this section of trail to be entirely shaded.

After you swing around the knob, the river comes into view just beyond the large, flat terrace or bar below you. The trail has a bit of deadfall on it along here, so your pace will be slower than expected. Duck, swerve, swat, step over, and look. Do not forget to sniff around occasionally. Skunk tracks are seldom seen, but you can somehow detect these animals' presence: they have made dens in the rock cavities along this section of the trail.

The decaying cabin of Ray Long stands to the left of the trail amid a jumble of downed trees. From the looks of it, Mumford and Long were both adept architects and builders. How they fared at finding gold is unknown. Cross a stream about a hundred feet past the cabin, and enjoy a nice vista. The sun shines through the leaves of bigleaf maple, adding a new light green hue to the forest.

Your trail is about 60 feet above the river, which you will rejoin in another ten minutes. Walk out of the tall trees into the understory, cross a couple of small streams, follow a fern glacier flowing out of a seep, and then enter an area on the right that is a bit more open. Blackberries have crowded the trail at eye-level here, so take appropriate precautions. Cross a jumble of bushes beneath Douglas fir and incense cedar before descending a short distance to a campsite at the river.

A fire ring and hewn-log bench occupy a central position above the river. There are also campsites in the trees close to the river, past the log bench. You can access the many pools from points to the left (downstream) and from the campsites upstream. A small cascade and pool occupy the channel just a bit downstream. Across the river is an imposing gravel pile left over from hydraulic miners in the 1850s. How the original channel looked before black powder, chisels, drills, and dynamite were used on it is somewhat hard to imagine. A lot of the vegetation has grown back—with Douglas fir claiming much of the territory held by oaks—and the river has been cleansing itself one deluge at a time.

Fill your canteens and get ready for a hill. It is more than 2,600 feet uphill from the river to the peak point above the trailhead, if you follow the Beacroft Trail. The route described here ascends the Beacroft Trail, which will reach the Foresthill Divide in 2.5 miles. Alternatively, the American River Trail continues slightly more than 4 miles farther, to Sailor Flat, passing New York Canyon on the way. You could then ascend 2,300 feet on the 3.25-mile Sailor Flat Trail to the divide. Another alternative is to hike 4 more miles, to Sailor Flat, covering the entire American River Trail, and then retrace your steps to the Mumford Bar trailhead.

From the camp, the American River Trail continues slightly uphill to the right of the log bench and fire ring. Head east and ascend 150 feet in the next 200 yards. The trail junction is easy to miss, despite its being signed on both trails; both signs are above eye level in the Douglas firs. The junction elevation is 3,050 feet above sea level.

The trail is going to ascend the 0.25 miles to Tadpole Creek and then turn southwest for about a mile before turning and traveling an equal distance to the southeast, after which it continues 0.25 miles south to the trailhead.

With the best vistas at your back, there are still lots of things to see. Naturally, at every rest, you will turn around, place your hands on your knees, lift your head, and say, "Ahhh!"

Streams and seeps are common on this slope. Shade is provided by the Douglas fir and ponderosa pine, which are surrounded by kit-kit-dizze and poison oak. There are some nice groves of bigleaf maple and black oak among the conifers. Start out by ducking under the bigleaf maple that grows under the weight of a downed Douglas fir. Cross a couple of streams crowded with ferns, and meander around the upturned root ball of an enormous fallen snag.

Head straight uphill for a while until you reach some nice vistas at the edge of a slight clearing. Your elevation at this rest stop is about 4,200 feet. There is another vista at the top of the rock-filled chute bound by manzanita and kit-kit-dizze that you are about to walk through. You can stretch your hamstrings shortly where sierra iris grows around the trail in a moderately flat area. Another vista to the west of Big Valley Bluff is at the bottom of a scree field, where the trail skirts to the left before reentering the trees at about 4,400 feet.

As you start to head southeast, you will walk past a trio of grand trees—two cedars and a fir. From this point, you have about a mile to hike, ascending just another 900 feet; there will be some excellent views upriver in about ten minutes. As you near the trailhead, the terrain will level out, and you will walk south across this broad, tree-studded area. The trail enters and follows the Iowa Hill ditch for about 50 feet and then exits it to the right. The trailhead is downhill at the end of a logging road, and Foresthill Divide Road is 0.25 miles beyond to the south.

NEARBY ACTIVITIES

A good overnight hike, with a shuttle, begins by descending the Sailor Flat Trail and concludes with an easy ascent of the Mumford Bar Trail. Good campsites are available along the trail and close by to the river. Alternatively, if you continue driving out Foresthill Road, French Meadows Reservoir offers camping in developed sites and has good fishing.

SUGAR PINE MOUNTAIN TRAIL 49

IN BRIEF

Nestled in the foothills near Meadow Vista, the Sugar Pine Mountain Trail makes a loop that circumnavigates the Winchester Country Club. This is an excellent training trail for anyone needing to prepare for rocky Sierra Nevada trails.

DESCRIPTION

Sugar Pine Mountain Trail circumnavigates Sugar Pine Mountain, coming closest to it at the halfway point on this hike. Your trail starts out on the left side of the entrance to Winchester Country Club and ends behind you on the right side of the entrance.

Just as its name implies, this mountain is home to sugar pines. The sugar pine trees you see here are growing at their lowest extent in elevation. The sugar pine is mainly found a bit higher up, usually in the mixed-conifer belt that starts at about 3,500 feet. The crest of Sugar Pine Mountain is barely more than 2,000 feet. The forest here is packed with the mixed conifers that are normally associated with sugar pines: ponderosa pine, foothill pine (at its upper limit), and incense cedar.

Head south, in the shade, from the 0-mile marker. Frequent trail markers on this

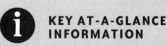

KEY AT-A-GLANCE INFORMATION

LENGTH: 6.5 miles
CONFIGURATION: Loop
DIFFICULTY: Moderate
WATER REQUIRED: 2 liters
SCENERY: Mixed-conifer forest
EXPOSURE: Shade and sun alternate on this trail
TRAIL TRAFFIC: Light
TRAIL SURFACE: Dirt and rock
HIKING TIME: 3 hours
SEASON: Year-round, sunrise–sunset
ACCESS: No fees or permits
MAPS: USGS Auburn, Lake Combie
WHEELCHAIR TRAVERSABLE: No
FACILITIES: None
DRIVING DISTANCE: 31 miles
SPECIAL COMMENTS: For an easy downhill to the North Fork of the American River, the Stevens Trail (Hike 51, page 262) leads to a picturesque stretch of emerald pools.

Directions

From the junction of Capital City Freeway and Interstate 80 East, take I-80 toward Reno and drive 30 miles to Exit 125, Clipper Gap. Drive 1 mile north on Placer Hills Road, and turn left on Sugar Pine Road. Turn left and drive 0.1 mile on Sugar Pine Road. Park at the turnout on the left. The trailhead is 0.15 miles around the curve, up the road on the left side of the Winchester Country Club entrance. It is signed with a 0-mile trail marker.

Sugar Pine
Mountain Trail
UTM Zone (WGS84) 10S
Easting: 0670781
Northing: 4316756
Latitude: N 38° 58' 59"
Longitude: W 121° 01' 41"

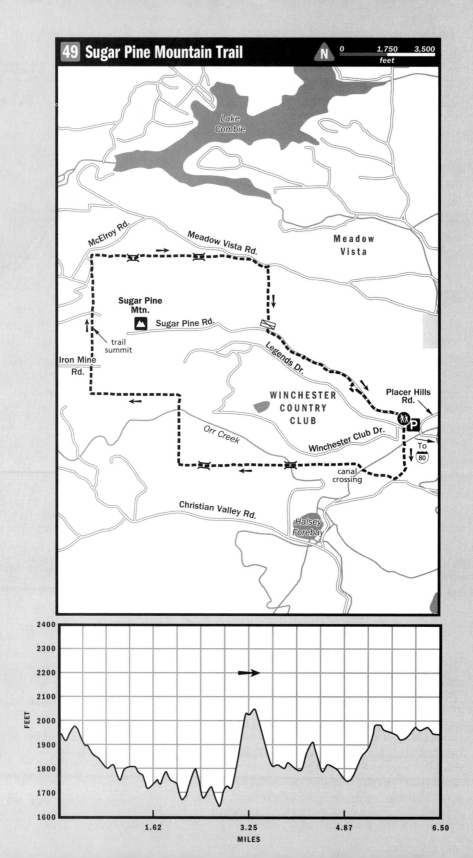

49 Sugar Pine Mountain Trail

N

0   1,750   3,500
feet

Lake Combie

McElroy Rd.

Meadow Vista Rd.

Meadow Vista

Sugar Pine Mtn.

Sugar Pine Rd.

trail summit

Iron Mine Rd.

Legends Dr.

Placer Hills Rd.

WINCHESTER COUNTRY CLUB

Orr Creek

Winchester Club Dr.

To 80

canal crossing

Christian Valley Rd.

Halsey Forebay

FEET

2400
2300
2200
2100
2000
1900
1800
1700
1600

1.62   3.25   4.87   6.50

MILES

Prints in the dirt show that turkey, quail, deer, and raccoon frequently use these trails.

route make navigation easy; thanks go to the Placer County Parks and Recreation Department and the Meadow Vista Trails Association. This is a multiuse trail that accommodates equestrians, bikers, and hikers. Frequent signs depict the expected trail courtesy between the three.

Sugar Pine Mountain Trail begins with a brief climb followed by a bit more in elevation loss. Gain 50 feet, then lose 75 feet; gain 100, lose 150. This continues as you move along the perimeter of Winchester Country Club. Your duff-and-dirt trail soon changes to dirt and boulder as you pass by toyon and black-oak trees. Wildlife do employ a number of camouflage techniques. One clever turkey stood ramrod straight next to a tree, neck stretched upward in imitation of the tree. Eyes unflinching. Motionless. It must have worked: The turkey remained safe.

Quail and turkey pass across this trail, leaving clusters of prints in the soft dirt of this single-track. A sign marks your turn to the west amid a cluster of eight or nine black oaks. Now the path is a double-track, where trail maintenance consists mainly of mowing the grass, keeping the poison oak at bay. After passing the soccer field on your left, pass the 0.5-mile marker, then, after about 150 feet, cross the cart path and road. You can hear the sound of rushing water ahead in the grasses about 100 feet before you cross the Bear River irrigation canal, which is hidden from view until you are almost on top of it.

Ascend from the canal by climbing up the dirt path. Raccoons have joined the turkeys in their gatherings along the trail. Now, your single-track is bordered—or,

Manzanita provides trailside cover for wildlife.

rather, confined—by a barbed-wire fence on the right and a white board fence on the left. An overgrown horse pasture to the left borders your path downhill past an enormous valley oak. An inviting blackberry thicket, ripe with berries that are obviously shared with raccoons, will slow you down a bit as you cross a footbridge over Orr Creek before climbing again.

Your next hill tops out in a small grove of ponderosa pine, where you have a nice vista of the surrounding area. One of the homeowners has posted a graphic, informal, but informative message (perhaps based on a recent personal experience) regarding rattlesnakes. Heed the advice: Rattlesnakes live in and around rocky places. Watch where you put your hands.

This level section, bordered on both sides by wire fencing, looks like it played host to a turkey-versus-raccoon match. Judging by the trail adornments, the raccoon went away the victor. Head downhill, being careful not to touch the electrified fence to your left. Pass under the power lines as you reach the 1.5-mile point. In a moment, yet another footbridge crosses a marshy area thick with blackberries. Stop here for an outdoor treat—jam on a stick. By the time you reach the top of the hill, you will be ready for more.

Black-tailed jackrabbits are easily spotted when their long ears stand out above the grasses and they leap, startled by the slightest movement. Deer, on the other hand, are so accustomed and habituated to humans that you will probably walk right up on one before noticing it at least once on this hike.

After 2 miles, power lines stretch overhead again. But you need to keep your head down along here: The trail is rutted and rocky and footing is dicey. You will cross Orr Creek again as you pass under the lines, but not for the last

time. Follow the trail to the west as you move away from the road a bit. Initially, some boulders will help you climb as you make your way back into the shade. Follow the fence line straight downhill and cross a small drainage after the big boulder in the middle of your trail.

You may find yourself feeling a bit like a coyote, moving from shade to shade for a little respite from the sun. A nice grove of live oak offers the next bit of shade. Descend to your next right turn, heading north across a footbridge spanning a marshy area. Watch your step on the trail after passing the outbuildings. Apparently, the steel fence posts were cut at ground level and now protrude from the trail by an inch or so.

After a climb of about 75 feet, you will cross a stone culvert. Now at the western border of the route, begin the 300-foot ascent to Sugar Pine Mountain. This normally is not a bother, but this is a steep climb with 24 (yes, I counted) switchbacks, none of which was longer than 20 feet. The good news is that when you reach the crest, you have hiked exactly half the route. The bad news is that, after you cross the fire road where the telephone lines end, there are 21 downhill switchbacks. Pass a failed homestead to the left and a downed ponderosa pine on the right, near the end of the golf course. Then cross a paved road just before making a right turn to face east. Walk along with the fence to your left, under the shade of sugar pines.

Another blackberry magnet (posing as a footbridge) stands next to a huge moss-encrusted black oak. Amid tall foothill pines grows a stand of fresh incense-cedar seedlings. This new growth leads you up to the cart path, which you will walk along for a moment before ducking back into the forest. More deer are resting in the shade at the next footbridge. Head down into and up from the next ravine, where you will maneuver around a big obstruction—a downed black oak across the trail. Walk along the road a short distance, crossing Ridgemoor Drive, and continue along the road.

At the next house on the right, the trail turns right, taking you south and away from the road. A trail marker about 75 feet away will confirm your route. With the house to your left, follow the fence line uphill—again barbed wire on the left and smooth wire on the right. Cross a small stream and continue to ascend this rocky trail. On your left is a gate, which is an alternate access point to the trail. There is room for one car to be parked here at this gate on Sugar Pine Road.

Surrounded by manzanita and foothill pine, you will cross an emergency-access road and then take a raised walkway across a marshy area as you parallel Sugar Pine Road for the final mile of your hike. Coveys of California quail often cause a commotion and sometimes flush out browsing deer while they reveal themselves. The soft, loose dirt on the trail highlighted not only turkey and quail tracks but also the telltale wiggly line of a snake crossing the path.

Walk around the water facility as you hike 0.3 miles to the entrance of Winchester Country Club. The trailhead is across the street as you reach the artificial cascades at the entrance. A marker points out that you have hiked 6.5 miles.

50 WINDY POINT TRAIL

KEY AT-A-GLANCE INFORMATION

LENGTH: 3 miles

CONFIGURATION: Out-and-back

DIFFICULTY: Moderate

WATER REQUIRED: 2 liters

SCENERY: Spectacular vistas of the North Fork of the American River

EXPOSURE: In and out of shade and sun; southern exposure

TRAIL TRAFFIC: Light

TRAIL SURFACE: Dirt, duff, rock, scree

HIKING TIME: 3 hours

SEASON: Year-round

ACCESS: No fees or permits

MAPS: USGS Colfax; ASRA local trails map

WHEELCHAIR TRAVERSABLE: No

FACILITIES: Pit toilets at Mineral Bar campground

DRIVING DISTANCE: 50 miles

SPECIAL COMMENTS: This trail offers a bit of vertical exposure; children may encounter some difficulties and should be watched closely.

Windy Point Trail

UTM Zone (WGS84) 10S

Easting: 0679804

Northing: 4328909

Latitude: N 39° 05' 26"

Longitude: W 120° 55' 15"

IN BRIEF

Breathtaking views of the North Fork begin about halfway down the Iowa Hill Road, and they don't stop until you reach the river at the end of this trail. After you ascend from the crystal-clear pools below, drive up to Iowa Hill to explore the pioneer cemetery.

DESCRIPTION

Windy Point is perched more than 600 feet above the trailhead to this old miner's trail leading down to quartz-laden greenstone bedrock at the river. The trail begins behind the four boulders along the road, one of which has a bore hole through which you can see down the trail. The flat-topped boulders are situated perfectly for you to adjust your boots for a steep downhill hike across some dodgy sections.

Bigleaf maple and valley oak shade the overgrown double-track at the outset and then yield to ponderosa pine and Douglas fir as you ascend a short hill. Just about the time that your eyes become accustomed to the dark

---

Directions ———————————➤

From its junction with the Capital City Freeway, drive 40 miles east on Interstate 80 to Colfax. Leave the highway at Canyon Way (Exit 133), and turn left onto Canyon Way and drive 1 mile toward Colfax. Turn right onto Iowa Hill Road, which is paved but extremely narrow, rarely offering room for cars to pass. Iowa Hill Road is not passable to RV's or vehicles with trailers. Continue downhill about 8 miles, and then uphill another 0.8 miles past the bridge at the Mineral Bar Campground. The trailhead is on the right and is marked with four large boulders and a 4 x 4 post with no sign. There is space for a few cars to park at the trailhead.

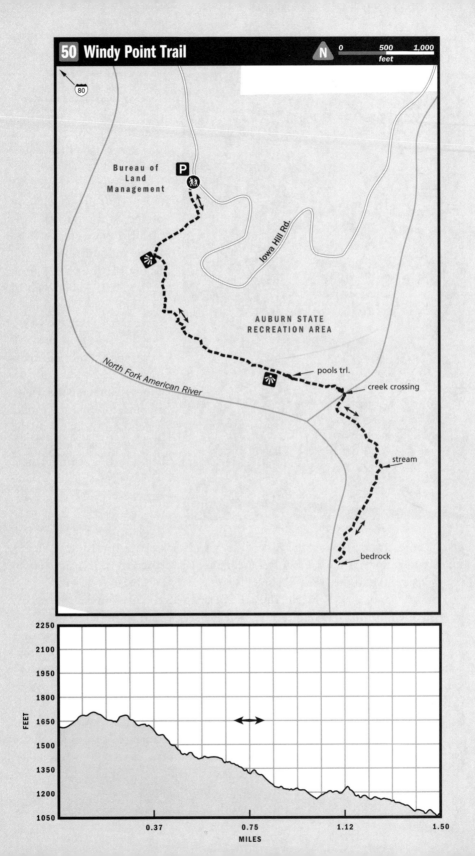

trail, it narrows to a tight single-track and breaks into the sun. Just as you step into the open—at about 0.2 miles—a small rock outcrop on the right serves as a stable platform from which to frame this wide-open vista. Below, the river flows from right to left, generally north to south with some high-angle turns along the way.

In fewer than 500 feet, your trail will narrow to the width of two boots. Although the views are nonstop for a half mile, watch your footing as the trail steepens and its camber is to the downhill side. It is very scrabbly along here, especially where it's the steepest. Using your trekking poles on this trail gives you a distinct advantage as you start into a series of steep switchbacks followed by more of the same. After a couple of large outcrops, you have about 0.5 miles to hike to the creek crossing.

A nice panorama of the North Fork opens up just before you descend across a fairly open hillside on this steeply angled, narrow, scree-littered, slanted and uneven trail with crumbly edges about 400 feet above the river. Take pictures and then descend. This is not where you want to have any distractions. Stop, stand, and look around. Lupine, buttercups, popcorn flower, poppy, and brodiaea splash color over the entire hillside. From up over your shoulder down to the scour line at the river, you are treated to a blanket of blue and white, purple, orange and yellow, accentuated with the green of live oak and foothill pine.

Continue past a side trail that descends steeply to a pair of clear pools in the North Fork. The described hike continues past the creeks ahead before descending to the river. If the first creek is impassable, take this side trail that leads to the river.

Descend some short, steep switchbacks into the darkness of a ravine's foliage and then down a short flight of natural stairs to the creek. In high-water

Morning light pierces the North Fork canyon at Windy Point.

runoff, this crossing may be impassable. Whenever you do cross, the boulders and rocks that you must cross over are always very slick when your boots are wet. Use caution here. The trail crosses the creek at a slight angle from right to left, exiting uphill through blackberries and poison oak. The latter occupies much of the trail margins from this point on.

A second stream ahead is easily stepped over, but it is surrounded by poison oak, and the trail leading up to it is fairly crumbly. Buckeye, toyon, laurel, alder, and live oak provide cool shade along here. This stretch of trail is not well maintained, but it remains quite distinct all the way to the river. It is reported that the trail continues downstream, joining the Indian Creek Trail to Yankee Jim's Bridge, but there is no sign of the trail further downstream.

As you hike out, keep in mind that the poison oak that was at your knees on the downhill hike in will now be at arm level on the uphill hike out. Some soap and water or a wet wipe can be very useful.

NEARBY ACTIVITIES

The Iowa Hill Cemetery has more than 100 decedents in it. Historic documents have left records of their lives, and these notes have been posted at the cemetery entrance for all to read.

51 STEVENS TRAIL

KEY AT-A-GLANCE INFORMATION

LENGTH: 7.4 miles
CONFIGURATION: Out-and-back
DIFFICULTY: Moderate
WATER REQUIRED: 3 liters
SCENERY: Waterfalls, wildflowers, and panoramas of the North Fork
EXPOSURE: Some shady respites but largely exposed on a south-facing slope
TRAIL TRAFFIC: Moderate
TRAIL SURFACE: Dirt and rock
HIKING TIME: 4 hours
SEASON: Year-round
ACCESS: No fees or permits
MAPS: USGS **Colfax**; ASRA map
WHEELCHAIR TRAVERSABLE: No
FACILITIES: Parking lot for about 15 cars; trash receptacle
DRIVING DISTANCE: 42 miles
SPECIAL COMMENTS: Easy descent to river on gold-rush-era trail. Colfax–Iowa Hill Road winds 9 miles up to a gold-era town and a historic cemetery with informative notes regarding each of the deceased. While you can no longer cross the North Fork on Stevens' footbridge, the trail does continue on the south side of the river and leads to its original destination, Iowa Hill. The trailhead for the Stevens Trail South (Hike 52, page 267) is next to the Iowa Hill Store.

- -

Stevens Trail
UTM Zone (WGS84) 10S
Easting: 0677494
Northing: 4330485
Latitude: N 39° 06' 19"
Longitude: W 120° 56' 50"

IN BRIEF

Created nearly a century and a half ago as a foot- and horse-trail between Colfax and Iowa Hill, this vista-packed walk must be the easiest route down to the beautifully wild and scenic North Fork of the American River. Chinese-built railroad beds, hard-rock mine shafts, waterfalls and cascades, crystal-clear pools, and a flock of leopard lilies are all within easy reach of this historic trail.

DESCRIPTION

This descent to the North Fork is enjoyably easy. Of course, the hike in is easier—but the slope on the hike out is gentle enough for hikers of any age to enjoy. One attraction here is the wall-to-wall view of the North Fork of the American River from above Iowa Hill Road and the bridge at Mineral Bar to the extreme close-ups of the crystal-clear water at trail's end.

The Stevens Trail descends about 1,150 feet to the North Fork of the American River. It was built in 1859 by Truman Stevens, who ran a livery stable in Colfax and a ranch in Iowa Hill. No freight was ever hauled on this foot- and stock-path, but anyone could cross the river for a toll.

Your hike begins at the parking lot set aside and marked by the Bureau of Land Management on the left side of the dirt-and-gravel

- -

Directions ──────────→

From Interstate 80 and Capital City Freeway, drive 40 miles east to Colfax, then take the Canyon Way exit and turn left on Canyon Way. Drive 1.5 miles on Canyon Way and, just before Canyon Way reenters the interstate, bear slightly right onto Canyon Court. In 0.5 miles, look for the signed parking lot on the left.

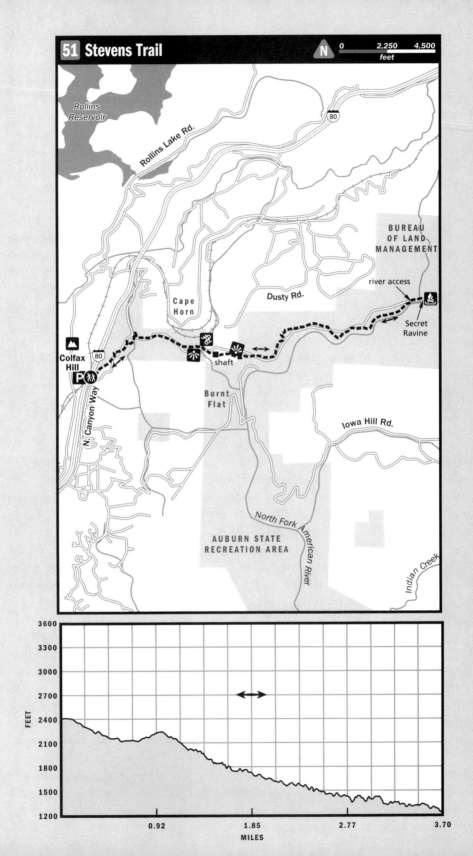

0   2,250   4,500
feet

N

Rollins
Reservoir

Rollins Lake Rd.

80

BUREAU
OF LAND
MANAGEMENT

river access

Cape
Horn

Dusty Rd.

Secret
Ravine

Colfax
Hill

P

shaft

80

N. Canyon Way

Burnt
Flat

Iowa Hill Rd.

North Fork American River

AUBURN STATE
RECREATION AREA

Indian Creek

3600
3300
3000
2700
2400
2100
1800
1500
1200

FEET

0.92   1.85   2.77   3.70
MILES

road. The trailhead is clearly marked at the north end of the lot. There is no water available at the trailhead, but you will have plenty to treat or filter on the way.

As you adjust your pack's straps, the trailhead markers—two signs and two metal posts—will guide you onto a picturesque duff trail that glides down into a cool forest. You will descend about 200 feet and weave in and out of a ravine and over two streams before the sound of the interstate fades behind you. If you are here in the right season and stop at the massive blackberry patch, you will hear plenty of birdcalls.

The trail is quite well defined at the outset. Shaded by fir and oak, your path is marked by signs, which seem to pop up just about whenever you think one would be handy. Just after you cross a creek over a four-by-four footbridge almost 0.75 miles along, be on the watch for a trail sign directing you to the right. Head east on this uphill trail, walking 120 feet up this exposed four-wheel-drive road, which, unfortunately, leads directly into the sun on early-morning hikes.

Pass by the blackberries and buckeye and head for the manzanita and oak at the top of the hill, where a very small trail sign directs you left. The double-track you are leaving continues ahead before veering off to the south across Burnt Flat. (One map lists it as Stevens Trail and shows it tying into the Iowa Hill Road at Slaughter Ravine.) Another four-wheel-drive road turns right and heads uphill to the south along the ridge. You are going to head toward Robbers Ravine to the east at the sign marked TRAIL.

Just ahead, under the shade of some midtrail foliage, is a perfect place to adjust your bootlaces and sip water. Cool manzanitas also shade this spot, which offers great seating on several large, flat boulders. After your eyes adjust to the light, you should see a profusion of bush monkeyflower all around. This spot will seem more precious for its shaded seating when you are on your hike out. So far, you have walked slightly more than 1 mile. Shortly, the trail will divide: bikers take the trail down to the right; hikers stay on the upper trail to the left.

Continue to walk southeast. As you pass beneath Cape Horn, look up and you should be able to see the dry-stacked rock walls laid by Chinese workers who were often suspended in baskets by their coworkers to accomplish these dangerous tasks. Their meticulous engineering and building skills literally supported the railroad across and through the Sierra Nevada Mountains and serve the railroad to this day. Cape Horn has two tracks: the almost-visible one skirting the edge and clinging to the cliffs above, and another that makes a tighter turn through a tunnel under the plateau above.

Look off to the right, across Burnt Flat. An outcrop of upturned shale offers a great vista point for excellent views of the hillsides downriver. You should begin to hear the sounds of cascades in Robbers Ravine. Slow down before entering the narrow slot in the rocks: every rock here is wet and slippery. The drop-off to the right would make a fall very unpleasant. But don't spend all your time watching your step. Keep your eyes open for clusters of brilliant orange leopard lilies right alongside the trail in this moist area. When you find them, look to the slope above, where you will likely find even more color.

Mineral Bar bridge stands midway between the Stevens Trail and the Windy Point trailhead.

Your trail hugs the uphill slope. You have a gentle descent across a talus field, with a steep drop to the right. It is short and likely to be covered with golden poppies and Indian paintbrush. The trail along here is outfitted with the officially required number of toe-stubbing immovable rocks, so watch your step while you are watching the flowers. Delicate, purple clarkia flow across the trail, revealing several minute watercourses.

Your trail is exposed to sun over the next 0.25 miles; just as it snakes along the hillside into some shade, look left and you will see a mine shaft cut horizontally into the rock face. USGS maps do not show this shaft. A more spectacular vista lies ahead another 0.25 miles. From this point, you can see the Iowa Hill–Colfax Road Bridge and the Mineral Bar Campground.

The exposed sections of the trail are conveniently interrupted by the shade of foothill pine and black oak. Large seeps form at joints in the rock, feeding mosses and ferns that grow surprisingly large.

Over the next mile, you will descend along an exposed slope. A trail to the right drops to the river, but the one described here continues left. From this vantage, it is easy to see the water below. There are crystal-clear pools lined by greenstone bedrock, reflecting green light, seemingly unmarred by a single ripple. The scour zone reveals boulders the size of houses, which channel the river back and forth across the canyon, across shallow gravel bars, and through willows, straining the water before aerating it again in a rapid before repeating it all again farther downstream.

As your trail descends through thickets of blackberries, you can see through the trees that the greenstone looks bleached. The still water looks cool and inviting. The steep slopes and blackberries might be reasonable deterrents to diving into the pools right now. You only have about 0.25 miles until you reach the crossing at Secret Ravine. Just before reaching the creek, though, you will pass an easy trail to the rocks at the river's edge below. In low-water years, the drop into the pools may be much easier than the scramble out. So plan your exit point and keep in mind that your hands will be wet and the rocks will be slippery.

The creek at Secret Ravine is very picturesque, but it is most memorable for being as refreshing as walking into an air-conditioned room. The confluence of the creek and the river is less than 100 feet to your right. Air flows over the pools above the trail, cooling the air as it falls toward the river; the air is speeded up at that confluence, creating a cool, refreshing breeze. Voilà. It's a natural swamp cooler.

Walk across the conveniently placed boulders and turn toward the river, where there is a well-established campsite and fire ring. It, like others along Secret Ravine, may be used by miners routinely working upriver. A trail is shown on the USGS map continuing upriver for another 4,000 feet along the water's rocky margin. The original bridge that crossed this fork has long since been washed away, leaving only pieces of foundation and sections of rusting steel cables. Secret Ravine's name seems enough to warrant an exploration upstream from the trail crossing.

An almost-distinct trail ascends the creek on the east side of Secret Ravine. Miners' camps, both historic and current, can be found here among the laurel and cottonwood overlooking some convenient, rockbound pools of crystal-clear water. Tarps and logs provide scant cover for the equipment being used today, or tomorrow, and rust covers the equipment used in earlier days.

Another cluster of leopard lilies is seen on the hillside here, above the moss-and-leaf covered rocks below the trail. As well, other clusters are growing about 200 feet upriver along the margin of the trees. These wonderful fragrant flowers, picturesque in early summer, are vividly orange when other spring flowers have already faded to paler colors.

The pools and shallows of the river east of the creek make great places to cool off. Beach attire here might take into account if miners are at work or the trail is very busy—the area sees the most hikers and miners after noon. However you do it, cool off before heading back uphill. This trail has about 2,800 feet of total elevation gain and loss. The gradual uphill grade rarely requires too much effort, but the shade is always appreciated.

STEVENS TRAIL SOUTH 52

IN BRIEF

This is a wonderful hike to the Wild and Scenic North Fork of the American River. When T. A. Stevens built this trail in the 1860s, his plan was to move people and livestock easily between Colfax and Iowa Hill. Now you can mosey down and up with the same ease on this historic thoroughfare.

DESCRIPTION

This is the forgotten side of the Stevens Trail. In the 1860s, travelers descending from Colfax would have crossed the suspension bridge that Stevens built at Secret Ravine and then would have continued to the gold fields at Iowa Hill, which was a town of more than 10,000 people. The suspension bridge has long since carried its last toll-paying horse and rider. However, at the end of this hike, you can still see the cables that attached the bridge to the bedrock.

Start at the signed trailhead to the right of the store. Be aware that the trail is on private property for the next 500 feet. Walk 25 feet straight downhill to the next trail sign,

KEY AT-A-GLANCE INFORMATION

LENGTH: 7.24 miles
CONFIGURATION: Out-and-back
DIFFICULTY: Moderate
WATER REQUIRED: 2–3 liters
SCENERY: Foothill woodland, Wild and Scenic River
EXPOSURE: Few patches of sun
TRAIL TRAFFIC: Light
TRAIL SURFACE: Duff and dirt
HIKING TIME: 5–6 hours
SEASON: Year-round
ACCESS: No fees or permits
MAPS: USGS Colfax, Foresthill
WHEELCHAIR TRAVERSABLE: No
FACILITIES: Parking on Iowa Hill Road opposite the store
DRIVING DISTANCE: 49 miles
SPECIAL COMMENTS: Easy access to the North Fork of the American.
Gold-rush-era history is vividly portrayed in the display at the Iowa Hill Cemetery, on the left, about 500 feet north just before you leave the north end of town. There you can read how the deceased lived their lives, how they died, and how their peers remembered them.

Directions ———————→

From its junction with the Capital City Freeway, drive 38.3 miles on Interstate 80 East toward Colfax. Take the Canyon Way ramp to the right and turn left on Canyon Way. In 1.1 miles turn right onto Iowa Hill Road. Drive 8.5 miles to Iowa Hill and park across from the store. Note: Iowa Hill Road is a narrow mountain road, often with no place to pass. Curves are tight and no guardrails protect cars from the steep drop-offs. It is advised that large vehicles and trailers stay off of this road. The Iowa Hill Store does not operate full-time. Prepare all your supplies in advance. The marked trailhead is to the right of the store.

Stevens Trail South
UTM Zone (WGS84) 10S
Easting: 0685013
Northing: 4330864
Latitude: N 39° 06' 26"
Longitude: W 120° 51' 36"

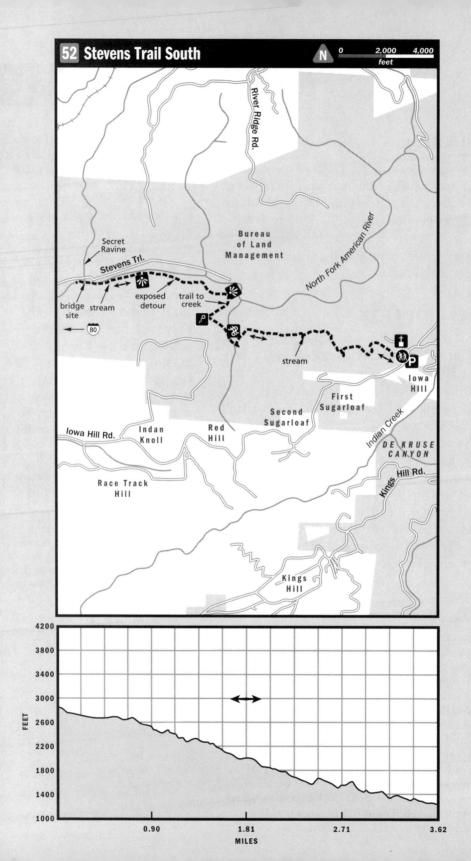

N

0	2,000	4,000

feet

River Ridge Rd.

North Fork American River

Secret
Ravine

Stevens Trl.

Bureau
of Land
Management

bridge
site

stream

exposed
detour

trail to
creek

80

stream

Iowa
Hill

First
Sugarloaf

Indan
Knoll

Red
Hill

Second
Sugarloaf

Indian Creek

DE KRUSE
CANYON

Iowa Hill Rd.

Kings Hill Rd.

Race Track
Hill

Kings
Hill

FEET						
4200						
3800						
3400						
3000						
2600						
2200						
1800						
1400						
1000						

0.90	1.81	2.71	3.62

MILES

and you are now on a line for the break in the trees ahead, where the trail enters the forest. An apple tree with large green fruit will be next to your right shoulder, and a mass of sweet blackberries will be to your left.

Zigzag down among the Douglas fir and ponderosa pine as you notice old, riveted iron pipes—part of the legacy of hydraulic mining that will soon become more evident. The trail is well signed and leads you northwest and then around the debris field, even occupying its outlet stream for a bit. Next you head southwest, where you will begin descending along a ravine. At 0.5 miles, a line of rocks and a new BLM trail sign direct you to the right if you are a hiker, rider, or biker. When you turn right, the bullet-riddled, wooden Stevens Trail marker verifies you are heading the right way (northwest).

The ravine to the right, now choking with shade-tolerant Douglas fir seedlings, was once used as a runoff. The trail is bordered by kit-kit-dizze, poison oak, and manzanita. Some red-skinned madrones shade the path. As you admire them, be careful not to trip on a sugar-pine cone, and be on the lookout for the 12-pound squirrels that eat the seeds in one sitting! No small feat, that: sugar-pine cones weigh up to four pounds and yield about 2,100 corn-sized seeds per pound of seeds. When you walk down into the crux of the next ravine, you will run into a fallen Douglas fir that straddles the gap from trailside to trailside. There is another trail sign on the other side of the ravine just after the treetop.

Your gentle descent takes you past some surprisingly huge black oaks on the slopes above the trail, a huge ponderosa pine next to the trail, and skyscraping Douglas firs below it. A toppled bigleaf maple lives on, despite being bent sideways by a fallen black oak.

Ponderosa pine

When wet, this next stream crossing—steep to both sides—would be a tumultuous cascade, with slippery, moss-covered rocks covering the trail. When dry, it offers a skunk shelter in the deep rock crevices below the path. As you walk along, notice the moss, nearly half an inch thick, growing over the rocks above and below the trail. A century and a half ago, those rocks were exposed and bare. You may look behind the moss and be surprised to see stacked rocks forming a wall: Stevens built a good, long-lasting trail. In fact, a large boulder broke off of the outcrop next to the path ahead and landed on a section of trail supported by a wall that Stevens built. The wall held and the boulder rests in place.

Continue your gentle descent, roughly paralleling the river below until you turn away from it and enter a ravine that comes down from Red Hill. This beautiful copse of dogwood, bigleaf maple, bracken ferns, and mosses is like an air-conditioned room on a hot day. The steep slope above the trail channels the water over large, slick blocks of blackened bedrock so that it cascades down to trail level, pooling before falling over a similarly steep and rocky descent. Large blocks of rock on either side may provide some dry footing.

The pools below you to the right slip away as the creek plummets and you move northwest again. When you can see back through the trees to the opposite side of the ravine, it's apparent that the bigleaf maple, live oak, black oak, and even the dogwood and laurel all share a very shallow vertical space on the hillside. The Douglas fir, however, starts beneath and ascends far above all other trees on the slope.

The ravine some 600 feet down the trail also offers plunging cascades in the spring. Fifty feet after crossing the creek, you can see the water cascade off the hill. The next ravine, 0.2 miles farther, features a spring that flows year-round. As the trail approaches it, ferns become so thick that the trail is obscured. This small yet picturesque seep is a nice place to wet your kerchief on a hot climb out.

In another five minutes, you will see a small trail descending sharply to your right. This trail is not mapped here and appears to lead to the creek in the ravine below. Hiking three minutes more on your trail takes you to an excellent vista point at the 2.2-mile point. The view upstream from here, about 450 feet above the river, looks down on the gravel and cobble arrayed on the river's bedrock channel. That little silver strand gleaming in the sun is framed by the diagonal walls of the canyons towering above it.

There is another fine example of wall building about ten minutes down the trail. At this same spot, there is an example of trail falling. Look for a detour up to the left that goes above and behind the outcrop, or scramble carefully up the face of the rock to follow the trail. Aside from a bit of exposure here, this is an easy maneuver because there are lots of natural rock steps, and the detour is very brief. The river is now only about 200 feet below your position.

Look on the opposite slope for signs of trail building. This is the portion of the Stevens Trail that extends past Secret Ravine to enable miners to reach upstream bars. Cross another small stream as you draw within about 75 feet of the river, then cross a jumble of rocks as you continue descending to the junction of the trail with the river.

Stevens built his suspension bridge here, and you can see the cables at your feet in the duff and brush. Although they may not be the Golden Gate variety, they stood long enough for Mr. Stevens to collect a toll of 25 cents from walkers and 50 cents from riders that allowed him to retire and live in Colfax until he was 80. He was buried in the historic Colfax Cemetery, which is just 0.5 miles from the Colfax threshold of his historic trail.

Thanks to a partnership between the U.S. Bureau of Land Management and the Trust for Public Lands, the private property around the trail was purchased and protected for hikers and other outdoors enthusiasts to enjoy.

There are two different worlds at this point on the river. One is calming, and the other is raucous. If you walk west past the cables, there is an easy access to the bedrock-lined pools in front of you and farther downstream. You can slip into the crystal-clear water by descending to the boulder the size of an SUV—right in front of the garage-sized one. Here you can walk across bedrock into the water.

If you turn back to the right of the cables, you can descend fairly easily to the rocks leading over to the cobble-covered bars. At this spot, not rapids but riffles churn the water into a noisy frenzy. Colorful, mineral-laden rocks line the river bottom and create beautiful images in the sunlight. There is also a small, sandy beach upstream about 100 feet. This area cannot be accessed easily and, judging by the debris discarded there, is not worth the effort.

Swim, wade, explore, and generally lounge until you are rejuvenated and inspired to hike back up to the trailhead. Wave to any fellow hikers on the opposite slope, and wave so-long to Secret Ravine on your ascent. You will find that it is as gentle going up as it was coming down.

53 EUCHRE BAR TRAIL TO HUMBUG CANYON

KEY AT-A-GLANCE INFORMATION

LENGTH: 8.88 miles
CONFIGURATION: Out-and-back
DIFFICULTY: Difficult
WATER REQUIRED: 4–5 liters
SCENERY: Foothill woodland and river canyon
EXPOSURE: Well shaded
TRAIL TRAFFIC: Light
TRAIL SURFACE: Duff, dirt, rock
HIKING TIME: 8 hours
SEASON: Year-round
ACCESS: No fees or permits
MAPS: USGS Dutch Flat, Westville; Tahoe National Forest map
WHEELCHAIR TRAVERSABLE: No
FACILITIES: Pit toilet but no water at trailhead parking area
DRIVING DISTANCE: 55 miles
SPECIAL COMMENTS: Be aware and respectful of private property.

IN BRIEF

If you're looking for an easy way down to the North Fork of the American River, this one is a sweetheart. The word *switchback* has a good name on this well-graded trail. Descend to the river and cross it on the only suspension footbridge across the wild and scenic North Fork. You can discover mining relics and campsites if you continue upriver to Humbug Canyon.

DESCRIPTION

The sign at the parking area points you in the right direction for the trailhead—just 500 feet east. Look to the right for a baby-blue sedan parked backward on the right side of the road. Just beyond that on the right is the sign for the Euchre Bar Trail. Your route to the river descends 1,525 feet in just 1.5 miles. So turn right and begin descending the dirt- and leaf-covered trail. Watch your footing on this trail. The duff is slippery along the entire route.

A trail sign 75 feet down on your left confirms that you have the right route. Rocks line the dirt track, which is covered here with live-oak and black-oak leaves. The rocks intrude on the trail in earnest when the bay laurel and foothill pines begin to appear. When the rocks thin out, the oaks thicken on

---

Euchre Bar Trail to Humbug Canyon

UTM Zone (WGS84) 10S
Easting: 0692603
Northing: 4340625
Latitude: N 39° 11' 36"
Longitude: W 120° 46' 11"

Directions ———————————➤

From the junction of Interstate 80 and Capital City Freeway, drive 51.5 miles on I-80 East to the Alta (#146) exit. Turn right on Morton Road and make an immediate left on Casa Loma Road. Drive 2.7 miles to the second railroad crossing. Continue across the tracks. The trailhead is 0.75 miles down the dirt road. A pit toilet marks the parking area, which fits about six cars.

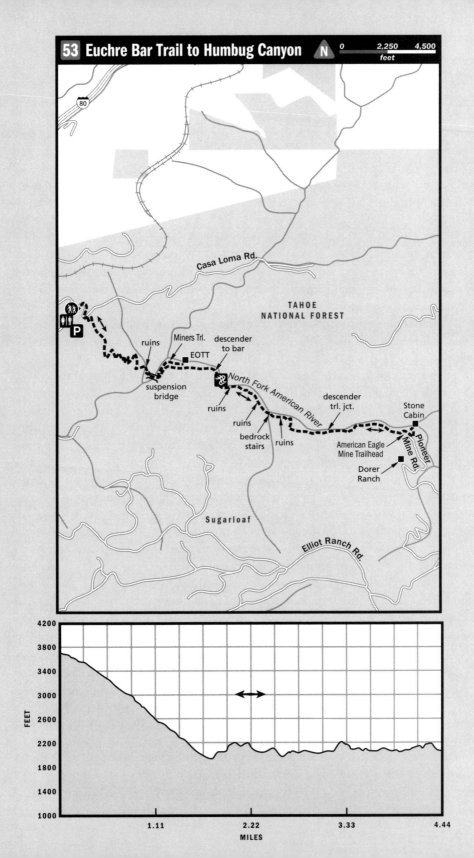

N

0   2,250   4,500
feet

80

Casa Loma Rd.

TAHOE
NATIONAL FOREST

ruins   Miners Trl.   descender
                                to bar
EOTT

suspension
bridge   North Fork American River

ruins   descender
                                             trl. jct.   Stone
ruins   Cabin
bedrock
stairs   ruins   American Eagle
                                             Mine Trailhead
                                             Dorer
                                             Ranch

Sugarloaf

Elliot Ranch Rd.

Pioneer Mine Rd.

FEET

4200
3800
3400
3000
2600
2200
1800
1400
1000

1.11   2.22   3.33   4.44

MILES

the slopes. Face flies and gnats swarm around you all along the trail, so it would be a good idea to apply repellent by the first switchback. The trail flattens a bit after 20 minutes of hiking.

You can see Sugarloaf Mountain and Sawtooth Ridge to the south and east when the trees cooperate. The eastbound train to Reno passes directly overhead as it rounds the point at Casa Loma. Walls built by Chinese railroad workers still support the tracks as they bend around points and span ravines. You can just hear the sound of the whistle fade through the trees as you continue to descend past the first mile.

By 1.25 miles, the trail has enough bare dirt to allow you to follow the tracks of raccoon and squirrel. Switchbacks help your downward journey under Douglas fir, black oak, and foothill pine. In 45 minutes you will see the first remains of gold-mining camps. Concrete pads and bed frames hint at what was a busy endeavor here.

Some rock steps help you over a sizable outcrop surrounded by large river cobble. It is hard to tell mining rubble from alluvial deposits around this heavily mined site. Still above the river, you will see the bridge come into view below, where it spans the river just past some random campsites to the right of the trail. Poison oak stands sentry at each end of the bridge.

When you cross the bridge, built in 1965, turn left and then stop immediately at the fork. If you are feeling adventurous, you can take a miner's trail to its end above Euchre Bar. The route described, and shown on the map, takes the trail uphill to the right, which leads you to Humbug Canyon.

The miner's trail involves 20 minutes of hiking on an unmaintained and somewhat overgrown trail that ends unceremoniously at a sheer drop where a spike remains driven into the rock above a glistening pool at Euchre Bar. A memorable point on the trail is the site of a memorial sign, placed with care on a foothill pine growing horizontally from the slope, declaring the young deceased miner to have been "a good miner, but a better friend."

From the junction of the miner's trail, head uphill on the Euchre Bar Trail and ascend through the fern, laurel, live oak, and dogwood until the trail levels a bit. You can view the Wild and Scenic River down the steep slope on the side of this rocky trail. Thick moss and ferns coat the rocks and boulders at the trail's side. A faint path leads steeply downhill to the river, but you continue straight, as your trail—occupying tracks perhaps built only for mining crews—levels.

While you are hiking at about 40 feet above the river, you can spot cabin sites and campsites all along the trail. Crystal-clear water glides through the pools below you. Look to the left to spot the old mining ditch to the left of the trail. In a moment, the ditch crosses the trail and continues on the right for some distance. There are a number of platform sites above the trail, where cabins or equipment stood. Duck when passing beneath a fallen Douglas fir, and if you did not, sit on the flat boulder just beyond it to rub your head.

Crystal-clear water at Humbug Bar

You can mentally sort among the debris, ruins, and remains to create a picture of life and industry along here. Very little remains of personal life, because the area's vegetation has regrown and occasional floods have washed away light materials and objects. Discarded or abandoned heavy equipment gives the best idea of the sights and sounds in this canyon during the 1850s.

You can view the remains of someone's porch and retaining walls, now holding back the laurel and scrub oak, on the right. Springtime has brought the color of sierra iris, brodiaea, clarkia, and penstemon to these front yards that sit 30 feet above the water. Cross the creek and mount the steps in the bedrock as you leave Euchre Bar behind and head to Humbug Canyon.

Bedsprings, frames, stove parts, broken mugs and plates, and bits of glass are the remains of a formerly tidy camp to the left. A platform of rocks may have supported the pulley and a wide belt as it passed upslope and then returned down to the equipment directly below on the bar. As you look at the wheels and pulleys, the compressors and pipes, the tramway parts, and the scoop buckets, you can only guess which piece performed which operation. More gear and cabin sites dot the trail on both sides as you continue.

Step up over bedrock to cross another creek, and then walk through a forest of Douglas fir saplings. The whipping branches are slightly less annoying than the spiderwebs strung across the crowded path. Use your trekking poles to clear the way.

The trail leads east past vertical slopes that drop from the left side of the trail to the sun-drenched emerald pools. A large seep on the right is cloaked

> Cross the bridge and turn left—
> twice if you want to go to the End of
> the Trail (EOTT).

in oversized ferns. Then cross a narrow cascade that bounces over the trail and begin to descend to the river as the canyon walls widen. A large round metal sheet is attached to a Douglas fir on the left: no writing, no drawing, just a blank white sheet of round metal.

The trail widens to road width as you approach the Dorer Ranch. The large Douglas fir in the center of a cluster of roads and trails is the trailhead for the American Eagle Mine Trail. Uphill to the right is the ranch, and it should be avoided as it is private property. Turn left and head down any of the roads or trails toward the river. Here, at Humbug Creek and the North Fork, you can rest before the return trip.

The ranch owner has made some improvements at the river's confluence with Humbug Creek. Respect this private property as you enjoy the pools and slides. Refresh yourself for the hike back to the bridge, and then prepare for an uphill hike to the trailhead.

NEARBY ACTIVITIES

The American Eagle Mine Trail, Hike 54 (see facing page), begins where this hike ends. If you have the energy, it is an exciting trail to interesting mining sites.

AMERICAN EAGLE MINE TRAIL  54

IN BRIEF

American Eagle Mine Trail takes off where Euchre Bar Trail ends. Hiking east on this section of Wild and Scenic River offers hikers choices of relaxing in the river's pools, exploring century-and-a-half-old mining operations, and observing the plentiful flora and fauna along the trail.

DESCRIPTION

If you followed the Euchre Bar Trail to its end below Dorer Ranch, you have had a taste of the river, the flora, and some of the antique mining contraptions. The trailhead for the American Eagle Mine Trail is located at the Douglas fir in the middle of the trail and road junctions below Dorer Ranch where the Euchre Bar Trail ends (Hike 53, previously profiled). Continue downhill to the river and its confluence with Humbug Creek.

If you are hanging around the pools on the river, the rope will help you scramble up its slick sides. The trail crosses Humbug

KEY AT-A-GLANCE INFORMATION

LENGTH: 2.14 miles
CONFIGURATION: Out-and-back
DIFFICULTY: Moderate
WATER REQUIRED: 1 liter
SCENERY: Wild and Scenic River, gold-rush-era remains
EXPOSURE: Shaded trail, with some sunny patches
TRAIL TRAFFIC: Light
TRAIL SURFACE: Duff, dirt, and rock
HIKING TIME: 2.5 hours
SEASON: Year-round
ACCESS: No fees or permits
MAPS: USGS Westville; Tahoe National Forest map
WHEELCHAIR TRAVERSABLE: No
FACILITIES: None
DRIVING DISTANCE: 55 miles
SPECIAL COMMENTS: Mining equipment and cabin sites

Directions

The best way to reach the trailhead is from the end of Euchre Bar Trail. From the junction of Interstate 80 and the Capital City Freeway, drive 51.5 miles on I-80 East to the Alta (#146) exit. Turn right on Morton Road and make an immediate left on Casa Loma Road. Drive 2.7 miles to the second railroad crossing. Continue across the tracks. The trailhead is 0.75 miles down the dirt road. A pit toilet marks the parking area, which fits about six cars.

An alternate approach to the trailhead is from Foresthill Divide Road: take Elliott Ranch Road to a trailhead on the gated Dorer Ranch Road. This is a dusty and sun-drenched road with few views.

American Eagle
Mine Trail
UTM Zone (WGS84) 10S
Easting: 0696290
Northing: 4338960
Latitude: N 39° 10' 39"
Longitude: W 120° 43' 39"

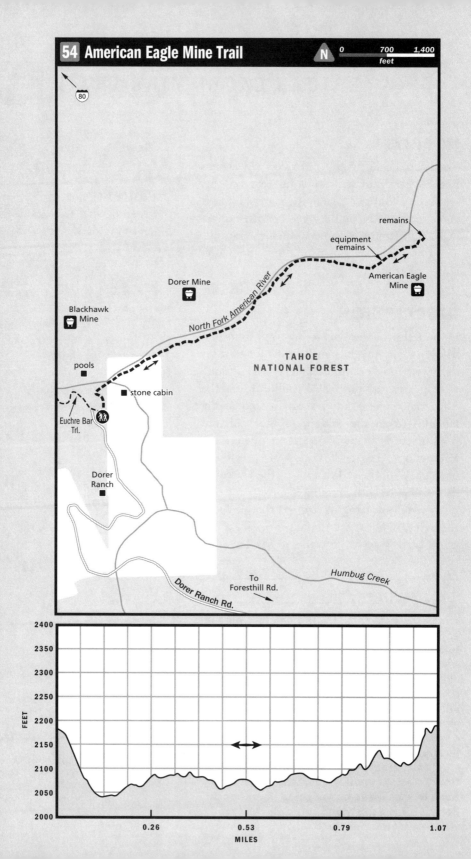

N

0   700   1,400
feet

80

remains

equipment
remains

American Eagle
Mine

Dorer Mine

North Fork American River

Blackhawk
Mine

T A H O E
N A T I O N A L   F O R E S T

pools

stone cabin

Euchre Bar
Trl.

Dorer
Ranch

Humbug Creek

To
Foresthill Rd.

Dorer Ranch Rd.

2400
2350
2300
2250
2200
2150
2100
2050
2000

FEET

0.26   0.53   0.79   1.07
MILES

Trekking poles can be used to support heavy mining equipment.

Creek at its mouth. Walk past the hammock strung next to the trail—without stopping—and ascend the bank on a short, sandy path. Within about 75 feet, look for a faint path leading slightly uphill and back to the right into some patchy bushes. Push on through, and within 50 feet you will see a roofless stone cabin standing on the bank above Humbug Creek.

Square on the inside, with doors, windows, and a hearth, this cabin is solid, if not windproof. It appears as if someone was trying to make a nice appearance here—perhaps for an understanding partner—by building a comfortable, albeit temporary, home. The most treasured and missed "accoutrement" of the gold camps was a wife, or a woman of any sort, actually. Trails lead to the creek and river, which was probably the builder's workplace.

Return to the trail and head east past some scrawny blackberries, where the trail broadens considerably. The path is clear for a few minutes, making for easy hiking as it contours alongside the river. Then, just like that, the trail becomes overgrown with bushes, seedlings, poison oak, face flies, and mosquitoes. Cross some logs, and the trail once again widens. California sisters butterflies linger trailside, providing color above the tree-shaded and duff-covered forest floor.

Rock walls built to support the fills the trail crosses still hold their position. These improvements on the local trails enabled the workers to move around the diggings efficiently: these were the miners' sidewalks and thoroughfares.

The river is about 15 feet below the trail now as you travel east. Wider and much calmer in this flat section, the pools look very inviting. Side trails will take you down for a brief dip. After that, keep following the old iron pipe that runs at least 500 feet alongside the trail on the right. It looks as if it was hastily sunk into the slope and then laid on top of the ground to bring spring water to those living along the river, near their claims.

Climb a bit and barge forward when the trail closes in on you. The river canyon's walls are vertical now, and you pass above them on the narrow trail. Mining remains lie mostly above the trail. A large fremontia, with its softball-mitt-sized leaves, crowds the trail on the right. Pass this bush, then pass a seep emerging from above the trail. Continue east for another ten minutes. The apparatus you see now is from the American Eagle Mine, which is technically about 200 feet above you.

Equipment, strange and primitive, rusting and overturned, is scattered about beneath the mine site. Well above the trail is a very large steel pipe, purpose unknown, held in place by laurel and oak. Adjacent to the trail, on the river side, is another mysterious mechanism. A steel octopus may best describe this possible exhaust manifold cowering beneath a bigleaf maple. There is another interesting piece of gear on the uphill side of the trail. This equipment, possibly an air compressor, looks as if it was once housed beneath a roofed enclosure and ran a belt of some kind on each side. Similar devices and wheels are also seen downslope.

Heading farther up the trail, the route east becomes crowded with underbrush and dissolves into the forest in another ten minutes. You may consider the trail to have ended when you discover another piece of overturned gear. An air compressor, manufactured in 1911 by Gardener Gov. Co., sits idle and rusting. Nearby, some iron spikes have been pounded into the rock, and then the forest closes off further travel.

On your return to the trailhead at Euchre Bar, look around for more remains. You will find tramway equipment manufactured in San Francisco, steel cables, flywheels, shovels and buckets, stove parts, and rockworks. The trek down was pretty easy. The trip up is not much more difficult since you have discoveries to talk about while you slowly ascend to your car.

NEARBY ACTIVITIES

The Green Valley Trail (Hike 46, page 239) takes hikers down a ridgeline from the trailhead on the Foresthill Divide to the Wild and Scenic River downstream from the Euchre Bar footbridge and just upstream of Giant Gap with spectacular views of Lovers Leap.

HARDROCK TRAIL

IN BRIEF

The Hardrock Trail loops around the 800-acre Empire Mine State Historic Park, guiding hikers through the relics of the region's richest gold-mining area. Additional loops adjoin this trail, allowing hikers to create their own routes for exploring some of the many other mine operations.

DESCRIPTION

Hardrock mining came to Nevada County in 1850 when George Knight discovered gold—literally a mountain of it. The Mother Lode he unearthed not only was one of the richest gold deposits in the world but also became the descriptive name for the entire region. More than half of California's gold production came from the mines in this area, with the Empire Mine and the North Star Mine yielding the greatest share of riches.

The Hardrock Trail begins at Penn Gate, which is close to the old Pennsylvania Mine site. The Pennsylvania Mine was one of many dotting the park grounds. In the 1850s, mine shafts were blasted, drilled, and dug in every direction to extract gold-bearing ore for further processing. Ore was crushed to sand by the numerous and noisy stamp mills. The resulting ore dust was treated with

KEY AT-A-GLANCE INFORMATION

LENGTH: 4.2 miles

CONFIGURATION: Connected loops

DIFFICULTY: Easy

WATER REQUIRED: 1 liter

SCENERY: Foothill woodland, historic mining relics and buildings

EXPOSURE: Mostly shaded

TRAIL TRAFFIC: Moderate

TRAIL SURFACE: Dirt and duff, gravel and sand

HIKING TIME: 2 hours

SEASON: Year-round, sunrise–sunset

ACCESS: $6 fee at visitor center

MAPS: USGS Grass Valley; local trail map available in visitor center

FACILITIES: Parking at Penn Gate is free; restrooms at visitor center

WHEELCHAIR TRAVERSABLE: No

DRIVING DISTANCE: 48 miles

SPECIAL COMMENTS: Hazardous-waste cleanup has temporarily closed some portions of the trails.

Directions ———————→

From Interstate 80 East and the Capital City freeway, drive 24 miles east to Auburn. Take the CA 49 exit northbound to Grass Valley. Drive about 22 miles to the Empire Street exit and turn right, onto West Empire Street. Cross South Auburn Street and continue 0.3 miles on East Empire Street to the Penn Gate trailhead parking area on the right.

Hardrock Trail

UTM Zone (WGS84) 10S

Easting: 0667753

Northing: 4341808

Latitude: N 39° 12' 33"

Longitude: W 121° 03' 25"

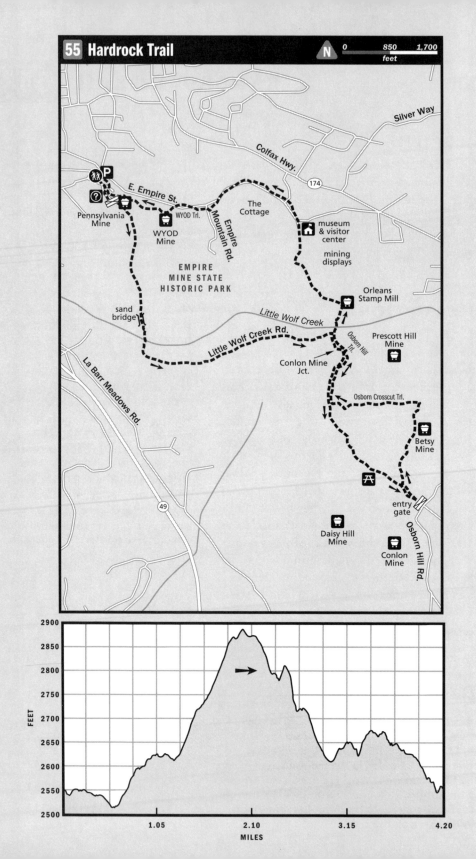

N 0   850   1,700
feet

Silver Way

Colfax Hwy.

174

E. Empire St.

The Cottage

Pennsylvania Mine

WYOD Trl.

WYOD Mine

Empire Mountain Rd.

EMPIRE MINE STATE HISTORIC PARK

museum & visitor center

mining displays

Orleans Stamp Mill

sand bridge

Little Wolf Creek

Little Wolf Creek Rd.

Osborn Hill Trl.

Prescott Hill Mine

Conlon Mine Jct.

Osborn Crosscut Trl.

La Barr Meadows Rd

Betsy Mine

49

entry gate

Osborn Hill Rd.

Daisy Hill Mine

Conlon Mine

FEET

2900
2850
2800
2750
2700
2650
2600
2550
2500

1.05   2.10   3.15   4.20

MILES

> **Mountain lions are a very real threat, even in urbanized areas.**

chemicals—the most hazardous of which were mercury and cyanide—to capture the gold. Your trail passes by the stamp mills, tailings piles, and slurry ponds, which are currently being cleaned up so they can be reclaimed by nature.

An information kiosk at the trailhead displays a map giving an overview of the trails. It also houses a very active colony of carpenter bees, which encourages speed-reading. It is best to pick up a current trails guide from the visitor center. Heed the warnings about both rattlesnakes and mountain lions: they are very real threats here.

Hikers, runners, bicyclists, and horseback riders share these trails as they tour this foothill woodland in the shade of Douglas fir, ponderosa pine, foothill pine, sugar pine, live oak, black oak, big leaf maple, and incense cedar.

The interpretive signs along the trail help visitors appreciate the area's history. What may look like a pile of useless rock turns out to be, well, a pile of useless rock that was placed there on purpose by individual miners toiling in the Work Your Own Diggins Mine. Operated somewhat like a time-share scheme, the mine was finally abandoned in 1912.

A chain-link fence on your left borders the trail as you walk south toward Little Wolf Creek. Keep close to the fence and cross over the sand dam to the left. Then cross a small footbridge over the creek before turning east on Little Wolf Creek Road. Under shade of ponderosa pine and a huge stand of big leaf maple, walk at a leisurely uphill pace to contour above the creek to your left.

After walking east for 1 mile, you will encounter a junction with the Osborn Loop Trail and the Union Hills trails. With the promise of several abandoned mines—the Conlon, the Betsy, Prescott Hill, and Daisy Hill—turn right, and then at the next junction follow the right-hand fork uphill. This is the apex of the Osborn Hill Loop when all the trails are open. Hazardous waste cleanup is ongoing, and trails may be rerouted from time to time.

The next south-bearing section of trail is exposed, as it gains about 200 feet in elevation over the next half mile. You'll pass the Daisy Hill Mine on the right. For observant hikers, there is a fenced-off mine shaft to the left. Pass under the power lines and note the trail beneath it. The described hike will later return you to this point.

Just in time for a brief water break, you will find a picnic table shaded by pine and fir. Despite the park-service sign, there is no scenic lookout but rather a trail downhill to Daisy Hill Mine. If you want to take this side trip, it is only 0.25 miles to the site, but dense whiteleaf manzanita makes it difficult to find the actual site remains. If you hit the fence, turn back 100 feet for the mine site. Stay on the main trail to continue toward Conlon Mine, which is just 500 feet past the next intersection. There is a gate adjacent to the mine site that allows access from Osborn Hill Road and Comet Lane.

When you return to the junction from the Conlon Mine site (which may be fenced off for cleanup), turn right on the Osborn Loop Trail, heading south, in the direction of the Prescott Hill Mine and the Hardrock Trail. On the way, you will pass the trail to the Betsy Mine on your right. A fence at Osborn Hill Road will turn you around if you explore this side trail.

An area closure around the Prescott Hill Mine abbreviates the Osborn Hill Loop. So, turn to the west when you reach the Osborn Crosscut Trail (underneath the power lines) until you zigzag to the left and right at the Power Line Trail. This is an unpleasant hilly stretch of cruddy trail that is very exposed to the sun. You will recognize the point you passed earlier and you will turn right to head north back toward the Hardrock Trail.

Follow the trail signs toward an easily crossed Little Wolf Creek. At the top of the brief uphill, the trail turns left to pass by the foundations of the Orleans Stamp Mill. Your trail continues to the back of the visitor center. The outdoor exhibits of the mining museum to your right are very interesting and often feature demonstrations. The Hardrock Trail continues on East Empire Street along the stone wall in front of the Bourne mansion. Penn Gate is only 0.5 miles ahead.

Before you reach your destination, you will pass the Mule Corral; here mules awaited their descent into the mines, where they worked out their lives and birthed generations of new stock. You will again walk through the Pennsylvania Mine remains as the trailhead comes into view.

NEARBY ACTIVITIES

Empire Mine's owner, William Bourne, built his family's home, which he called The Cottage, on the site in 1898. Tours of the mansion and grounds are available through the park's visitor center.

The mining museum itself is worth a trip. The displays of the mine shafts and side tunnels dramatically illustrate the engineering expertise of the Cornish miners who engineered and built them.

56 INDEPENDENCE TRAIL: West Branch

KEY AT-A-GLANCE INFORMATION

LENGTH: 4.6 miles (West Trail only)

CONFIGURATION: Out-and-back

DIFFICULTY: Easy

SCENERY: Foothill forest, canyon overlooks

EXPOSURE: Always shaded

TRAIL TRAFFIC: Moderate

TRAIL SURFACE: Leaf-covered duff and dirt

HIKING TIME: 1–3 hours

SEASON: Year-round

ACCESS: No fees or permits

MAPS: USGS Nevada City; local trail map available at Tahoe NF Ranger Station on CA 49

WHEELCHAIR TRAVERSABLE: Yes; all facilities are accessible.

FACILITIES: Restrooms at trailhead and 2 spots along the trail; no water available

DRIVING DISTANCE: 57 miles

SPECIAL COMMENTS: This is the nation's first wheelchair-accessible wilderness trail. Groups may take a docent-guided tour by calling (530) 272-0298. The East Branch is temporarily closed for extensive trail maintenance and flume reconstruction. Fortunately, of the two branches, the West Branch is the more scenic.

Independence Trail:
West Branch

UTM Zone (WGS84) 10S

Easting: 0664097

Northing: 4350854

Latitude: N 39° 17' 29"

Longitude: W 121° 05' 49"

IN BRIEF

Just ten minutes from Nevada City, this pleasant hike makes use of the first wheelchair-accessible wilderness trail in the United States. The builders created the path from the remains of an abandoned mining and irrigation canal originally built in 1854. The level grade makes it ideal for hikers of all ages and abilities. Interpretive and identifying signs highlight the diversity of flora along the trail. A sharp eye will spot a California newt among the trail duff (and the sharp hiker will not touch it—its slimy coating is toxic). The cascades at Rush Creek, which has a superior ramp-access system, is the glamour spot on this route.

DESCRIPTION

Gold Country trails certainly offer foothill hikers some diverse and lush flora. The trail itself runs along a mining relic: In 1854 the Excelsior Mining and Canal Company constructed the Excelsior Ditch to transport water from the South Yuba River 17 miles to join another canal near the present-day Lake Wildwood dam. This nearly level ditch and the maintenance trail beside it are now your route.

Directions ⟶

From its junction with the Capitol City Freeway and Interstate 80 East, drive 24 miles to Auburn. Exit I-80 at the CA 49 exit and drive 27 miles north to Nevada City, then turn left—following CA 49—at the split with CA 20. Immediately to your right is the Tahoe National Forest ranger station, where you can obtain additional trail information and a simple map. The trailhead is 6.2 miles past the ranger station. A parking area with enough room for a dozen cars is on the right side of CA 49, in front of the trailhead and restrooms.

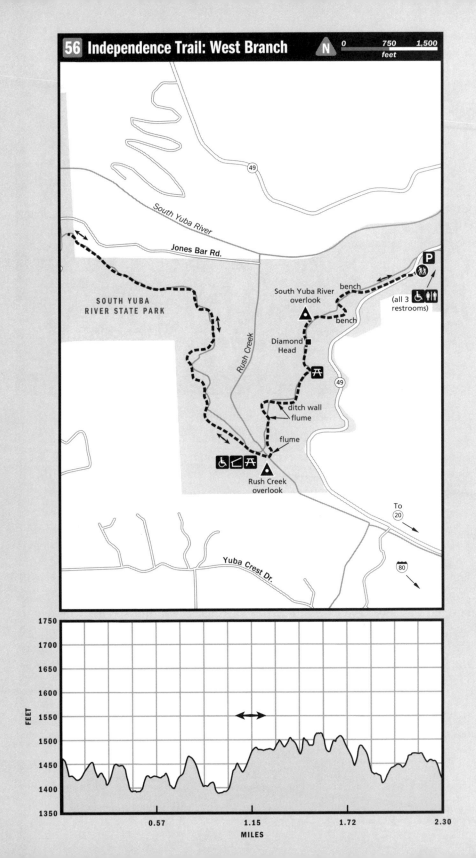

South Yuba River

Jones Bar Rd.

49

SOUTH YUBA
RIVER STATE PARK

Rush Creek

South Yuba River
overlook

bench

bench

Diamond
Head

(all 3
restrooms)

P

49

ditch wall
flume

flume

Rush Creek
overlook

To
20

Yuba Crest Dr.

80

FEET

1750
1700
1650
1600
1550
1500
1450
1400
1350

0.57   1.15   1.72   2.30

MILES

A ramp built in the style of a trestle and flume allows all hikers to access the stream and enjoy the cascades of Rush Creek.

The East and West branches share a common trailhead. Your trail, the West Branch, is the more scenic of the two. Signs on the information board will direct you if you forgot your compass.

You almost immediately enter a short tunnel to pass safely underneath CA 49. Signs there inform hikers that leashed dogs are permitted on the trail, but bicycles, motorcycles, camping, and fires are not. And beware of the poison oak.

The reinforced fence borders this initial stretch, separating hikers from exposed, steep hillsides. The trail has three distinct segments, which you will notice from the outset. In the first 0.1 mile, you will see the stone wall (probably covered with moss and lichen), which is the original wall of the ditch. Adjacent to and slightly above the ditch path is the path for the ditch tenders who monitored the water flow and made repairs. The most unusual features along the path are the flumes—wooden troughs standing on trestles, which carried the water across ravines and other streams.

A bench fashioned from a large tree trunk sits next to the first bridge at the 0.2-mile point. Within another 50 feet, Jones Bar Trail leads off to the north. Stay left on Independence Trail. Notice the incense cedar mixed in with Pacific madrone as you make your way down to the next bridge and another log bench.

Look closely for the interpretive signs for the towering ponderosa pine, the canyon live oak, and Kellogg black oak, which happen to surround the excellent South Yuba River Overlook, which you will reach after 0.4 miles. Here is a nice shelter in case of sudden showers.

As you walk 500 feet on, notice the deerbrush and manzanita bushes shading you from even the low morning sun. A series of ramps lead you to Diamond Head—a class-A outhouse at the 0.5-mile point in your hike.

You will have the sensation of descending into the canyon, but it is an illusion caused by CA 49 climbing up the hill as the trail stays level. As the sound of cars falls away, you will notice more and more ferns, mosses, and lichens along the rock walls. Amble 500 feet more and you will encounter an outhouse and a nice picnic table. So far you have traveled 0.6 miles.

Look up at the Douglas fir now towering over you and the bigleaf maple shading you when its leaves are full. In the next few hundred feet, you are going to notice the air becoming cooler where moist, moss-covered rocks surround you. These rocks remain as they were when laid over 150 years ago. Although reconstructed, Flumes 26 and 27 are identical in design to the water-carrying structures of the gold-rush days. By the time you reach Flume 27 you will have walked just about a mile.

Your south-facing trail still gets plenty of shade from the surrounding manzanita and may be muddy in some spots along here. If you look carefully, you will probably spot a California newt. The male newt may puff himself up, showing his reddish abdomen; but his defense is in his skin, which has a coating toxic to humans. Shoot a photo and leave the newt alone.

California buckeyes line the path here as you come upon another small shelter allowing a shaded overlook to the South Yuba River below. The best site is still ahead about 500 feet, where you will come upon Flume 28. Its horseshoe shape illustrates exactly how the ditch builders shortcut most ravines by building a trestle with a flume atop it.

This flume is special in that it allows easy access to the pool at the base of the cascades of Rush Creek. This is truly an idyllic spot for everyone. In winter the ice clings to the rocks surrounding the pond, and in the spring, water shoots with a roar across the rocks these ramps overlook. Benches, a shelter, wide shallow ramps, and a tree-shaded pool. Spectacular. This is where you are sure to linger, where children will run and splash, and where everyone can reach the stream below the cascades.

As you leave Rush Creek the trail turns north, contouring along the opposite side of the ravine. If you're ready for a snack, picnic tables are about 200 steps ahead. Ramps lead to the tables and to an outhouse at the end of the platform.

The trail ends at Jones Bar Road, an obvious turnaround spot. Retrace your steps to the trailhead or drop down to Jones Bar and the beaches along the river.

NEARBY ACTIVITIES

The Empire Mine State Park in Grass Valley features a museum and visitor center displaying a complete mining history for the Mother Lode and specifically the Empire Mine. The Hardrock Trail (Hike 55, page 281) explores the Empire Mine and several others that were operated in the same area.

57 BUTTERMILK BEND TRAIL

KEY AT-A-GLANCE INFORMATION

LENGTH: 2.5 miles
CONFIGURATION: Out-and-back
DIFFICULTY: Easy
WATER REQUIRED: 0.5 liters
SCENERY: Spectacular views of the South Yuba River
EXPOSURE: Partially shaded trail with exposed areas
TRAIL TRAFFIC: Moderate
TRAIL SURFACE: Dirt and rock
HIKING TIME: 1.5 hours
SEASON: Year-round; parking sunrise–sunset
ACCESS: No fees or permits
MAPS: USGS French Corral
WHEELCHAIR TRAVERSABLE: No
FACILITIES: Toilets in parking area and at nearby visitor center
DRIVING DISTANCE: 62.5 miles
SPECIAL COMMENTS: For more information about the South Yuba River State Park, see www.ncgold.com/ Museums_Parks.syrp. If you want more exercise and a different view of the river, take the Point Defiance Trail (Hike 58, page 294) 1 mile to Englebright Lake and return. The Point Defiance Trail begins across the road and about a 100 yards down at a signed trailhead adjacent to the covered bridge.

Buttermilk Bend Trail

UTM Zone (WGS84) 10S

Easting: 0655872

Northing: 4350874

Latitude: N 39° 17' 35"

Longitude: W 121° 11' 33"

IN BRIEF

Prepare for extraordinary views of the South Yuba River from rock benches along this easy trail. Here, the riparian zone holds somewhat closely to the river's edge, quickly transitioning to a foothill woodland zone upslope. The result is a transition zone that boasts the best of both zones. The abundance of flowers and trees along this short, friendly trail makes this a favorite foothill hike for all ages.

DESCRIPTION

Starting your trip from the second parking lot is easiest, but whether you park here or back across the river next to the bridge, take time to cross the Bridgeport Bridge.

The Bridgeport Bridge has the distinction of being the longest single-span covered bridge in America. Built in 1862, it is one of only ten covered bridges left in California. Made from Douglas fir and covered with sugar-pine shingles, the bridge's double-truss and hoop construction is unique. The only other bridge of its design was built in New York. Information in the visitor center will explain how this bridge's architecture is responsible for its strength, durability, and beauty.

Directions ————————➤

From the junction of Interstate 80 East and the Capital City Freeway, drive approximately 24 miles east on I-80 to the CA 49 north exit in Auburn. Drive about 23 miles toward Grass Valley, and exit toward Marysville on CA 20. Head 7.5 miles on CA 20 to Pleasant Valley Road, then bear right and drive 7.7 miles to the Bridgeport Visitor Center. You can park in the lot on your left just past the large barn or continue across the bridge and park in the lot on your right, on the road, or directly in front of the trailhead, next to the toilets.

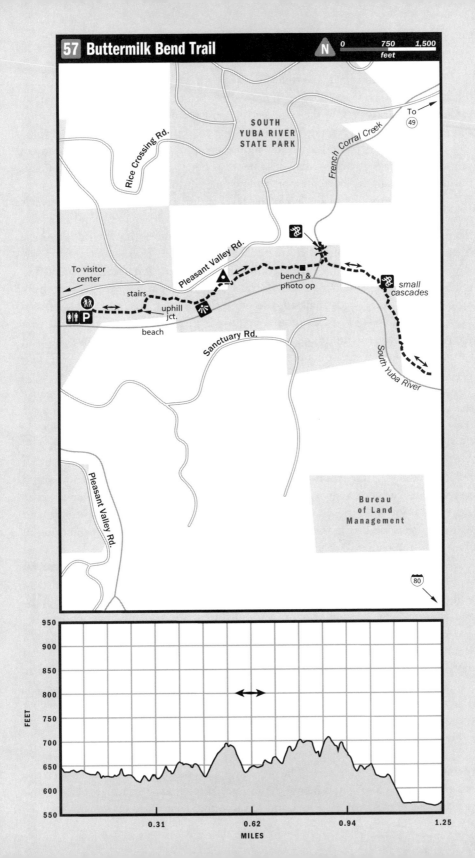

57 Buttermilk Bend Trail

N

0   750   1,500
feet

Rice Crossing Rd.

SOUTH
YUBA RIVER
STATE PARK

French Corral Creek

To
49

To visitor
center

Pleasant Valley Rd.

stairs

uphill
jct.

beach

bench &
photo op

small
cascades

Sanctuary Rd.

South Yuba River

Pleasant Valley Rd.

Bureau
of Land
Management

80

FEET

950
900
850
800
750
700
650
600
550

0.31   0.62   0.94   1.25

MILES

Your trailhead is near the toilets in the north parking lot. If you parked here, the trail is obvious. However, if you parked next to the visitor center, traverse the bridge and turn right onto the path leading past the picnic table and information sign, then walk through the gate and cross the road to the north lot.

Signs warn of rattlesnakes and mountain lions along this trail. These are sensible warnings for this area, despite this being such an easy trail. Colorful poison oak is particularly common along spots of this trail as well.

The trail initially rises above the river so gradually that you might miss some of the interpretive signs that identify the flora along the trail and hillsides. Beginning in March, California poppies, popcorn flowers, larkspurs, shooting stars, fiddlenecks, and blue dicks are splashed across the slopes above and below you and at every seep and spring coming in from your left. Stop frequently to read about them. Smell them endlessly. But leave them to grow, as the park requests. The more seeds that fall, the more flowers that spring.

The trail you are on is about 75 yards below an alternate trailhead that starts in the original flume dug in the hillside in 1877. Looking above the trail to the left, you may see some of those original flume works. Your trail will join with that leg shortly.

The smooth wire fence to your right is there to steady your nerves because the trail runs above the river along an abrupt precipice. As you begin to notice the enormous cobble littering the river in front of you, the trail will ascend a short hill. At the top of this rise, a side trail to the right descends to the river.

Follow the trail uphill to the left, past the miner's lettuce and flowering redbud. Directly after this junction, you should be able to see some stairs ahead of you. Get ready for a quick elevation gain—these 35 stairs pop you up to some switchbacks on an exposed slope. The dirt path is quite well defined now and will soon be joined from the left by the upper trail. You are now in the original flume and the trail will remain level to its end.

When you can distinctly hear the river, just as the trail turns northeast, you will have a great view of the pools and beach below. In another 20 steps, there will be a bench cut into the rock. Purple spring vetch, orange California poppy, and white canyon nemophila grow around you at this up-canyon viewpoint.

Another side trail, with stairs at the top, leads down to the river. Your path continues northeast, where you will find a stone bench right at the bend in the trail marked by the large foothill pine. The view overlooking the cascades is fantastic.

Continue eastward, with miniature lupine and bird's-foot fern lining the trail. A small ravine has been strengthened by some recent rockwork above and below the trail. Another vantage point—allowing you to see around Buttermilk Bend—is equipped with a stone bench. The cascades below make for a great picture.

After walking north for a few minutes, you will cross a bridge over the ravine at French Corral Creek. The bridge is wide and you can linger to watch the water cascading above and below the bridge. You can also head left after crossing the bridge to sit on the rocks and observe the streamside insect activity.

The Bridgeport Bridge is the longest wooden single-span covered bridge in America.

After crossing the bridge, make a U-turn to exit the ravine. Look back to the obvious stonework on the opposite side of the bridge, and now look on your side for similar formations. These are the abutments for the original flume that crossed the ravine.

As you leave the ravine, look for the deep purple of the zigzag larkspur, popcorn flower, and blue dick around the rock outcropping. The toyon has been trimmed back but still shades much of the trail. Blue oak and foothill pine also ensure a cool hike.

Depending on the season, you may be able to see some relics of the gold-mining era—other than your trail. This is reported to have been a mining area, and so large numbers of people were encamped right below your path. The stone fireplace, just about 50 feet below the trail, may indicate a dwelling more permanent than a tent—a home or a boarding house. The large metal pieces that look like monitor pipes are said to be sections of a hoist for moving rocks.

Just 1.25 miles on, the South Yuba River State Park ends. You can descend one of two trails that angle toward boulders as big as midsize cars. After exploring at the river, retrace your steps to the trailhead.

NEARBY ACTIVITIES

The Kneebone Family Cemetery and the Bridgeport Barn are on the grounds of the nearby Bridgeport Visitor Center.

58 POINT DEFIANCE TRAIL

KEY AT-A-GLANCE INFORMATION

LENGTH: 2 miles
CONFIGURATION: Out-and-back
DIFFICULTY: Easy
WATER REQUIRED: 1 liter
SCENERY: Riparian woodland and close-up river views
EXPOSURE: Well-shaded
TRAIL TRAFFIC: Busy
TRAIL SURFACE: Sand, dirt, and rock
HIKING TIME: 1 hour
SEASON: Year-round; parking sunrise–sunset
ACCESS: No fees or permits
MAPS: USGS **French Corral**
WHEELCHAIR TRAVERSABLE: No
FACILITIES: Toilets at visitor center; picnic area and toilet at destination
DRIVING DISTANCE: 62.5 miles
SPECIAL COMMENTS: Combine this hike with the Buttermilk Bend Trail for spectacular up-canyon views. The trailhead is at the end of the longest wooden single-span covered bridge in America.

Point Defiance Trail
UTM Zone (WGS84) 10S
Easting: 0655667
Northing: 4350866
Latitude: N 39° 17' 35"
Longitude: W 121° 11' 41"

IN BRIEF

Point Defiance Trail is a cool riverside adventure with side trips to pebble-covered beaches. Watch the Yuba as it swings from bank to bank toward Harry L. Englebright Lake.

DESCRIPTION

The Point Defiance Trail is a straight, short shot downriver and back. A mere 1 mile long, this trail takes you by beaches, rapids, and quiet riffles as you hike over river cobble, through rockslide debris, and under a pleasant riparian-woodland canopy.

Finding the trailhead is rarely this straightforward. As long as you can park anywhere within sight of both the barn and the covered bridge, it's a cinch. With the barn to your back, walk through the bridge to the opposite side of the river. The trailhead is uphill to your left.

This trail is also known as the Englebright Lake Trail because Point Defiance is actually a point on the South Yuba where the lake reaches farthest upriver. The dam itself was built in 1941 to catch the debris from mining operations in the South Yuba drainage.

Directions ⟶

From Interstate 80 East at the Capital City Freeway, drive 24 miles on I-80 East to the CA 49 north exit in Auburn. Head 23 miles toward Grass Valley, and exit toward Marysville on CA 20. Drive 7.5 miles on CA 20 to Pleasant Valley Road, then bear right and drive 7.7 miles, passing Lake Wildwood, to the Bridgeport Visitor Center. Park in the lot on the left, just past the large barn, or continue across the bridge and park in the lot on your right, or on the road. Your trailhead is through the bridge, on the left as you emerge on the opposite bank.

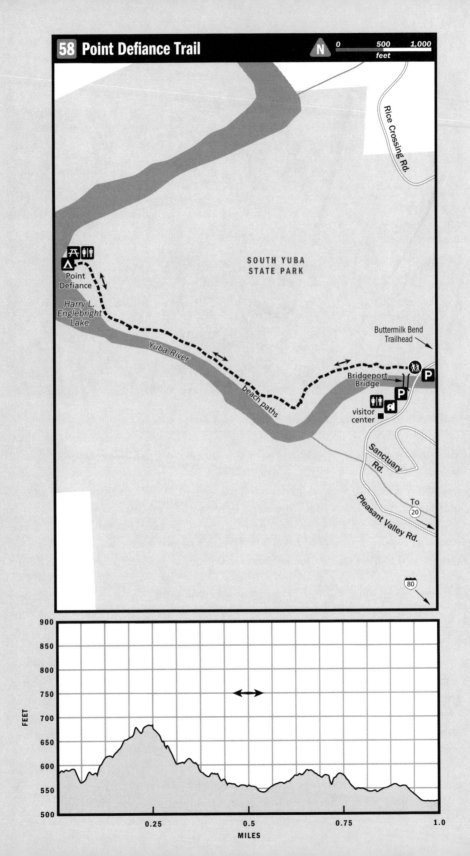

58 Point Defiance Trail

N   0   500   1,000
feet

Rice Crossing Rd.

SOUTH YUBA
STATE PARK

Point
Defiance

Harry L.
Englebright
Lake

Yuba River

beach paths

Buttermilk Bend
Trailhead

Bridgeport
Bridge

visitor
center

P

P

Sanctuary
Rd.

To
20

Pleasant Valley Rd.

80

900
850
800
750
700
650
600
550
500

FEET

0.25   0.5   0.75   1.0

MILES

Sugar-pine shingles cover the Bridgeport Bridge's hoop-and-truss frame.

Your hike takes in the last portion of the South Yuba before the river is slowed by the lake.

Your dirt-and-rock trail will wind along within 30 feet of the river among manzanita, toyon, and foothill pine. There really is no way to wander off this trail unless you take one of the many side trails down to the beaches. Some easy access points are noted here. The first access point that you will come to is within 100 feet of the trailhead. Note that dogs are generally not invited onto the beaches.

After you spot the initial warning about mountain lions and rattlesnakes in the area, you can look across to the opposite shore through the live oak and madrone. Your trail may be damp in places because the ravines entering from the right fill each spring.

As you come upon the rapids, the trail will follow the river. You can get some nice views of the bar as the river turns southwest. As you overlook the bar after the riffles, you can see another beach that would be quite pleasant after spring runoff. Watch your footing on the loose rock in this area as you gain elevation. When you cross the jumble of rocks and boulders around 0.25 miles, you are crossing the result of rockslides rather than flooding.

Just after the river and the trail turn northwest (after about 0.4 miles), you may notice a nice single-track footpath down to the river. Another, easier path is ahead. The beach is a nice strand of coarse sand and river cobble.

As the river approaches your trail to within about 15 feet, you will see boulders the size of compact cars signaling a quiet area. Flood debris can be seen above your head in the oak and madrone branches. When the trail gains height on the river, notice how the channel narrows between your bank and the bar—water squeezing into such a small gap causes it to accelerate and shoot out downstream. That's the basic theory of the hydraulic-mining technique that uses a monitor: Large intake pipes upstream and successively smaller diameter pipes farther and farther downstream build pressure, which is released at the monitor at a very high speed and pressure capable of decimating the hillsides.

As you near the end of the trail, the river is noticeably broader and calmer. You will also catch sight of a broad patch of blackberry bushes just before you cross another jumble of boulders. A junction with a path angling left signals the picnic area. Enjoy the beach just past the composting toilet. Your return is the way you came in.

NEARBY ACTIVITIES

If you would like to get a much different view of the South Yuba River, hike the Buttermilk Trail, which starts from the parking lot across the road. See Hike 57 (page 290) for details on this view of the river.

It is interesting to walk through the historic remains around the visitor center. Original forty-niners with a very colorful story—but one not uncommon at the time—founded Bridgeport: in 1849 William Thompson, a ship's captain, abandoned his ship in San Francisco Bay to go with his wife to the gold fields. They settled here, and their descendants live nearby and maintain the cemetery to the southwest of the visitor center.

59 DIGGINS LOOP TRAIL

**KEY AT-A-GLANCE
INFORMATION**

LENGTH: 5.4 miles

CONFIGURATION: Connected loops

DIFFICULTY: Moderate

WATER REQUIRED: 2 liters

**SCENERY: Views of hillsides
removed by hydraulic-mining
operations**

EXPOSURE: Very sunny

TRAIL TRAFFIC: Light

**TRAIL SURFACE: Gravel; dirt
and duff**

HIKING TIME: 2.5 hours

**SEASON: Year-round, sunrise–
sunset**

ACCESS: $6 parking

**MAPS: USGS North Bloomfield, Pike.
A local trail map and brochure are
available at the museum.**

**FACILITIES: Restrooms, picnic
tables, telephone, and snacks
available at town site**

WHEELCHAIR TRAVERSABLE: No

DRIVING DISTANCE: 77 miles

**SPECIAL COMMENTS: Pay parking
fee or self-register at the museum.**

Diggins Loop Trail
UTM Zone (WGS84) 10S
Easting: 0680829
Northing: 4359707
Latitude: N 39° 22' 04"
Longitude: W 120° 54' 03"

IN BRIEF

Your hike begins at the historic town of North
Bloomfield then passes the old school, church,
and cemetery on the way to a loop through
Diggins Pond, the scene of intense hydraulic
mining. Your trail then climbs to the rim overlook and returns to the town site and your
original trailhead.

DESCRIPTION

Gold was discovered in the creeks and hills in
the surrounding area, but its extraction from the
ore-bearing gravels was inefficient and uneco-
nomical. When three mining partners devised
a method to deliver water to their diggings to
process the gravels, a new and cheap method
of mining was born. Hydraulic mining came to
North Bloomfield (which was originally called
"Humbug" because of its poor production),
and the landscape soon changed forever.

Walk around the town of North Bloomfield, which boasts several original and restored
buildings along with displays of the huge water
cannons known as monitors. Your trailhead
sits across the street from two of the giant

Directions ⟶

**From the junction with the Capital City Freeway,
take Interstate 80 East 24 miles to Auburn and
take the CA 49 exit. Turn left at the light and
drive 26 miles north on CA 49 toward Nevada
City. Continue on CA 49 by turning left toward
Downieville. Drive 11 miles, then turn right onto
Tyler–Foote Road, where you will see a sign for
the Malakoff Diggins State Historic Park. Continue on Tyler–Foote Road 17 miles to the park.
The name of the road will change to Cruzon
Grade Road and then to Backbone Road. Turn
right on Durbec Road into the park. Signs will
lead you to the North Bloomfield town site.**

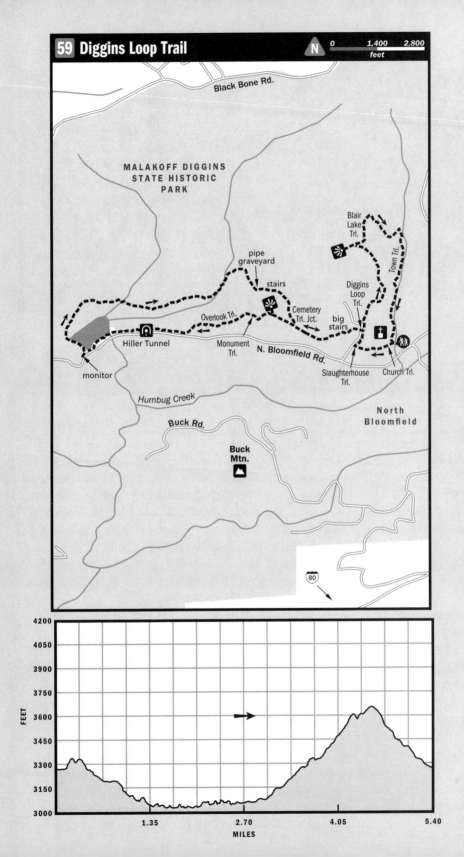

N   0   1,400   2,800
feet

MALAKOFF DIGGINS
STATE HISTORIC
PARK

Black Bone Rd.

Blair
Lake
Trl.

Town Trl.

pipe
graveyard

stairs

Diggins
Loop
Trl.

Cemetery
Trl. Jct.

Overlook Trl.

big
stairs

Hiller Tunnel

Monument
Trl.

N. Bloomfield Rd.

Church Trl.

monitor

Slaughterhouse
Trl.

Humbug Creek

North
Bloomfield

Buck Rd.

Buck
Mtn.

80

FEET

4200
4050
3900
3750
3600
3450
3300
3150
3000

1.35   2.70   4.05   5.40
MILES

Monitors such as the Hendy Giant blasted water at the hillsides, where benches held ancient gold-bearing gravels.

monitors, to the left of the 1870 McKillican and Mobley General Store, at the bridge among the "Clampicnic" grounds (erected by E Clampus Vitus, a fraternal organization). The trail begins across the footbridge next to yet another monitor.

There are two trailheads at this point. One leads uphill on the Town Trail. You will be returning via this trail. The other trail leads to the cemetery via Church Trail. Walk 0.2 miles up to the cemetery, with the fence to your right. The church and schoolhouse are off to the left, and a trail sign at the corner of the fence indicates your trail goes to the right onto Diggins Loop Trail. Five hundred feet down the trail is your marker to turn left to Diggins Loop. Your trail winds downhill under foothill pine, white fir, and Douglas fir. A set of large steps cut into the trail will help you down toward the floor of the diggings.

As you pass some large piles of cobble and gravel, the trail is very distinct. This is not always the case. You are entering what is essentially a giant bathtub, with a drain at the far west end. After every rain, the sand-and-gravel trail can get washed and shifted around. The trail is mostly distinguishable because it is made of compacted gravel that often looks like a sidewalk, but it can become rather indistinct at times. The park has done a good job of placing trail signs just about everywhere that a hiker would wonder where the trail goes.

At the obvious crossing, continue to walk straight across the road. A trail sign will help you, but it is not visible until you cross. Another sign, just ahead, will direct hikers onto either the north or south portions of the trail. The described hike takes the south fork and proceeds clockwise around the basin.

Pass by some old discarded mining gear, nozzles, and pipes as you walk to a vista point on the right. While you are still a bit above the floor, this vantage point gives a breathtaking view of the basin and surrounding hills. As you hike west along the gravel path, watch for rattlesnakes, said to be plentiful in the diggings.

Bear-proof garbage bins have been added in the town recently, for only one reason: bears frequent this area and will take your food. Follow all warnings posted about not storing food in your vehicle and help eliminate the problem by disposing of garbage and recyclables in the receptacles provided.

Trail signs will keep you going in the right direction as you continue to head west past a side trail to the monument regarding the North Bloomfield Gravel and Mining Company, the "creators" of the Malakoff Diggins site. After a junction with another spur trail coming from the overlook parking, you again pass by discarded and rusting pipes, monitor stands, and other mining gear surrounded by the encroaching manzanita.

After walking 2 miles, notice the sign on the right of this packed-dirt trail, which points out the entrance to the Hiller Tunnel. Water that entered the diggings was drained through this small tunnel. Just downhill to the right, in a shaded growth of grass, is the opening to the tunnel; during dry times, you can walk its entire length. The Hiller Tunnel was insufficient for the amount of water needed to be drained and so was replaced in 1874 by the 8,000-foot-long North Bloomfield Tunnel, an engineering feat at the time.

Another trail sign at the west end of the loop marks the intersection with the West Point Trail. Leave the loop for a few hundred feet to see another monitor, which appears to have been left in the position it was on the day operations ceased. The water-supply pipe runs downhill and is still connected to the monitor. (Contemporary photos of the diggings match up closely to the facts on the ground today.) Continue north along the stark white "hillsides." These are excellent displays of the alluvial sands and gravels that contained gold.

Your walk along the north side of the loop is less well defined and requires a bit more route finding than does the trek along the south side. The local map and a compass will help, though they are not a necessity. Trail markers have been placed quite frequently but only a few are visible from one marker to the next. Generally, you will follow the base of the cliffs as you walk across wet, sandy stretches of trail. When the trail turns away from the cliffs, it follows a gravel stream (or the trail merely becomes a gravel stream) for several hundred feet. Again, four-inch-square posts topped with yellow paint serve as markers to help guide you. The thick willows here are fringed with bush lupine; both often conceal the markers. Keep your eyes open and anticipate the path's course, and you will not have any real difficulty. Waterproof footwear is a real bonus on the north side.

When you can see a large white needle of sandstone, you have hiked about 3.5 miles. The trail along here is quite indistinct (especially so the day after a rain), and you will need to mind the markers to stay on the route. Take a look at the small metal tab on the side of each post. The tabs are labeled N-15, N-16, N-17, and so on. When you reach N-18, turn south southeast to stay on track.

Another pipe graveyard follows the trail's uphill turn to the east. It is interesting to see pipes made from riveted steel that are one to two feet in diameter. Follow some trail signs up a stony wash and a nice set of stairs in the hill. When you reach the next intersection, you will recognize it as the north–south split you crossed earlier. Take the big steps uphill to the junction with the slaughterhouse trail. You can return to the trailhead via the Church Trail by retracing your steps, or you can hike up the Slaughterhouse Trail to get an excellent view of the diggings from the rim.

Turning left at this junction, hike uphill for about a half mile. The last few hundred feet will have you huffing a bit as you intersect the road. Turn left onto this paved road. The overlook is marked another few hundred feet up to the left. After your side trip to the overlook, turn left again when you return to the pavement, and walk past the group campground, which will be on your left.

Your trail to return to the town site is opposite the covered assembly area next to the group campground. A trail sign past the toilets marks the head of the Town Trail and points the way to Blair Lake Trail. Turn right and head downhill, passing the amphitheater on your left. The dirt-and-duff trail is a cool and shady respite from the openly exposed trail in the diggings but still offers plenty to discover. Rusted scoops, buckets, pipes, and cables—some partially buried, some not—are hard evidence that the mining here was not done by individuals (like panning) but rather undertaken on an industrial scale.

Just before you cross a small footbridge, you will see a marker indicating your right turn onto the Town Trail. You will descend along a creek to your left through thick cover of Douglas fir, foothill pine, and incense cedar. In about a half mile, you will emerge from the trees at the trailhead bridge where your hike originated.

Gold was first plucked by hand from the rivers, then it was drilled for and dug from hard rock. Here is the best example of how the hills were blown apart and washed away by water to reach the gold-bearing gravels. Your trail loops through floor of the diggings and then heads up to the rim to give you a bird's-eye view of the area, its devastation, and its recovery.

NEARBY ACTIVITIES

The Humbug Creek Trail leads inquisitive hikers down 1000 feet over the course of three miles from the diggings to the South Yuba River. Historic mining relics can be seen along the way and good pools adorn the river.

The South Yuba River Trail is a 15-mile river route from Washington to Edward's Crossing. It can be lengthened by trekking to Purdon's Crossing. It is reported to be an excellent overnight hike.

The South Yuba River State Park, The Malakoff Diggins State Historic Park, the Bureau of Land Management, or the Tahoe National Forest have jurisdiction at some point over the lands of these hikes.

FAIRY FALLS TRAIL 60

IN BRIEF

This hike to Fairy Falls takes you along an easy route through an area of intense geologic history to a set of waterfalls—all of which will be flooded if the proposed Waldo Dam is constructed. Fairy Falls (also known as Shingle Falls on topos) sits astride the ill-named Dry Creek and drops 60 feet to the pool before tumbling over Lower Fairy Falls.

DESCRIPTION

This easy hike to Fairy Falls includes something for a wide variety of interests. Following the old Spenceville Road where the lone oak stands, you will walk past what was once Spenceville, founded in the 1850s and abandoned in 1915. Copper mines dot the lower trail, and gold fields can be found in the hillsides. Mines are especially dangerous and should never be entered.

The trail is bordered by the Spenceville Wildlife Area, and so it is home to a vast

KEY AT-A-GLANCE INFORMATION

LENGTH: 5.8 miles

CONFIGURATION: Out-and-back

DIFFICULTY: Moderate

WATER REQUIRED: 2 liters

SCENERY: River, pools, cascades, two waterfalls, and foothill woodlands

EXPOSURE: Lots of exposure to sun; the route in provides some shade

TRAIL TRAFFIC: Light

TRAIL SURFACE: Dirt and gravel; dirt and duff

HIKING TIME: 4–5 hours depending on lunch, photos, and wading time

SEASON: Year-round

ACCESS: No fees or permits

MAPS: USGS Camp Far West, Wolf

FACILITIES: None

WHEELCHAIR TRAVERSABLE: No

DRIVING DISTANCE: 63 miles

SPECIAL COMMENTS: The large, clear pools below the lower falls make this an ideal destination on a hot summer day.

Directions ———————→

Starting at the split of Interstate 5 North and CA 99 North after Arco Arena, take CA 99 (which turns into CA 70) north 35 miles toward Marysville. In Marysville, turn right onto CA 20 and drive 0.2 miles, then turn left onto CA 20 and proceed 0.2 miles. Make another right turn to continue on CA 20. Follow CA 20 for 18.5 miles to Smartville Road, on the right (Beale AFB sign). Turn right on Smartville Road and go 5.5 miles, staying to the left, to reach Waldo Road. Turn left onto this gravel road and drive 1.8 miles to Spenceville Road. Be careful when crossing over the wooden-decked Waldo Bridge. Stay on Spenceville Road 2.3 miles to its end. Your trailhead is across the old wooden bridge that crosses Dry Creek.

Fairy Falls Trail
UTM Zone (WGS84) 10S
Easting: 0649630
Northing: 4330819
Latitude: N 39° 06' 49"
Longitude: W 121° 16' 09"

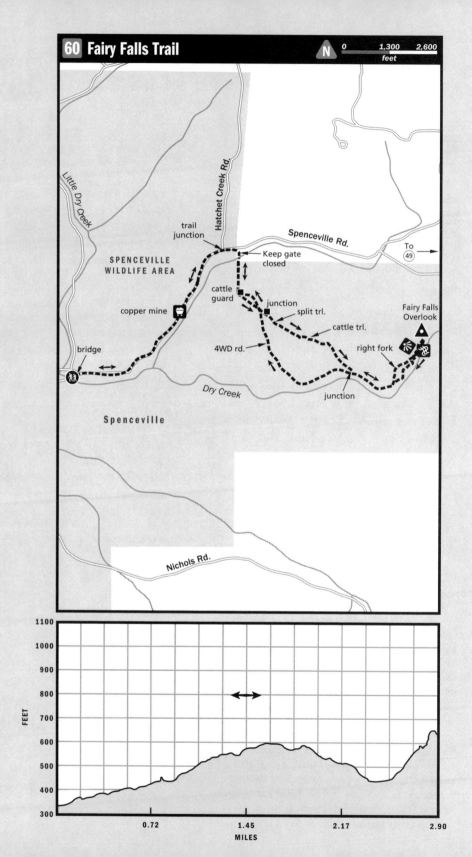

60 Fairy Falls Trail

N
0   1,300   2,600
feet

Little Dry Creek

Hatchet Creek Rd.

Spenceville Rd.

trail
junction

SPENCEVILLE
WILDLIFE AREA

Keep gate
closed

To
49

cattle
guard

junction

copper mine

split trl.

Fairy Falls
Overlook

cattle trl.

4WD rd.

right fork

bridge

Dry Creek

junction

Spenceville

Nichols Rd.

FEET

1100
1000
900
800
700
600
500
400
300

0.72   1.45   2.17   2.90
MILES

This dilapidated bridge crosses Dry Creek at the original Spenceville site.

number of migratory birds. If you are interested in rocks, Fairy Falls and Dry Creek's canyon expose geologic features that are within easy reach. You will find typical flora of the riparian and foothill woodlands, but the blossoming flowers alone are worth a springtime hike here. They are at their peak from March through May.

Watch your step as you head across the wooden bridge at the trailhead— aside from spotting seriously sagging timbers, you will see that holes have burned completely through the deck. Within 50 feet of the bridge, I almost stepped on a medium-sized northern alligator lizard as it sat motionless in a sunny patch in the trail. Before traveling a half mile, you might also spot a two-toned green Pacific tree frog as this little fellow bellows from a seep located on the left side of the trail.

Look across Dry Creek at the exposed rock; the result of the heating and melting of several minerals metamorphosed this rock into what we know as serpentine, California's state rock. This greasy-looking, dark-green rock is very common in the western foothills largely due to the geologic forces that also created the gold here.

In fact, as you drove just south of the town of Smartville, you entered a geologic area that was formed just about 200 million years ago and is now known as California. An island 600 miles out in the Pacific Ocean began moving east at the same time that the North American continent began moving west.

Fairy Falls, on Dry Creek, is called Shingle Falls on some maps.

When they inevitably met, the resulting faulting created favorable conditions for gold and other metals to be formed and exposed.

Geologists call that arc-shaped island, which stretches from Oroville to Auburn and extends about 25 miles west into the Central Valley, the Smartville block. This formation is largely responsible for California's legacy of gold.

This area was settled not only for its rich gold veins but also for its copper-bearing ore. Copper is so concentrated in the Smartsville block that Native Americans were able to dig it directly out of the earth. After about 0.75 miles, look for an opening in the roadcut that appears to be covered by stacked blocks. That is one of the sealed copper mines, further evidenced by the red stained clays in the path.

Walk generally northeast along old Spenceville Road, bypassing a trail that enters from the north and leads to private property. You will soon encounter a gate blocking your road, so turn to the south and walk toward the gate you see there. Now, you have a brief but unrelenting south-facing uphill climb. Turn around to look at the scenery of the surrounding hills to lift your spirits.

When you reach the top of the hill after 1.4 miles, you will see a cattle guard standing as lonely as the tollbooth in *Blazing Saddles*. You can ignore the road that goes off to the southwest. The two trails by the cattle guard are your trails. They split and wrap around the knoll to your southeast. You will hike in on one and out on the other.

On this hike, the distinct cattle trail is your path going into the falls. After visiting the falls, you are going to exit on the four-wheel-drive road on the left. The cattle trail shortcuts the road before entering the hillside which is forested with live oak, manzanita, toyon, and foothill pine.

Remember: this is a cattle trail, so mind your steps. Pick a path around either side of this fallen oak and avoid going off to the right on the smaller trails. You should head southeast with a small knoll to your right as you descend to Dry Creek. Nearing the creek, you will join the road that skirted the knoll on the creek side. If you are here at the right time, you will see the popcorn flowers flood the hillside with white.

Now down next to the creek, you can find lots to dawdle over at the cascades and pools before you climb up to the falls. When you are done here, continue on up the road heading north until a distinct trail leads off to the right as the road continues its steep rise. Follow this dirt path as it is joined by the trail from the pools. The trail ascends sharply to the viewpoint overlooking the falls, where an old fence offers some protection.

As you ascend, you will see Lower Fairy Falls, but it is difficult to get a close look from above. There are good views of Fairy Falls both above and below. If you scramble around past the fences, you can get some impressive views of the pool 60 feet below. Climb back up toward the trail and take the footpath toward the pools.

If you want to avoid the noise of the cascades below at the pools, you will find a broad, flat hillside covered with California poppies, where you can enjoy a quiet picnic before heading back to the four-wheel-drive road and along the creek to the trailhead.

NEARBY ACTIVITIES

The South Yuba River State Park is about 15 miles to the north and offers miles of river recreation as well as hiking, biking, and equestrian trails. The Buttermilk Bend Trail (Hike 57, page 290) and the Point Defiance Trail (Hike 58, page 294) highlight pioneer engineering along a scenic river.

APPENDIXES
AND INDEX

APPENDIX A:
OUTDOOR SHOPS

Adventure Sports
1609 Watt Avenue
Sacramento, CA 95864
(916) 971-1800
www.gearcloset.com

Big 5 Sporting Goods
6608 Laguna Boulevard
Elk Grove, CA 95758
(916) 691-9112

6251 Mack Road
Sacramento, CA 95823
(916) 427-0978

980 Florin Road, Suite A
Sacramento, CA 95831
(916) 393-1831

3420 Arden Way
Sacramento, CA 95825
(916) 488-5060

10755 Folsom Boulevard
Rancho Cordova, CA 95670
(916) 852-0898

4794 Manzanita Avenue
Carmichael, CA 95608
(916) 972-1067

3637 Elkhorn Boulevard
North Highlands, CA 95660
(916) 332-6511

1301 West Covell Boulevard
Davis, CA 95616
(530) 758-7731

7833 Greenback Lane
Citrus Heights, CA 95610
(916) 726-5566

2411 West Kettlemen Lane
Lodi, CA 95242
(209) 366-1514

606 East Bidwell Street
Folsom, CA 95630
(916) 984-7148

1909 Douglas Boulevard
Roseville, CA 95661
(916) 773-4773

431 Pioneer Avenue
Woodland, CA 95776
(530) 669-7013

2030 Harbison Drive
Vacaville, CA 95687
(707) 452-0168

1053 March Lane
Stockton, CA 95207
(209) 957-3095

1902 North Texas Street
Fairfield, CA 94533
(707) 426-5026

2556 Grass Valley
Auburn, CA 95603
(530) 887-8326

284 Placerville Road
Placerville, CA 95667
(530) 295-8290

Big 5 Sporting Goods *(continued)*
123 West McKnight Way
Grass Valley, CA 95949
(530) 274-1562

1252 Colusa Avenue
Yuba City, CA 95991
(530) 671-3410

REI
1790 Expo Parkway
Sacramento, CA 95815
(916) 924-8900
www.rei.com/stores/21

2425 Iron Point Road
Folsom, CA 95630
(916) 817-8944
www.rei.com/stores/86

1148 Galleria Boulevard
Roseville, CA 95678
(916) 724-6750
www.rei.com/stores/74

Sierra Outfitters
2100 Arden Way
Sacramento, CA 95825
(916) 922-7500

Sport Chalet
8511 Bond Road
Elk Grove, CA 95624
(916) 714-5740

10349 Fairway Drive
Roseville, CA 95678
(916) 773-6828

2401 Butano Drive
Sacramento, CA 95825
(916) 977-1730

Sports Authority
6005 Madison Avenue
Carmichael, CA 95608
(916) 338-7183
www.sportsauthority.com

8217 Laguna Boulevard
Elk Grove, CA 95758
(916) 691-4380

2799 East Bidwell Street
Building M-10
Folsom, CA 95630
(916) 983-5821

6740 Stanford Ranch Road
Roseville, CA 95678
(916) 789-8436

1700 Arden Way
Sacramento, CA 95815
(916) 564-3400

3631 North Freeway Boulevard
Sacramento, CA 95834
(916) 419-3140

APPENDIX B:
MAP SOURCES

Alpenglow Sports
Tahoe City, CA
(530) 583-6917

Bassett's Station
Sierra City, CA
(530) 862-1297

Bookends Bookstore
Napa, CA
(707) 224-7455

Calaveras Ranger District
Hathaway Pines, CA
(209) 795-1381

California Surveying and Drafting Supply
Sacramento, CA
(916) 344-0232

Chico Sports Ltd.
Chico, CA
(530) 894-1110

El Dorado National Forest
El Dorado, CA
(530) 622-4666

Georgetown, CA 95634
(530) 333-4312

Pioneer, CA
(209) 295-4251

Placerville, CA
(530) 622-5061

Pollock Pines, CA
(530) 644-2349

Forest Stationers
Quincy, CA
(530) 283-2266

Granite Chief, Inc.
Truckee, CA
(530) 587-2809

Grant Plumbing and Hardware
Foresthill, CA
(530) 367-2327

Jackson Family Sports
Jackson, CA
(209) 223-3890

Kittle's Outdoor and Sport Co.
Colusa, CA
(530) 458-4868

Miners Emporium
Sierra City, CA
(530) 862-0630

Mi-Wok Ranger District
Mi-Wuk Village, CA
(209) 586-3234

Mountain Recreation Inc.
Grass Valley, CA
(530) 477-8006

Mountain Sports
Chico, CA
(530) 345-5011

Mountain True Value Hardware
Truckee, CA
(530) 587-4844

Oars Dories Inc.
Angels Camp, CA
(209) 736-4677

Ogden Survey Equip Co.
Sacramento, CA
(916) 451-7253

Paradise Sporting Goods
Paradise, CA
(530) 877-5114

Paradise Surplus
Paradise, CA
(530) 872-9307

Pioneer Mining Supplies
Auburn, CA
(530) 885-1801

Placerville News Co.
Placerville, CA
(530) 622-4510

REI
Folsom, CA
(916) 817-8944

Roseville, CA
(916) 724-6750

Sacramento, CA
(916) 924-8900

Sierra Gold
Downieville, CA
(530) 289-3515

Sierra Mountain Sports
Quincy, CA
(530) 283-2323

Sierra Nevada Adventure Co.
Arnold, CA
(209) 795-9310

Sierra West Surveying
Paradise, CA
(530) 877-6253

Soda Springs General Store
Soda Springs, CA
(530) 426-3080

Soper Wheeler Co.
Strawberry Valley, CA
(530) 675-2342

Sportsman's Den
Quincy, CA
(530) 283-2733

Superfast Printing
Marysville, CA
(530) 742-4223

Surplus City
Oroville, CA
(530) 534-9956

Tahoe National Forest
American River Ranger District
Foresthill, CA
(530) 367-2224

APPENDIX B:
MAP SOURCES (CONTINUED)

Tahoe National Forest *(continued)*
Nevada City, CA
(530) 265-4531

Sierraville Ranger District
Sierraville, CA
(530) 994-3401

Truckee Ranger Station
Truckee, CA
(916) 587-3558

Tahoe Sports Ltd.
South Lake Tahoe, CA
(530) 544-2284

Valley Sporting Goods
Modesto, CA
(209) 523-5681

APPENDIX C:
HIKING ORGANIZATIONS

American River Conservancy
348 Highway 49
P.O. Box 562
Coloma, CA 95613
(530) 621-1224
www.arconservancy.org/xoops

Auburn State Recreation Area
Canyon Keepers
(530) 885-3776
www.canyonkeepers.org

Chico Hiking Association
2411 Notre Dame Boulevard
Chico, CA 95928
www.chicohiking.org

High Sierra Hikers Association
P.O. Box 8920
South Lake Tahoe, CA 96158
www.highsierrahikers.org

Pacific Crest Trail Association
5325 Elkhorn Boulevard, PMB #256
Sacramento, CA 95842
(888) 728-7245
www.pcta.org

Placer Group Sierra Club
(916) 781-4926
www.sierraclub.org

Sacramento Backpackers Meetup Group
backpackers.meetup.com/121/?gj=sj6

Sacramento Dads and Kids Hiking Group
hiking.meetup.com/336

Sacramento Hiking Meetup Group
hiking.meetup.com/20

Sequoya Challenge–Independence Trail
P.O. Box 3166
Grass Valley, CA 95945
(530) 477-4788
www.sequoyachallenge.org

Sierra Buttes Lakes Basin Coalition
6180 Wycliffe Way
Sacramento, CA 95831
(916) 428-8910

Sierra Club–Mother Lode Chapter
1116 Ninth Street
Sacramento, CA 95814
(916) 557-1100, ext. 119
motherlode.sierraclub.org

APPENDIX D:
MANAGING AGENCIES

American River Ranger District
Foresthill, CA
(530) 367-2224

Bureau of Land Management
Folsom Field Office
63 Natoma Street
Folsom, CA 95630
(916) 985-4474
www.blm.gov/ca/st/en/fo/folsom

Cache Creek Natural Area
Bureau of Land Management
Ukiah Field Office
2550 North State Street
Ukiah, CA 95482
(707) 468-4000
www.blm.gov/ca/st/en/fo/ukiah/
cachecreek.2

California Department of Fish and Game
P.O. Box 47
(7329 Silverado Trail)
Napa, CA 94558
(707) 9445500
www.dfg.ca.gov/regions/region3

California Department of Parks and
   Recreation
American River District
7806 Folsom–Auburn Road
Folsom, CA 95630-1797
(916) 988-0205

Auburn State Recreation Area
P.O. Box 3266
Auburn, CA 95604
(916) 885-4527
auburn.parks.state.ca.us

Camanche Lake South Shore
   Recreation Area
P.O. Box 206
Burson, CA 95225
(209) 763-5178

Caswell Memorial State Park
28000 South Austin Road
Ripon, CA 95366
(209) 599-3810
www.parks.ca.gov

Cosumnes River Preserve
Bureau of Land Management
7100 Desmond Road
Galt, CA 95632
(916) 686-6982

13501 Franklin Boulevard
Galt, CA 95632
(916) 684-2816
www.cosumnes.org

East Bay Municipal Utility District
Mokelumne Watershed and Recreation
   Division
5883 East Camanche Parkway
Campo Seco, CA 95266
(209) 772-8204
www.ebmud.com

Empire Mine State Historic Park
10791 East Empire Street
Grass Valley, CA 95945
www.empiremine.org

Folsom Lake State Recreation Area
7806 Folsom–Auburn Road
Folsom, CA 95630-1797
(916) 988-0205
www.parks.ca.gov/?page_id=500

Grizzly Island Game Refuge
2548 Grizzly Island Road
Suisun City, CA 94585
(707) 425-3828

Indian Grinding Rock State Historic Park
Chaw'se Regional Indian Museum
14881 Pine Grove–Volcano Road
Pine Grove, CA 95665
(209) 296-7488

Malakoff Diggins State Historic Park
North Bloomfield, CA 95959

**Marshall Gold Discovery
   State Historic Park**
P.O. Box 265
Coloma, CA 95613
(916) 622-3470

New Hogan Lake
U.S. Army Corps of Engineers
2713 Hogan Dam Road
Valley Springs, CA 95252
(209) 772-1343

Placer County Parks Division
11476 C Avenue
Auburn, CA 95603
(916) 889-7750

**Sacramento County Department of Parks
   and Recreation**
3711 Branch Center Road
Sacramento, CA 95827
(916) 366-2066

Sly Park Recreation Area
P.O. Box 577
Pollock Pines, CA 95726
(916) 644-2545

Spenceville Wildlife Area
California Department of Fish and Game
1701 Nimbus Road
Rancho Cordova, CA 95819
(916) 355-7010

Tahoe National Forest
Nevada City, CA 95959
(530) 265-4531

UC Davis Arboretum
University of California, Davis
One Shields Drive
Davis, CA 95616
(530) 752-4880
www.arboretum.ucdavis.edu

APPENDIX E:
ADDITIONAL READING

The American River. Auburn, CA: Protect American River Canyons, 2002.

Arno, Stephen F. *Discovering Sierra Trees.* Yosemite, CA: Yosemite Association, 1973.

Basey, Harold E. Discovering *Sierra Reptiles and Amphibians.* Yosemite, CA: Yosemite Association, 2004.

Halfpenny, James. *A Field Guide to Mammal Tracking in North America.* Boulder, CO: Johnson Books, 1986.

Hill, Mary. *Geology of the Sierra Nevada.* Berkeley: University of California Press, 2006.

Horn, Elizabeth L. *Sierra Nevada Wildflowers.* Missoula, Montana: Mountain Press Company, 1998.

Miller, Millie, and Cyndi Nelson. *Talons: North American Birds of Prey.* Boulder, CO: Johnson Books, 1989.

Murie, Olaus J. *Peterson Field Guide: a Field Guide to Animal Tracks.* Boston: Houghton Mifflin Company, 1974.

Niehaus, Theodore F., and Charles L. Ripper. *Peterson Field Guide: a Field Guide to Pacific States Wildflowers.* Boston: Houghton Mifflin Company, 1976.

Russo, Ron, and Pam Olhausan. *Mammal Finder.* Berkeley, CA: Nature Study Guild, 1987.

Storer, Tracy I., Robert L. Usinger, and David Lukas. *Sierra Nevada Natural History.* Berkeley: University of California Press, 2004.

Thomas, John H., and Dennis R. Parnell. *Native Shrubs of the Sierra Nevada.* Berkeley: University of California Press, 1974.

Underhill, J. E. *Sagebrush Wildflowers.* Blaine, WA: Hancock House, Inc., 1986.

Whitman, Ann H., ed. *Audubon Society Guide: Familiar Trees of North America: Western Region.* New York: Alfred A. Knopf, 1988.

INDEX

DEAR CUSTOMERS AND FRIENDS,

SUPPORTING YOUR INTEREST IN OUTDOOR ADVENTURE, travel, and an active lifestyle is central to our operations, from the authors we choose to the locations we detail to the way we design our books. Menasha Ridge Press was incorporated in 1982 by a group of veteran outdoorsmen and professional outfitters. For 25 years now, we've specialized in creating books that benefit the outdoors enthusiast.

Almost immediately, Menasha Ridge Press earned a reputation for revolutionizing outdoors- and travel-guidebook publishing. For such activities as canoeing, kayaking, hiking, backpacking, and mountain biking, we established new standards of quality that transformed the whole genre, resulting in outdoor-recreation guides of great sophistication and solid content. Menasha Ridge continues to be outdoor publishing's greatest innovator.

The folks at Menasha Ridge Press are as at home on a white-water river or mountain trail as they are editing a manuscript. The books we build for you are the best they can be, because we're responding to your needs. Plus, we use and depend on them ourselves.

We look forward to seeing you on the river or the trail. If you'd like to contact us directly, join in at www.trekalong.com or visit us at www.menasharidge.com. We thank you for your interest in our books and the natural world around us all.

SAFE TRAVELS,

Bob Sehlinger

BOB SEHLINGER
PUBLISHER